Interurban Knowledge Exchange in Southern and Eastern Europe, 1870–1950

AF723221

Around 1900, cities in Southern and Eastern Europe were persistently labeled "backward" and "delayed." Allegedly, they had no alternative but to follow the role model of the metropolises, of London, Paris or Vienna. This edited volume fundamentally questions this assumption. It shows that cities as diverse as Barcelona, Berdyansk, Budapest, Lviv, Milan, Moscow, Prague, Warsaw and Zagreb pursued their own agendas of modernization. In order to solve their pressing problems with respect to urban planning and public health, they searched for best practices abroad. The solutions they gleaned from other cities were eclectic to fit the specific needs of a given urban space and were thus often innovative. This applied urban knowledge was generated through interurban networks and multi-directional exchanges. Yet in the period around 1900, this transnational municipalism often clashed with the forging of urban and national identities, highlighting the tensions between the universal and the local.

This interurban perspective helps to overcome nationalist perspectives in historiography as well as outdated notions of "center and periphery." This volume will appeal to scholars from a large number of disciplines, including urban historians, historians of Eastern and Southern Europe, historians of science and medicine, and scholars interested in transnational connections.

Eszter Gantner (1971–2019) was a research fellow at the Herder Institute for Historical Research on East Central Europe from 2013 through 2019.

Heidi Hein-Kircher is head of the department "academic forum" at the Herder Institute for Historical Research on East Central Europe in Marburg, Germany.

Oliver Hochadel is a historian of science and a tenured researcher at the Institución Milá y Fontanals de Investigación en Humanidades (CSIC, Barcelona).

Routledge Advances in Urban History
Series Editors: Bert De Munck
(Centre for Urban History, University of Antwerp)
Simon Gunn
(Centre for Urban History, University of Leicester)

This series showcases original and exciting new work in urban history. It publishes books that challenge existing assumptions about the history of cities, apply new theoretical frames to the urban past, and open up new avenues of historical enquiry. The scope of the series is global, and it covers all time periods from the ancient to the modern worlds.

3 **Urbanizing Nature**
Actors and Agency (Dis)Connecting Cities and Nature Since 1500
Edited by Tim Soens, Dieter Schott, Michael Toyka-Seid and Bert De Munck

4 **Cities, Railways, Modernities**
London, Paris, and the Nineteenth Century
Carlos López Galviz

5 **The Materiality of Literary Narratives in Urban History**
Edited by Lieven Ameel, Jason Finch, Silja Laine and Richard Dennis

6 **The Rise and Fall of London's Ringways, 1943–1973**
Michael Dnes

7 **New Approaches to Governance and Rule in Urban Europe Since 1500**
Edited by Simon Gunn and Tom Hulme

8 **Migrants and the Making of the Urban-Maritime World**
Agency and Mobility in Port Cities, c. 1570–1940
Edited by Christina Reimann and Martin Öhman

9 **Interurban Knowledge Exchange in Southern and Eastern Europe, 1870–1950**
Edited by Eszter Gantner, Heidi Hein-Kircher and Oliver Hochadel

For more information about this series, please visit: www.routledge.com/Routledge-Advances-in-Urban-History/book-series/RAUH

Interurban Knowledge Exchange in Southern and Eastern Europe, 1870–1950

Edited by
Eszter Gantner, Heidi Hein-Kircher and Oliver Hochadel

Routledge
Taylor & Francis Group
NEW YORK AND LONDON

First published 2021
by Routledge
52 Vanderbilt Avenue, New York, NY 10017

and by Routledge
2 Park Square, Milton Park, Abingdon, Oxon, OX14 4RN

Routledge is an imprint of the Taylor & Francis Group, an informa business

© 2021 Taylor & Francis

The right of Eszter Gantner, Heidi Hein-Kircher and Oliver Hochadel to be identified as the authors of the editorial material, and of the authors for their individual chapters, has been asserted in accordance with sections 77 and 78 of the Copyright, Designs and Patents Act 1988.

All rights reserved. No part of this book may be reprinted or reproduced or utilised in any form or by any electronic, mechanical, or other means, now known or hereafter invented, including photocopying and recording, or in any information storage or retrieval system, without permission in writing from the publishers.

Trademark notice: Product or corporate names may be trademarks or registered trademarks, and are used only for identification and explanation without intent to infringe.

Library of Congress Cataloging-in-Publication Data
Names: Gantner, Eszter B. honoree. | Gantner, Eszter B., editor. | Hein-Kircher, Heidi, 1969– editor. | Hochadel, Oliver, 1968– editor.
Title: Interurban knowledge exchange in Southern and Eastern Europe, 1870–1950 / edited by Eszter Gantner, Heidi Hein-Kircher and Oliver Hochadel.
Description: 1st Edition. | New York : Routledge Taylor & Francis Group, 2020. | Series: Routledge advances in urban history ; vol 9 | Includes bibliographical references and index.
Identifiers: LCCN 2020025820 (print) | LCCN 2020025821 (ebook) | ISBN 9780367333294 (hardback) | ISBN 9780429319235 (ebook) | ISBN 9781000207637 (adobe pdf) | ISBN 9781000207644 (mobi) | ISBN 9781000207651 (epub)
Subjects: LCSH: Cities and towns—Europe, Southern—Effect of technological innovations on. | Cities and towns—Europe, Eastern—Effect of technological innovations on. | City planning—Europe, Southern—History. | City planning—Europe, Eastern—History. | Cities and towns—Growth. | Civilization, Modern.
Classification: LCC HC244.5 .I58 2020 (print) | LCC HC244.5 (ebook) | DDC 307.1/1609409041—dc23
LC record available at https://lccn.loc.gov/2020025820
LC ebook record available at https://lccn.loc.gov/2020025821

ISBN: 978-0-367-33329-4 (hbk)
ISBN: 978-0-429-31923-5 (ebk)

Typeset in Sabon
by Apex CoVantage, LLC

In memoriam

Eszter Gantner (1971–2019)

Contents

Figures

Preface

This book is dedicated to the memory of our esteemed colleague and dear friend Eszter Gantner. She passed away in August 2019 as the manuscript for this book neared completion. In fact, her last e-mail reached us a few days before her death, resolving some final details concerning the images and captions for her chapter. The idea for this book owes very much to Eszter's vision of how to invigorate urban history and Eastern European history with new ideas and interdisciplinary alliances. Thanks to her initiative, two historians of Eastern Central Europe and one historian of science from Barcelona formed a team. We were interested in urban history from different but complementary viewpoints. What brought us together was the "periphery perspective" – and what might connect urban spaces in Eastern and Southern Europe.

We organized a double conference inviting historians of science, urban historians and historians of public health and urban planning to talk about the interurban knowledge exchanges taking place in "their" cities. The first part of the conference took place at the Institució Milà i Fontanals (CSIC) in Barcelona in September 2016. The second part, with more advanced drafts of the papers, was hosted at the Herder Institute for Historical Research on East Central Europe in Marburg in May 2017. Both events were funded by the Fritz Thyssen Stiftung, and we are most grateful for their support (Ref. 30.16.0.074GE).

In the years leading up to this publication, Oliver Hochadel benefited from the following projects: "Science and the City. Natural History, Biology and Biopolitics in the Divided City: Barcelona and Buenos Aires (1868–1936)"; Ministerio de Economía y Competitividad (HAR2013-48065-C2-1-P); "¿Ciencia en la periferia? La cultura científica de ciudades en el Sur y el Este de Europa alrededor de 1900: paralelismos, contextos y redes" (201510I030) "Proyecto intramural especial" Consejo Superior de Investigaciones Científicas; and "Science, Technology and Medicine in modern Catalonia (18th–20th centuries)"; Grup de recerca consolidat i finançat (SGR 2014-1410 and SGR 2017-1138,) AGAUR-Generalitat de Catalunya.

Heidi Hein-Kircher was inspired by the discussions and contribution to this project and in turn she could contribute ideas from her project on local government in Lviv (Lembergs "polnischen Charakter" sichern. Kommunalpolitik in einer multiethnischen Stadt der Habsburgermonarchie zwischen 1861/62 und 1914, Stuttgart: Steiner 2020) and ideas stemming from methodological and conceptual discussions within the collaborative projects "SFB/TRR 138 Dynamics of security. Types of Securitization from a Historical Perspective." She and Eszter Gantner were also enriched by the conceptual discussions of the Hessian Loewe-focus project "Conflict regions in Eastern Europe."

Much needed support and input in different ways came from our colleagues Sean Brady, Miquel Carandell, Andras Hecker, Goran Hutinec, Christine Krüger, Agustí Nieto-Galan, Harald R. Stühlinger, Ned Sumerville and Jan Surman. William Connor proved to be an excellent proofreader and Iryna Dolnytska did a great job on the index. We thank Iryna Dolnytska for indexing. We also would like to thank the anonymous reviewers for their critical and constructive feedback and Bert De Munck and Simon Gunn for including our book in their series "Routledge Advances in Urban History."

This book is also about interurban knowledge exchanges in a different sense. Scholars from a dozen countries participated in it and exchanged knowledge, ideas and methods. We tried – pretty successfully, we dare say – to learn from each other. Adaptation, eclecticism, local circumstances, national particularities, transnational networks – all these factors shaped our articles, just like they had transformed the urban spaces we were studying. All this pleased Eszter very much.

Heidi Hein-Kircher and Oliver Hochadel
Marburg/Barcelona, December 2019

Introduction

Searching for Best Practices in Interurban Networks

Eszter Gantner, Heidi Hein-Kircher and Oliver Hochadel

In March 1904, Spanish entomologist Manuel Martínez de la Escalera reported in the popular journal *Alrededor del Mundo* about the journey he had undertaken the previous summer. Escalera and his superior Ignacio Bolívar visited numerous museums in Western and Central Europe to inform themselves about the latest advances of others working in their field. They were looking for inspiration for their soon-to-be-built museum in Madrid. At the time, it had been decided to move the national natural history collections from its cramped quarters to a new site overlooking the Paseo de la Castellana, where the Museo Nacional de Ciencias Naturales (as it was called since 1913) still resides today.

Surprisingly, at least from our present-day-perspective, the two Spanish emissaries were quite underwhelmed by the Muséum National d'Histoire Naturelle in Paris. Escalera complains about the gallery of mammals, describing it as the "most ludicrous and bad" that one might get to see. Obviously, the metropolis did not offer the model the Spanish naturalists had hoped for. Yet they found what they were looking for in other cities, in:

> Brussels and Altona and Dresden, and now in Leyden. There is a whole series of buildings for museums of natural history being built. This highlights that it is no longer Paris, London and Berlin, but ten other cities of the second and third order, not happy with their old museums, that are following the movement that the times demand and are constructing new ones, swiftly and generally well.[1]

This episode comprises in a nutshell some of the central themes of this book: study travels across Europe backed by an urban institution for the purpose of gathering models for reform "at home"; the imperative of modernization, that is, the "movement that the times demand"; doubts with respect to models provided by the major metropolis; instead learning from "ten other cities of the second and third order"; the crucial role of well-connected experts such as Escalera and Bolívar using their international networks; and the public dimension of this discourse on the improvement of the urban space, as Escalera published his travel report in a popular illustrated magazine.

This example highlights the closely-knit interurban networks and the search for best practices we would like to address in this volume. In its first part, this introduction will try to build a theoretical and conceptual framework, using different strands of urban history as well as the scholarship on knowledge transfer. Equipped with these concepts and tools, we shall then try in the second part to highlight the numerous connections and common themes between the 12 case studies of the volume.

The Modern City and Applied Urban Knowledge

The modern city (more on this notion later) took shape in the second half of the nineteenth century. What made it modern was not only the exponential growth of the population and the creation of a new urban infrastructure. The urban space was marked by a high concentration of short-distance relations, multi-directional exchanges within and the acceleration of movement and communication; for example, through the replacement of horse-drawn carriages by tramways or local trains. This modern city faced a whole range of interrelated problems such as rapid industrialization, a new working world, a serious housing crisis, "uncontrolled" immigration, high mortality, social inequality, crime and shocking poverty. These two factors – the "densification" within the city and the numerous social challenges – were instrumental for the development of new fields of "applied urban knowledge" such as urban planning, hygiene and "cultural infrastructures" (these three fields serve as headings for the three parts of this book). In other words, the inherent dynamic of the urban space and the production of applied urban knowledge entered a dialectic relationship.[2] The municipal administrations had to tackle the long list of problems they faced by modernizing the city in a comprehensive and informed way. The construction of a well-functioning sewage system and sufficient drinking water supply, providing city-dwellers and the growing industry with gas and later electricity and devising a tightly knit public transport system (trains, trams and trolley-buses) were the most pressing challenges city councils had to face. "Knowledge became a major resource for the future of urban development."[3]

This leads us to our central questions: Which models did the cities try to follow in their reforms? How did they inform themselves about the newest advances in, say, tuberculosis treatment or museum architecture? In short: how was this applied urban knowledge produced, communicated and appropriated?

Transnational Municipalism and Best Practices

Solutions were sought after in the form of "best practices" from other urban contexts. They were esteemed as "recipes for success" in order to modernize the cityscape according to a city's specific conditions.[4] In the decades after 1850, an interurban network emerged in Europe (and beyond) in which urban knowledge in its different forms was being constantly exchanged. Urban historians have coined the concept "transnational municipalism" which will be central for our book.[5] Disregarding national borders, urban reformers in different cities became increasingly aware that they were facing similar problems with respect to public health and urban planning. Many city councils reached out to other cities all over Europe or even across the Atlantic in order to modernize their own. There existed "a kind of European market in urban ideas, strategies and models."[6] In fact, best practices could literally be found around the globe. Through study trips of specifically appointed commissions, participation in international congresses and exhibitions, architectural competitions and other available sources of information, cities searched for best practices and then tried to adapt them back home. Reception and appropriation are two complementary processes of city-making, according to historians of technology Mikael Hård and Thomas Misa.[7] Or as Jens Lachmund put it: "Appropriation is always a selective process through which circulating concepts and objects get mixed with locally existing traditions."[8]

Thus, city councils and other municipal institutions were quite eclectic in their choice of best practices. They were well aware that the metropolis – as Escalera found out in Paris – might not always have the proper solution for their specific urban problems, or one they could afford. Cities of comparable size and with similar structural problems might have developed concepts that would fit their own needs and parameters much more suitably. This distinctly pragmatic approach also promised to avoid errors that had been committed elsewhere. Being "late" or "backward" might turn out to be advantageous, and could be used by reformers rhetorically as political leverage to demand new technologies or urban planning concepts in order to modernize their city.

This volume posits that the knowledge that circulated in this interurban space is "knowledge in transit," a concept from the history of science.[9] This concept argues against the so-called top-down model (or deficit model) in science communication. In this hierarchical model, scientific knowledge is produced in a clearly delimited space (such as a laboratory) and then transmitted in a simplified way to an allegedly ignorant audience. Yet this assumption does not do justice to the complexities of the generation of scientific knowledge. Rather, historians of science argue that knowledge is "co-produced" in the act of its communication. They stress the diversity of audiences, who may appropriate the transmitted knowledge in their own specific – and productive – ways.[10]

Applied to urban history and transnational municipalism, "knowledge in transit" implies that urban knowledge is permanently altered, combined, hybridized and adapted to fit the specific needs of a city. Empirical research will have to show to what degree this transfer was successful or not. Obviously, there is no guarantee that the interurban exchange of knowledge was going to work out. Time and again, the chapters in this volume will highlight the crucial importance of the local urban context and its specific political, social, economic and cultural characteristics in the analysis of this transfer of urban knowledge. Each city will appropriate best practices from elsewhere in creative ways, produce new knowledge through their syntheses and serve as a testing ground of new technologies.

This search for best practices can surely be found well before the mid-nineteenth century. And in the time span covered by this volume, cities were not the only actor eager to glean useful knowledge from homologous actors abroad. Searches for best practices may be found at a state-level or in transnational contexts,[11] but also at different institutional levels; for example, between prisons or in the realm of education to name but two examples.[12]

Yet as the rapid growth of the cities led to ever more pressing problems with regard to public health and dire living conditions from around the 1870s onwards, this interurban search is more problem-driven and systematic than earlier attempts. It is intrinsically connected with the formation of large bureaucracies at both the municipal and national levels at the same time. Local governments changed in character from a pure financial administration to a diversified administrative body defining new tasks and responsibilities in which the state did not intervene. Municipal government forms part of the increasing administrative penetration of the state ("Durchstaatlichung")[13] at the local and regional level, whereby more and more areas of public life became state-regulated and controlled. At the same time, municipal government was increasingly politicized and developed its own agendas. Hence, the modernization processes could be interpreted as a result of this politicization of local affairs. For this very reason, the applied urban knowledge in question is intrinsically political, marked by ideologies as well as distinct and often conflicting ideas of "modernity," "progress," "morality" and "nation."

The growth of municipal administration and the need for specific urban expertise created a new group of historical actors: experts in urban reform. These local politicians, council members, city planners, architects, physicians, hygienists, engineers, museum directors, journalists and business men are, in a sense, the protagonists of this book.[14] We will try to show that these actors were deeply embedded in both local and transnational networks.

Apart from transnational municipalism as practiced by these urban elites, we would also like to add another important but rather informal and indirect mechanism of knowledge exchange, the "interurban matrix."[15] This concept was coined by Nathaniel Wood, taking as a case study the city of Cracow. From the mid-nineteenth century onwards, both the number of newspapers and the literacy rates increased vastly across most of Europe. Wood argues that, through the ubiquitous daily press urbanites learned what was going on elsewhere, often comparing Cracow with other cities. The idea of the interurban matrix helps us to pursue the ideas of urban improvement beyond the circles of urban elites. Millions of newspaper readers became aware that they shared a very similar urban space with millions of other city-dwellers across Europe. They were bound together by a set of experiences, aspirations and values that found its most condensed form in the expression of the "European civilization," which was both a role model and point of reference, meaning modern transport systems, public health services, and cultural institutions such as the opera or the theater; in short: "modernity."

Modernity and Modernities

The terms modern, modernity and modernization seem omnipresent in the discourse about the city around 1900, both in the sources and in the secondary literature. The concept of "the modern city" is often used synonymously with the "European city" (and sometimes the "Western City" to include North America).[16] Often implicitly rather than explicitly, it posits the metropolis – "Paris, London and Berlin," in Escalera's words – as the urban model per se. Depending on the discourse, the "modern city" may also stand for the close link between industrialization and urbanization, with Manchester as the archetype.

Such a concept presupposes a historical teleology and thus a center-periphery model that is both hierarchical and normative. In particular, cities outside of the United Kingdom, France and Germany seem to be relegated by definition to an "inferior" position, "backward" and "delayed." (Urban) historians, trained to think anti-teleologically, have long been weary of these models. Yet in actual historiographical practice, it is quite hard to shake off these preconceptions, not least because much of the relevant scholarship has focused on the – supposedly – technologically more advanced Western European cities, the alleged vanguards of modernity.

"European history was dressed as universal development and treated as a yardstick and a model," as Sebastian Conrad put it.[17] And this is maybe even more the case in urban history. The "plot" of teleological modernization is deeply ingrained in our vision of the "modern city." It is this assumption that established the European (and North American) city as *the* model of reference in urban history and beyond. Even in their critique of this master narrative of modernity, many historians often still move within the Western world. Despite the recognition of the differences that other cities represent, there appears to be a strong tendency to treat them – in one way or another – as "deficient."

Some urban historians have suggested post-colonial theory as the best antidote in order to deconstruct the claim that Western civilization is the one and only root of modernity. It highlights the ubiquitous "othering" in a binary discourse of "modern/European" and "underdeveloped," "civilized" and "uncivilized," "advanced" and "backward," that marks – often more implicitly than explicitly – urban history.[18]

In the meantime, it has nearly become commonplace to criticize a monolithic understanding of "modernity." The idea of "multiple modernities," formulated two decades ago by sociologist Shmuel Eisenstadt, has been influential here.[19] He criticizes the notion that there was only one "cultural program of modernity" that was supposed to spread from Europe to the rest of the world. Many accounts of urban history establish a tight link between the concept of modernization and technological progress. The most recent technologies seemed to pave the way to a better urban future. For local actors, becoming modern meant applying the latest technologies and promising to make the city "healthier" and more "beautiful," a link that some of the chapters address. In the same vein, urban historians have long been attentive to the particularities of non-European cities and speak of "alternative" or "different modernities." Beatriz Sarlo, for example, refers to Buenos Aires as representing a "peripheral modernity."[20] The historiography about the evolution of Indian cities around 1900 is enormous. Urban historians describe the negotiation with and resistance to British models, thus stressing the unique character of Indian cities and their own contributions to urban modernity.[21] In these municipal networks, there was "at no stage a limited 'one-directional' flow of knowledge from Britain to the outer reaches of the Empire."[22]

Other scholars, while agreeing with the critique of one master narrative of modernity, have warned that this might lead to the idea of a fragmentation of modernities, as if they existed parallel to each other but were not intrinsically connected. Sociologist Göran Therborn therefore suggests the concept of "entangled modernities." Similarly, global historian Sebastian Conrad takes issue with Eisenstadt's concept of "multiple modernities" and instead proposes to speak of "variations on modernity i.e., one modernity with a diversity of cultural manifestations."[23]

Within cultural studies modernization is nowadays understood as a tightly interwoven and interdependent "clew of strings." These processes do not only transform economic conditions, but also social and cultural life, including mentalities.[24] Hence, different paths and understanding of "modernization" developed, depending on the starting point. As modernization is a dynamic process of diversification, each city could find and define its own way to become modern.

Particularities of Eastern and Southern Europe

Much of the scholarship cited so far is attentive to the opposition of "the West and the rest," vindicating the active role of, for example, "the

Global South," that may in no way be reduced to a simple receiver of preordained models. Buenos Aires, Calcutta (now Kolkata) and Bombay (now Mumbai) obviously lay outside Europe. But what about the cities located just around the "West," i.e. the United Kingdom, France and Germany? "The European city" used in an emphatic sense, as mentioned previously, tends to exclude Southern and East Central European cities.[25] Because they are not "central" enough for Western history and not sufficiently "distant" for global approaches, they end up in the blind spot of historical research, as Katalin Szende put it recently.[26] How do we as historians conceptualize these regions?

If, for a moment, we allow for some sweeping and obviously problematic generalizations: how was Southern Europe perceived around 1900? Spain and Portugal, once dominant colonial powers, and Italy, once Europe's leading cultural force, had lost touch with progressive enlightenment ideas and therefore, in the nineteenth century, struggled hard to catch up with the countries situated to their north. By contrast, societies in Eastern Europe, never had a leading role, being dominated by the large empires around them. To repeat: these categorical (dis)qualifications describe the perception of the historical actors, both in the center and at the periphery.

Research on Eastern (Central) European cities has gained momentum in recent years.[27] Scholars have pointed out their specific features: "It was particularly this ethnic-national, religious, and cultural diversity which would become a defining characteristic of East Central European cities until the twentieth century."[28] Urban historians argue that these cities found their own way to modernity, which indicates a paradigmatic shift in their reassessment of the history of these cities.[29]

The "Southern European city" is a far less used category in urban history. Historians have struggled to come up with a definition that comes to grips with the immense variety of potential candidates of Southern European cities. There is, for example, no clear consensus on how far the South extends and which cities to include. What about cities in the Ottoman Empire?[30] Most of the research, for example on Barcelona, Madrid and several Italian cities, focuses on the post-1945 era and the problem of uncontrolled suburban growth.[31] There is hardly any literature that attempts to situate Southern European cities within interurban networks around 1900.

As this book also shows, the tight and dynamic interconnections between urban modernization, transnational knowledge transfer and nationalization were perhaps the most important characteristics in the age of nationalism, of modernization and of technological and structural changes with respect to improvements in Eastern and Southern European cities.

We have now neared the starting point of the research project that culminated in this edited volume. From the very beginning, the three editors of this book were wondering: What should we call these cities that, allegedly, were not at the vanguard of urban modernization in the late nineteenth and early twentieth centuries? Our first workshop was entitled "'Urban Peripheries?': Emerging Cities in Europe's South and East, 1850–1945." We were well aware of the problematic connotations of "periphery" and thus put it in inverted commas and added a question mark. Yet in the end, we realized in the many discussions with our authors and other colleagues that even with these two qualifications the semantic "baggage" of a term such as "periphery" became too heavy. Even if it is not the historian's intention, the term tends to "downgrade" these cities, carrying connotations such as "backward" and "delayed."[32] Quite a number of (urban) historians have used the term "second cities," and with different slants. The basic idea of this term is to distinguish these second cities from the large metropolises and to identify characteristics unique to them.[33] Therefore, we entitled our second workshop "Interurban Knowledge Exchange. Emerging Cities in Southern and Eastern Europe, 1870–1945." Yet another concept is "emerging cities," a term that two of us, Eszter Gantner and Heidi Hein-Kircher, have coined.[34] It refers in particular to Eastern European cities developing into modern regional metropolises in the late nineteenth century and in some cases into national capitals after 1918. The concept of emerging cities stresses their proper agency. They understood that it was essential to compete and that, while it was important to learn from other cities, the metropolis, be it London, Paris or Berlin, was not by default the role model to follow due to the difference in scale and general predisposition.

In our view, the concepts "second city" and "emerging city" certainly carry analytical and conceptual merit. Yet in a sense they presuppose the center-periphery hierarchy they would like to question. It seems to be very hard to get rid of normative and teleological conceptions that posit the Western metropolis as the ultimate goal. Ultimately, all these adjectives – peripheral, second and emerging – define the city in reference to the metropolis and not independently.

In order to avoid that, we decided to deploy a neutral expression for the title of the book, simply calling it "Interurban Knowledge Exchange in Southern and Eastern Europe, 1870–1950," leaving aside semantically charged adjectives such as "second" and "peripheral." Even seemingly affirmative terms such as "emerging" may still evoke ideas of hierarchies and of having to "catch up." What is more, a larger historical perspective, dissolves quickly any kind of ranking. In the late Middle Ages and into the early modern period, Barcelona, Milan, Buda, Prague and Warsaw – to name but a handful of the cities that feature in our book – were centers of political power and economic prowess well beyond their region and hardly peripheral or secondary.

We would thus like to situate our research program in line with the global turn in recent historiography that intends to "decenter" space, and rather advocates concepts such as the mobility of actors and objects and the circulation of ideas and practices.[35] Yet this focus on interconnectivity does not imply that all interurban hierarchies simply disappear. First: while the historian may probably be well advised to avoid terms such as center (or metropolis) and periphery, in an analytical sense, they are highly relevant as actors' categories.[36] Searching for new ideas to build the natural history museum in Madrid, Escalera initially thought of Paris as providing the model and spoke of "cities of the second and third order." How historical actors perceived their cities and their relation to the large European metropolises is clearly important.

Second: in trying to use neutral terms, we in no way intend to gloss over the fact that in terms of political power, economic development or technological capacities highly unequal relations between cities existed around 1900 – and well before and well after that. The task of the historian thus consists in continuously questioning narratives that ascribe a monolithic version of modernity as represented by London, Paris, Berlin and Vienna, while still acknowledging the strong influence of these metropolises on so many cities and citizens in Eastern and Southern Europe.

The solution this book proposes is to think in terms of networks. Equipped with concepts such as transnational municipalism, knowledge in transit and the interurban matrix, the focus on individual cities should give way to concentrate on the multi-directional interchanges. A mere comparative approach might be insufficient, as it tends to essentialize the units of comparison, as the proponents of the *histoire croisée* have argued.[37] This is not simply a book about Eastern and Southern European cities, but rather about what is connecting them. It assembles an array of cities that generally do not appear side by side: Barcelona and Berdyansk, Milan and Lviv, for example. At the start of this research project, we felt that there was something experimental about our perspective, combining two large and apparently very distinct regions, Eastern and Southern Europe. What patterns of interurban knowledge exchanges would we find, if any?

The Structure and Chapters of This Volume

For systematic reasons, this book is divided in three sections: (1) urban planning, (2) public health, and (3) "cultural infrastructures." Yet it goes without saying that these three topics are generally closely interconnected in the urban space. Rather than simply listing the 12 chapters in order, in the remainder of this introduction, we will identify their common themes: the multi-directionality of interurban exchanges, the relationship between urban planning and nationalism, the tension between universal versus local models and identities, the role of interurban actors and the material dimension of interurban knowledge exchange. We thus hope to answer at least some of the questions raised earlier. More than this, in the following pages, we would like to draw attention to the historical complexity of each case study, of each urban space and interurban network. Indeed, there are numerous themes these chapters have in common, yet what this spectrum of case studies also brings to the fore, just as importantly, is the enormous variety of interurban knowledge exchanges.

Multi-Directionality of Exchanges

Knowledge is not produced in one space, and this is *a fortiori* the case with respect to urban knowledge. A number of chapters in this book exemplify the bi- or multi-directionality of interurban knowledge exchanges in which the large metropolises such as London or Paris feature little if at all. These transfers always changed what was being transferred, because the knowledge and the associated practices needed to be adapted to the local circumstances of a different urban space.

For example, in the 1880s, Moscow's city administration launched important urban reforms to improve appalling sanitary conditions, most notably a complete overhaul of the sewage system. Due to their "late" start, the sanitary reforms in Moscow could benefit from a paradigmatic shift in the understanding, prevention and treatment of epidemic diseases. Rather than "older" European metropolises, Moscow followed "smaller" cities in their reform of urban sanitation. New forms of sewage systems had been successfully tested, for example, in Toulon (France) and Memphis (United States), and relevant aspects were adopted by Moscow (Mazanik, Chapter 5). The other cases studies underline this finding: when Czech experts pondered how to reconstruct Prague's Jewish ghetto just before 1900, they studied urban renewal practices in cities such as Toulon, Naples, Florence, Berlin, Frankfurt-am-Main, and Nuremberg (Giustino, Chapter 1). Eclecticism but also selectivity mark the case of the planning of a modern tuberculosis dispensary in Barcelona in the early 1930s. Dissatisfied with the "Northern European" model, Catalan physicians and architects contemplated the architectural models in both the Soviet Union *and* Mussolini's fascist Italy. In the end, they built a dispensary according to the "Mediterranean" model, conceived of as a sort of multi-cultural melting pot. In this case, identity politics, ideologies, avant-garde discourses of innovation (functionalism) and medical theories around how to best fight tuberculosis were enmeshed – and hard to separate (Miralles Buil, Chapter 7). All these cases show, *mutatis mutandis*, that the transfer of best practices created new ways to reform the urban space.

Unknown except to specialists, prior to the Spanish Civil War, Barcelona had a thriving car industry and was home to several Spanish car companies and foreign company subsidiaries. The strong influence the US automobile industry had on Europe and on Spain in particular is undeniable. Yet the transfer of technology and design was, in fact, bi-directional. Spanish high-end cars were held in high esteem on both sides of the Atlantic, in Europe *and* the United States. Some of their features were even copied. The automobile industry is also by definition interurban, disposing of production sites in a number of cities. The Hispano-Suiza subsidiary in France near Paris is an example of the international projection of Barcelona-based companies. And in the 1920s the Czechoslovakian brand Škoda had a license to make Hispano-Suiza cars for the Eastern European market at their factory in Pilsen (Stiefel, Chapter 11).

On occasion, the assumed center-periphery-hierarchy is even inverted. When in 1902 Swiss hygienist Friedrich Erismann became a member of the Zurich City Council, he was able to use his vast experience in urban sanitary reforms gathered during 27 years in Russia (mainly Moscow) to spur on the reforms back home (Mazanik, Chapter 5). In 1907, Gustave Loisel searched for models and best practices with respect to the planned reforms of the Paris zoo and found them, among others, in some animal parks in Northern and Eastern Europe. He suggested to his French superiors to take note of the exemplary features of institutions in Breslau (Wrocław), Budapest, Stockholm and Pilawin in tsarist Russia. Hence the so-called "periphery" could provide ideas and blueprints considered worthy of emulation for the "center," in this case Paris (Hochadel, Chapter 9).

In a chronological sense, the last chapter in this volume describes the efforts of the Italian industrialist Guido Ucelli to create a Museum of Technology in Milan before and after World War II. In his search for best models and inspiration, Ucelli contacted and visited a large number of technological museums. This included several Eastern European ones, such as Prague, Warsaw and Budapest. Interurban knowledge exchange between Eastern and Southern Europe did not stop even after the Iron Curtain had cut the continent apart (Canadelli, Chapter 12).

In sum, applied urban knowledge did not circulate in linear or hierarchical ways but rather in multi-directional ways via horizontal connections between administrations, institutions and experts. Bi- or multi-directionality also means that, through the import and adaptation of foreign ideas, models and practices the local actors inserted themselves in interurban networks. Thus they were able to position themselves as players by presenting their results, for example Moscow's new sewage system, Barcelona's new tuberculosis clinic or Milan's new Museum of Technology not only to their publics "at home," but also within their interurban networks.

Urban Planning and Nationalism

The burgeoning scholarship on transnational history[38] of the last two decades aspires to overcome "methodological nationalism."[39]

"Transnational" or "transurban" histories even have become buzzwords. In particular, transurban studies seem to be a much needed counterweight to balance looking at this crucial period only through the lens of the "age of nationalism." "European cities are seen as nodes in communication networks that created a transurban public sphere," and therefore it is doubtful whether the emerging nation-state of the late nineteenth century should be the main frame of historical analysis.[40] We subscribe to this analysis, yet at the same time these two historical dynamics, nationalism and transurbanism, are by no means exclusive or strictly opposed. They are part of the same modernity, tightly interconnected, certainly not without friction but often spurring each other one, as many of the case studies illustrate.

In the late nineteenth and early twentieth centuries, cities were focal points – engines, really – of national movements. In particular, Eastern European regional and/or provincial capital cities played a central role in the nation-building process.[41] This volume deals with cities such as Warsaw, Budapest, Prague and Zagreb that became capitals of new nation-states after 1918 and thus political, economic and cultural centers. So, the connection between nationalist discourse and urban reform is, in most cases, self-evident. The point this volume would like to make is that this connection comes in all kinds of forms.

Why did municipalities and other actors select certain models and not others? This was in fact a complex process in which various interdependent factors played a role. We need to ask: what were the concrete needs of the city? In which pre-existing or emerging networks was the city situated? And possibly most importantly: to what degree did the local political constellations of the time shape the choices concerning urban reform? Around 1900, the city council of Lviv tried to reform the public health system, most urgently its sewers. In their search for technical solutions, the councilors consciously avoided the models from the Habsburg Empire (to which their city formed part of) but looked rather to Germany. Yet when it came to questions of identity politics, the Lviv aldermen tried to follow Warsaw and other Polish cities. The city council, dominated by ethnic Poles and their nationalist agenda, was eager to transform Lviv into a "Polish town" (Hein-Kircher, Chapter 6). This case study gives a clear hint that adopted best practices were "tinted" by the locally dominant nationality with their own national agenda.

Similarly, in Croatia, historical actors were reticent to be influenced by Hungarian architects and town planners due to their experience of feeling dominated by Hungarians at the time of the Austro-Hungarian Empire. Originally, urban planning and architectural models were imported directly from Vienna to Zagreb. Yet already around 1900, networks with centers of urban planning in Germany and also in France emerged. These networks proved long-lasting, well beyond World War I. In the interwar period, Croatian politicians and town planners relied heavily on foreign expertise in their quest to devise a plan for "Greater Zagreb." Yet, the international competition for this plan in 1933 raised questions about expertise and authority. Who should be entitled to sit on the board of the competition and make decisions? Does it matter which nationality they are? (Bjažić Klarin, Chapter 4). The reformers of Moscow's public health system, too, needed the expertise of foreigners but avoided nationalist overtones. Real "patriotism," they argued, cared about providing Muscovites with the proper "conditions for healthy life," not the nationality of the engineer (Mazanik, Chapter 5).

Czech nationalism weighed in on the reform of Prague's castle in the interwar period, leading to tensions with Jože Plečnik, the Slovenian architect in charge. Yet there were other, "non-nationalist," factors in play as well, all such as shifting local priorities and the personalities of the experts. These factors affected how receptive or reticent the municipal bodies were with respect to the import of foreign ideas and practices (Giustino, Chapter 1).

Nation-building agendas were not necessarily incompatible between "emerging nations," in particular if they both came from "peripheral" contexts. A highly instructive example is the intense collaboration between Catalan art historian, architect and politician Josep Puig i Cadafalch and his Romanian interlocutors, the historians Nicolae Iorga and Constantin Marinescu and the architects Petre Antonescu, Marica Cotescu and Maria Irineu in the 1920s and early 1930s. In their work on medieval history and architecture and the spread of Romanesque art and architecture, they helped each other in laying intellectual foundations in their respective projects of nation building in Catalonia and Romania. This "transnationally produced national history" challenges the widespread view that national history is disinterested in these kinds of intellectual exchanges with foreign colleagues, as in this case between Barcelona and Bucharest (Mallart, Chapter 10). Thus, caution is called for. The connection between urban reform and nationalist agenda is never uniform and straightforward as the various – quite different – cases in this volume show.

Universal Versus Local/National

Many of the chapters in this book address the growing tension between universal ideals on the one hand and the forging of local and national identities on the other hand. The processes of modernization and nationalization were deeply intertwined. Particularly in multi-national and multi-confessional contexts, this often led to the exclusion of the (ethnic or denominational) "other," i.e. of minoritarian and subordinate groups. In some of our Eastern European case studies, anti-Semitic attitudes were virulent in the discourses on how to modernize the cities of Prague, Lviv and Warsaw. Jewish communities (and quarters) are often identified as "backward," "unhygienic" and as an "obstacle" to the urban reform agenda.

Around 1900, cities in Eastern and Southern Europe had to straddle what turned out to be two interdependent, but also often contradictory, agendas: on the one hand, the modernization of the urban space by following metropolitan models from abroad and, on the other hand, an emerging sensitivity toward their own "cultural heritage" that might be in need of preservation.[42] With respect to the topic of this book, this might be translated into the embrace of or the resistance to knowledge transfer.

In their modernizing attempts, many cities aspired to a general notion of "Europe" or the "myth of Europe."[43] This manifested itself, for instance, in the spread of Hausmannian boulevards. In the case of Lviv and Budapest this import from Paris served as a conscious – and highly visible – defense against the urban model of the Austro-Hungarian capital Vienna. Other examples are the strong influence of German urban planning in Zagreb and the implementation of sewage systems by British engineer William Lindley in Budapest, Prague, Warsaw, and Moscow, to name only the cities that feature in this volume.[44]

Yet architects, engineers, journalists and local politicians often felt uneasy. Would this import of standard models in the name of modernization not have an irreversible homogenizing effect on urban spaces all over Europe? And would the tearing down of entire quarters not lead to an irretrievable loss of historic architecture and thus national identity?

The Prague case study illustrates very well these tensions between modernization and preservation. The ghetto was considered unhygienic beyond salvation, its flattening in the 1890s a necessary step. Yet the awareness for the historical value of urban structures increased. Novelist Vilém Mrštík feared that the city's attempt to "catch up" might lead to a "headlong collapse of our national individuality, so that in a short time, we will not understand what exactly about us is so valuable," as he warned in 1897.[45] This specter of losing something specifically Czech also marked the debate in the interwar years on how to reform Prague's famous castle (Giustino, Chapter 1).

We previously introduced Nathaniel Wood's idea of the interurban matrix made up by the increasingly large numbers of media and readers since the mid-nineteenth century. This interurban matrix was crucial in making city-dwellers aware of developments in other urban spaces. At the same time, these media also looked inward, pointing out deficiencies but also achievements at home. Periodicals were thus spreading the imperative of modernization well beyond the governing elites. Warsaw's popular magazines, for example, were constantly assessing and discussing the grade of modernization that their city had achieved. Seemingly paradoxically, the issue of urban poverty was part of the discourse on urban modernity. Yet, it did not go unnoticed that this modernization effort may turn the city into a denationalized and standardized European urban space. This was plainly at odds with the idea of Warsaw representing the "heart of Polishness," in particular given the fact that there was no Polish state at the time and Warsaw under Russian rule (Frysztacka, Chapter 8).

Catalan architect Josep Puig i Cadafalch rejected the geometrical grid of the Cerdà Plan (1859) that had been implemented in the large extension in Barcelona called Eixample. For Puig, due to its "universality," the Cerdà Plan lacked any kind of cultural (i.e. Catalan) specificity. Yet modern urban planning was not incompatible or strictly opposed to the historical fabric of a city. Puig designed a modern urban layout with an inspiration in the vernacular. His transformation of the square Plaça de Catalunya connected the new with the historic quarters of Barcelona and aimed at reinstalling hierarchy in the urban space by creating a clear center (Mallart, Chapter 10).

Hence, the "local" and the "universal" are not necessarily at odds with one another. An instructive example of their hybridization is the career of Hungarian artist Géza Maróti. His artistic "tool-kit" was gleaned from a particular regional or national culture, but became easily adaptable elsewhere, even in culturally very different urban settings, such as Mexico City and Detroit. The motifs and patterns Maróti developed and transferred between continents were at the same time universally decipherable, but also offered a specific reinvented urban and/or national identity for his customers. This demonstrates that neither the universal nor the local are static but in constant change, and in the case of Maróti, the local and the universal appear inseparable (Gantner, Chapter 3).

In the case of the port city of Berdyansk, situated at the southern margin of the Russian Empire, the constellation is quite different. Founded only in 1827 on the shores of the Sea of Azov, Berdyansk had no historical past to refer to while attempting to chart its path toward modernization. Trying to find its urban identity, this port city was rather torn between defining its proper place within the Russian Empire (and vis-à-vis its rival Odessa) and its multifold connections with Europe, in particular through trade, enterprising businessmen and the considerable number of foreign consuls from well over a dozen countries (Lyman and Konstantinova, Chapter 2).

(Inter-)Urban Actors

Historical actors of different kinds were crucial for the processes of knowledge production and exchange this volume tries to describe. This includes urban actors such as mayors, city councilors and leading civil servants in the cities' administrations, as well as interurban actors such as architects, urban planners, physicians and engineers working abroad and well situated in international networks. New professional elites – mainly technicians, but also bureaucrats – emerged in these local contexts. Due to their common education, interests and networks, they were often well connected with colleagues from other cities.

Urban and interurban actors are, of course, to be understood as ideal types. In practice there was a considerable overlap between the two types. These actors were ambitious, outward-looking and eager to modernize the(ir) urban space. The exchanges they pursued were multi-directional. In some cases, they deliberately eschewed the role model of the (imperial) capital in their reform schemes. Not only applied urban knowledge, but also historical actors, circulated in a multitude of ways and directions between urban centers in Southern and Eastern Europe – and beyond.

Four chapters of this volume have a clear protagonist: the Italian museum maker Guido Ucelli, the Hungarian artist Géza Maróti, the Catalan art historian Josep Puig i Cadafalch and the French reformer of zoological gardens Gustave Loisel. Other chapters feature "supporting actors" such as the Czech hygienist Isidor Soyka, instrumental in transferring the latest German best practices in hygiene to Prague, Swiss hygienist Friedrich Erismann working in Moscow, the tuberculosis-fighting physician Lluís Sayé in Barcelona and the British entrepreneur John Edward Greaves, who set up a reaper factory in Berdyansk. In one way or another, these historical actors operated as cultural brokers between institutions, cities and countries. As mediators, they were also crucial contributors to these processes of interurban knowledge exchange. Thus, it seems important to conceptualize the role of these interurban actors. The question is how, given their enormous diversity in terms of their background and agendas. They were by necessity multilingual and frequent travelers, mobile and flexible, often insiders and outsiders at the same time, and clearly aware of the potential advantages of inserting themselves in interurban networks. How did they negotiate their individual aspirations (professional career or business interests) alongside their "institutional" commitments, working for a municipal body, a ministry or a museum? What made them interchange ideas with other interurban actors? When and why did they decide not to? Clearly, more research, both on a conceptual and empirical level is needed to adequately characterize these interurban actors.[46]

The Material Dimension of Interurban Knowledge Exchange

We previously stressed that best practices were always adapted, altered, combined and improved in order to fit the specific local circumstances. It is thus of considerable interest to look at the concrete mechanisms by which these best practices were "translated" into a different urban context. This concerns the material dimension of knowledge exchange; that is to say, the large spectrum of media that gather, convey and discuss this genuinely urban knowledge. As we have seen, interurban networks of knowledge exchange, both formal and informal, existed between municipal governments, academics of all disciplines, engineers, architects, physicians, institutions such as museums and zoological gardens and other kinds of associations. These networks were sustained by study trips, exhibitions, international congresses and fairs, prize competitions, private letters and publications of all sorts ranging from books, expert reports and catalogs to articles in journals and newspapers.

Many chapters in this volume pay attention to the material dimension in which information circulated. In most cases, this will be written records, but it also includes all sorts of visualizations (maps, plans, models) and quantitative information. Such a focus will allow us to investigate how knowledge was received and appropriated by different audiences. Archival evidence shows, for example, how Catalan architect Puig i Cadafalch strategically sent his programmatic booklet *La Plaça de Catalunya*, bursting with plans and maps, to a larger number of his international contacts, while Catalan physician Lluís Sayé selected and used statistical data on tuberculosis from at least half-dozen countries, and received numerous cut-out articles from both specialist and general media through his international network. In order to write his three fact-packed *Rapports* totaling almost 600 pages for the French Ministry of Education, zoo reformer Gustave Loisel had to devise a complex agenda of gathering and preparing "raw" information from nearly 100 foreign animal-keeping institutions, mostly zoos, including their budgets, architectural drawings of animals' enclosures and photos, including postcards of their exhibits. Warsaw's popular weekly magazines, some of them richly illustrated, helped their large readership to understand their own urban space by constantly comparing and contrasting it with reports on other European cities. The reports of consuls from the port city of Berdyansk provided their governments in London, Brussels, Athens, Rome, Madrid, Oslo and many other capitals with up-to-date information, pointing out business opportunities that in turn helped to modernize the city on the Sea of Azov. The international competition on the urban master plan for Zagreb generated over 50 entries containing architectural drawings and city maps, and thus served as an important platform for interurban knowledge exchange. Even buildings such as the tuberculosis dispensary built in the Raval quarter of Barcelona in the mid-1930s reflect the multiple influences and adaptations of both medical theories and architectural styles. A focus on the materiality of interurban knowledge exchange should be very fruitful with respect to future investigations in this field.

Conclusion

From our particular perspective from Eastern and Southern Europe, the notions of center and periphery, of a dominating metropolis, and merely receptive second cities, have dissolved. (The afterword of Cor Wagenaar asks for the implications of this dissolution, going beyond our European framework and fin-de-siècle focus). To be sure, they remain important as actors' categories, as they have shaped the perception and actions of our protagonists, and we would like to stress that the symmetrical approach we pursued should never lose sight of the multiple asymmetries of political and economic power or the cultural influence that persisted.[47] Thinking in terms of networks seems crucial, yet hierarchies of all sorts need to be taken into account. As historians, we must try to grasp the dynamic of the period in question.

The circulation of applied urban knowledge followed its own logics und undercut center-periphery relationships. Often, this exchange of knowledge bypassed the metropolis and on occasion even inverted center-periphery trajectories. These logics of circulation are multifold, as this introduction has tried to show, and as the chapters of this volume describe in great detail. The interurban knowledge exchange included a large number of fields addressing concrete problems; it was multidirectional, highly eclectic and very much shaped by local factors (covering the entire spectrum between embracing and resisting knowledge from outside); it was also propelled by a new class of interurban actors and depended on networks of different sorts (institutional, personal and combinations thereof); and it was characterized by a constant tension between a transnational municipalism and processes of forging urban and national identities. This eclectic appropriation of ideas and practices from other cities often proved productive and innovative. We therefore consider our experiment of looking at two putative peripheries to be fruitful and promising with respect to future investigations. Our focus on knowledge exchange has brought to light both the numerous interurban connections and the individuality of urban spaces between Barcelona and Berdyansk.

Notes

1. Manuel Martínez de la Escalera, "Los museos a la moderna," *Alrededor del Mundo* (March 10, 1904): 149–150; our translation. For the context see Santiago Aragón Albillos, *En la piel de un animal. El Museo de Ciencias Naturales y sus colecciones de taxidermia* (Madrid: Consejo Superior de Investigaciones Científicas, Ediciones Doce Calles, 2014), 155–157.
2. Daniel T. Rodgers, *Atlantic Crossings: Social Politics in a Progressive Age* (Cambridge, MA: Harvard University Press, 1998).
3. Heidi Hein-Kircher, "The City and the Knowledge in East Central Europe: Plea for a Stronger Tie-Up in Research," *Journal of Urban History* 43, no. 4 (2017): 625–638, p. 633, https://doi.org/10.1177/00961442177053478.
4. Eszter Gantner and Heidi Hein-Kircher, "'Emerging Cities': Knowledge and Urbanization in Europe's Borderlands 1880–1945 – Introduction," *Journal of Urban History*, 43, no. 4 (2017): 575–586.
5. This historiography started off with Marjatta Hietala, *Services and Urbanization at the Turn of the Century: The Diffusion of Innovations* (Helsinki:

Finnish Historical Society, 1987). Instructive case studies are to be found in Pierre-Yves Saunier and Shane Ewen, eds., *Another Global City: Historical Explorations into the Transnational Municipal Moment, 1850–2000* (New York: Palgrave Macmillan, 2008); Nicolas Kenny and Rebecca Madgin, eds., *Cities Beyond Borders: Comparative and Transnational Approaches to Urban History* (Farnham: Ashgate, 2015).

6. Felix Driver and David Gilbert, "Imperial Cities: Overlapping Territories, Intertwined Histories," in *Imperial Cities: Landscape, Display and Identity*, eds. Felix Driver and David Gilbert (Manchester: Manchester University Press, 1999), 1–17, p. 9.
7. Mikael Hård and Thomas J. Misa, "Modernizing European Cities: Technological Uniformity and Cultural Distinction," in *Urban Machinery: Inside Modern European Cities*, ed. Mikael Hård and Thomas J. Misa (Cambridge, MA: MIT Press, 2008), 1–20, pp. 10–11.
8. Jens Lachmund, "The City as Ecosystem. Paul Duvigneaud and the Ecological Study of Brussels," in *Spatializing the History of Ecology. Sites, Journeys, Mappings*, ed. Raf de Bont and Jens Lachmund (London and New York: Routledge, 2017), 141–161, p. 142.
9. James A. Secord, "Knowledge in Transit," *Isis* 94, no. 4 (2004): 654–672. For three recent (and very different) examples of case studies see Anna Nilsson Hammar et al., eds., *Circulation of Knowledge: Explorations into the History of Knowledge* (Lund: Nordic Academic Press, 2018); John Krige, ed., *How Knowledge Moves: Writing the Transnational History of Science and Technology* (Chicago and London: The University of Chicago Press, 2019); Johannes Feichtinger, Anil Bhatti, and Cornelia Hülmbauer, eds., *How to Write the Global History of Knowledge-Making: Interaction, Circulation and the Transgression of Cultural Difference* (Dordrecht/London/New York: Springer, 2020).
10. Agustí Nieto-Galan, *Science in the Public Sphere: A History of Lay Knowledge and Expertise* (London and New York: Routledge, 2016).
11. Eszter Gantner, Heidi Hein-Kircher and Aleksander Łupienko, "On the Search for Best Practices: Emerging Cities and Their Transatlantic Relations," *Yearbook of Transnational History* 3 (2020): 1–13. The Japanese state, for example, sent several fact-finding missions to Europe from the 1860s onward, see Jürgen Osterhammel, *Die Flughöhe der Adler. Historische Essays zur globalen Gegenwart* (München: C.H. Beck, 2017), 109.
12. Martina Henze, "Transnational Cooperation and Criminal Policy: The Prison Reform Movement 1820s to 1950s," in *Shaping the Transnational Sphere: Experts, Networks, and Issues (c. 1850–1930)*, ed. Davide Rodogno, Bernhard Struck and Jakob Vogel (New York: Berghahn, 2014); Damiano Matasci, *L'école républicaine et l'étranger: Une histoire internationale des réformes scolaires en France, 1870–1914* (Lyon: ENS Editions, 2015).
13. On the general process: Jörg Ganzenmüller and Tatjana Tönsmeyer, "Einleitung: Vom Vorrücken des Staates in die Fläche. Ein europäisches Phänomen des langen 19. Jahrhunderts," in *Vom Vorrücken des Staates in die Fläche: Ein europäisches Phänomen des langen 19. Jahrhunderts*, ed. Jörg Ganzenmüller and Tatjana Tönsmeyer (Köln: Böhlau, 2016), 7–32.
14. The literature on these new experts is considerable. See for example: Rodgers, *Atlantic Crossings*; Martin Kohlrausch, Stefan Wiederkehr, and Katrin Steffen, eds., *Expert Cultures in Central Eastern Europe: The Internationalization of Knowledge and the Transformation of Nation States Since World War I* (Osnabrück: Fibre, 2010); Davide Rodogno, Bernhard Struck, and Jakob Vogel, eds. *Shaping the Transnational Sphere: Experts, Networks, and Issues (c. 1850–1930)* (New York: Berghahn, 2014).

15. See Nathaniel Wood, “Urban Self-Identification in East Central Europe Before the Great War: The Case of Cracow,” *East Central Europe/ECE* 33 (2006): 11–31; Nathaniel Wood, *Becoming Metropolitan: Urban Selfhood and the Making of Modern Cracow* (DeKalb: Northern Illinois University Press 2010), in particular 74–78 and 192–202.
16. Urban historians have discussed this issue at large, e.g. Friedrich Lenger and Klaus Tenfelde, eds., *Die europäische Stadt im 20. Jahrhundert. Wahrnehmung – Entwicklung – Erosion* (Köln: Böhlau, 2006).
17. Sebastian Conrad, *What is Global History?* (Princeton: Princeton University Press, 2017), 25.
18. Pedram Dibazar et al., “Questioning Urban Modernity (Introduction Special Issue),” *European Journal of Cultural Studies* 16, no. 6 (2013): 643–658, p. 655.
19. Shmuel N. Eisenstadt, “Multiple Modernities,” *Daedalus* 109, no. 1 (2000): 1–29, pp. 1–2.
20. Beatriz Sarlo, *Una modernidad periférica: Buenos Aires 1920 y 1930* (Buenos Aires: Nueva Visión, 1999).
21. To cite but two recent monographs: Anindita Ghosh, *Claiming the City: Protest, Crime, and Scandals in Colonial Calcutta, c. 1860–1920* (Oxford: Oxford University Press, 2016); Prashant Kidambi, *The Making of an Indian Metropolis: Colonial Governance and Public Culture in Bombay, 1890–1920* (London: Routledge, 2016).
22. John Griffiths, “Were There Municipal Networks in the British World c.1890–1939?” *The Journal of Imperial and Commonwealth History* 37, no. 4 (2009): *575–597*, p. 581.
23. Göran Therborn, “Entangled Modernities,” *European Journal of Social Theory* 6, no. 3 (2003): 293–305: Conrad, *What is Global History?* 60.
24. Hans van der Loo and Willem van Rijen, *Modernisierung. Projekt und Paradox* (München: dtv, 1992), 11–12, 45.
25. This has been pointed out by a number of urban historians, e.g. Martin Baumeister and Rainer Liedtke, “Probleme mit der ‘europäischen Stadt’: Städte in Südeuropa,” *Informationen zur modernen Stadtgeschichte* 1 (2009): 5–14, p. 7.
26. See the abstract of her paper “Medieval Cities and Towns in East Central Europe as Trading Hubs in a Global Perspective,” for the conference “The Pursuit of Global Urban History: A Dialogue Between Two Fields,” Leicester, July 2019.
27. Markian Prokopovych et al., Special Issue “Urban History in East Central Europe,” *East Central Europe/ECE* 33, no. 1–2 (2006); Kohlrausch, Wiederkehr and Steffen, eds., *Expert Cultures in Central Eastern Europe*; Markian Prokopovych, ed., Special Issue: “Thematic Block on East European Cities,” *Urban History* 40, no. 1 (2013); Jan C. Behrends and Martin Kohlrausch, eds., *Races to Modernity: Metropolitan Aspirations in Eastern Europe, 1890–1940* (Budapest and New York: Central European University Press, 2014).
28. Hein-Kircher, “The City and the Knowledge,” 3.
29. Ibid., and see the case studies of Jörg Gebhard, *Lublin: Eine polnische Stadt im Hinterhof der Moderne, 1815–1914* (Köln: Böhlau, 2006); Frank Henschel, *“Das Fluidum der Stadt . . .” Urbane Lebenswelten in Kassa / Košice / Kaschau zwischen Sprachenvielfalt und Magyarisierung 1867–1918* (Göttingen: Vandenhoeck & Ruprecht, 2017).
30. Cities in the Ottoman Empire were certainly also part of interurban knowledge exchanges; see Nora Lafi, “Mediterranean Connections: The Circulation

of Municipal Knowledge and Practices at the Time of the Ottoman Reforms, c.1830–1910," in *Another Global City: Historical Explorations into the Transnational Municipal Moment, 1850–2000*, ed. Pierre-Yves Saunier and Shane Ewen (New York: Palgrave Macmillan, 2008), 35–50.

31. See, for example, Baumeister und Liedtke, "Probleme"; Martin Baumeister, "Grenzen der Stadt: Masseneinwanderung und Öffentlichkeit in Barcelona und Turin 1950 bis 1975," in *Die europäische Stadt im 20. Jahrhundert. Wahrnehmung – Entwicklung – Erosion*, ed. Friedrich Lenger and Klaus Tenfelde (Köln: Böhlau, 2006), 417–436; Anna Pelka, *Urbaner Wandel und Öffentlichkeit: Die Peripherien Madrids und Barcelonas in der Zeit der Franco-Diktatur* (Köln: Böhlau, 2019), 20–22.
32. For a more detailed discussion of the term "periphery" in the urban history (of science), see Oliver Hochadel, and Agustí Nieto-Galan, "How to Write an Urban History of STM on the 'Periphery'," *Technology and Culture* 56, no. 4 (2016): 978–988; Oliver Hochadel, "Introducción: Circulación de conocimiento, espacios urbanos e historia global. Reflexiones historiográficas sobre las conexiones entre Barcelona y Buenos Aires," in *Saberes transatlánticos. Barcelona y Buenos Aires: Conexiones, confluencias, comparaciones (1850–1940)*, ed. Álvaro Girón, Oliver Hochadel and Gustavo Vallejo (Aranjuez: Doce Calles, 2017), 15–37.
33. Maiken Umbach, "A Tale of Second Cities: Autonomy, Culture, and the Law in Hamburg and Barcelona in the Late Nineteenth Century," *The American Historical Review* 110, no. 3 (2005): 659–692; Shane Ewen, "Transnational Municipalism in a Europe of Second Cities: Rebuilding Birmingham with Municipal Networks," in *Another Global City: Historical Explorations into the Transnational Municipal Moment, 1850–2000*, ed. Pierre-Yves Saunier and Shane Ewen (New York: Palgrave Macmillan, 2008), 101–117; Jerome I. Hodos, *Second Cities: Globalization and Local Politics in Manchester and Philadelphia* (Philadelphia: Temple University Press, 2011); Juliana Adelman, "Second City of Science? Dublin as a Centre of Calculation in the British Imperial Context, 1886–1912," in *Urban Histories of Science*, ed. Oliver Hochadel and Agustí Nieto-Galan (London: Routledge, 2018), 122–140.
34. Gantner and Hein-Kircher, "Emerging Cities."
35. Conrad, *What is Global History?*; for the history of science, see Kapil Raj, *Relocating Modern Science: Circulation and the Construction of Knowledge in South Asia and Europe, 1650–1900* (London: Palgrave Macmillan, 2010).
36. Hochadel and Nieto-Galan, "How to Write an Urban History"; Oliver Hochadel, "Periphery and Metropolis: Some Historiographical Reflections on the Urban History of Science," in *Science in the Metropolis. Vienna in Transnational Context, 1848–1918*, ed. Mitchell G. Ash (London: Routledge, 2020), 43–63.
37. Michael Werner and Bénédicte Zimmermann, "Beyond Comparison: Histoire Croisée and the Challenge of Reflexivity," *History and Theory* 45, no. 1 (2006): 30–50, p. 37.
38. The literature is enormous. See, among the more recent publications, e.g. Andrew K. Sandoval-Strausz and Nancy H. Kwak, eds., *Making Cities Global: The Transnational Turn in Urban History* (Philadelphia: University of Pennsylvania Press, 2017). A good guide is Conrad, *What is Global History?*
39. Matthias Middell and Katja Naumann, "Global History and the Spatial Turn," *Journal of Global History* 5, no. 1 (2010): 149–170, p. 155.
40. Claus Møller Jørgensen, "Nineteenth-Century Transnational Urban History," *Urban History* 44, no. 3 (2017): 544–563, p. 558.

41. Emily Gunzburger Makas and Tanja Damljanovic Conley, eds., *Capital Cities in the Aftermath of Empires: Planning in Central and Southeastern Europe* (London: Routledge, 2010).
42. Cathleen M. Giustino, "Prague," in *Capital Cities in the Aftermath of Empires: Planning in Central and Southeastern Europe*, ed. Emily Gunzburger Makas and Tanja Damljanovic Conley (London: Routledge, 2010), 157–173, p. 164; Nathaniel Wood, "Conclusion: Not Just the National: Modernity and the Myth of Europe in the Capital Cities of Central and Southeastern Europe," in idem, 258–269, p. 264.
43. Wood, *Becoming Metropolitan*, 193; Wood, "Conclusion: Not Just the National," 260.
44. Harald R. Stühlinger, "Jean-Charles-Adolphe Alphand: Les Promenades de Paris, 1867–1873," in *Manuale zum Städtebau. Die Systematisierung des Wissens von der Stadt 1870–1950,* ed. Vittorio Magnago Lampugnani et al. (Berlin: DOM Publishers), 30–49.
45. Vilém Mrštík, "Bestia Triumphans," *Rozhledy* 6 (1896–1897): 588.
46. For a possible starting point, see the dossier edited by Antje Dietze and Katja Naumann, "Revisiting Transnational Actors from a Spatial Perspective," *European Review of History: Revue Européenne d'histoire* 25, no. 3–4 (2018): 415–430. Also see David Pretel and Lino Camprubí, eds. *Technology and Globalisation: Networks of Experts in World History* (Cham: Palgrave Macmillan, 2018).
47. As Nygård and Strang put it with respect to intellectual exchanges: "the emphasis on hybridity, entanglement, and reciprocity that has dominated recent discussion on transnational history should be complemented with an acknowledgment of center – periphery tensions and the asymmetrical nature of transnational cultural interaction"; Stefan Nygård and Johan Strang, "Facing Asymmetry – Nordic Intellectuals and Center-Periphery Dynamics in the European Cultural Space," *Journal of the History of Ideas* 77, no. 1 (2016): 75–98, p. 96.

Part I

Building a Modern City

Networks in Urban Planning

1 The Ghetto and the Castle

Modern Urban Design and Knowledge Transfer in Historic Prague Before and After 1918

Cathleen M. Giustino

Prague is an old city with a long history. It dates back to the ninth century when Prince Bořivoj built the first castle on one of the surrounding hills while below it, alongside the Vltava River, settlement and trade began to develop. In the decades leading up to World War I, Prague was the capital of Bohemia, a province in the multi-national Habsburg Monarchy. By then, centuries of native and foreign rulers had bequeathed the historic urban center a dense network of winding streets and stone buildings dating from the Romanesque, Gothic and Baroque eras. The late nineteenth century was a time of growing national conflict in Prague. During it, Czechs dominated the levers of municipal power in the Bohemian capital, while Germans were far less involved in City Hall decisions, but not entirely absent. Local medical experts were eager to learn about modern urban design practices in foreign countries and apply the most useful of them to municipal plans for the improvement of public health in Prague.

After World War I, Prague was named the capital city of the new independent state of Czechoslovakia. In the interwar period, Czechs continued to dominate decision-making about Prague's built landscape, but by then, the constellation of professional interest groups active in the shaping of the city's physiognomy had changed. Architects and others interested in the preservation of built heritage were now very involved. Their reception of foreign ideas about modern urban design was mixed compared to that of the pre-war medical experts; some were very enthusiastic, others were resistant.

Both before and after 1918, nationalism played a role in the construction of Czech attitudes toward the transfer of knowledge on urban matters but, as this chapter will show, so did a number of other important factors, including both the positions of experts, who competed for authority on a playing field of power, and the abilities of insiders and outsiders to work together.[1] To shed light on these reasons for differing Czech stances toward foreign modern urban design practices, this chapter will discuss two important projects in historic Prague – one carried out prior to World War I and the other conceived during the interwar period. For the pre-war example, the late nineteenth-century urban redevelopment of Josefov, Prague's former Jewish ghetto, will be examined. This significant modernization project, which tremendously changed the architectural and social composition of part of the city center, was mostly completed by 1914.[2] For the interwar example, the work of the now world-renowned Slovenian architect Jože Plečnik on the reconstruction of the Prague Castle, a former imperial seat of power overlooking the symbolic city center, will be explored. While Plečnik's brilliant designs for renovations inside the Castle walls were largely realized, his plans for streets leading to those walls remained unbuilt.[3]

At first glance, it might seem incongruous to compare the modern urban design histories of a former ghetto and a castle, one once the home of a persecuted minority and the other a past residence of kings and Holy Roman Emperors. Yet, the two projects shared something significant in common: both were perceived as important for the projection of Czech national status and power through the architecture of the capital city, and both garnered attention from university-trained experts who used the spaces of the Bohemian capital in their quests for leverage and authority.[4]

Through examination of urban plans for Prague's former Jewish ghetto and the Castle, we can observe a process in which professionals, some emerging and some established, used the architecture of a historic city to promote and empower a consolidating nation and also themselves.[5] Studying expert interest groups is also a useful way to move beyond reifying notions of monolithic nations and expand appreciation of negotiation and struggle in the construction of national identities. Additionally, it opens up methodological possibilities for the study of knowledge transfer by calling attention to ways in which the shifting priorities, positions and personalities of experts inside and outside of nations can affect receptivity to foreign ideas and practices.[6]

Historic Prague and Its Place in the Modernizing World

In the decades before World War I, the Austrian Municipal Statute of 1850 specified the duties and powers of Prague's local government.[7] The Statute gave municipal managers in the Bohemian capital significant autonomy over the administration of public health, sanitation, streets and buildings, all important aspects of modern urban design. It created two elected representative bodies, the City Council and the Board of Aldermen. They met in the City Hall on the Old Town Square, a political and symbolic center in historic Prague and an important place for the gathering and dissemination of knowledge about science and the city.

Prior to World War I, representatives of municipal Prague were elected according to a very narrow suffrage, allowing only a small oligarchy of men access to local parliamentary power. Annual tax payments and gender determined who enjoyed the citizens' right to vote or run for municipal positions. In the second half of the nineteenth century, Czechs always controlled Prague's elected municipal bodies. Their domination over the levers of local power was further strengthened following Mayor Tomáš Černý's 1882 "Golden Slavic Prague" speech. His words so affronted the small number of German elected representatives in the Aldermen Council (five out of a total of 90 representatives) that they gave up their seats, with only one German again holding elected municipal power between then and the start of the First Czechoslovak Republic in 1918.[8]

The German absence made Prague's City Hall a local bastion of Czech power used to shape the city's spaces as its managers argued best promoted their nation's interests. Still, this was no system of monolithic control. Two Czech political parties, the Old Czechs and the Young Czechs, competed against one another for domination over municipal resources. The parties, both of them liberal and national, argued heatedly over many issues, most notably over the role of religion in education and government. The Young Czechs, in contrast to the Old Czechs, wanted strict separation of church and state.

Still, despite their differences, the two political parties had something in common. They were united in their desire to participate in the advances of the industrializing, modernizing West – or at least in their readiness to use the idea of belonging to the progressive world order as a political resource. The Old Czechs were not so "old" that they spurned participation in scientific progress; the Young Czechs were not so nationalist that they refused to learn from other parts of Europe, including Germany.[9] The fact that neither of these pre-war Czech political parties was averse to foreign knowledge can be seen in the history of the urban redevelopment of Prague's former Jewish ghetto, where the city's poorest residents lived – many of them Christians – after the full emancipation of Prague's Jews in 1859. This was a "sanitation" project entailing extensive demolition and reconstruction, in addition to population transfer.[10]

In order to appreciate the history of the tearing down of Prague's Jewish town, it is necessary to consider the physical borders of historic Prague prior to 1918. In the final decades of Austro-Hungarian rule, the Bohemian capital consisted of a much smaller area than after the breakup of the old monarchy and the creation of Czechoslovakia. Under the terms of the 1850 Municipal Statute, its borders included the five historic wards of Old Town, New Town, the Little Side, Hradčany and Josefov. The latter, Josefov, contained Prague's former Jewish ghetto. By 1910, the borders of municipal Prague, a relatively small urban area, had expanded to include the new wards of Vyšehrad, Libeň and Holešovice.

During the latter half of the nineteenth century, Bohemia was a place of intense industrialization and migration from the countryside to the city, as people sought work following the abolition of serfdom under the monarchy in 1848. These momentous changes contributed to the growth of an "iron ring" of suburbs with factories and workers' housing that encircled historic Prague. The surrounding suburbs, which sat at a higher elevation than the center, each had their own independent municipal governments.

The industry and population growth in the "iron ring" challenged public health conditions in the historic city, which was built down along the banks of the polluted Vltava River where stone houses, narrow streets and shallow, wooden sewers had been constructed to accommodate the needs of a much smaller, pre-industrial population. The historic city and the new industrial suburbs made little effort to coordinate their municipal projects. Streets were built in the new areas of development without considering their relations to established arteries in the historic core and in a manner that obstructed the flow of traffic and fresh air to the increasingly toxic center, contributing to worsening health conditions for its residents.

The declining level of public hygiene in historic Prague, particularly in the ward of Josefov, the former Jewish ghetto, led municipal leaders to raise concerns about the well-being of the local population. Very importantly, those concerns became linked to dire warnings about the Czech nation lagging behind the progressive world order. This language of backwardness, while undoubtedly at times the result of genuine worry, also functioned as a tool of interest-group struggle when members of the Young Czech and Old Czech parties competed against one another for municipal power.

Leaders of both parties compared their city to other urban centers in Europe and elsewhere in the world, painting a bleak picture. For example, in a speech he gave in December 1878, Julius Grégr, a leading Young Czech, told his audience,

> Even when one does not consider the number of dead in hospitals, Prague appears to be, in spite of everything, the fourth most unhealthy city in Europe. Only three cities compete with Prague for this sad precedence and, moreover, even two cities outside of Europe that are famous for their unusually poor health, Bombay and Madras, sometimes demonstrate more favorable death rates.[11]

In their struggle for power, both parties made announcements about how they would not only improve health in the Bohemian capital, but also advance the Czech nation's standing in the progressive world order. This contributed to their willingness to pursue the urban redevelopment of Josefov, Prague's former Jewish ghetto, a project that local medical experts, using scientific measures and foreign knowledge, eagerly promoted.

Medical Experts and the "*Finis Ghetto*" Plan

Prior to 1900, medical experts were the university-trained specialists with the most interest in and most influence over urban planning in municipal Prague. In 1877, Czech medical experts called for the institutionalization of their knowledge in the City Hall. In response, in May 1878, the City Council created the Municipal Health Commission, which was given responsibility for monitoring public health challenges and pursuing solutions to them. Initially, the commission included only representatives elected to positions in the City Hall, but before long, experts in medicine, most of them Czech, were appointed to join its deliberations. Czech architects and others who were knowledgeable and passionate about historic Prague, including art historians and archeologists, were not asked to participate; nor at that time did they show much interest in being involved or in aspects of urban planning.

In March 1879, a report put out by the new commission called on science to help ease Prague's plight. It stated that,

> Should the public sanitation service not fall into stagnation, but rather experience a continuous transformation corresponding to progressive science and experience, then the constant contact with scientific powers, which promote and strive for better hygienic standards in various areas, appears urgently required.[12]

The institutionalization of medical expertise in Prague deepened in November 1880 when the municipality appointed its first public health director, the Czech physician Dr. Ignác Pelz. In 1884, Dr. Jindřich Záhoř, also a Czech physician, replaced him. Záhoř, like other medical experts in Prague, was familar with contemporary theories about the spread of disease, including those of Max von Pettenkofer and Robert Koch in Germany. He learned much about these theories from Isidor Soyka.

Soyka played an important role in the transfer of foreign knowledge about public health and hygiene to Prague. As a Jew who could write in Czech, but primarily worked in the German language and with German institutions, Soyka did not neatly fit into standard categories used to describe Prague's complex ethnic mix. Regardless of his German ties, he had a good relationship with Záhoř and other Czech members of the Municipal Health Commission, helping them to appreciate and spread the ideas of von Pettenkofer and Koch from Germany to the Bohemian capital.

In 1874, Soyka completed his studies in medicine at Prague's Charles-Ferdinand University, which had not yet been divided along national lines. From 1879–1884, he worked as an assistant to von Pettenkofer in the latter's Institute of Hygiene, which formed part of the Medical

Faculty at the University of Munich. There he focused on the study of the spread of disease through soil and water, synthesizing information from von Pettenkofer's and Koch's theories. In 1880, he also earned a degree in construction hygiene (*Bauhygiene*), which involved studying building from the perspective of public health and sanitation, at the Technical University in Munich, going on to teach the subject there from 1880–1883.[13]

By the time that Soyka returned to Prague in 1884, the Charles-Ferdinand University had been divided into Czech and German halves. He was appointed professor at the German half, where he founded the first Institute of Hygiene in the Bohemian capital. There he taught "sanitation" (*die Assanierung*; *asanace*), among other subjects. After his appointment in Prague, he traveled abroad to various meetings pertaining to public health. For example, in 1884, he attended the Hygiene Exhibition in London, and in 1885, he spent two weeks at Robert Koch's institute in Berlin. In addition to his teaching and research activities, Soyka also regularly participated in municipal meetings regarding public hygiene. He served as a respected and respectful member of the Municipal Health Commission and helped to transfer foreign knowledge important for modern urban design and public health to Prague until his death in 1889.[14]

In 1885, Soyka helped Záhoř, who was still Prague's director of public health, and Václav Janovský, a Czech physician in the Municipal Health Commission, to write the annual report on that year's commission activities. Using records from municipal health inspectors, who gathered statistics about illnesses in the individual wards of municipal Prague, the participants in this collaborative effort counted and compared cases of infectious diseases and deaths resulting from them in each part of the city. The diseases included smallpox, scarlet fever, diphtheria, measles, whooping cough and typhus.

Based on this comparison and knowledge about the growing science of hygiene at home and abroad, the report concluded that Josefov had more than twice the number of cases of sickness and death due to infectious disease than the other wards in Prague, and that the diseases threatening residents throughout the urban center had, in many cases, developed in the former ghetto and spread from there. In order to improve public health in the Bohemian capital, the report argued that it was necessary to completely demolish and rebuild Josefov. This was a bold and striking conclusion. In summarizing it, the report stated, "Only a radical method can help, that is, tearing down the ward and rebuilding it on the foundation of modern hygiene and at state expense."[15]

In the call for the radical urban redevelopment of Josefov, Záhoř and his colleagues in the medical profession made reference to examples of promising modern urban design and public health practices taking place in other European cities, including Toulon, Naples and Florence. Záhoř had not studied or worked abroad, as Soyka had, but he wanted to deepen his knowledge of the science of hygiene in other cities, so in

July 1885, he traveled to Berlin, Frankfurt-am-Main and Nuremberg to investigate public health measures in those cities.[16] Reports on his travels were published on the front pages of the newspaper *Pokrok* (*Progress*), one of the daily publications of the Old Czech Party, thereby helping to share knowledge of foreign urban practices with the public. While his reports did not state why he had traveled to those particular cities and skipped others, they provided insights into what he had learned from – and what he wanted other Czechs to learn from – his travels. For example, he described his visit to the modern sanitation and water works of Berlin with the important German engineer, James Hobrecht, as one of his guides. He shared his great enthusiasm for how successful this modern technology was at cleaning the polluted waters of the German capital. "If I had not seen it with my own eyes. . . . I would never have been convinced that so much waste water could be without local health problems," he wrote. He was impressed that he barely noticed any bad smell. From his trips to Berlin and Frankfurt-am-Main, Záhoř concluded that, on account of Prague's hilly terrain, the Bohemian capital would need a different solution for its sanitation and water works.[17]

After accepting the Municipal Health Commission's radical conclusion that Josefov needed to be torn down and rebuilt, in October 1886, City Hall officials announced that they would hold a competition for the best plan for the urban redevelopment of the former ghetto and neighboring parts of the Old Town. Four months later, on 22 February 1887, the winning design was announced. It was entitled "*Finis Ghetto*" or "The End of the Ghetto." Alfred Hurtig (a municipal geometrician), Matěj Strunc (an architect), and Jan Hejda (a municipal engineer) designed it. They left no records about what inspired their design. It included a wide, straight boulevard that ran through the middle of Josefov in a manner reminiscent of Hausmann's Paris and a street that encircled the western side of it in a way that shared some resemblance to Vienna's Ringstrasse (see Figure 1.1).

A picture of Hurtig's "*Finis Ghetto*" plan was printed in only one place. This was the April 1887 issue of the illustrated weekly *Golden Prague* (*Zlatá Praha*), a middle-class Czech publication. The brief and anonymous commentary accompaning the plan is worth noting, as it included statements that projected an image of the Czech nation's inferior position within a progressive world order. It suggested that Josefov was an embarassment to Czechs and a cause of loss of respect for them among advanced Westerners. The author denigrated the old ghetto as a pocket of Oriental backwardness near the heart of Prague, saying:

> on the right bank [of the Vltava] stands the monumental building of the Rudolfinum and behind this rich entrance to a modern city, in close proximity, is the repulsive labyrinth of twisting, narrow streets

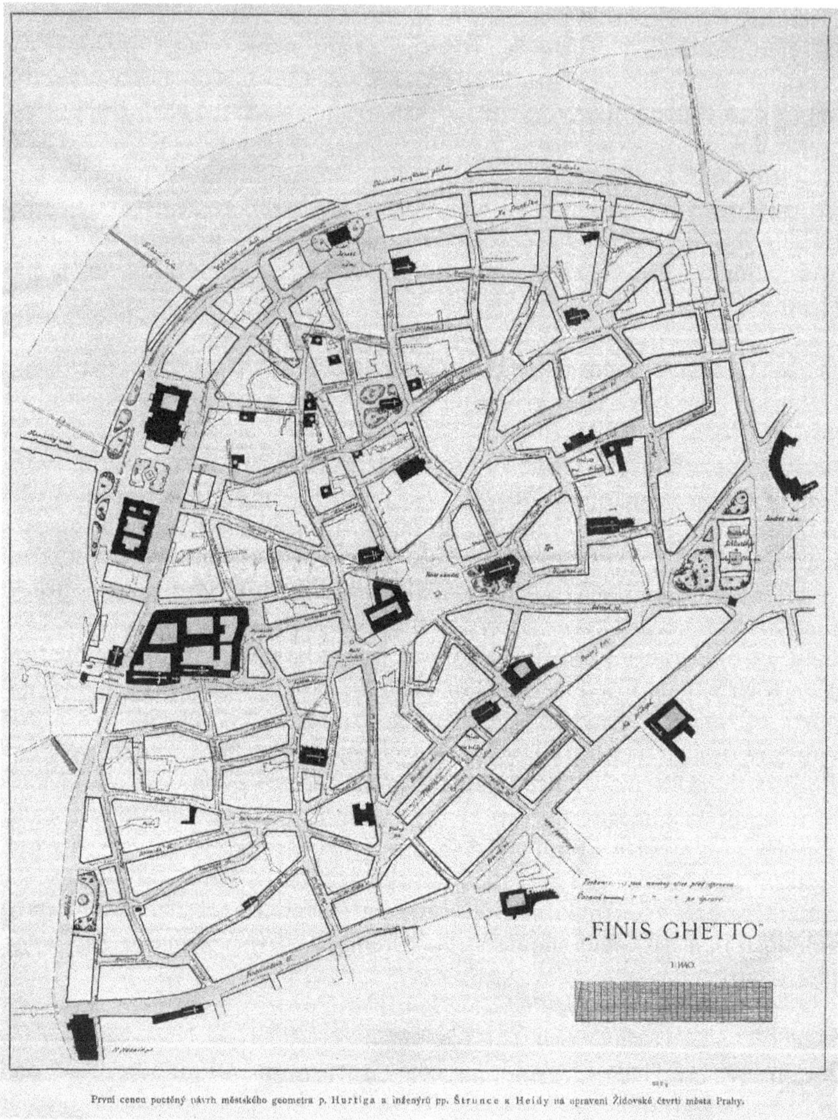

Figure 1.1 The "*Finis Ghetto*" plan, Prague 1887.

Source: From *Zlatá Praha*, 4 (1887): 348; private collection of Cathleen M. Giustino

filled with foul-smelling odors from gutters, smoke gushing forth from low chimneys, and animated figures and scenes, which look as if they were carried to Prague straight from the Orient, from somewhere in Baghdad.[18]

Using a disparaging view of the non-Western world to build support for the tearing down of Prague's Jewish town, the commentary rhetorically asked, "Why travel to the Far East, when it is possible to find the most neglected corner of Istanbul here in the middle of the capital city of the Kingdom of Bohemia!"[19]

By the time these passages were written, many of the former ghetto's Jewish residents had moved to more salubrious parts of Prague, and poor Christians, who were often migrants from the countryside during an age of rapid industrialization, lived there in overcrowded rooms with scant sanitary facilities.[20] Still, as words in these passages suggest, anti-Semitism, in addition to worries about national backwardness and public health, was a force behind the urban redevelopment plan, albeit in a complex manner that cannot be unpacked in this article about knowledge transfer and modern urban design in Prague before and after World War I.[21]

Architects and the Call to Preserve Historic Prague

On the eve of World War I, most of the "*Finis Ghetto*" plan had been transformed into built reality and the British engineering firm of William Lindley had laid new modern sewers under the old ghetto. Of the 260 stone structures that had existed in Josefov in 1895, only a dozen or so remained, including six of the former nine synagogues and the Jewish Town Hall.[22] A section of the historic Old Jewish Cemetery had vanished, too. New straighter, wider streets lined with fashionably ornamented luxury apartments for the upper-middle class appeared on land previously covered with winding alleyways, closed-end courtyards and the unhygienic housing in which Prague's poorest denizens had resided during the final decades of the nineteenth century.[23]

As the implementation of the "*Finis Ghetto*" plan commenced, opposition to it and to the destruction of historic architecture resulting from it began to emerge. Among the leaders of this opposition were Czech architects who now wanted a voice in decisions regarding the Bohemian capital's built landscape. The architects, who were not involved in the creation of the urban redevelopment project, had become anxious and fearful that their artistic knowledge, some of it learned through study in Vienna, Rome and Athens, was unappreciated in the face of medical experts' scientific knowledge.[24] They made a new appeal for the role of historic Prague's architecture in the advancement of the Czech nation and, as a result, better positioned themselves to win leverage and authority in decisions about urban planning. They did not evoke anxieties about backwardness in the progressive world order, as champions of the "*Finis Ghetto*" plan did. Instead, the architects projected different urban and national fears. They argued that, because the plan was based on foreign ideas, it threatened the historic city with a loss of distinctiveness and the Czech nation managing the municipality with a loss of identity and power.

The Czech architects wanted their expert opinions to be heeded. In April 1895, they sent the City Council "The Memorandum in the Name of the Alteration of Prague (Pamětní spis ve příčině úpravy Prahy)." It called for the creation of a municipal commission that would oversee the urban planning of Prague "from the artistic point-of-view" and "examine legally approved regulation plans, especially the one for the sanitation zone, from the artistic perspective." This commission was to be the center of knowledge within the City Hall for experts in architecture and art history. The new body was also to help Czech architects to gain an institutional foothold in the local government that could be used for negotiating with and competing against other interests, including medical experts.[25]

In October 1896, local elected representatives replied to the architects' request for the institutionalization of their expertise by creating the Municipal Artistic Commission. This new consulting body consisted of 11 members, including six architects, three professors of ornamental drawing, one building engineer and one builder. All members were Czechs, with the exception of Friedrich Ohmann, a German from Lviv, who at the time taught at Prague's Academy of Fine Arts.[26] The commission identified the artistic improvement of Hurtig's "*Finis Ghetto*" plan as its first priority. In June 1897, it presented the City Council with a new design for the streets of Josefov, one that required far less demolition. The following December, the City Council rejected the plan, saying that it was too expensive, it did not promote public hygiene and that the municipality was legally bound to work with the "*Finis Ghetto*" plan. After failing to convince local representatives to revise their decision, the Artistic Commission's members all resigned and went looking for a new way to secure influence and authority for their expertise.[27]

It was at that point that the architects joined forces with other members of Czech society who were both opposed to municipal plans for modern urban design and increasingly devoted to the preservation of historic Prague. Among them were celebrated writers, university students and middle-class women. The members of this growing community were not anxious about their nation's belonging to the progressive world order, because they did not perceive their nation as backward. They worried that, if historic Prague were to be modernized, the city would come to look indistinguishable from other European cities and thereby lose its uniqueness and authenticity. They argued that, without a distinct capital city, the Czech nation could be threatened with diminished power and even extinction.

Opposition to chasing after belonging in the advanced world order was best expressed in the article "*Bestia Triumphans*," written in 1897 by the novelist Vilém Mrštík, a friend of some important Czech architects and artists. Mrštík did not mince his words when he criticized the champions of foreign-knowledge transfer:

> The City Council, when making excuses for its infamous machinations, usually gives various reasons – now transportation, now health, now interest in some sort of revival of the city and, now again, a *fata morgana* of Greater Prague, just like a trade mission from Berlin or Vienna would imagine it. These reasons are generally summarized in one grand phrase: "The interest of Prague as the world capital city of the Kingdom of Bohemia demands."[28]

Expressing his fear of the homogenizing logic of the race for world-nation status and its implications for the Czech nation, he wrote,

> All of that [imitation of foreign developments] supports and accelerates the headlong collapse of our national individuality, so that in a short time we will not understand what exactly about us is so valuable, when we no longer exist as an independent nation with its own culture, when our entire way of life, inside and out, is derived from others and nothing more than language distinguishes us from Germans.[29]

Attention to the preservation of Prague's architectural heritage only slightly halted the imposition of urban redevelopment onto the landscape of Josefov.[30] The "*Finis Ghetto*" plan was mostly realized. The far greater lasting success of the architects lay in their founding of the Club for Old Prague in January 1900.[31] The club was a Czech civil society dedicated to ensuring that modernization plans did not harm the city's architectural heritage and unique character. During the interwar period, it strove to keep the Czech public informed about threats to historic Prague. Leading members included university-trained experts in architecture and art history. They read and disseminated the ideas of foreigners knowledgeable about historic preservation, including Viollet-le-Duc, John Ruskin and Georg Dehio.[32]

Through the Club for Old Prague, Czech architects, along with Czech experts in art history, historic preservation and archeology, increased their authority and influence in government positions important for the shaping of the city's built landscape. For example, before the war, the club's first president, Luboš Jeřábek, won a seat in the Alderman Council based on appeals for the protection of historic Prague and then went on to direct the Czech half of the Provincial Office of Monument Care for Bohemia, a position within the Austrian Ministry of Culture and Education.[33] During the interwar period, another club member, Zdeněk Wirth, secured employment in the new Czechoslovak Ministry of Education and

Enlightenment, where he was responsible for the administration of archeology, museums, archives, libraries and monument care until 1938, the year of the Munich Agreement.[34]

The remainder of this chapter will seek understanding of Czech attitudes toward foreign knowledge about urban planning after World War I. It will examine reactions of Czech experts in architecture and historic preservation to the modern urban designs of the Slovenian architect, Jože Plečnik, official architect of the Prague Castle for most of the interwar period. It will reveal resistance to knowledge transfer and provide insight into reasons for that resistance.

The First Czechoslovak Republic and President Masaryk's Vision for the Prague Castle

During the 1920s, jurisdiction over the urban planning of Prague was very different than it had been while the Habsburg Monarchy existed. After the creation of Czechoslovakia, responsibility for the capital city's built development was transferred out of the offices of the municipal government to the State Regulation Commission, a new urban planning authority within the Ministry of Public Works which was a central government body.[35] Vocal and influential experts in architecture, engineering and health met in the State Regulation Commission to discuss and decide on plans for Prague's development.[36] Some of them belonged to the Club for Old Prague, which grew in influence and remained greatly concerned about protecting the historic city. Adding to their worries was the rise after 1918 of a new generation of modernist Czech architects who had no reservations about or objections to demolition in historic Prague for the sake of modernization. Jaromír Krejcar was a modernist Czech architect during the interwar period. He called opposition to demolition in historic Prague "the Old Town taboo" and equated that opposition with:

> the reign of terror . . . imposed by several sentimental art historians, not only over architects with modern views and sensibility . . . but also over the population of the city by forcing their lives into a tangle of old, narrow streets.[37]

The significant transfer of urban planning authority from the municipality to the central government in the new country of Czechoslovakia occurred as part of the creation of Greater Prague. In Greater Prague, historic Prague and all surrounding suburbs were incorporated within one large municipal government. The City Hall on the Old Town Square remained a central meeting place for local politicians and administrators. In contrast to the very limited voters' rights of the Habsburg period, in Greater Prague there was universal adult suffrage for municipal representatives. Czechs remained in control of municipal power, reduced though it was due to the State Regulation Commission, and with some Germans returning to elected positions in the city government.[38]

Rising above downtown Prague on one of the city's many hills is the Prague Castle, a centuries-old architectural complex of ecclesiastical and secular structures revealing multiple layers of spiritual, architectural and political history. In contrast to the historic wards of Old Town and Josefov situated below it, during the decades before World War I, when Habsburg administrators had offices in the Castle, few efforts were made to modernize this monumental site, where there was no sewer system, many rooms lacked electricity, courtyards were unpaved and adjacent buildings and gardens needed repair.[39]

In November 1918, the Castle became the office and the home of the first President of Czechoslovakia, Tomáš Garrigue Masaryk. In those early days of the new independent state, before the ratification of the republic's democratic constitution with multiparty rule and universal suffrage, the National Revolutionary Committee made important decisions for the young government. Among other decisions, it placed two Czechs, Kamil Hilbert and Jindřich Čapek, in charge of renovating and updating the Castle. Hilbert was the architect supervising the completion of the St. Vitus Cathedral, started by Holy Roman Emperor Charles IV, and Čapek was a sculptor. Both men resigned in July 1919 after they were accused of mismanaging funds for the reconstruction project. A newspaper report about the accusation revealed the Castle's profound meaning for many Czechs, calling it "a monument to the glory and suffering of the nation" and "a stone poem singing a secret, mysterious, but most stirring song in the heart of every Czech."[40]

In December 1919, the National Revolutionary Committee permanently entrusted care of the Castle to the Office of the President, giving Masaryk, "the President-Liberator," the power to appoint the architect responsible for renovating the Castle. Masaryk selected Jože Plečnik for this position, which he held from 1920 until 1935. Plečnik (1872–1957) was a native of Ljubljana, the capital city of the one-time Austro-Hungarian province of Carnolia (now Slovenia). He was also a well-respected foreigner who had studied architecture in Vienna with Otto Wagner during the 1890s. Plečnik's original use of forms from early civilizations and deep respect for materials were inspired by his admiration of German architect Gottfried Semper, whose book *Stil* lauded ancient cultures, and by the opinion of some experts that his beloved Slavs were related to the Etruscans.[41]

After completing his studies in Vienna with Otto Wagner, Plečnik worked as a freelance architect and then, in 1911, he was appointed professor at the School of Decorative Arts in Prague. In the Bohemian capital, he gained admirers among modernist Czech architects, including the cubist designers Pavel Janák and Josef Gočar, although he had some criticisms of their work and did not make many friends among them.

He wrote to his brother, "I have no real ties or friends here – the people are strange – they are gentle and kindly, but they are strange."[42] After World War I, Plečnik often lived in Ljubljana, holding a professorship there while simultaneously serving as the architect of the Prague Castle.

The president admired Plečnik's work and reputation, and he was comfortable with the fact that the architect was a foreigner. He liked that Plečnik was a fellow Slav. Furthermore, Masaryk hoped that, as someone who was largely an outsider among Czechs, the Slovenian's work on the Castle would not suffer from the growing conflicts among Czech architects due to disagreements about the role of history and tradition in design. Alice Garrigue Masaryková, the president's daughter, sometimes assisted Plečnik, urging him to think of the Prague Castle as a Slavic Acropolis.[43] He also received help from Otto Rothmayer, a former student of his, who handled conflicts for him.[44] For the most part, though, Plečnik preferred to work on his own. The Castle had an Artistic Commission with which he could consult, although he showed little interest in it. His sympathetic and highly respected biographer, Damjan Prelovšek, wrote, "In his work Plečnik always tried to remain totally independent."[45]

Masaryk gave the foreign architect tremendous freedom to make plans for the Prague Castle without input from Czech experts. Plečnik's extensive latitude was the result not only of his own independent nature, but also of Masaryk's fear that Plečnik would quit if Czech architects, with their different views, upset him – something that almost happened when one of them, Karel Fiala, "tried to break Plečnik's creative energy."[46] The great freedom that Masaryk gave to him, along with the Slovenian architect's desire to work alone, concerned Czech experts. While they admired some of his designs, they also worried about the impact of his architectural choices on their capital city's built heritage; and, very importantly, they wanted influence and leverage on the playing field of professional power in Prague. Plečnik was not like Isidor Soyka, who, despite being largely an outsider among Czechs due to his work with German institutions, consulted and collaborated with Czech medical experts on the Municipal Health Commission. Plečnik's personality, combined with his power, threatened the authority of Czech architects and contributed to local resistance to his foreign ideas and knowledge transfer.

Masaryk served as president of Czechoslovakia until 1935, two years before his death. He and other Czech organizers of the new state had a distinct ideology, one that proudly asserted at home and abroad that their country was a democracy. They worked hard to create and project images, narratives and symbols of the new state's democratic character.[47] Reality and representation were not fully synchronized, however, with Czechoslovak democracy sometimes falling short of its lofty claims. For example, Czechs dominated state power and resources, while the country's Germans and Slovaks had less influence and fewer benefits.

Prague's castle, as well as other spaces in the capital city, were resources used in efforts to construct the new state's identity. Masaryk had a specific symbolic goal in mind for the Castle and he believed that Plečnik had the vision necessary for realizing it. Masaryk wanted the Castle, a former seat of kings and emperors, to represent Czechoslovak democracy. He also wanted the environs surrounding the Castle to serve this goal.

The president expressed his desire in a speech that he gave before the National Assembly, the country's highest law-making body, on 28 October 1923, the fifth anniversary of Czechoslovakia's founding. There he announced his "wish that the Castle and its surroundings become not only a seat of the President, but also a symbol of our national democratic ideals."[48] He repeated this wish in the 1925 draft of his will, which stated:

> The purpose of these requests is to make the Castle into the seat of a democratic president; all the adaptations outside and inside the Castle must be simple, but artistically noble, symbolizing the idea of state independence and democracy. The same spirit must govern the Castle's immediate surroundings.[49]

For Masaryk, democratic architecture included built forms that drew inspiration from antiquity, particularly ancient Greece, and, very importantly, that eliminated or at least reduced built evidence of former Habsburg rule in the new independent Czechoslovakia.[50]

Jože Plečnik's Urban Plans for Historic Prague

It was in the interior rooms of the Castle where Plečnik had the most freedom to create according to his independent vision and without the watchful eyes of Czech experts in architecture. He redesigned passageways and rooms, including the president's apartments, where, borrowing from classical architecture, he placed an impluvium. When his work extended beyond the Castle's interior, especially beyond its outer walls, it was more difficult for Plečnik to avoid attracting the attention of others, particularly members of the Club for Old Prague who worried about preserving the city's architectural heritage. This held true for his designs of ways to improve physical connections, including streets and bridges, between the Castle and other parts of Prague and for the environs immediately surrounding the centuries-old Castle complex. With these proposals, conceived also with the goal of grandly displaying the Castle and intensifying its symbolic impact, Plečnik became involved in the modern urban design of historic Prague.

Plečnik's first urban designs for the Czechoslovak capital date from 1920 and 1922. The goal of these proposals was to better connect the Old Town on the right bank of the Vltava River with the Castle on the left bank. Both proposed the development of thoroughfares that began at Wenceslas Square, passed through the historic Old Town, and then crossed the river either via an existing bridge, or in the case of the 1920 plan, also via a proposed new bridge.[51] Realizing either of these early proposals by Plečnik would have been very difficult given Prague's built history. Both required the destruction of parts of the Old Town. Razing structures in this historic district was an idea that amounted to sacrilege for Czechs who associated the city's built heritage with the power and prestige of the nation, including members of the Club for Old Prague. They were supporters of what, as was mentioned previously, the Czech modernist architect, Jaromír Krejcar, critically called the "Old Town taboo."[52]

In the early 1920s, the State Regulation Commission began its own plans for the development of land near the Castle. These plans pertained to efforts to erect a Czechoslovak National Parliament Building on the Letná Plain, a large flat expanse overlooking downtown Prague and stretching out from the northeast end of the Castle grounds. The commission held a number of competitions to select the best location on the Letná for the parliament building. Competition rules stated that only citizens of Czechoslovakia could submit proposals, and all of the winning designs were by Czechs. Earlier competition entries were more traditional in nature; some later entries were inspired by international modern designers, including the French modernist, Le Corbusier, who lectured in Prague in 1925 and 1928.[53]

The parliament building was never erected, in significant part due to Plečnik's opposition to placing it near the Castle and Masaryk's strong advocacy of his castle architect. Plečnik did not want views of the Castle obstructed by or interrupted with any sort of development, traditional or modern. He wanted it to stand in "splendid isolation."[54] He paid little mind to the fact that the State Regulation Commission, with advice from members of the Club for Old Prague, was working to ensure that any construction on the Letná Plain would protect the city's panorama and not disturb views of the Castle.[55] The State Regulation Commission invited Plečnik to meet and discuss plans for locating the parliament building in the vicinity of the Castle. The castle architect, who wanted to work alone, did not meet with the commission.

Plečnik also resisted working with his Czech colleagues when he redesigned the Castle. This was seen especially well in controversy surrounding changes he made in the third courtyard, where the St. Vitus Cathedral stands. Experts in the Club for Old Prague opposed his plans due to worries about archeological discoveries underneath the courtyard, and they tried to insist that the space's historic character be preserved. Plečnik removed the old, ornate Baroque base and basin beneath the Gothic statue of St. George fighting the dragon. He gave the legendary pair a new modern base and basin with clean straight lines and resting within a thin circular bronze railing suggestive of a halo. He had the courtyard paved with large slabs of smooth stone, more in keeping with Italian piazzas than with Prague's cobblestone-encrusted squares and streets.

In 1930, experts in the Home Council of the Club for Old Prague published a statement in which they defended themselves from the criticism of not having done enough to protect the Castle, particularly the third courtyard, from Plečnik. They agreed that the Slovenian architect's alterations were "an irreparable error, which has, perhaps forever, devastated a monumental and, for all Czechs, precious space." They explained that they were limited in their abilities to protest and stop Plečnik's intervention on account of the tremendous independent power that Masaryk had given to him. More specifically, they complained of "complete absolutist interference in the alteration of the Castle, especially in the last two years, when the Castle Commission, which alone could oppose this totally undemocratic conduct, was not convened." Still, the Club maintained that its members had stood for and would "always stand for the time-honored nature of the Castle."[56]

In the 1930s, Plečnik was still conceptualizing designs for how best to plan the environs around the Castle. In 1931, he created a new dramatic and ambitious plan that was never constructed. In it, he showed that he was now unconcerned about physically connecting the right and left banks of Prague. Thus, this design only treated the Castle side of the river and its realization would not have required any destruction of parts of the historic Old Town across the water. In the 1931 plan, Plečnik envisioned a grand, upward-curving boulevard in the shape of a loop that partly rested on stone arches reminiscent of Roman aqueducts (Figure 1.2). In the process of moving around the loop, the drivers and passengers of cars and trams were to see different impressive views of the Castle environs and the historic city stretching below it. The experiences of viewing those vistas were to serve as visual or virtual bridges connecting parts of the city, including the Castle, to one another. At the top of the loop, there was to be an intersection with a wide east-west artery running along the Castle's northern face.[57] The State Regulation Office rejected Plečnik's 1931 plan, acknowledging that it did show how difficult it was to solve the urban challenge of connecting the Castle with the city below it.[58]

In 1934, a year before Masaryk's retirement, Plečnik created his last urban design for the environs surrounding the Castle. This plan, concerned only with an area very close to the Castle, was focused on the creation of an east-west artery running alongside the historic site's northern face. It was to be a 40-meter-wide, 1-kilometer-long straight ceremonial route with no mechanized traffic. Cars and trams were to drive on a new street that Plečnik planned to develop parallel to the monumental boulevard. Plečnik added elegant geometric forms to the 1934 plan, which were similar to classical elements he had placed in Castle gardens. A large oval pool was to be constructed at the eastern end of the boulevard, a

Figure 1.2 Model of Jože Plečnik's design for a boulevard looping upwards toward the Prague Castle, 1931.

Source: Used with kind permission of Plečnik's Collection, Museum and Galleries of Ljubljana

cylindrical cupola was to stand at its far western end and, between them, a square pool was to be created near the old Baroque riding school. The ceremonial boulevard was to be connected to the Castle's northern entry with a new bridge and a new opening into the third courtyard (see Figure 1.3). The 1934 plan faced resistence from Czech experts concerned about Prague's historic architecture, and it alarmed 245 Czech women who signed a petition aiming "To save the Castle from interference by a foreigner who is ruthlessly destroying Bohemian monuments."[59]

In 1935, architects and others in the Club for Old Prague held a meeting regarding Plečnik's 1934 plan, which they opposed. Wirth, who was still responsible for the administration of archeology, museums, archives, libraries and monument care at the Ministry of Education and Enlightenment, spoke at the meeting. He praised Plečnik's designs for the president's apartments inside the Castle. He was less positive when discussing Plečnik's work on the third courtyard, and he was critical of the 1934 plan. Wirth thought that the latter required too much alteration of the Castle environs and maintained that it had been completed without sufficient study and measurement. He requested that local Czech experts in

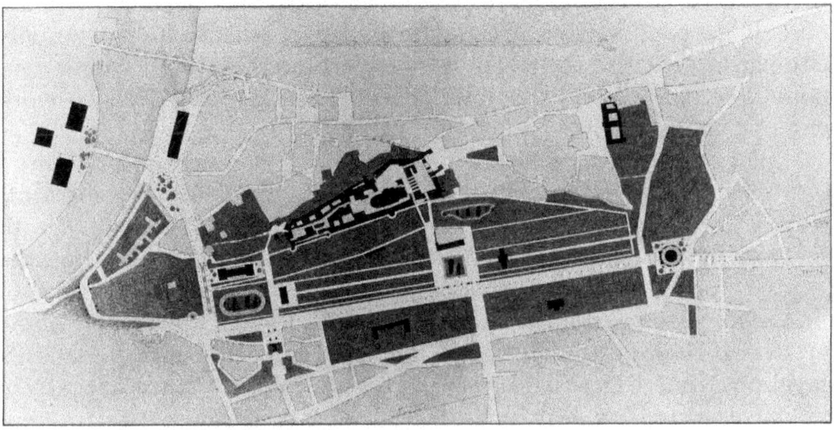

Figure 1.3 Jože Plečnik's design for a boulevard running alongside the Castle's Northern face, 1934.

Source: Used with kind permission of Plečnik's Collection, Museum and Galleries of Ljubljana

architecture be allowed to review the plan and discuss it with Plečnik.[60] No review or discussion occurred.

In 1935, Masaryk stepped down as president, and shortly afterwards, Plečnik resigned from his position as castle architect. Even if the Slovenian architect had kept his position, it is unlikely that he would have met with his Czech colleagues, given his reluctance to work with them before then. Pavel Janák, the Czech cubist designer who renovated Prague's Baroque Czernin Palace and was a student of Plečnik's, was selected to be the new castle architect, a position he held for nearly 20 years, despite the regime changes in Czechoslovakia during and after World War II.

Conclusion: Aids and Obstacles to Knowledge Transfer in Historic Prague

A comparison of the urban redevelopment of Josefov in late-nineteenth–century Prague and Plečnik's designs for the Prague Castle during the interwar period reveals different attitudes among Czech experts toward knowledge transfer. There was less enthusiasm for ideas from abroad among architects and others concerned about the historic attributes of the Castle than there was among medical experts involved in the creation of the "*Finis Ghetto*" plan. This single juxtaposition should not be used to reduce the entire history of modern urban design in Prague to one argument or narrative about change over time because, certainly, there are more projects with other dynamics to be considered. Still, it can serve to advance thinking about contexts and elements that are more or less conducive to foreign-knowledge transfer, including not only nationalism, but also the positions of expert interest groups within non-monolithic nations and the abilities of insiders and outsiders to work with one another.

Clearly, both before and after World War I, national loyalty played a significant role in knowledge transfer, albeit not always in the same manner. It helped sometimes with the embrace of and sometimes with the resistance to the spread of ideas from abroad. In late-nineteenth–century Prague, Czech medical doctors promoting the urban renewal of the Josefov district enthusiastically drew from foreign knowledge. In the interwar period, influential Czech architects and art historians opposed the imposition of Plečnik's urban plans onto Prague's landscape. Given the different ways in which national identity could affect Czech reception of foreign ideas, it is clear that other historical circumstances or elements must be considered when seeking to explain differing Czech stances regarding foreign ideas. In order to gain a deeper understanding of forces that aid or obstruct knowledge transfer in any context, we need to look more closely at expert interests, including their positions of influence and authority; their motivations for sharing, borrowing and/or blocking foreign ideas; and their personalities.

The two nineteenth- and twentieth-century modern urban design projects discussed here reveal a changing constellation of experts involved in the shaping of Prague's built landscape. Initially, Czech medical experts, in cooperation with a colleague who had strong ties to Germany's scientific community, had dominant voices in discussions and decision-making about modern urban design. Architects and other experts interested in heritage, including art historians, were not involved in the creation and implementation of the "*Finis Ghetto*" plan. In time, though, the project, which destroyed part of historic Prague, encouraged them to pay more attention to urban planning – not only to defend what they perceived as their national interests, but also to promote what they saw as their professional interests.

The Czech architects and other experts who worried about Plečnik's designs for the Prague Castle were not out-and-out opposed to foreign modern urban design. However, they did try to obstruct the transfer of the Slovenian architect's ideas onto their capital city's historic landscape. They wanted those changes to be carried out with respect for their capital city's heritage as they perceived it and with respect for their professional knowledge and authority. When creating and implementing the "*Finis Ghetto*" plan, Czech medical doctors did not have a foreigner imposing his ideas onto their capital city's built landscape without their input. Soyka, who was largely an outsider among Czechs due to his work using German language and with German institutions, worked with Czech colleagues. Perhaps Czech architects and others would have had more enthusiasm for Plečnik's urban design ideas if the Slovenian architect had been amenable to more collaboration with them. In sum, the ability of insiders and outsiders to collaborate with one another, together with individuals' personalities and their positions on playing fields of power, are important contextual elements to consider when studying the transfer of knowledge across borders.

Notes

1. For information on urban development, architecture and public space in modern Prague, see Klára Brůhová, *Praha nepostavená: Vltavské břehy jako urbanistické téma moderní metropole* (Prague: Czech Technical University Publishing House, 2017); Kryštof Drnek, *Nerealizovaná Praha* (Prague: Scriptorium, 2019); Cathleen M. Giustino, *Tearing Down Prague's Jewish Town: Ghetto Clearance and the Legacy of Middle-Class Ethnic Politics Around 1900* (Boulder: East European Monographs, 1993); Cathleen M. Giustino, "Prague," in *Capital Cities in the Aftermath of Empires: Planning in Central and Southeastern Europe*, ed. Emily Gunzburger Makaš and Tanja Damljanović Conley (New York: Routledge, 2010); Cynthia Paces, *Prague Panoramas: National Memory and Sacred Space in the Twentieth Century* (Pittsburgh: University of Pittsburgh Press, 2009); Ines Koeltzsch, *Geteilte Kulturen: Eine Geschichte der tschechisch-jüdisch-deutschen Beziehungen in Prag, 1918–1938* (Munich: Oldenbourg, 2012); Jiří Pešek, *Od aglomerace k velkoměstu: Praha a středoevropské metropole, 1850–1920* (Prague: Scriptorium, 1999); Rostislav Švácha, *The Architecture of New Prague, 1895–1945* (Cambridge, MA: MIT Press, 1995).
2. Publications focusing on the history of the urban redevelopment (the "*asanace*") of Josefov are Cathleen M. Giustino, *Tearing Down Prague's Jewish Town*; *Pražská asanace: K 100. výročí vydání asanačního zákona pro Prahu*, ed. Kateřina Bečková (Prague: Museum of the Capital City of Prague, 1993).
3. Books focusing on Plečnik's architecture and design, including his work for the Prague Castle and its environs, are *Josip Plečnik: Architekt Pražského hradu*, ed. Zdeněk Lukeš, Damjan Prelovšek and Tomáš Valena (Prague: Prague Castle Administration, 1996), which is also in English translation (all citations here come from the Czech edition); Damjan Prelovšek, *Jože Plečnik, 1872–1957* (New Haven: Yale University Press, 1997).
4. An excellent set of chapters about professional interest groups in the late Habsburg Monarchy and its successor states remains *Professions in Modern Eastern Europe*, eds. Charles E. McClelland, Stefan Merl and Hannes Siegrist (Berlin: Duncker & Humblot, 1992). Works on experts and Prague include Rudolf Kučera, *Rationed Life, Science, Everyday Life, and Working Class Politics in the Bohemian Lands, 1914–1918* (New York: Berghahn, 2016); Vojtěch Pojar, "Quality Over Quantity: Expert Knowledge and the Politics of Food in Prague, 1914–1918" (Master's Thesis, Central European University, 2017). For information on experts in interwar Czechoslovakia, see Elisabeth van Meer, " 'The Nation Is Technological': Technical Expertise and National Competition in the Bohemian Lands, 1800–1914," in *Expert Cultures in Central Eastern Europe: The Internationalization of Knowledge and the Transformation of Nation States Since World War I*, ed. Martin Kohlrausch, Stefan Wiederkehr, and Katrin Steffen (Osnabrück: Fibre, 2010), 85–104; van Meer, "The Transatlantic Pursuit of a World Engineering Federation:

For the Profession, the Nation, and International Peace," *Technology and Culture* 53, no. 1 (2012): 120–145.

5. Oliver Hochadel and Agustí Nieto-Galan, "How to Write an Urban History of STM on the 'Periphery'," *Technology and Culture* 57 no. 4 (2016): 978–988.
6. My thinking about the shifting positions of different expert groups in the history of urban planning in Prague is partly inspired by the concept of the "intellectual field" found in Pierre Bourdieu, *The Field of Cultural Production* (Cambridge: Polity Press, 1993).
7. The text of Prague's 1850 Municipal Statute, which remained in place with few revisions until the dissolution of the Habsburg Monarchy, is in *Landesgesetzblatt für das Königreich Böhmens*, April 27, 1850, nr. 85.
8. Specifics from Mayor Černý's controversial speech are discussed in Giustino, *Tearing Down Prague's Jewish Town*, 42–44.
9. For information about Old Czech and Young Czech politics, see Bruce M. Garver, *The Young Czech Party, 1874–1901, and the Emergence of a Multi-Party* System (New Haven: Yale University Press, 1978); Giustino, *Tearing Down Prague's Jewish Town*, chap. 3.
10. Czechs called the radical destruction and reconstruction of Josefov "*asanace*," which comes from the German term "*Assanierung*" and can be translated as "sanitation." I am using the term urban redevelopment, because it suggests the complexity and intensity of the spatial and social transformation entailed in this "sanitation" project. Given that the poor residents who were forced to leave their homes in the Jewish district could not afford to return to the luxury apartments built on the cleared land, I think the term gentrification also applies.
11. Julius Grégr, "Rozprava o obecních záležitostech pražských v Klubu národní strany svobodomyslné, *Národní listy*, December 12, 1878. See also Giustino, *Tearing Down Prague's Jewish Town*, 79.
12. "Referate des Comités der erweiterten Sanitäts-Commission der städt [ischen] Commune Prag," *Prager Medicinische Wochenschrift* 4, no. 1 (January 2, 1879): 195. See also Giustino, *Tearing Down Prague's Jewish Town*, 82.
13. František Kožíšek, "Hygienik, na kterého se mělo zapomenout: Ke 165. výročí narození Isidora Soyky," *Hygiena* 60, no. 1 (2015): 25–29. See also the works of Petr Svobodný, including, "Isidor Soyka: Pettenkoferův žak," *Dějiny věd a techniky* 28, no. 1 (1995): 1–14; "Isidor Soyka: Zakladatel Hygienického ústavu německé lekářské fakulty v Praze," *Dějiny věd a techniky* 28, no. 3 (1995): 145–166. Kožíšek calls Soyka "a Czech Jew who, for professional reasons, got into a German environment" (28). In the first of his articles cited here, Svobodný says Soyka was "a Bohemian German of Jewish origin [český Němec židovského původu]" (1).
14. Soyka's death was a suicide and scholars are not sure why this happened. Evidence suggests contributing factors were health issues, the death of his brother and perhaps challenges at the university, including anti-Semitism and views that he was "not German enough." See Kožíšek, "Hygienik," 27.
15. *Bericht über die Thätigkeit des Prager städtischen Gesundheitsrather im Jahre 1885*, eds. Václav Janovský, Isidor Soyka, and Jindřich Záhoř (Prague: Verlag der Gemeinderenten der königlichen Hauptstadt Prag, 1887), especially 54–62. It is interesting that the Czech-controlled municipality published this and other medical reports in German. That Czechs used German when publishing medical articles and books became a public issue as can be seen in "Český vědec v německém rouše," *Národní listy*, 1 January 1901. Here too, though, we should keep in mind that, along with nationality politics, a professional struggle for leverage and authority was at work.

16. The travels of Záhoř and the work of Soyka speak to the concept of transnational municipalism examined in *Another Global City: Historical Explorations into the Transnational Municipal Moment, 1850–2000*, ed. Pierre-Yves Saunier and Shane Ewen (New York: Palgrave Macmillan, 2008).
17. Záhoř's articles discussing his knowledge-gathering travels include, "O zdravotných poměrech v Berlině," *Pokrok*, November 21, 1885; "Zdravotní ústavy ve Frankobrodě nad Mohanem," *Pokrok*, December 5, 1885; "Norimberk: Jeho hřbitov a kanalisace," *Pokrok*, December 8, 1885. See also his book *Ze čtvrté vědecké cesty fysika pražského do hlavních a sídelních měst: Stuttgartu, Štrasburku, Nancy, Remeše, Paříže, Lyonu, Ženevy, Lausannu a Curychu* (Prague: Řivnáč, 1890).
18. R. Hurtig, "*Finis Ghetto*," *Zlatá Praha* 4 (1887): 438.
19. Ibid. Other Orientalist thinking in Prague's past is seen in Cathleen M. Giustino, "Rodin in Prague: Modern Art, Cultural Diplomacy, and International Display," *Slavic Review* 69, no. 3 (Fall 2010): 591–619.
20. Cathleen M. Giustino, "Municipal Activism in Late-Nineteenth-Century Prague: The House Numbered 207-V and Ghetto Clearance," *Austrian History Yearbook* 34 (2004): 247–278.
21. For more on anti-Semitism as a causal force contributing to the urban redevelopment of Josefov, see Giustino, *Tearing Down Prague's Jewish Town*, especially chaps. 7–8.
22. A work devoted to Lindley and his firm's work on Prague's sewers is Jaroslav Jásek, *William Heerlein Lindley a pražská kanalizace* (Prague: Scriptorium, 2006).
23. Because the original impoverished residents could not afford to return to live in Josefov after its destruction and reconstruction, I think this urban redevelopment project can also be called gentrification.
24. The late entry of Czech architects into discussions about urban planning and modernization in Prague is discussed in Cathleen M. Giustino, "Architects and the Task of Urban Planning in Late Imperial Czech Prague, 1866–1900: Winning Jurisdiction 'From Below'," in McClelland, Merl, and Siegrist, eds., *Professions in Modern Eastern Europe*, 499–528.
25. "Pamětní spis ve příčině úpravy Prahy," *Zprávy Spolku architektů a inženýrů v Čechách* 29 (1895): 113–117.
26. Names of all commission members are in "Za příčinou zachování starobylého rázu Prahy," *Věstník obecní královského hlavního města Prahy* 3 (1896): 147.
27. More information on the the Municipal Artistic Commission is in Giustino, *Tearing Down Prague's Jewish Town*, 275–279.
28. Vilém Mrštík, "*Bestia Triumphans*," *Rozhledy* 6 (1896–1897): 588. Mrštík's statement, which was also published and circulated in pamphlet form, is presented in more detail in Giustino, *Tearing Down Prague's Jewish Town*, 284–289.
29. Mrštík, "*Bestia*," 636.
30. Examples of small, but significant, moments of victory for the preservationists are in Giustino, *Tearing Down Prague's Jewish Town*, chap. 11.
31. Kateřina Bečková, *Sto let Klubu Za starou Prahu, 1900–2000* (Prague: Schola ludus-Pragensia, 2000).
32. Efforts to transfer knowledge about German and Austrian preservation theory to Czech experts are discussed in Kristina Uhlíková, *Zdeněk Wirth: První dvě životní etapy, 1878–1939* (Prague: Národní památkový ústav, 2010), 27–33.
33. Ibid., 56–57.
34. Ibid., 62–69.

35. For more on Czech technocrats during the interwar period, see van Meer, "'The Nation Is Technological.'"
36. Members of the first Commission were Eustach Mölzer (engineer), Josef Záruba-Pfefferman (engineer), Otto Knot (municipal advisor), Ladislav Procházka (physician), Jiří Stibral (architect), Jan Záhorský (engineer), Antonín Engel (architect) and Antonín Balšánek (architect). Found in V. Dk., "Státní regulační komise pro hlavní města Prahy a okolí," *Styl* 1 (1920–21): 62.
37. Jaromír Krejcar, "Cesta k moderní architectuře," *Disk* 2 (1925): 26–30. Quotation found in Švácha, *Architecture of New Prague*, 149–150.
38. On ethnic relations in interwar Prague, see Koeltzsch, *Geteilte Kulturen.*
39. Martin Halata, Daniela Karasová, and Michal Šula, *Na slunečné straně: Městský trakt Pražského Hradu jako Habsburské sídlo, 1800–1918* (Prague: Gallery, 2013).
40. "Památný pražský [*sic*] hrad obětí vandalismu," *Večerník práva lidu*, July 8, 1919.
41. Archeological finds near Ljubljana bolstered this view among experts. See Prelovšek, *Plečnik*, 118–119.
42. Ibid., 115. An important exception was his friendship with the Czech architect Jan Kotěra, which can be observed in *Kotěra/Plečnik: Korespondence*, ed. Jindřich Vybíral and Damjan Prelovšek (Prague: Vysoká škola uměleckoprůmyslová, 2001).
43. The relationship between Alice Masaryková and Plečnik is discussed in Bruce Bergland, *Castle and Cathedral in Modern Prague: Longing for the Sacred in a Sceptical Age* (Budapest and New York: Central European University Press, 2017).
44. Prelovšek, *Jože Plečnik*, 125, 361.
45. Ibid., 139.
46. Ibid.
47. Works analyzing efforts to construct and mobilize symbols for political ends in the First Czechoslovak Republic include Andrea Orzoff, *Battle for the Castle: The Myth of Czechoslovakia in Europe, 1914–1948* (Oxford: Oxford University Press, 2009); Nancy M. Wingfield, *Flag Wars & Stone Saints: How the Bohemian Lands Became Czech* (Cambridge, MA: Harvard University Press, 2007), chap. 5.
48. "Presidentovo poselství," *Národní listy* (*Večerní vydání*), October 29, 1923.
49. For the Czech original see Marco Pozzetto, "Plečnik a Hradčany: Architektura pro novou demokracii," in Lukeš, Prelovšek, and Valena, eds., *Josip Plečnik*, 51; Věra Malá, "Hradní architekt a řízení stavební činnosti na Pražském hradě," also in Lukeš, Prelovšek, and Valena, eds., *Josip Plečnik*, 132.
50. Prelovšek, *Jože Plečnik*, 120.
51. "Prof. J. Plečníka [*sic*] komunikační studie ku regulaci Letné a okolí hradu," *Styl* 2 (1921–1922): 33, xxi; *Styl* 3 (1922–1923): 32, 43.
52. Švácha, *Architecture of New Prague*, 149–150.
53. Le Corbusier's influence on Czech architects, and sometimes exaggerated claims about that influence, are discussed in Martina Hrabová, "A Reverse History of Modernism: What Connects Prague to Le Corbusier?" *Room One Thousand* 2 (2014), http://escholarship.org/uc/item/1678061j#page-1.
54. The use of the term "splendid isolation" in regard to Plečnik's plans for the Castle is in Prelovšek, *Jože Plečnik*, 153.
55. Efforts to protect Prague's panorama, including views of the Castle, from plans to locate a National Parliament Building on the Letná Plain is the subject of Cathleen M. Giustino, "Parlament, Letenská pláň a panoráma Prahy za první republiky," *Zprávy památkové péče* 78, no. 5 (2018): 466–478.

56. Home Council of the Club for Old Prague [Domácí rada Klubu za Starou Prahu], "Klub Za starou Prahu a úprava třetího nádvoří Pražského hradu," *Za starou Prahu: Věstník pro ochranu památek* 14, no. 1 (February 1930): 1. The article to which the Club was responding is J.R. Marek, "Svatý Jiří se vrátil," *Národní listy* (*Příloha*), October 20, 1929.
57. Photos of a number of Plečnik's plans for the urban design of Prague are in Lukeš, Prelovšek, and Valena, eds., *Josip Plečnik*, 457–465.
58. Jörg Stabenow and Jindřich Vybíral, "Projekty pro Prahu: Urbanistické návrhy Josipa Plečnika pro okolí Hradu," in Lukeš, Prelovšek, and Valena, eds., *Josip Plečnik*, 436–437.
59. Prelovšek, *Jože Plečnik*, 155.
60. Emanuel Poche, "Anketa Klubu Za starou Prahu o návrzích arch [itekta] Josefa Plečnika na úpravu severní strany Pražského hradu," *Za starou Prahu: Věstník pro ochranu památek* 19, no. 3–4 (August 1935): 17–19.

2 In Search of Best Practices Within the Confines of the Russian Empire

The Port City of Berdyansk

Igor Lyman and Victoria Konstantinova

Introduction

In 1872, James Ernest Napoleon Zohrab, the British consul in Berdyansk, sent a report about "Southern Russia" (a region encompassing the Black Sea and the Sea of Azov) back to London:

> The towns are, as a rule, well laid out as regards plan, and that is all. The streets are unpaved, undrained; there are no sewers to carry off the sewerage of the houses, and all filth is thrown into the streets, which are, in wet weather, beds of deep and foully tainted mud, and in dry weather, thick in equally foul dust. The villages are, if possible, more filthy than the towns. It is a matter of surprise that towns and villages, which are centres of filth and decomposed matter, where no sanitary precautions are adopted, are not hotbeds of malignant fevers. They are, on the contrary, very free from diseases of the zymotic class. This must be attributed to the streets being all very wide, to the houses not being crowded together, and to the almost constant prevalence of winds from the west, north, or east. No sanitary measures are adopted of any kind to secure the public health, and the immunity which the towns enjoy from disease is due entirely to accidental causes.[1]

Of course, as a representative of Western Europe, the British consul was well acquainted with Western patterns of modernization, which he and his contemporaries saw as a yardstick for the assessment of "modern" and "backward." At the same time, Zohrab, as well as many other British, having imperial and trade interests here and being among the "actors" of modernization in the region, was rather skeptical of its achievements. Was this attitude prejudiced, or was the region and hence the city of Berdyansk really backward and peripheral?

The period from the mid-nineteenth to the early twentieth century, beginning with the "Great Reforms" (a large-scale attempt at improving social and economic conditions, undertaken by Emperor Alexander II in the 1860s–1870s) and culminating with the Revolution of 1917, for the Russian Empire is usually regarded as the era of the search for modernization. This search was rather contradictory and inconsistent. In this process, the "Russian" port cities of the Black Sea and the Sea of Azov, i.e. imperial ports from Odessa to Batumi, played an important role as imperial "windows to Europe." We could assume that Berdyansk constitutes an important case study with regard to interurban knowledge exchange during the era of modernization because of its status as a seaport; located on the imperial periphery, the city acted as a "gate" for the transferal of ideas because of its port functions.

Another reason why the case of Berdyansk is so interesting is its age. Founded in 1827, at the beginning of the reform era, Berdyansk, which received official city status, was one of the youngest settlements in the region. Moreover, because the number of official city settlements increased very slowly, distorting the real picture of urbanization, Berdyansk remained among the youngest cities of the region until the end of the imperial period. This was quite important from the point of view of potential opportunities for the introduction of modern innovations: unlike old cities, Berdyansk did not need to break away from a traditional way of life. Or, more precisely, the pre-modern way of life in Berdyansk had not yet managed to take root as deeply as in the cities that had been established earlier.

The fact that Berdyansk, almost from the very beginning, was a port city aimed at foreign trade and had direct contacts with European cities gave rise to optimism about its potential to effectively adopt "the best practices" of modernization. While Odessa remained the main port city of the Russian Empire on the Black Sea,[2] Berdyansk as an emerging city was considered as a potential "second Odessa," that is, as the main city on the coast of the Sea of Azov. However, the reality turned out not to be so rosy, and Berdyansk's journey of modernization not so certain. We may formulate a hypothesis that the realities of Berdyansk's progress on the road of modernization were, to a large extent, determined by the possibilities of realizing the great initial potential of the city under circumstances of bureaucratic upheaval and inconsistency as major changes took place in the Russian Empire. What exactly was Berdyansk's trajectory along the path of modernization? How did the realities of the Russian Empire affect it? Who were the "actors" of the city's modernization? Which cities were models or points of reference for Berdyansk? What was the image of Berdyansk in the context of best practice adaptation from the point of view of "insiders," "outsiders" and "foreigners"? These are just some of the questions that arise when considering the case study of Berdyansk in the context of the topic of interurban knowledge exchange.

None of these issues has yet been the subject of a special study. At the same time, the historiography is quite representative, which makes it possible to get closer to answering the questions. In this context, we should mention publications in the fields of urban history and urban theory by Jan De Vries,[3] Harry Jansen,[4] Simon Parker[5] and John Rennie Short,[6] as well as studies in the fields of social history and modernization theory by Boris Mironov[7] and Igor Poberezhnikov,[8] and research about the modernization of the Black Sea and the Sea of Azov region by Roger L. Thiede,[9] Frederick W. Skinner,[10] Patricia Herlihy[11] and Evrydiki Sifneos.[12] It seems reasonable to adopt Natalia Yakovenko's definition of "modernization" as "a successful metaphor" for the description and explanation of the past, the core of which is the synthesis of the past into a certain entity on the basis of a number of fixed features of transformation of the traditional societies into "modern" and "industrial" ones, with urbanization as one of the basic criteria.[13] Reiner Lindner's interpretation of modernization of the Russian Empire in general and Southern Ukraine in particular is also far from seeing it as linear and general.[14] Books by Igor Lyman and Victoria Konstantinova directly concern the history of Berdyansk during the period of imperial modernization.[15]

The Trajectory of Berdyansk's Progression Along the Path of Modernization

It is generally assumed that the Russian Empire started to move along the road of modernization in 1861, when the implementation of the "Great Reforms," beginning with the emancipation of serfs, began to affect social, administrative, financial, educational and military spheres. However, there are many reasons to assert that the Black Sea and the Sea of Azov region (the Southern Ukraine), to which Berdyansk belonged, began this journey much earlier, because the tasks of rapid economic development and attracting the largest possible number of settlers had already long been a priority. Having extraordinary geopolitical and economic importance for the Russian Empire, this region, beginning with the coastal areas, had been developing for decades before the abolition of serfdom, partially adopting and transforming Western models in order to encourage trade.

A certain role in this was played by individuals who held positions of power in the region – in particular by Novorossiysk and Bessarabian Governor General Mikhail Vorontsov, who is considered the "father" of Berdyansk. Vorontsov personally participated in the survey of the area near Berdyansk Spit to evaluate the possibility of constructing of a port. He was educated in Great Britain. This background influenced his vision of the ways in which the region could be developed: one of the priorities he identified was increasing the role of the port cities and the close connection "of land and sea," involving a large-scale economic development that would provide opportunities for the export of agricultural products by sea. Thus, a proposal was made for a new port on the Sea of Azov, which was to become an important component in the network connecting the Russian Empire with other countries.[16]

Patronized by Vorontsov, Berdyansk already began to develop rapidly in the period from the 1830s to the 1850s. During this time, the city experienced a boom in the areas of urban construction and foreign trade. It was in these spheres that Berdyansk, adopting the best practices of the time, most impressed contemporaries. In 1830, only three years after the construction of Berdyansk began, the regional press reported that, in an area where there had previously been an open, desolate steppe, more than 200 beautiful and neat houses had already been built.[17] Berdyansk, as well as older imperial cities of the region – Odessa, Nikolaev, Kherson – was projected taking into account prospects for their territorial expansion and development. During the initial stage of their construction, none of these cities was very densely built up; there were mainly single-story houses in the central districts at first – only later did the cities begin to grow upwards, adding a number of floors. So, their initial measures allowed these cities, for more than a century and a half, to maintain the comfort of space without significant transformations.[18]

On 19 April 1862, Emperor Alexander II approved a plan for the city of Berdyansk. This plan shared many similarities with earlier plans for other port cities of the region. The coincidence was not accidental: the same architects who worked in other cities of the Black Sea and the Sea of Azov regions were involved in the development of the Berdyansk plan and in the designing of the city's buildings. In particular, Alexander Vahlenkamp,[19] who became Berdyansk's city architect in 1856[20] and later designed many houses in the city, applied for the position of academician of the Imperial St. Petersburg Academy of Arts in 1856. Along with his application, he submitted a number of designs for buildings that he had worked on over a period of ten years for various "colonies of the South of Russia."[21]

It is significant that there was a sharp and conspicuous difference in terms of planning and infrastructure between the coastal cities of the region and cities of the Ottoman Empire, a phenomenon that was often emphasized by foreigners. In particular, in his very colorful diaries, the British officer George Cavendish Taylor, who described a visit of the allied squadron to Berdyansk in May 1855, wrote that all the cities of the Russian Empire that he had seen in the region stood in stark contrast to the cities of the Ottoman Empire; no Ottoman city could be compared to, say, Kerch in the Crimea in terms of the quality of living it offered.[22]

The rapid development of foreign trade through the port of Berdyansk provided a strong economic basis for the introduction of best practices in urban planning. The number of foreign trade offices in the city grew very quickly. Entrepreneurs from Greek, Italian, Balkan and other port cities, who established these offices, brought a wealth of experience and knowledge about how to run businesses, which they had already applied

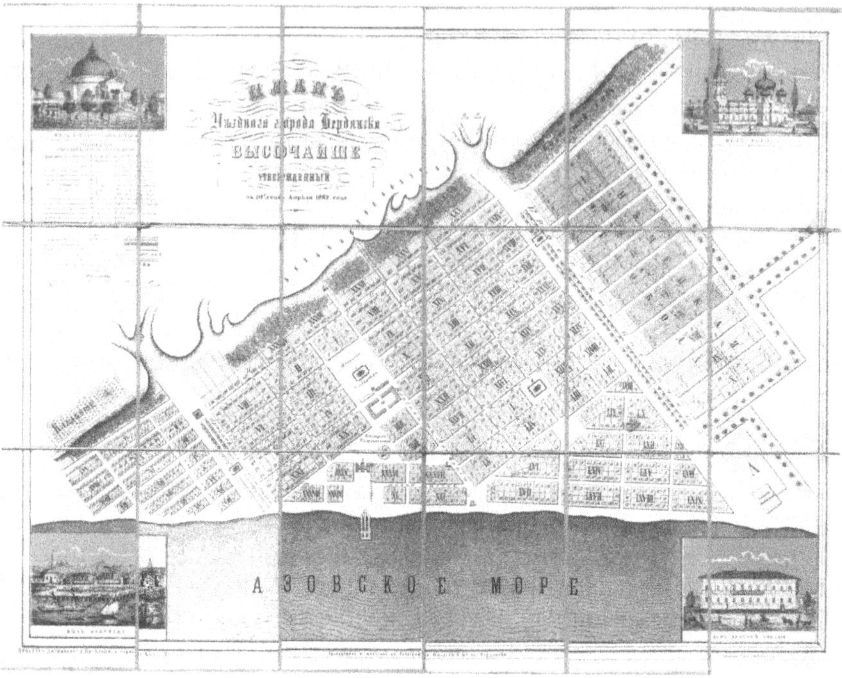

Figure 2.1 Plan of the city of Berdyansk, 1862.

Source: Private collection of Igor Lyman

in other countries and in other "Russian" ports around the Black Sea and the Sea of Azov.

Of course, foreign entrepreneurs had to take into account the specifics of the bureaucracy of the Russian Empire, which in many respects was an obstacle to more rapid development. In 1858, a British consulate was established in Berdyansk, and on 12 January 1858, Queen Victoria appointed Robert William Cumberbatch[23] to the post of British consul in the city.[24] Already in his first report, Cumberbatch expressed concern that the tariff and custom house regulations in the Russian Empire had not been revised; thus, many British manufacturers and merchants refrained from investing their capital due to the many formalities, unforeseen difficulties and expenses that it would entail.[25]

Despite this, at the start of the era of "Great Reforms," Berdyansk was already playing an important role in the export of grain from lands of the Russian Empire. Moreover, according to public opinion, it was a very promising city which had every chance of becoming the main port on the Sea of Azov and could, in some respects, serve as an example, a model for other cities of the region. In particular, in the context of the educational reform, the self-governments of Berdyansk and its *uezd* (an administrative subdivision of a province) were able to create and finance a network of educational institutions, which began to be considered one of the best in the south of the Russian Empire. Here, the most advanced pedagogical methods were implemented, and the most suitable and up-to-date buildings for schools were built. Indeed, it was in the Berdyansk *uezd* that the famous educator Baron Nikolai Korf, who had worked for many years in Switzerland, tested his pedagogical innovations, and it was at the Berdyansk Boys' Gymnasium that Korf organized his last Teachers' Congress, where questions of how to import and implement European experience in the educational sphere were discussed.[26] Consequently, new educational ideas were able to spread. The unique building of the Boys' Gymnasium, which was built on the initiative and with the money of the city and the *uezd*, was considered by various inspectors as the best (sometimes the second best, after Richelieu Gymnasium in Odessa[27]) across the entire territory of the Odessa Educational District, which included vast lands from Bessarabia in the west to the Don region in the east.[28]

Needless to say, these transformations of urban self-government were some of the most significant manifestations of the modernization processes of the second half of the nineteenth century, which reflected all the inconsistencies and contradictions of the process of modernization in the Russian Empire and its cities, including Berdyansk.[29] In general, in these transformations, Berdyansk moved in the mainstream of state-wide

Figure 2.2 Postcard: Berdyansk Boys' Gymnasium, early 20th century.

Source: Private collection of Igor Lyman

changes. Although other reforms did not produce such brilliant results as those in the educational sphere, a number of significant achievements were also noted. Moreover, a number of individuals from Berdyansk greatly contributed to the elaboration and introduction of best practices in other cities and countries. For instance, Vladimir (Waldemar) Haffkine, a graduate of Berdyansk Boys' Gymnasium,[30] became an outstanding scientist, bacteriologist and epidemiologist, and discovered the principle of and an effective method of inoculation against cholera and bubonic plague. He worked at the University of Geneva and the Pasteur Institute in Paris. From 1893–1915, Haffkine was in the service of the British Crown in India, being the official state bacteriologist of the Indian government (1893–1904).[31] He established the Plague Research Laboratory in Bombay and became its director. The laboratory was visited by scientists from many countries, including the Russian Empire, who studied the best practices proposed by Haffkine (primarily, methods of vaccine preparation and inoculation procedures). In 1925, the laboratory was reorganized into an institute and named after its founder (the Haffkine Institute). Now the Institute is the largest research center for the study of plague and cholera in Southern Asia.

The second half of the nineteenth century was thus an era of innovations and improvements in port infrastructure in Berdyansk, brought about by scientific and technological progress. The breakwater was officially put into operation on 24 March 1869. Significant work was

Figure 2.3 Postcard: Pier of Berdyansk, early 20th century.

Source: Private collection of Igor Lyman

also carried on lengthening and repairing the wharf. South Bay on the Berdyansk Spit was landscaped, and large amounts of money were spent on dredging. Furthermore, the "cultural face" of the city significantly changed.[32] Berdyansk acquired more and more components of the "gentlemen's set" of modernization.[33] But the city was still far away from "perfection."

Already at this time, a number of negative trends in the development of Berdyansk began to appear and manifested themselves increasingly, all of them posing challenges for the port city, the welfare of which directly depended mainly on the export trade of grain. One problem was the shallowing of the sea, which continued to worsen; permanent dredging was required for vessels to approach the pier. The "hinterland" of Berdyansk – that is, the area where cargoes for export arrived in the port city – was increasingly narrowed due to the growing competition from other ports of the region. An important component of this competition was "the struggle for the railway"; Berdyansk was only connected to the railway network of the Russian Empire in 1898, much later than the ports of Rostov, Taganrog and Mariupol.[34] Unsatisfactory conditions of dirt roads, obstacles to development created by the imperial bureaucracy, some inept actions of representatives of local government, crop failures and famine, changes in the global market of wheat and flour, and some other factors became the reasons for the fact that, already at the end of the nineteenth century, Berdyansk ceased to be a city of high hopes.[35] Despite having implemented a number of the "best practices" of modernization, the city could not make full use of the advantageous opportunities that had manifested themselves early on in its development.

The "Actors" of the City's Modernization

The promoters of modernization in Berdyansk can be classified into two groups: the first being immigrants and foreigners, the second being the "old" representatives of the local population and migrants from other areas of the Russian Empire. Probably the most remarkable representatives of immigrants' groups, who significantly changed the Berdyansk *uezd* as a whole and the city in particular, were Mennonites and Germans.[36] From the very beginning of the city's history, a German "*Slobodka*" (colony) had existed here. At a time when a significant part of the population – not only of the *uezd*, but also of the city – was involved in agriculture, settlers in the German *Slobodka* demonstrated unprecedented successes in economy, agriculture[37] and, in particular, in viticulture and gardening. Moreover, it was members of this group who founded and managed several of the city's most successful industrial enterprises.

It is noteworthy that, in the 1870s, a significant number of Mennonites had to leave Berdyansk and the *uezd* in connection with the military reform in the Russian Empire. Mennonites, being pacifists, initially had the privilege of not having to serve in the army. But in 1871, the British consul in Berdyansk, James Ernest Napoleon Zohrab, reported that:

> The country is threatened with a serious loss in the emigration of the German agricultural colonists. The new laws which have been passed by the Emperor abrogate the privileges under which the German have hitherto lived in this country, and which originally induced them to immigrate.[38]

In the following year, Zohrab reported that four Mennonites went to the United States and to Canada to examine those countries and sent back reports to their co-religionists in Berdyansk.[39] Over the next few years, thousands of Mennonites, who had been subjects of the Russian Empire, emigrated.[40]

Other actors potentially capable of bringing the "best practices" of modernization to Berdyansk were the representatives of the numerous countries with consulates in the city. The list of consulates was increasing – while those of Austria, Sicily and Sardinia had been present in the city since the 1840s, in the second half of the 1850s consulates of Greece, Denmark, and Belgium were established here. As mentioned earlier, a British consulate in 1858 was also established. Official representatives of Turkey, Spain and Italy were stationed in the city from around 1870,[41] while France, Germany and the Netherlands were represented from 1872,[42] and Sweden and Norway from 1890.[43] By 1915, there was a French consul, and vice-consuls of Great Britain, Greece, Denmark, Spain, Italy, Sweden and Norway in Berdyansk.[44] Their consular jurisdiction extended not only to the city itself, but also to the district and, in some cases, much further.

Some representatives of these countries were invited by the government of the Taurian Province and the Berdyansk self-government to help solve Berdyansk's most pressing problems. In particular, in 1869, British subjects Charles Grierson and Vilmot received permission to build a port jetty from which barges and towboats could deliver goods for loading onto ships.[45] Another important problem for Berdyansk was the lack of drinking water. So, in 1888, the city council appointed a Scottish contractor to construct an artesian well.[46] One year before, this contractor had achieved very satisfactory results in the artesian well boring in Melitopol, a city 129 km away from Berdyansk.[47]

Perhaps the most striking example of a foreigner who made a great contribution to the modernization of Berdyansk – not only applying other's "best practices," but also developing his own – was the British consul and industrialist John Edward Greaves.[48] Greaves was British pro-consul in Berdyansk from 1880–1907 and was appointed vice-consul on 10 December 1907.[49] Born in Sheffield[50] and trained as an engineer,[51] in

1876 he had already been appointed as a representative of the British company "Clayton & Shuttleworth," which had a warehouse of foreign agricultural machinery and a workshop at the warehouse in Berdyansk. The reference book of 1911 stated that, starting in 1876 and due to the energetic nature of John Greaves and "the extremely favorable moment in the history of agricultural machinery in Russia," production had begun to develop in Berdyansk, which was later characterized as the first operation of its kind in the Taurian Province. In 1883, Greaves opened a small factory on Vorontsovskaya Street in Berdyansk.[52] In 1894, the plant passed into the hands of the Trade and Industrial Association, but that did not mean that the founder had lost control over it: instead, he became a member of this association. While the characteristics of Greaves' plant ("the largest works in Europe")[53] by Vladimir Lenin were widely popularized in Soviet times, the similar characteristics, presented in a work by the famous theoretician of anarchism Peter Kropotkin, remained out of sight of Berdyansk inhabitants and the Soviet public in general. In his work "Fields, Factories, and Workshops," Kropotkin wrote in 1898 that "the town of Berdyansk . . . can now boast of the largest reaper manufactory in Europe, capable of turning out three thousand machines annually."[54]

At the All-Russia Exhibition in 1896, Greaves' plant was awarded with the right to use the coat of arms of the Russian Empire on its advertising and products. Two years later, John Greaves himself was awarded with the gratitude of the Emperor Nikolai II "for a very energetic and fruitful activity in the sphere of Russian agricultural machine building."[55] When the Belgian Anonymous Company bought the plant in 1899, John Greaves remained its manager. Being the president and manager of the Belgian Anonymous Company, Greaves received the Order of the Crown from the King of the Belgians.[56]

John Greaves was well aware of the benefits of an English technical education compared to a Russian one, and therefore sent his relatives (a son and two grandsons) to study at the Technical School of Sheffield. Later, all of them returned to Berdyansk and became managers at the Greaves plant, implementing the knowledge and technical skills they had gained in England. In 1904, the plant administration, by its own initiative and in line with modern European trends, reduced the duration of the working day for its employees to nine hours, and later arranged a reading room for workers, established dramatic and musical groups and introduced a number of other measures which improved the working and leisure conditions.[57]

At the same time, Greaves adopted the best European practices and the latest achievements of scientific and technological progress for his own comfort: his private house became the most modern in Berdyansk and surprised even sophisticated representatives of Western Europe. Amy

Evelyn Greaves, the niece of John Greaves who was born in Sheffield and grew up there in a middle-class family in comfortable conditions, was deeply impressed by her uncle's house when she visited Berdyansk at the end of the nineteenth century. She found electric lights everywhere, a very modern bathroom with a tub and shower, complete with hot and cold running water. She recollected that her father's house in Sheffield had all these facilities as well, though electric lights were installed there later, and the family still used gas incandescent lights; plumbing with hot and cold water could be found only in the newest houses in England. Greaves' niece believed that it was only her uncle's engineering skills that made these technological advancements possible in Berdyansk.[58]

The Greaves also brought European crazes to Berdyansk, including in some quite unexpected areas. In particular, it was the British consul's two grandsons who were responsible for the popularization of football in Berdyansk, having been fascinated by the game during their studies in England.[59] They created a football team at their grandfather's plant and became its leading players. Within two or three months, another team was formed at the plant.[60]

Yet the case of John Greaves was the exception rather than the rule. Generally, foreign entrepreneurs were not interested in Berdyansk, as they were aware that the modernization of the city would require them to invest large sums of their own money. In this regard, a very significant observation was expressed in 1879:

> The trading power of our port is a corporation of foreign merchants and commissioners, mostly temporary guests, who are solely and exclusively interested in the port. As for the city itself and its internal life, most foreigners do not deal with it, considering it completely (from their point of view, of course) neither more nor less as a profitable point of exportation, an overseas sales station. About the other elements of the population (those who lack power and influence) I will be silent.[61]

But in reality, it was not only foreigners who had a great influence in Berdyansk and affected the pace of its progress in modernization. Many Russian subjects, including "old" representatives of the local population and migrants from other areas of the Russian Empire, played a key role and cannot be characterized as "lacking power and influence." The most active individuals in this group were merchants. These subjects of the Russian Empire also brought and applied in Berdyansk experience they had gained in foreign port cities, as well as in other ports of the region. The obituary of the merchant Nikolai Popovich, who died in Berdyansk in 1842, stressed that he had studied in Richelieu Liceum in Odessa, later "became acquainted with the main ports of the Mediterranean and, enriched with commercial knowledge, returned to his fatherland." He became a patriot of the young city and was considered a founder of Berdyansk's foreign trade offices.[62] When, in 1854, another merchant, Nikolai Dzhurasovich, died, the *Odesskiy Vestnik* reported that he had been one of the first to settle in Berdyansk and that, from the very early stages, he had enriched the young city with his extensive foreign trade, adorned it with remarkable buildings and attracted many foreign companies to settle there.[63]

It is not surprising that it was merchants who, as a rule, held the post of mayor in Berdyansk, as well as significant positions as deputies of the Berdyansk City Council (*Duma*) in all its convocations. They worked hard to ensure that Berdyansk had those signs of "civilization" that already existed in other cities of Europe and the Russian Empire. For example, Nikolai Kobozev, who was mayor from 1841–1857 and again from 1860–1862, as well as a wealthy ship owner, realized the extreme importance of the railway as an achievement of scientific and technological progress and began to make efforts to obtain permission for Berdyansk to be connected to the railway network of the Russian Empire. He also funded the construction of the city theater with his own money, considering it an indispensable attribute of a civilized city. Konstantin Konstantinov (mayor in 1871–1875), one of the richest merchants in the city, was behind the initiative to open the Boys' Gymnasium and other educational institutions, established the city's public bank and arranged the building of a fire station.[64]

Bureaucratic functionaries (*chinovniki*) also became important actors of modernization in Berdyansk because of the gradual professionalization of the local administration. As a rule, these functionaries were less open to foreign "best practices" than merchants were. Instead, being part of the Russian bureaucracy, they preferred to look for such practices inside the empire. For instance, one of them, the titular councilor Vasilij Kryzhanovskyi, first served in the office of Odessa Governor, then became a warden of the Mariupol customs post, and, in 1840, by request of Novorossiysk and Bessarabian Governor General Mikhail Vorontsov, was transferred to the post of warden of the Berdyansk customs house. He became a patriot of Berdyansk, an initiator and an active participant in many improvements in the city, bringing to Berdyansk the knowledge and experience he had gained in other port cities around the region. At the same time, Kryzhanovskyi was not only known for his positive contributions: he was put on trial twice for embezzling bricks, which were state property, and for his involvement in smuggling.

Interestingly, Vasilij Kryzhanovskyi was, for several decades, the most active Berdyansk correspondent for the *Odesskiy Vestnik*, a newspaper that served as the main print source of information about events in the city during the nineteenth century and was read by the residents of

Berdyansk and other parts of the region (local newspapers only appeared in Berdyansk in the early twentieth century). In this way, Kryzhanovskyi served as a transmitter of the experience and knowledge that had been gained and produced in Berdyansk, including "best practices," to readers in other cities. In particular, he wrote about experiments in growing tobacco, mulberries[65] and grapes[66] in Berdyansk, as well as proposals for the use of the ten-year privileges granted to the city by the government for progressive ends,[67] local innovations in the salt trade,[68] experiments in organizing auctions for the lease of municipal lands[69] and best practices implemented in Berdyansk relating to the organization of the gymnasium and other educational institutions.[70]

It goes without saying that the circle of people who belonged to the second group of actors responsible for modernization in Berdyansk was not restricted just to merchants and administrative functionaries. Teachers, doctors, engineers and industrialists were also involved in this process. There were even enthusiasts and promoters of modernization among the urban peasant population: one of them, a self-taught mechanic named Akim Pirozhkov,[71] built a small steamboat of his own design in Berdyansk in the mid-nineteenth century.[72] At the same time, it would be very optimistic to conclude that knowledge transfer took place on all levels. The "broad" masses of the population simply followed the changes that had already taken place and adapted to the new realities. On the other hand, "traditionalists" and conservatives played a significant role in the urban community, advocating the preservation of existing practices. It is significant that many of these individuals were functionaries (*chinovniki*), who represented the cumbersome Russian bureaucracy. The attitude of the majority of Berdyansk's population toward innovations directly depended on whether these advancements could bring them immediate and tangible benefits. That is why people from various strata of the Berdyansk population ardently supported the idea of building the railway, realizing that it could dramatically increase exports of grain via the seaport and would thus guarantee the prosperity of the whole city. The *Odesskiy Vestnik* wrote about this unanimity, which was unusual for Berdyansk: "As they go about their everyday routines, despite the preoccupation with current affairs, local residents are interested in the very serious issue of the railway."[73]

Thus, because of its function and status as a seaport, Berdyansk became a "gateway" for the transfer of ideas and took part in the interurban knowledge exchange, which was mediated through a range of groups and individuals, not only "old" domestic "actors" who were oriented mainly toward the practices of "Russian" cities. Immigrants and foreigners brought international experience to Berdyansk directly. However, not all foreign "best practices" had a chance to be implemented in Russian imperial realities.

Imagining Berdyansk: Inside – Outside – Foreign Perception of the City and the Adaptation of Best Practices

When we analyze the ways that contemporaries saw the cities of the region and Berdyansk in particular, we do not see the conflict between a vision of the city "that was obsessed with symbols from the past and another that pointed resolutely toward its future,"[74] which, for instance, Nathaniel Wood noted for East Central European cities by analyzing the image of Cracow before 1914. In this regard, southern Russian cities differed to a certain extent from East Central European cities, which in turn leads us to a differentiating assessment of "modernity": while some inhabitants of the old cities appealed to a glorious past, which served as an argument for them to assume that modernization was not necessarily a welcome change, in contrast, inhabitants of the seaports of the Black Sea and the Sea of Azov – and Berdyansk in particular – did not feel the same piety toward the Ottoman, "pre-Russian" history.[75] In this respect, inhabitants of the region's ports were more open to modernizing changes than populations elsewhere that had a clear awareness of the deep historical roots of their cities. At the same time, local inhabitants were quite aware of the differences between their city and region and other parts of the Russian Empire. In the "Diaries" of Berdyansk resident Vasilij Kryzhanovskyi we can find many examples of clear distinctions between these territories: "From Russia they write that there is such a warm winter" (7 January 1865), "The sledge road, as in the deepest Russia" (9 February 1875), etc.[76] The port cities' inhabitants felt this distinction because of "Western" influences on city planning and hence of "modernity."

Of course, like those who lived in the old cities and towns, inhabitants of the seaports of the Black Sea and the Sea of Azov compared their cities with others; in this way they, as Nathaniel Wood formulated, "sought to show at once the uniqueness of their hometown and its familiar place in the firmament of urban civilization."[77] However, while some inhabitants of Cracow compared their city to Mecca, Athens or Rome in "an effort to make the most of the city's situation as a dilapidated, but relatively free city with a storied past,"[78] the region's ports were compared mostly with the advanced, innovative Odessa. The case study of Berdyansk, which was often called "the second Odessa," is revealing in this regard. It is interesting that, in descriptions of some buildings of Berdyansk, deliberate mention was made of the fact that they were built according to example of Odessa. In particular, Nikolai Popovich (a merchant who moved to Berdyansk in 1836 and became one of the first inhabitants of the city) built a house there that was considered to be a copy of the house of Duke de Richelieu in Odessa.

In general, over the course of the nineteenth and early twentieth century, the "cultural image" and urban landscape of Berdyansk significantly changed, in many respects following the example of Odessa. In particular, theater performances were one of the most visible components of the cultural life of Berdyansk. One of the residents of Berdyansk wrote in 1861: "We strive to keep up with the others. Proof of this is the theater that was built by Kobozev. It is much larger than the theater in Taganrog and in some sense can be compared with the theater in Odessa."[79] However, according to critics, the repertoire of the theater in Berdyansk was considerably poorer than in Odessa, and the professionalism of the local theater troupe left much to be desired. For this reason, the press paid great attention to visiting artists from Odessa and artists who were popular among Odessa spectators. For example, in 1857, the press reported on performances in Berdyansk: "Everyone was especially interested in the play of Zverev, who is the current favorite of the Odessa audience. The theater was almost always full"; "In October Moritz Gesheles, well-known in Odessa, was here and gave several of his optical performances, but they did not please everyone."[80]

Less frequently, Berdyansk was compared to other cities and towns. But these comparisons again focused not on the "glorious past," but on the current state of the city and its prospects. Soon after the foundation of Berdyansk, one of its residents wrote:

> Houses grow here like mushrooms, and we have already heard it said: "The small town of Berdyansk is like a piece of Moscow." It is not surprising: a ten-year privilege, habitation near the sea and the rich steppe, such active trade – all this attracts foreigners to us.[81]

At the same time, Berdyansk was compared with its nearest competitors – other ports of the Sea of Azov;[82] in this comparison the young age of the city, which was called "the grandson of Taganrog and the son of Mariupol," was regarded as an advantage rather than a drawback. Later, in the 1880s, Russian writer Nikolai Leskov compared Berdyansk to the Baltic town of Arensburg, writing that "Berdyansk, in comparison with Arensburg, was a city on a winning streak with regard to the prosperity of its citizens."[83] All of these cities and towns were within the territory of the Russian Empire. It is important to note that these comparisons did not just reflect an image of Berdyansk, but mostly reflected a real exchange of knowledge, especially with other ports of the Sea of Azov: Mariupol, Taganrog and Rostov-on-Don. In fact, every more or less important innovation in these ports, thanks to the press, rumors and other sources, became quickly known in Berdyansk and vice versa, and local "actors" of modernization pondered the possibilities of borrowing and adapting this new-found knowledge. This was quite logical, considering, in particular, both the similar specificity of these cities and their being in the same region.

In the eyes of many outside observers from the Russian Empire, Berdyansk and its *uezd* also were not (especially prior to the last decades of nineteenth century) an ordinary part of the empire, but could be compared with rapidly developing overseas regions. In this regard, the characterization given by the writer Grigory Danilevsky was very revealing: "Our Kentucky and Massachusetts." This is the title of one of the chapters of his popular novel *Fugitives in New Russia*,[84] in which there are many descriptions of Berdyansk and its *uezd*. The rapid development of bourgeois relations here on the eve of the reform of 1861 so impressed the author that he began to draw a direct parallel between this region and the states of the United States: Danilevsky shared the very widespread view that Berdyansk and its *uezd*, like the American states, gave almost every newcomer great opportunities for rapid enrichment.

It would be interesting to find out whether inhabitants of Berdyansk felt a sense of "belonging to Europe,"[85] not just to the Russian Empire. Among other tools, content analysis of the periodical press at this time, which is also featured in this issue, could help to shed some light on this. From around 600 articles that appeared in the most popular nineteenth century regional newspaper, the *Odesskiy Vestnik*,[86] between 1827 and 1893, and which were written by Berdyansk correspondents about the port city, we found just one mention of Berdyansk belonging to Europe:

> It is amazing that, over the course of only a decade, a city was created on a deserted beach, surrounded by villages of semi-wild Nogai, with 2,000 houses, 10,000 residents, a port, trade, revenue reaching the tens of millions of rubles, and with all the features of European life.[87]

As for representatives of European countries, in their minds, Berdyansk was clearly associated with the Russian Empire, not with Europe. However, this did not stop them from drawing parallels. This can clearly be seen, in particular in the reports of the British consuls in Berdyansk.[88] Among the various comparisons of Berdyansk with European cities, we will pay particular attention to one made by consul James Ernest Napoleon Zohrab in 1868: "Berdiansk is now, in many respects, a more costly place to live in than most of the capitals of Europe, and certainly more so than Odessa, which has world-wide celebrity for its expensiveness."[89] In 1894, acting vice-consul Greene wrote: "The town of Berdiansk can now boast of the largest reaper manufactory in Europe, capable of turning out 3,000 machines annually."[90]

Thus, by studying the foreign perception of the emerging Berdyansk – both from inside and outside the city – as well as the adaptation of best practices, we come to understand that Berdyansk dwellers did not cling to the past, nor did they accept innovations with the same suspicion as the inhabitants of the old cities. They compared Berdyansk mostly with the innovative Odessa and tried to learn from the experience of this port. Local people, as well as outsiders, understood the differences between Berdyansk and other cities of the Russian Empire. Berdyansk dwellers, on the one hand, maintained contacts with European countries and borrowed innovations from them, but, on the other hand, did not clearly attribute their city to European ones. At the same time, Europeans also associated Berdyansk not with Europe, but with the Russian Empire. This perception was closely interconnected with the vision of the differences in the possibilities of implementing modernization changes.

Conclusions

By analyzing the case study of the port city of Berdyansk, we are able to make some generalizations about the progress of modernization in the Black Sea and the Sea of Azov region and the search for "best practices." The pace of modernization in different urban spaces within the region varied considerably. There are reasons to conclude that the region was living simultaneously in several different time dimensions. While some (modernized) parts were moving fairly quickly, other (traditional) areas remained almost static. Redefining the theory of Braudel about the *longue durée* structures, it can be said that the largest port cities – first of all, Odessa – experienced the fastest changes, while "remote provinces" such as small inland towns were the slowest, remaining at a lower, unaffected level, where the "storms of change" had barely any impact. That is why Odessa became the main "role model" and an "example for imitation" for Berdyansk, as well as for most other "Russian" cities on the shores of the Black Sea and the Sea of Azov. This phenomenon was observed in virtually every component of the modernization processes.

At the same time, there was a mutual influence of ideas and "patterns" of modernization between port cities of the region, the hinterland of the Russian Empire and the cities (first of all, ports) of other countries. So, neither Berdyansk nor other cities in the region should be considered as a "unique, self-contained phenomenon." Instead, they should be regarded as a network with different levels of relations. In its turn, this network should be considered as a component of a wider network of European cities.

To some extent, the situation in the region with regard to the interchange of modernization experiences could be compared to the situation in the remote parts of the British Empire: according to John Griffiths, there was "at no stage a limited, 'one-directional' flow of knowledge from Britain to the outer reaches of the Empire."[91] We can talk about the combination of a direct Western influence and an interchange of modernization experiences among the cities of the region with influence coming through Russia, through the imperial capitals in particular. This last kind of influence was, however, less powerful in the cities of the Black and Azov seas region in comparison with other regions that remained under Russia's control due to the direct contact the south had with foreign lands though the ports.

So, the history of the modernization of Berdyansk – as well as that of other seaports on the Black Sea and the Sea of Azov – is, to some extent, the history of imperial connections. But it was not a donor-recipient metropole-colony model, determined only by center-periphery imperial connections. Rather, it was fusion of local, imperial and extra-imperial influences.[92] This fusion was largely dependent on how effectively distribution channels of modernization experiences and the exchange of knowledge operated. In Berdyansk, "periphery" did not have a negative connotation and was not perceived as a synonym for backwardness. On the contrary, its location on the edge (border) of the empire was perceived as advantageous, giving the city the leading edge, i.e. bringing it closer to innovations and their actors.

Its status as a seaport, together with the relative newness of the city – which meant that it was not so profoundly "tied down" by the experience and traditions of pre-modern life – made Berdyansk an extremely promising place for adapting the best foreign modernizing practices via the interurban knowledge exchange. At the same time, the realities of the Russian Empire significantly affected this process. The Berdyansk case study as a whole confirms the validity of the diffusion theory, as interpreted by Igor Poberezhnikov: the Western models, institutions and values were used as samples, which did not substitute the old (traditional) models, institutions, and values, but, in practice, entered a complex process of interaction leading to their transformation. Considering the influence of modern innovations developed on Russian soil, these advancements could never have been simple replicas of "the Western samples."

Notes

1. *Further Reports from Her Majesty's Diplomatic and Consular Agents Abroad Respecting the Condition of the Industrial Classes and the Purchase Power of Money in Foreign Countries: Presented to Both Houses of Parliament by Command of Her Majesty* (London: Harrison and Sons, 1872), 308.
2. Odessa was not just the largest city in the region. The "post-industrial" city of Odessa in the late nineteenth and early twentieth century remained one of the key administrative centers.
3. Jan De Vries, *European Urbanization, 1500–1800* (London: Methuen; Cambridge, MA: Harvard University Press, 1984).
4. Harry Jansen, *The Construction of an Urban Past: Narrative and System in Urban History*, trans. Feike de Jong (Oxford and New York: Berg, 2001).

5. Simon Parker, *Urban Theory and the Urban Experience: Encountering the City* (London: Routledge, 2004).
6. John Rennie Short, *Urban Theory: A Critical Assessment* (Basingstoke: Palgrave Macmillan, 2006).
7. Boris Mironov, *Sotsialnaja Istorija Rossii Perioda Imperii (18 – nachalo 20 v.) [Social History of Russia of the Period of the Empire (18th – Early 20th Century)]*, vol. I (Sankt-Petersburg: Dmitrij Bulanin, 2003).
8. Igor Poberezhnikov, "Modernizatsionnaja Perspektiva: Teoretiko-Metodologicheskie i Distsiplinarnye Podhody [Modernization Perspective: Theoretical-Methodological and Disciplinary Approaches]," in *The Third Ural Historical and Pedagogical Readings* (Ekaterinburg: Ural State Vocational Pedagogical Press, 1999), 16–25; Igor Poberezhnikov, "Dilemmy Teorii Modernizatsii [Dilemmas of Modernization Theory]," *Third Tatishchev Readings* (Ekaterinburg: Ural State Vocational Pedagogical Press, 2000), 6–15.
9. Roger L. Thiede, "Industry and Urbanization in New Russia from 1860 to 1910," in *The City in Russian History*, ed. Michael F. Hamm (Lexington: The University Press of Kentucky, 1982), 125–138.
10. Frederick W. Skinner, "Trends in Planning Practices: The Building of Odessa, 1794–1917," in *The City in Russian History*, ed. Michael F. Hamm (Lexington: The University Press of Kentucky, 1982), 139–159; Frederick W. Skinner, "Odessa and the Problem of Urban Modernization," in *The City in Late Imperial Russia*, ed. Michael F. Hamm (Bloomington: Indiana University Press, 1986), 209–248.
11. Patricia Herlihy, *Odessa: A History 1794–1914* (Cambridge: Harvard University Press, 1991).
12. Evrydiki Sifneos, *Imperial Odessa: Peoples, Spaces, Identities* (Leiden and Boston: Brill, 2018).
13. Natalia Yakovenko, *Vstup do istorii [Introduction to History]* (Kyiv: Krytyka, 2007), 272, 274.
14. Reiner Lindner, *Pidpryemtsi i misto v Ukraini 1860–1914 r. (Industrializatsija i sotsialna komunikatsija na Pivdni Rosijskoji imperiji) [Entrepreneurs and a City in Ukraine, 1860–1914 (Industrialization and Social Communication in the South of the Russian Empire)]* (Kyiv and Donetsk: Promin, 2008), 14.
15. Victoria Konstantinova and Igor Lyman, *Berdyanska Cholovicha Gimnazija (Ostannya Tretyna 19 Stolittya) [Berdyansk Boys' Gymnasium (the Last Third of the XIX Century)]* (Kyiv: Osvita Ukrainy, 2006); Victoria Konstantinova, Igor Lyman, and Anastasiya Ignatova, *European Vector of the Northern Azov in the Imperial Period: British Consular Reports About Italian Shipping* (Berdyansk: Tkachuk O.V., 2016); Igor Lyman, Victoria Konstantinova, and Eugene Danchenko, *British Consul and Industrialist John Edward Greaves* (Berdyansk: Tkachuk O.V., 2017); Igor Lyman and Victoria Konstantinova, *The Ukrainian South as Viewed by Consuls of the British Empire (Nineteenth – Early Twentieth Centuries). Volume 1: British Consuls in the Port City of Berdyansk* (Kyiv: Osvita Ukrainy, 2018); Igor Lyman and Victoria Konstantinova, *Nimetski konsuly v Pivnichnomu Pryazovyi [German Consuls in the Northern Azov Region]* (Dnipro: LIRA, 2018).
16. Gelina Harlaftis, Victoria Konstantinova, Igor Lyman, Anna Sydorenko and Eka Tchkoidze (eds), *Between Grain and Oil From the Azov to the Caucasus: the Port-Cities of the Eastern Coast of the Black Sea, Late 18th – Early 20th Century*, Black Sea History Working Papers, vol. 3 (Rethymnon, 2020), 305–316.

17. "Berdyanskaja pristan [Berdyansk pier]," *Odesskiy Vestnik*, 59, July 23, 1830, 234.
18. Victoria Konstantinova, *Urbanizatsija: Pivdennoukrainskij Vymir (1861–1904 roky) [Urbanization: Southern Ukrainian Dimension (1861–1904 years)]* (Zaporizhzhia: AA Tandem, 2010), 222; N. Melnik, "Arhitektura Kompleksiv Gromadsko-Zhytlovoji Zabudovy Mist Pivdnya Ukrainy kintsya 18 – pochatku 20 st. (na Prykladi Mist Khersona, Mykolaeva, Odesy) [Architecture of Complexes of Public and Residential Buildings of the Cities of the Southern Ukraine in the Late 18th – Early 20th Century (Case Studies of Kherson, Nikolaev, Odessa)]" (Ph.D. Diss., Lviv, 2007), 90.
19. Vasilij Kryzhanovskyi, "[Berdyansk]," *Odesskiy Vestnik*, 16 (January 23, 1864): 64.
20. State Archive of the Odessa region, fond 1, opys 194, sprava 258, "About the appointment of the painter Vahlenkamp as Berdyansk's city architect. 1856."
21. P. Petrov, *Sbornik Materialov dlya Istorii Imperatorskoj Sankt-Peterburgskoj Akademii Hudozhestv za Sto Let jeje Suschestvovanija [Collection of Materials for the History of the Imperial St. Petersburg Academy of Arts for a Hundred Years of Its Existence]*, Part III (Sankt-Petersburg, 1866), 262.
22. George Cavendish Taylor, *Journal of Adventures with the British Army, from the Commencement of the War to the Taking of Sebastopol*, vol. II (London: Hurst and Blackett, 1856), 8–20.
23. Incidentally, the great-great-grandson of the British consul in Berdyansk Robert William Cumberbatch is the contemporary world-famous British actor Benedict Timothy Carlton Cumberbatch.
24. Edward Hertslet (compiler), *The Foreign Office List, Forming a Complete British Diplomatic and Consular Handbook. January 1865* (London: Harrison, 1865), 75.
25. *Accounts and Papers: Thirty-Five Volumes (27). Statistic Tables. Colonial and Other Possessions; Foreign Countries. Session 24 January – 28 August 1860. VolumeLXV* (London: George Edward Eyre and William Spottiswoode, 1860), 42.
26. Konstantinova and Lyman, *Berdyanska Cholovicha Gimnazija (Ostannya Tretyna 19 Stolittya) [Berdyansk Boys' Gymnasium (the Last Third of the XIX Century)]*, 415.
27. "Berdyansk," *Odesskiy Vestnik*, 305, November 12, 1887, 3.
28. Konstantinova and Lyman, *Berdyanska Cholovicha Gimnazija (Ostannya Tretyna 19 Stolittya) [Berdyansk Boys' Gymnasium (the Last Third of the XIX Century)]*.
29. For the whole Russian Empire, Odessa was a testing ground for the search for an optimal management model within the city self-government modernization framework. This Black Sea port city became the site for the approbation of the city self-government reform, later introduced all around the Empire.
30. National Library of Israel, W.M.W. Haffkine Archive, ARC Ms. Var. 325/40, "Biographical notes . . . ," 1–7.
31. Selman Abraham Waksman, *The Brilliant and Tragic Life of W.M.W. Haffkine, Bacteriologist* (New Brunswick, NJ: Rutgers University Press, 1964).
32. Harlaftis, Konstantinova, Lyman, Sydorenko and Tchkoidze eds., *Between Grain and Oil From the Azov to the Caucasus*, 316–322.
33. State Archive of the Odessa region, fond 1, opys 194, sprava 353, "About the abolition of hospitals in Kerch, Yalta and Berdyansk, also about their

reopening, as well as in Evpatoria. 1856;" State Archive of the Autonomous Republic of Crimea, fond 27, opys 1, sprava 7257, "According to the report of the master of the city and the port of Berdyansk on the opening of the gymnastic club. 1863–1864," State Archive of Odessa region, fond 1, opys 82, sprava 85, "About new staff of Berdyansk city hospital. 1864;" State Archive of the Odessa region, fond 1, opys 44, sprava 54, "On the introduction of street lighting in the city of Berdyansk. 1869;" State Archive of Odessa region, fond 1, opys 44, sprava 106, "On the opening of a credit for the Berdyansk public bank for the discount of bills in the Odessa office of the state bank. 1869;" State Archive of the Autonomous Republic of Crimea, fond 26, opys 1, sprava 28071, "A book given by the Berdyansk city government to the temporary commission on the arrangement of the Berdyansk port for a record of received and spent money for work on the construction of the Berdyansk port. 1886;" State Archive of the Autonomous Republic of Crimea, fond 27, opys 13, sprava 1550, "About port facilities in Berdyansk, . . . about the offers of the master of the city and the port of Berdyansk for street paving and construction of the boulevard. 1879;" Russian State Historical Archive, fond 1288, opis. 6, delo 876, "Berdyansk, 1899–1901"; etc.

34. Even after obtaining a connection to the railway network, Berdyansk was put at a disadvantage in comparison with other ports because of a most unfavorable (so-called "export") railway tariff, which was applied to the city by the government.
35. Harlaftis, Konstantinova, Lyman, Sydorenko and Tchkoidze eds., *Between Grain and Oil From the Azov to the Caucasus,* 322–327.
36. Germans and Mennonites were not the same, although usually they did not differ in the perception of the local population.
37. In 1863, the acting British consul in Berdyansk, William George Wagstaff, wrote in relation to this: "These colonies present a striking contrast with the surrounding country. On entering their precincts, a different style of agriculture is at once remarked. The allotment of the land, the uniform buildings and methodical arrangement of the same, together with the fruit trees that are planted, all prove their superiority to Russian agriculturists." ("Berdiansk Report by Mr. Acting Consul Wagstaff on the Trade of Berdiansk, for the Year 1863," in *Commercial Reports Received at the Foreign Office from Her Majesty's Consuls Between July 1st, and December 31th, 1864* [London: Harrison and Sons, 1865], 118–127).
38. "Report by Consul Zohrab on the Trade and Commerce of Berdiansk for the Year 1871," in *Commercial Reports Received at the Foreign Office from Her Majesty's Consuls* (London: Harrison and Sons, 1872), 487–492.
39. "Report by Consul Zohrab on the Trade of Berdiansk for the Year 1872," in *Commercial Reports Received at the Foreign Office from Her Majesty's Consuls* (London: Harrison and Sons, 1873), 1002–1009.
40. The worst expectations, expressed by Zohrab, came true: "The contemplated Menonite emigration has attracted attention in Russia and America during the past year, and the question has been discussed in the papers. What was considered an idle threat to extort exemptions and privileges will shortly be shown to have been a firm resolve. A large number of Mennonite families from the neighboring districts and from the Crimea have completed all their preparations for departure, and they purpose leaving next spring. They are all well off, and being good agriculturists, thrifty, and hard-working, they will prove a valuable acquisition to the country they adopt as their new

home. Without doubt their departure will be followed by other bands of emigrants, and there will soon be a steady exodus. As his Imperial Majesty generally gives these people six years' time to elect to submit to the new laws and remain or to quit the country, the movement will not be hurried, and the emigration will be gradual but steady, and by the end of 1879 it is very probable that most of the Mennonites will have left this country" ("Report by Consul Zohrab on the Trade and Commerce of Berdiansk for the Year 1873," in *Commercial Reports Received at the Foreign Office from Her Majesty's Consuls* [London: Harrison and Sons, 1874], 853–860).

41. Konstantin Bakhanov and Igor Lyman, *Berdyansk v Dnevnikah Titulyarnogo Sovetnika V.K. Kryzhanovskogo. Kryzhanovskyi V.K. Dnevniki [Berdyansk in the Diaries of the Titular Counselor V.K. Kryzhanovskyi. Kryzhanovskyi V.K. Diaries]* (Zaporizhzhya: Prosvita, 2002), 166, 181.
42. *Novorossijskij Kalendar na 1873 God [Novorossia Calendar on 1873]* (Odessa, 1872), 97.
43. "Berdyansk," *Odesskiy Vestnik*, 65, March 10, 1890, 3.
44. *Torgovo-Promyshlennyj Ukazatel i Putevoditel po Gorodu Berdyansku [Industrial and Commercial Index and City Guide of Berdyansk]* (Berdyansk: Typography of M. Doroshenko, 1915), 15.
45. State Archive of the Odessa region, fond 1, opys 17, sprava 73, "Regarding the permission for the military engineer Colonel Pochinskiy with the participation of the British subjects Grierson and Vilmot to build in Berdyansk the port jetty and boathouse. 1869."
46. "26 Nojabrya [26 November]," *Odesskiy Vestnik*, 327, December 5, 1888, 2; *Foreign Office. 1889. Annual Series. # 536. Diplomatic and Consular Reports on Trade and Finance. Russia. Report for the Year 1888 on the Trade of the Consular District of Odessa* (London: Harrison and Sons, 1889), 23.
47. *Foreign Office. 1888. Annual Series. # 346. Diplomatic and Consular Reports on Trade and Finance. Russia. Report for the Year 1887 on the Trade of the Consular District of Odessa* (London: Harrison and Sons, 1888), 16.
48. Lyman, Konstantinova, and Danchenko, *British Consul and Industrialist John Edward Greaves*; Igor Lyman and Victoria Konstantinova, "British Vice-Consul in Berdyansk John Edward Greaves," *Scriptorium nostrum* 2, no. 5 (2016): 86–108; Igor Lyman and Victoria Konstantinova, "Zyednuyuchy Brytansku, Rosiysku i Nimetsku imperiyi: Rodyna brytanskoho vitsekonsula Dzhona Griyevza v avanhardi modernizatsiyi na Pivdni Ukrainy [Connecting the British, Russian and German Empires: Family of the British Vice-Consul John Greaves at the Forefront of Modernization at the Southern Ukraine]," *Ukraina Moderna* 25 (2018).
49. *The Foreign Office List and Diplomatic and Consular Year Book, 1917* (London: Harrison and Sons, 1917), 295.
50. Helmut T. Huebert, *Mennonites in the Cities of Imperial Russia. Vol. 1: Barvenkovo, Berdyansk, Melitopol, Millerovo, Orechov, Pologi, Sevastopol, Simferopol* (Winnipeg: Springfield Publishers, 2006), 172.
51. The National Archives, FO 655 (Foreign Office: Chief Clerk's Department and Passport Office: Collection of Passports), FO 655/269 "Place of Issue: ROSTOV. Name: John Edward Greaves, with wife Jane."
52. *Ves Berdyansk i Ego Uezd. Adresno-Spravochnaja i Torgovo-Promyshlennaja Kniga [The Whole of Berdyansk and Its Uezd. Address-Reference and Commercial-Industrial Book]* (Simferopol: Zvenigorodskiy, Veresotskaja & Brakhtman, 1911), 29.

53. Vladimir Lenin, *Razvitie Kapitalizma v Rossii [The Development of Capitalism in Russia]* (Moscow: Izdatelstvo Politicheskoj Literatury, 1971), 219.
54. Peter Kropotkin, *Fields, Factories and Workshops* (New Brunswick and London: Transaction Publishers, 1993), 37–38.
55. *Ves Berdyansk i Ego Uezd*, 30. The company with 1,500 workers had warehouses far away from Berdyansk: in Kharkov, Chelyabinsk, Omsk and Semipalatinsk.
56. In October of 1912, "The Edinburgh Gazette" informed that King George V "has been pleased to give and grant unto John Greaves, Esq., . . . His Majesty's Royal licence and authority to accept and wear the Insignia of Chevalier of the Order of the Crown, which Decoration has been conferred upon him by His Majesty the King of the Belgians, in recognition of valuable services rendered by him" ("Whitehall," October 22, 1912," *The Edinburgh Gazette*, October 29, 1912, 1100).
57. *Ves Berdyansk i Ego Uezd*, 30.
58. Amy E. Greaves Sudermann Enss, *Winding Trails: From Sheffield to the Steppes and Beyond: A Memoir 1899–1915*, ed. David P. Sudermann and Mary R. Blocksma (Northfield, MN: Small World Press, Privately Published; Corrected Unpublished 2nd Edition, 2001), 27.
59. Interestingly, the world's first-ever official football club was formed in 1857 exactly in Sheffield.
60. V. Mikhailichenko, E. Denisov, and N. Tishakov, *Berdyansk: Vzglyad Cherez Stoletija [Berdyansk: A Look Through the Centuries]* (Berdyansk: Pivdenna Zorya; Zaporizhzhya: Dyke Pole, 2010), 227.
61. Az, "Berdyansk," *Odesskiy Vestnik*, 59, March 17, 1879, 2–3.
62. N.X. "Popovich. Nekrologia [N.Kh. Popovich. Obituary]," *Odesskiy Vestnik*, 5, January 17, 1842, 22.
63. Vasilij Kryzhanovskyi, "[Berdyansk]," *Odesskiy Vestnik*, 52, 15 May 1854, 1.
64. Bakhanov and Lyman, *Berdyansk v Dnevnikah Titulyarnogo Sovetnika V.K. Kryzhanovskogo*, 41, 187.
65. Vasilij Kryzhanovskyi, "19 Marta [19 March]," *Odesskiy Vestnik*, 25, March 27, 1846, 126.
66. Vasilij Kryzhanovskyi, "Pervyj Opyt Razvedenija Vinograda na Berdyanskih Peskah [The First Experience of Growing Grapes on the Berdyansk Sands]," *Odesskiy Vestnik*, 64, August 15, 1851, 2.
67. Vasilij Kryzhanovskyi, "Pervaja Lgota Gorodu Berdyansku [The First Privilege for the City of Berdyansk]," *Odesskiy Vestnik*, 32, April 25, 1851, 1.
68. Vasilij Kryzhanovskyi, "4 Sentiabrja [4 September]," *Odesskiy Vestnik*, 75, September 9, 1844, 364; Vasilij Kryzhanovskyi, "22 Ijunja. O Torgovle Solju v Berdyanske [June 22, On the Salt Trade in Berdyansk]," *Odesskiy Vestnik*, 52, July 2, 1852, 2.
69. Vasilij Kryzhanovskyi, "20 Oktiabrja [20 October]," *Odesskiy Vestnik*, 120, November 3, 1860, 574.
70. Vasilij Kryzhanovskyi, "[Berdyansk]," *Odesskiy Vestnik*, 206, September 19, 1872, 854; Vasilij Kryzhanovskyi, "[Berdyansk]," *Odesskiy Vestnik*, 246, November 8, 1873, 1100; Vasilij Kryzhanovskyi, "Sentiabrja 25 [September 25]," *Odesskiy Vestnik*, 216, October 4, 1875, 2.
71. State Archive of the Odessa region, fond 1, opys 60, sprava 99, "At the petition of the Berdyansk mayor to release self-taught mechanic Akim Pirozhkov from recruitment. 1863."
72. "1 Aprelja [1 April]," *Odesskiy Vestnik*, 49, May 4, 1861, 215–216.

73. Abazali, "20 Maja [20 May]," *Odesskiy Vestnik*, 120, June 1, 1872, 488.
74. Nathaniel Wood, "The 'Polish Mecca', the 'Little Vienna on the Vistula' or 'Big-City Cracow'? Imagining Cracow Before the Great War," *Urban History* 40, no. 2 (2013): 243.
75. We cannot agree with the thesis about the absence of urban traditions in the region during "pre-Russian" times. Yet cities here developed in spite of, rather than in the continuation of, the old local traditions. These cities were the product and, at the same time, the factor of imperial expansion. That is why the urbanization of, in particular, the Ukrainian part of the Black Sea and the Sea of Azov coast had a distinct regional specificity in comparison with other Ukrainian regions, which came under Russian rule much earlier and were mostly much older. The majority of the cities of the region were thus "imperial" and not "historical," if we follow the typology of Reiner Lindner (Lindner, *Pidpryemtsi i misto v Ukraini 1860–1914 r.*, 19, 37–78).
76. Bakhanov and Lyman, *Berdyansk v Dnevnikah Titulyarnogo Sovetnika V.K. Kryzhanovskogo*, 15.
77. Wood, "The 'Polish Mecca'," 228–229.
78. Ibid., 231.
79. M-R., "21 Dekabrja [21 December]," *Odesskiy Vestnik*, 4, January 11, 1861, 16–17.
80. V. Serikov, "9 Yanvarja [9 January]," *Odesskiy Vestnik*, 8, January 21, 1858, 29–30.
81. Vasilij Kryzhanovskyi, "13 Iyulja [13 July]," *Odesskiy Vestnik*, 60, July 26, 1844, 300.
82. Harlaftis, Konstantinova, Lyman, Sydorenko and Tchkoidze eds., *Between Grain and Oil From the Azov to the Caucasus.*
83. Nikolai Leskov, "Temneyuschie Berega [Darkening Shores]," in *Collected Works in 11 Volumes. Volume 11* (Moscow: GIHL, 1958), 165.
84. Grigory Danilevsky, "Beglye v Novorossii [Fugitives in New Russia]," *Vremya* 1–2 (1862).
85. Nathaniel Wood, "Conclusion: Not Just the National: Modernity and the Myth of Europe in the Capital Cities of Central and Southeastern Europe," in *Capital Cities in the Aftermath of Empires: Planning in Central and Southeastern Europe*, ed. Emily Gunzburger Makas and Tanja Damljanovic Conley (London: Routledge, 2010), 267.
86. Igor Lyman and Andriy Pimenov, compilers, "*Yune misto." Litopys Istorii Berdyanska Ochyma Korespondentiv "Odesskogo Vestnika" (1827–1860) ["Young Town." A Chronicle of the History of Berdyansk Through the Eyes of the Reporters of the "Odesskiy Vestnik" (1827–1860)]* (Berdyansk and Rostov-on-Don: RA "Tandem-U", 2007); Igor Lyman and Victoria Konstantinova, compilers, "*Kraschyj Port Azovskogo Morya." Litopys Istorii Berdyanska Ochyma Korespondentiv "Odesskogo Vestnika" (1861–1875) ["The Best Seaport of the Sea of Azov." A Chronicle of the History of Berdyansk Through the Eyes of the Reporters of the "Odesskiy Vestnik," (1861–1875)]* (Berdyansk and Taganrog: RA "Tandem-U", 2007); Igor Lyman and Victoria Konstantinova, compilers, "*Povitova Stolytsya." Litopys Istorii Berdyanska Ochyma Korespondentiv "Odesskogo Vestnika" (1876–1893) ["The Capital of the Uezd." A Chronicle of the History of Berdyansk Through the Eyes of the Reporters of the "Odesskiy Vestnik" (1876–1893)]* (Berdyansk and Nevinnomysk: RA "Tandem-U", 2007).
87. M. Buhteev, "O Torgovom Znachenii Berdyanska [On the trade value of Berdyansk]," *Odesskiy Vestnik*, 38, May 10, 1847, 199–200.

88. Lyman and Konstantinova, *The Ukrainian South as Viewed by Consuls of the British Empire.*
89. *Commercial Reports Received at the Foreign Office from Her Majesty's Consuls* (London: Harrison and Sons, 1868), 128.
90. *Foreign Office. 1894. Annual Series. # 1375. Diplomatic and Consular Reports on Trade and Finance. Russia. Report for the Year 1893 on the Trade & c. of Taganrog* (London: Harrison and Sons, 1894), 26.
91. John Griffiths, "Were There Municipal Networks in the British World c.1890–1939?" *The Journal of Imperial and Commonwealth History* XXXVII, no. 4 (2009): 575–597, quote at 581; John Griffiths, "Civic Communication in Britain: A Study of the *Municipal Journal* c.1893–1910," *Journal of Urban History* XXXIV, no. 5 (2008): 775–794.
92. Ewen Shane, *What Is Urban History? What Is History Series* (Cambridge: Polity Press, 2015).

3 Traveling Architecture

Géza Maróti's Art Between the Regional and the Global

Eszter Gantner

At the Milan International world's fair in 1906, the planner of the Hungarian pavilion, Géza Maróti, was awarded five grand prizes among the 409 awards at the exhibition, in the categories of sculpture, architecture and applied art. The young artist, a self-made man, the son of a tenant farmer, and at the same time studying and working as business manager in the studio of the architectural sculptor Ignác Oppenheimer in Budapest, Maróti became one of the most successful artists of turn of the century in the fields of applied art and interior design. As a consequence, he was invited to design the Hungarian exhibition and pavilion at the international applied art exhibition in 1906 in Milan. However, the Hungarian pavilion and its exhibition told not only the story of a talented and ambitious self-made man, but also the story of Budapest, which emerged through transformation and modernization into a regional center of Austria-Hungary.

Within this framework, this chapter argues that Maróti's international success was rooted, on the one hand, in his network and the opportunities offered by Budapest at the very beginning of his career, and, on the other hand, in his easily decodable "regional–universal" art. This art was not only "transportable," but also allowed the cities that commissioned him, namely Budapest, Mexico City and Detroit – all cities with regional aspirations – to invent glorious "national" pasts. Thanks to this network and his artistic "tool-kit," he established strong links of communication and exchange between these cities and across continents.

Budapest and Géza Maróti

From the merging of three small cities (Pest, Buda, Óbuda), a new capital – Budapest – was established in 1873. The city developed rapidly into a metropolis of industry, media, science and culture, and consequently became a center of national power. Although, only decades earlier, the revolution and the struggle for liberation in 1848–1849 and over the following years saw a break in the development of the twin cities of Buda and Pest, they remained the objects of the Hungarian "national project," rooted in the era of romantic nationalism in the 1820s and 1830s. Before they were transformed into the nation's capital in 1873, the twin cities provided a home for the national movement and institutions of national culture, such as the national theater and national museum. In 1867, when the Habsburg administration reached a compromise with the Hungarian nobility, Hungary was granted a status equal to that of Austria within the Habsburg Empire, making Budapest the twin capital of a dual monarchy. It was this compromise, too, which opened the second great phase of development in the history of the city, which lasted until World War I. This was a period of rapid industrialization, urban growth and modernization, and became the most glorious era in the history of the city, before or since. This growth and development was pursued by the government, whose aim was to create both a national and regional economic and cultural center. However, the growth of emerging cities in Europe's borderlands, such as Budapest, Zagreb and Ljubljana, was not only the result of economic innovation and industrialization, but also due to these cities' national and cultural strategy, which involved the careful selection and transfer of best practices and knowledge from abroad.[1] These manifested also in the field of the urban development of Budapest, where various foreign practices and techniques were not merely adapted, but the possible advantages and disadvantages of applying them carefully measured.[2]

This process allowed modernization to take place in a way that was sensitive to local needs and conditions, while at the same time embracing the latest European developments.[3] This was a paradigmatic development in cities with regional aspirations, as they emerged as important centers at the intersection of national and regional interests, and within both imperial and European frames.[4] Many of these cities had a young, well-educated generation of experts,[5] who became – in addition to the politicians – the driving force, the "engineers" of the modernization there. This can be regarded as a specific modernization, too, which was influenced and shaped by the strategies, interests and decisions of local agents and institutions, as well as by the quality and quantity of the transformed practices, techniques and methods, as Shmuel Eisenstadt pointed out in his work on *Multiple Modernities*.[6] Within this context, the conscious adaptation or rejection of best practices was of great importance. Furthermore, a "specific local knowledge" was produced through the transfer of best practices. This knowledge related to how a city could be transformed into a national capital and regional center and was communicated between the emerging cities in the form of exhibitions, expert meetings and study visits. But the "official" networks and channels maintained by associations, municipalities and expert groups was rooted in the individual networks of people who were devoted to architecture, urban development and planning, as the career of Géza Maróti[7] illustrates.

Maróti belonged to a generation of Hungarian intellectuals that emerged after the political compromise between Austria and Hungary in 1867, at a time when national culture was taking shape.[8] This generation not only included many representatives of marginal groups in ethnic terms, but also proved to be socially heterogeneous. The newly conceived liberal education policy, the introduction of incentive programs by the government and the capitalist economic transformation offered the chance of social mobility and modernization, regardless of people's ethnic or social affiliation. Both Maróti's career and working ethos had been influenced by these developments and contained features, such as the strong "Hungarian feeling" that characterized the biographies and careers of many of his contemporaries.[9]

Maróti (Rintel) was born into a Jewish family in Nitra, in the northern part of Hungary, in 1875. Like many Jewish families at this time, his family was willing to exploit the opportunities that were opening up and decided to move to Budapest, as did thousands of people from the rural part of the country. This era saw increased migration, especially Jewish migration, into towns with rapidly developing economies and to Budapest in particular. In 1850, Pest had 17,500 Jewish inhabitants; by 1857, this number had risen already to 23,000. In 1869, the Jewish population in the city was 45,000, by 1880 this number had increased to 71,000, by 1890 to 103,000 and around the turn of the century Budapest had 166,000 Jewish residents.[10] Increasing urbanization ultimately promoted the formation of a Jewish middle class, too. This middle class played a crucial role in the formation of a sensitive urban population that was open minded toward the arts. Having been involved in the Hungarian economy since the beginning of the 1860s and accepting several elements of the assimilationist ideas put forward by the Hungarian political elite, these people did everything to "become Hungarian." This enthusiasm for the "Hungarian national culture" also characterized the life and career of Géza Maróti – who changed his name from Rintel to the more Hungarian sounding Maróti in 1905 and became Roman Catholic, too – and was a crucial element of his work.

After moving to Budapest, he started his career in the workshop of the stucco plasterer Ignác Oppenheimer as an apprentice stonemason. In 1900, Maróti established his own studio, and he soon became a successful artist and a well-known figure of the Budapest art world. Many of the main buildings such as the Music Academy (1904–1907) and Gresham Palace (1905) were decorated with his figures. But he painted too, and during World War I, his sketches and paintings from the front in Galicia were printed and published Europe-wide.[11]

Alongside his design activities, he was deeply involved in the work of the young architects associated with Károly Kós and Béla Lajta, who wanted to reinvent Hungarian architecture on the basis of folk art.[12] Maróti went with Kós and Lajta to Kalotaszeg, Transylvania, in 1908 in order to collect and record folk art motives. By doing so, they followed a similar path as their friends and colleagues in Finland, Eliel Saarinen and

Figure 3.1 Budapest, Abonyi Street 1; decoration by Maróti, 1911.

Source: Photo by Fortepan/Makovecz Benjamin, 1985; Photo ID 108297 FORTEPAN© 2010–2014, under Creative Commons CC-BY-SA-3.0 license

Akseli Gallen-Kallela, and others throughout Europe's borderlands with emerging national culture and cities.[13]

Maróti's art was a clear manifestation of this approach: he designed the Hungarian pavilion for the Milan International in 1906 and, three years later, for the exposition in Venice in 1909.[14] On these two occasions, he developed an easily identifiable, very decorative and attractive style, incorporating national motifs. This design led not only to the international breakthrough at the Milan Exposition, but provided the fundament for his international network and career, as well. The exposition was a turning point: on the one hand, his work was reviewed internationally, and on the other hand, it served as a point of departure for his international career and networking.

Becoming International I: Milan and Mexico City

In 1906, Milan hosted a world's fair. Also known as the Great Expo of Work and Transportation, the Milan International was created with the aim to make a great international exhibition for transportation to inaugurate the Paris – Milan railway on the occasion of the completed alpine tunnel of Sempione.[15] Although Milan was known already both nationally and internationally as one of the key protagonists in global trade at that time, the decision to set up an exhibition was made on the basis of the aim to highlight the city's growing industry. The construction of the Sempione Tunnel, a 20-km long railway tunnel that connected Milan to the great capitals of Europe, provided the prefect occasion for celebrating this achievement of local industry. The Expo opened on 28 April and ran until 31 October 1906. It was held in the Sempione Park, where a fine arts exhibit was set up, and in the Piazza d'Armi, where there were engineering and industrial exhibits and various pavilions showcasing foreign nations, including the Hungarian pavilion, which was mainly the work of Maróti. The two areas were linked by an electric railway, highlighting the main theme of the Expo, which was transportation. The Expo was organized into 200 stands and attracted approximately 10 million visitors from all over the world. Most countries from Western Europe were represented, but the exhibition also provided the possibility for nations and empires such as Turkey, Japan, Russia, China and the United States to exhibit their "industrial progress," as well.[16] However, the exhibition was far more than that: it also provided a platform for exchange, networking and the transfer of knowledge and techniques, as well as of ideas and best practices.[17] Maróti recognized this, too, and he would later include in his memoirs reports of the various meetings, visits and parties that he attended.[18]

Despite the claims of Maróti and the other Hungarian participants regarding the low quality of the pavilion constructions and the chaos before the opening,[19] this exposition offered a special opportunity for the multi-talented Maróti to introduce himself on the international stage. He became one of the "rising stars" of the exhibition, as he recalled in his memoirs:

> I was loved by the jury. . . . I received the big gold medal at the Milan Chamber of Commerce and Industry. . . . We were notified that the Italian royal couple came to visit our exhibition.[20]

The Hungarian pavilions[21] of Milan and, three years later, of Venice, both of which were mainly designed by Maróti, combined folk art elements with contemporary high-tech solutions. The most popular attraction of the 1906 Hungarian pavilion was the main hall, which featured marble and special tiles produced by the Zsolnay factory. In the middle stood the Duck Fountain, which made a particularly vivid impression on visitors due to its unique ceramic technique. The pavilion, through its richly decorative and exclusively "Hungarian" design, earned fame and attention for Maróti.

His art and style combining folk art with universal aesthetic forms matched the expectations of those urban architects and planners who were working on cities where the "national" had to be physically

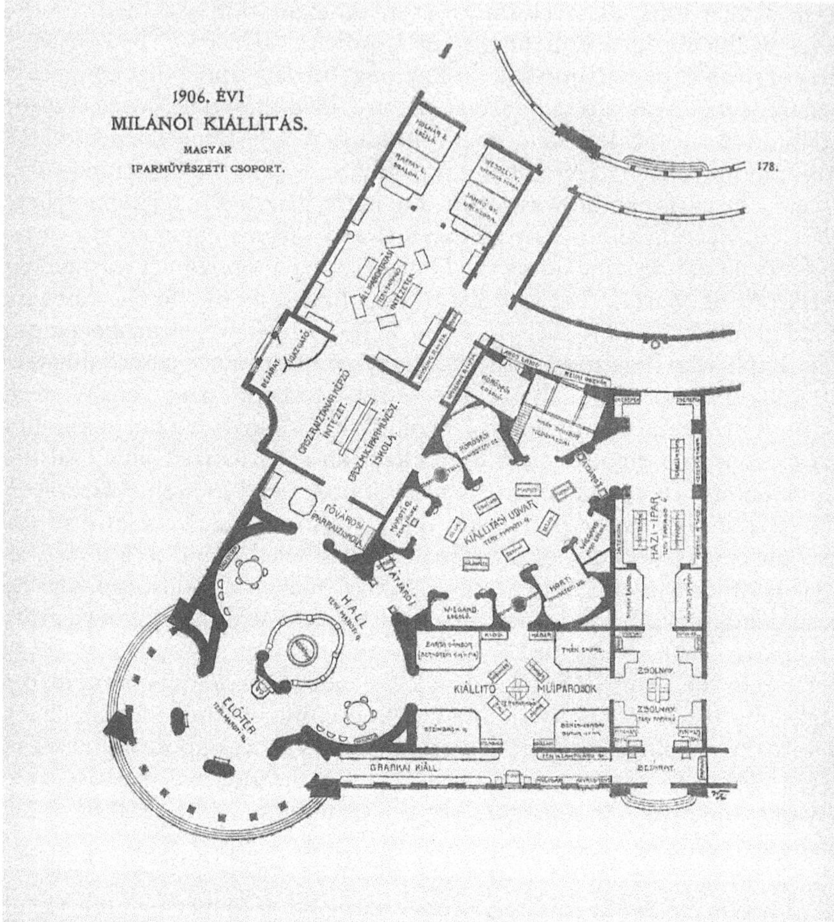

Figure 3.2 Map of the Hungarian pavilion at World Fair in Milan, 1906.

Source: epa.oszk.hu/01000/01059/00050/pdf/1906_04–05_161–219.pdf; accessed and downloaded 12 December 2017, open access

imprinted on the urban landscape. The Hungarian arts and crafts journal *Magyar Iparművészet*[22] (*Hungarian Industrial/Applied Art*) published many photographs of Maróti's pavilion in Milan, documenting not only the halls, but also the interiors and the various objects within. These photographs possess a special value today because the entire pavilion, including the objects and designs, was destroyed by a fire on 3 August 1906. "It was horrible in Milan, that . . . ruin. I simply burst into tears."[23] Having financed the Hungarian exhibition in advance,[24] and being insured for only a part of the pavilion and its contents, Maróti lost the major part of his wealth. Although he and his colleagues succeeded in reconstructing the pavilion to some extent, his loss was still immense.

Despite this tragic episode, Maróti benefited in every other possible way from the Milan International: he not only won five "*grands prix*" as sculptor, as architect and as artist for his great design, but also, through the press and the numerous reports and reviews worldwide,[25] and through the various meetings and invitations, he rose to prominence in the international scene. As he later wrote: "I made a lot of interesting acquaintances in Milan."[26] In his memoirs, he listed who invited him where and how many times, and how he met Joseph Maria Olbrich, Vittorio Pica and, most importantly, Adamo Boari at the exhibition.[27] Adamo Boari, who was at that time already an established architect with commissions in both North and South America, visited the pavilion and was very impressed by Maróti's style. He subsequently invited him to design the interior of the planned Teatro Nacional in Mexico City.

Boari himself belonged to the generation of globally active architects who were now enjoying the advances of rapidly developing continental and intercontinental communication and transport infrastructure.[28] Trained at the universities of Ferrara and Bologna, Boari traveled to Brazil in 1899 to pursue new professional opportunities and soon began work on several railway and road building projects in the regions of Santos and Campiñas (near São Paulo). These large-scale infrastructure projects became catalysts for Boari's new interest in town planning. In 1888, despite now residing in Brazil, Boari made a submission to the design competition for the Italian parliament building in Rome.[29] In 1890, Boari also prepared drawings for a Universal Exposition that was commended by its assessors. While working in Brazil, Boari also traveled to Montevideo and Bueno Aires. Visits to the Uruguayan and Argentinean capitals undoubtedly heightened his interest in urbanism. In parallel, Boari continued to develop his abilities as an architect. In 1892, he moved to the United States and settled in Chicago. In Chicago, the civil engineer began formal training in architecture at the University of Chicago and became a licensed architect in 1899. At the time of Boari's arrival, the burgeoning metropolis was gaining national recognition as an epicenter of progressive architecture and urbanism. In preparing to host the World's Columbian Exposition in 1893, Chicago became the locus of considerable design activity. It was at this time that Boari apparently gained employment with the fair's consulting architects, Daniel Hudson Burnham and John Wellborn Root, and became involved with the project.[30] The path that would lead Boari and later Maróti to Mexico City began in Chicago. In 1897, his entry in the international design competition for Mexico's "National Capitol" building (Palacio Legislativo) was awarded first prize. Boari's success in the Mexican capitol competition led to him visiting the country and meeting the president, Porfirio Díaz, around 1898. Boari's time in Mexico and direct contact with Díaz resulted in a series of projects there. He was commissioned to design the Palacio de Bellas Artes and the Palacio de Correos de México in Mexico City. In 1901, he began work on the Palacio de Bellas Arte, inviting Maróti to join the project in 1906.

In his memoir, Maróti described the first meeting with Boari in Milan as follows:

> Two Mexican ministers and two secretaries of state and Adam Boari, an Italian architect living in Mexico, who has been on a study trip in Milan paid for by the Mexican government, invited me for dinner. . . . One of the gentlemen, who was the Minister de los Educationes et las Obras publicas (sic!) asked me during the dinner to come to Mexico City to design the interior of the Teatro Nacional.[31]

The turn of the century brought a very productive period in Mexico's development. One of Porfirio Diaz's primary objectives was to promote extremely fast modernization in the newly independent country. Like the national states and their capital cities in Eastern Europe in the second half of the nineteenth century, the focus here was also on creating an infrastructurally and technically modern state with a strong national culture, representation and identity.[32] The most important state institutions were built in this period.[33] These approaches enabled Boari to invite people such as Maróti, whose art and design and experiences with developing a unique "language" at the intersection of national and international interests was a guarantee to fulfill the expectations and national program of the Mexican government.[34]

The work in Mexico, especially the design of the stained-glass windows of the national theater, also enabled Maróti to transfer applications and practices developed in Budapest. An example was the cooperation with Miksa Róth, who ran one of the most advanced and well-known glass-painting factories in Central and Eastern Europe.[35] The application of highly decorative stained glass in public buildings started during the *Belle Époque* period in Europe. Developed in European cities like Budapest and Prague where there was "feverish" construction in the last third of the nineteenth century, this technique arrived in Latin America due to the direct commissioning of European architects and artists or due to their migration. Among the most influential stained-glass artists in Latin America,[36] 11 had European background and training, Maróti being one of them. In 1907, he traveled to Mexico City and signed a contract for works such as the proscenium mosaic arch and glass ceiling, the iron framework for the glass ceiling, and models for a glass stage curtain in the national theater.[37] Maróti was also commissioned to make the sculptures for the cupola of the building. These works established a further link to the factories and know-how in Budapest, as his design was realized and completed in the Budapest-based studio of Ármin and Ferenc

Steiner,[38] and was transported in March 1910 to Mexico City. As he later recalled, "It had a huge effect to transport these giants to Mexico, along with the separate iron structure from the Nicholson factory. Beforehand, of course, photographs were taken."[39]

Despite the success in Mexico City, he could not continue to work there after World War I. Facing the revolutions in Hungary (1918–1919) and the unstable political and economic situation there, Maróti desperately wanted to leave the country, and he hoped for new commissions in Mexico and for the possibility of staying there long enough to gain Mexican citizenship.[40] But, despite his attempts to revitalize his previous network and gain a foothold in Mexico through his previous commissions, he failed completely. The reasons for this failure were manifold;[41] however, one of most important factors seems to have been the political change in Mexico and, with it, the emergence of a new "revolutional" aesthetic approach with new artists and styles, such as those of Diego Rivera, which made it clear that there was no interest anymore for Maróti's more art nouveau-based style rooted in the pre-war period.[42]

Despite the break with Mexico, the friendship with Boari and the job in Mexico had a twofold impact on Maróti's career: on the one hand, he extended his network toward North America, and on the other hand, his reputation increased enormously, especially in Europe and in Hungary, where many art journals ran articles on his design work in the Palacio de Bellas Artes.[43]

Becoming International II: Detroit

Maróti's connection and friendship with Eliel Saarinen began in 1907 when Maróti visited Finland and their mutual friend, the artist Akseli Gallen-Kallela.[44] Eliel Saarinen, like Maróti and Boari, belonged to an international network of architects and artists, which emerged at the turn of the nineteenth and twentieth centuries.[45]

Trained at the University of Helsinki between 1893 and 1897, Saarinen designed the Finnish Pavilion at the Paris World Fair in 1900, where he achieved early fame for its design. Saarinen gained international prominence two years later when he won the competition for the design of the Helsinki railway station. In 1911, he started his career in city planning, visiting Budapest and consulting the mayor over the various master plans and advising Tallinn on a town planning competition.[46] A year later, in 1912, Saarinen took part in the international city planning competition for the new Australian capital, Canberra. In 1922, his participation in the design competition for the Chicago Tribune Tower made his name better known in the United States, so Saarinen moved there with his family. In 1925, he was asked by George G. Booth to design buildings for his new and ambitious project, the Cranbrook Educational Center near Detroit.

When the telegram from Saarinen arrived in 1926, Maróti was more than happy and grateful to accept the invitation to design the interiors of the college. At this time, after the dissolution of the Habsburg Monarchy, Hungary was a ruined country, both politically and economically. Furthermore, due to increasing anti-Semitism and a right-wing, conservative political and cultural turn under Miklós Horthy, Maróti experienced increasing marginalization and aggression, partly due his Jewish origin. Hungary could not offer him opportunities anymore. His decorative art, which aimed to strike a balance between the national and universal, no longer had a place in a country and society that were becoming more and more isolated.[47] Although he was able to realize some smaller commissions, such as the interior of the Csepel Works in 1918 and the pavilion of the Hungarian exhibition in Monza, fewer and fewer possibilities opened up for him.[48] From this perspective, the invitation to Detroit was more than Maróti dared to hope for. When he accepted the invitation in 1927, he was not planning on emigrating to the United States, however Saarinen had long-term plans for him. In 1926, Saarinen had even sent him a telegram, offering him – with Booth's approval[49] – the position of lecturer for sculpture in the new art school in Cranbrook.

The city in which Maróti arrived at the end of January 1927 had already become one of the industrial hubs of the United States. Detroit was an important center for transportation, linking the waterways of the Great Lakes system with the Erie Canal and the railway.[50] The rise of manufacturing led to a new class of wealthy industrialists, entrepreneurs and professionals who were interested in decorative architecture for their buildings. One of them, George Booth, was the founder of the Cranbrook Educational Community, where a special focus was given to arts and crafts. In 1925, he asked the already internationally respected architect, Eliel Saarinen, to design the campus in Bloomfield Hills, Detroit. Saarinen personally recommended Maróti to Booth and invited him to collaborate on the commission. George Booth referred to this invitation and recommendation in a letter to the secretary of the Society of Arts & Crafts, describing Maróti as follows:

> I have trusted entirely the judgment of Mr. and Mrs. Saarinen. I have learned also that he has some reputation outside of his country. . . . I think you can see that, with very little knowledge of him or his work, it was simply a "gamble" in art, but I had a great deal of faith in the Saarinens' opinion. . . . At least on one point I can speak from experience, and say that he proves a most agreeable gentleman, speaks English well[51]

Soon after his arrival, Maróti became an active member of the artistic community in Detroit and received more and more commissions in the city through Booth. Booth also introduced him to the architect Albert Kahn, who at that time already had a design for a skyscraper on his drawing board. The meeting ended with Maróti being invited to work as the decorative architect on one of the greatest buildings in Detroit: the Fisher Building. Besides the Fisher Building, Maróti also contributed to the architecture of the Foreman Bank Building, the Hurison (Hudson?) Motor Co. Building[52] and the Times Building with his rich, colorful and symbolist decorative art. His style – shifting from art nouveau to art deco – and many of his applied motives derived from the heritage of his conceptual, folk art-based art. However, while in Budapest, at the world exhibitions and in Mexico City, his art – with its motifs and symbols – represented and manifested the ambitions of the emerging cities, in Detroit his symbols and decorations emphasized the wealth and the power of the United States and its cities through commerce and transportation. In this way, the symbols and motifs shifted away from the national and particular, gaining a more global meaning.

In 1928, at the peak of his success in Cranbrook and Detroit, Maróti was already in possession of the permanent residency he needed to apply for American citizenship. Nonetheless, in 1929, after finishing his work on the Fisher Building, he sailed to Europe and moved to the Middle East, only returning to Detroit in 1931. Here, at the Detroit Institute of Arts, he exhibited the artworks he had produced during his Middle East journey in 1930. His drawings and paintings, which incorporated motifs from Cairo, Jerusalem, Athens, Thebes, Gaza and other places, attracted positive reviews, though only a few of them ended up being sold; most of the works are today to be found in the Hungarian Museum for Applied Arts. Despite the friends, prospects, opportunities, success and material security he had enjoyed in Detroit, Maróti ultimately chose to return to Hungary. As he had written in a number of letters to his daughter in Hungary, his years living in America had been tainted by acute homesickness.[53]

Conclusion

Cities with regional aspirations like the ones mentioned in this chapter, i.e. those which transformed themselves into economic, political and cultural hubs with an influence over neighboring areas,[54] were connected to each other via a constant stream of traveling experts. These people maintained networks that were often rooted in personal relationships such as friendships. The activities and mobility of Géza Maróti demonstrated this phenomenon clearly. Moreover, his plans and works, which manifested in a number of buildings and interiors around the world, show us that these emerging cities received fresh impulses not exclusively from the "centers," but often from other cities that have often been labeled "peripheral." These cities faced the same challenges of modernization[55] as did their inhabitants, and the lessons and skills gained from these experiences were able to be turned into advantages on the international stage, as Maróti's activities demonstrated. His flexibility and multilingualism, but also his skill in combining the particular with the universal in his art, were some of the factors that led to his international success and his ability to adapt his art to various urban and cultural settings.

By analyzing Maróti's activities and networks, we can also identify those processes and forms of knowledge transfer that emerged at the intersection of the national culture and contemporary European trends. Maróti's work was an interaction between these two, and it can be assumed that this was an additional element underlying his international success. Another characteristic of this process was its close relationship with the urbanization of the country, and thus of the whole region. Without the emerging cities such as Budapest, Prague and Zagreb becoming cultural, economic and political centers and metropolises, Maróti's generation in Central Europe might never have gained access to the opportunities, infrastructures and experiences described in this chapter.

He and many of his contemporaries managed to develop an artistic "tool-kit" derived from their own particular national culture, which became "transportable" and adaptable elsewhere, even in very different environments. Furthermore, their networks, which were established and developed through the mutual aim of combining national elements with European and international trends, enabled links between those emerging cities, where artists, planners and architects faced the same challenges and tasks.

Notes

1. Jan C. Behrends and Martin Kohlrausch, "Races to Modernity: Metropolitan Aspirations in Eastern Europe, 1890–1940. An Introduction," in *Races to Modernity: Metropolitan Aspirations in Eastern Europe, 1890–1940*, ed. Jan C. Behrends and Martin Kohlrausch (Budapest: Central European University Press, 2014), 1–20, pp. 13–15.
2. Eszter Gantner and Heidi Hein-Kircher, "Introduction – Emerging Cities: Knowledge and Urbanisation in Europe's Borderlands 1880–1945," Special Issue Emerging Cities. *Journal of Urban History* 43, no. 4 (July 2017): 575–586, p. 577.
3. Ibid., 579.
4. Emily Gunzburger Makas and Tanja Damljanovic Conley, *Capital Cities in the Aftermath of Empires* (New York: Routledge, 2015).
5. Laura Kolbe, "Imperial and National Helsinki: Shaping an Eastern or Western Capital City?" in *Races to Modernity: Metropolitan Aspirations in Eastern Europe, 1890–1940*, ed. Jan C. Behrends and Martin Kohlrausch (Budapest: Central European University Press, 2014), 267–289.
6. Shmuel Eisenstadt, "Multiple Modernities," *Daedalus* 129, no. 1 (Winter 2000): 1–29.

7. András Hadik, "Maróti Géza tevékenysége az I. világháborúban," in *Maróti Géza*, ed. Piroska Ács (Budapest: Ernst Múzeum, 2002), 72–82.
8. György Spira and Károly Vörös, ed., *Budapest története IV: A márciusi forradalomtól az őszirózsás forradalomig* (Budapest: Akadémiai Kiadó, 1987), 221.
9. Ibid.
10. Gábor Gyáni, "Uses and Misuses of Public Space in Budapest," in *Budapest and New York. Studies in Metropolitan Transformation 1870–1930*, ed. Thomas Bender and Carl E. Schorske (New York: Russell Sage Foundation, 1994), 85–108.
11. Hadik, "Maróti Géza tevékenysége az I. világháborúban," 72–82.
12. Tamás Csáki, "A finn építészet és az 'architektúra magyar lelke'- Kultúrpolitika, építészet, publicisztika a századelő Magyarországán," *Múltunk* 29, no. 1 (2006): 200–230.
13. Jeremy Howard, *Art Nouveau: International and National Styles in Europe* (Manchester: Manchester University Press, 1996).
14. Piroska Ács, "Maróti Géza pavilonművészete," in *Maróti Géza 1875–1941. Mi vagyunk Atlantisz*, ed. Piroska Ács (Budapest: Ernst Múzeum, 2002), 54–64.
15. John Findling and Kimberly Pelle, "Milan 1906," in *Encyclopedia of World's Fairs and Expositions*, ed. John Findling and Kimberly Pelle (Jefferson: McFarland & Company, 2008): 185–187, p. 185.
16. Ibid., 186.
17. See on this aspect: Evelyn Kroker, *Die Weltausstellungen im 19. Jahrhundert: Industrieller Leistungsnachweis, Konkurrenzverhalten und Kommunikationsfunktion unter Berücksichtigung der Montanindustrie des Ruhrgebietes zwischen 1851 und 1880* (Göttingen: Vandenhoeck & Ruprecht, 1975).
18. Maróti Géza, Emlékiratai, *Lapis Angularis IV* (Budapest: Ernst Múzeum, 2002), 13–22.
19. Ibid.
20. Ibid., 16.
21. See Figure 3.2.
22. Ibid., 169–216.
23. Maróti, Emlékiratai, *Lapis Angularis IV*, 20.
24. Ibid., 16.
25. N.N. "Kulföldi Vélemények a Magyar kiállítás iparművészeti osztályáról," *Magyar Iparművészet*, no. 4–5 (1996): 220–225, pp. 220, 223.
26. Maróti, Emlékiratai, *Lapis Angularis IV*, 18.
27. Ibid., 16–19.
28. See David Arnold, "Europe, Technology, and Colonialism in the Twentieth Century," in *History and Technology* 21, no. 1 (2005): 85–106.
29. Annette Condello and Christopher Vernon, "Adamo Boari, Mexico City and Canberra," in *11th Conference of the International Planning History Society (IPHS): Planning Models and the Culture of Cities*, ed. Francisco-Javier Monclus and Manuel Guardia, vol. 1 (Barcelona: Escola Tecnica Superior d'Arquitevtura del Valles, 2004), 1–14, www.etsav.upc.es/personals/iphs2004/, accessed August 10, 2019.
30. Ibid.
31. Maróti, Emlékiratai, *Lapis Angularis IV*, 18.
32. On this aspect, see Mauro F. Guillén, "Modernism Without Modernity: The Rise of Modernist Architecture in Mexico, Brazil, and Argentina, 1890–1940," *Latin American Research Review* 39, no. 2 (January 2004): 6–34, p. 6.

33. On the construction of Mexico City, see, among others: Emily Wakild, "Naturalizing Modernity: Urban Parks, Public Gardens and Drainage Projects in Porfirian Mexico City," *Mexican Studies/Estudios Mexicanos* 23, no. 1 (2007): 101–123 or Claudia Agostoni, *Monuments of Progress: Modernization and Public Health in Mexico City, 1876–1910* (Calgary: University of Calgary Press, 2003).
34. Guillén, "Modernism Without Modernity."
35. Jacek Purchla and Piotr Krakowski, eds., *Art Around 1900 in Central Europe: Art Centres and Provinces* (Kraków: International Cultural Centre, 1999).
36. A.M. Corrêa Pinto et al., "The Conservation of Stained-Glass Windows in Latin America: A Literature Overview," *Journal of Cultural Heritage* 34, no. 11–12 (2018): 172–181.
37. Hadik, "Maróti Géza tevékenysége az I. világháborúban," 13.
38. The Steiner company was present in Budapest already at the beginning of the twentieth century. According to the 1907 Industrial List, Steiner Ármin and Ferenc Imperial and Royal Court Producers manufactured, among other things, bronze building decorations and business portals at their premises at 6 Köztelek Street.
39. Maróti, Emlékiratai, *Lapis Angularis IV*, 39.
40. Mónika Szente-Varga, "Maróti Géza és más magyar művészek a mexikói nemzeti színház építésében," in *Maróti Géza*, ed. Piroska Ács (Budapest: Ernst Múzeum, 2002), 108–113, p. 110.
41. See on that: János Sturcz, "Ami megmaradt . . . Maróti Géza megvalósult munkái az Egyesült Államokban 1927–1932," in *Maróti Géza*, ed. Ács Piroska (Budapest: Ernst Múzeum, 2002), 132–148, p. 132.
42. Szente-Varga, "Maróti Géza és más magyar művészek a mexikói nemzeti színház építésében," 108–113.
43. Eg.: Magyar művészet Mexikóban. (Maroti Rintel.) Jeltelen cikk. A Nap, January 23, 1908.
44. Csáki, "A finn építészet és az 'architektúra magyar lelke' " 200–230, p. 224.
45. Michael Saler, ed., *The Fin- De-Siécle World* (New York: Routledge, 2015), 404.
46. He won this competition in 1913 with his plan for Tallinn. Karin Hallas-Murula, "Diffusion of European Modern City Planning Around 1910: Transferring and Implementation of International Knowledge in Tallinn, Estonia," in "Emerging Cities, Knowledge and Urbanisation in Europe's Borderlands 1880–1945," ed. Eszter Gantner and Heidi Hein-Kircher, *Journal of Urban History* 43, no. 4, Special issue (July 2017): 615–624.
47. On Hungary's history after World War I, see Ignác Romsics, *A Short History of Hungary* (Budapest: Osiris Kiadó, 2016).
48. Sturcz, "Ami megmaradt . . . Maróti Géza megvalósult munkái az Egyesült Államokban 1927–1932," 132–148, p. 132.
49. Ibid., 133.
50. Arthur M. Woodford, *This Is Detroit (Michigan) 1701–2001: An Illustrated History* (Detroit, MI: Wayne State University Press, 2001); Scott Martelle, *Detroit: A Biography* (Chicago: Review Press, 2012).
51. George Booth to Helen Plumb, February 1, 1927. Henry Scripps Booth and Carolyn Farr Booth Papers, Cranbrook Archives, Bloomfield Hills, MI.
52. "Hurison" is mentioned in some contemporary sources, but researchers believe today, that it was probably conceived instead of "Hudson." Sturcz, "Ami megmaradt . . . Maróti Géza megvalósult munkái az Egyesült Államokban 1927–1932," 132–148, p. 151, mentions that there are some sketches of

a projected Hudson building in the Budapest Museum for Applied Arts, so that possibly the project was not realized.

53. Idem. After his return to Hungary in 1932, Maróti faced growing discrimination, poverty, marginalization and isolation due to his Jewish origin. He died in 1941 at his home in Zebegény.
54. Condello and Vernon, "Adamo Boari, Mexico City and Canberra."
55. Gantner and Hein-Kircher, "Introduction – Emerging Cities," 575–586.

4 The Exchange of Urban Planning Theory and Practice Along the Austro-Hungarian Periphery

Zagreb as a Case Study

Tamara Bjažić Klarin

Along the Austro-Hungarian "periphery," such as that of present-day Croatia (then the Kingdom of Croatia, Slavonia and Dalmatia), the import of knowledge in the field of urban planning and architecture was a necessity. Croatian architects, prominently from Zagreb, looked across borders to arm themselves with knowledge at the forefront of contemporary theory and design in order to best apply these theories to the current situation in their homeland. The sources and methods of the transfer and import of knowledge changed during the period from the 1860s to World War II.

Within the territorial borders of the dual monarchy, architectural education, like all the other technical sciences, was controlled and determined exclusively by Vienna, Prague, Graz and Budapest, while the underdeveloped periphery received the knowledge and products created in and by these cities. Under these circumstances – where knowledge production was controlled by the monarchy centers – the majority of urban planning and architectural models were imported by Croatian professionals directly from Vienna. The situation started to shift in the 1880s, owing to the Društvo inženjera i arhitekta (Society of Engineers and Architects, founded in 1878). The Society had the leading role in establishing "horizontal" networking – a flexible and democratic network among experts in the field of architecture and civil engineering. The knowledge exchange was achieved through collaboration with other professional associations, journals, congresses, exhibitions, study trips and competitions. This was actually a precondition for the next stage, at the beginning of the twentieth century, when the professionals, for the first time, started to selectively and critically approach the knowledge they imported and turned toward Germany in search for more advanced planning practices. That "luxury" was concurrent with the emancipatory processes of Croatian architects and the crisis of urban planning within Austro-Hungarian borders. After the 1890s, Austro-Hungarian architects in monarchy centers were not able to produce new models, as remarked by Renate Banik-Schweitzer.[1]

It should be taken into account that established processes did not change substantially even following the collapse of the monarchy, when Croatia belatedly founded the long-awaited Visoka tehnička škola (Technical School), resulting in a reduction of knowledge imported and mediated by education. This break took place at a critical moment for cities such as Split and Zagreb, a period marked by housing crises and the emergence of slums due to the transformation of these cities from provincial centers of the Austro-Hungarian monarchy to commercial, traffic and industrial centers of the Kingdom of Serbs, Croats and Slovenes. These shifts required a new way of looking at contemporary urban planning methods and the import of knowledge, which led to the launching of international competitions – the most "luxurious model" of knowledge exchange, which, until World War I, was exclusively reserved for centers of power such as Vienna, Barcelona, Berlin and Paris. It was through this model that Zagreb took primacy for the first time. It adopted the concept of a functional city in an official planning document as early as 1932. Furthermore, the urban planning practices and institutions established during this period enabled the complete emancipation of the architectural and urban planning profession after World War II, when architects were once again faced with dramatic and demanding tasks, those of a reconstruction of an entire country. Covering the period from the 1880s until World War II, this essay discusses the import of knowledge in the area of urban planning, deliberating on the origin of planning models and the choices that were made.

Inherited Nineteenth-Century Urban Planning Models and Practices

With reference to a shared body of East Central European knowledge, Zagreb authorities provided basic urban planning documents, building codes and regulatory plans in order to meet the challenges of transforming a medieval city into a modern metropolis in the second half of the nineteenth century. There were two directions of knowledge transfer on urban planning and architectural models and practices. One, from Vienna, owed to architects almost exclusively educated by Friedrich von Schmidt at the Academy of Fine Arts,[2] while the second one came from other parts of East Central and Central Europe and was achieved through work of the Croatian Society of Engineers and Architects – the leading authority in the field. The Society established fruitful collaboration with fellow associations in Prague, Budapest, Lviv and Trieste, organized study trips and visits to the international and professional exhibitions such as the Millennial Exhibition in Budapest (1896) and the Czech Exhibition of Architecture and Engineering in Prague (1898), and eventually participated in international congresses itself.[3] One of the Society's most outstanding achievements beyond Austro-Hungarian borders was that of Martin Pilar, who attended the Fifth International Congress of Architects held for the occasion of the Exposition Universelle in Paris in 1900.[4] Professional journals and publications were an omnipresent medium of knowledge transfer. Therefore, the Society founded its own library and launched *Viesti društva inžinira i arhitekta* (*The Gazette of the Society of Engineers and Architects*).[5] The journal was exchanged with those of Austrian, Galician and Czech societies, while among the purchased ones were *Zeitschrift für Praktische Baukunst*, *Zeitschrift für Bauwesen*, *Zeitschrift für Bauhandwerke*, *Neubauten und Concurrenzen*, *Wochenblatt für Architekten und Ingenieure*, *Annales des ponts et chaussées*, etc. The urban planning publications were limited mostly to issues of infrastructure and building codes including those of Vienna, Zurich, Hannover and Berlin.[6]

The *Građevni red za grad Zagreb* (*Building Code for the City of Zagreb*, 1857) and the first regulatory plan (1865), on the one hand, and the *Propisi za izgradnju zgrada na Josipovcu* (*Rules for the Construction of Summer Houses at Josipovac*, 1888) and second regulatory plan of Zagreb (1887), on the other hand, marked two stages of city development – the proto-urban and *Gründerzeit*. The two stages had significantly different goals, ambitions and ways in which the city was conceptualized. The proto-urban stage started with the merging of the twin medieval settlements of Kaptol and Gradec on the southern hills of Medvednica with the inhabited area below them into a single city in 1850 and continued until the earthquake of 1880, while the second stage shaped the Donji grad (Lower Town) – the main urban substance of the city.[7]

The first regulatory plan was elementary both in its solutions and execution (Figure 4.1). The plan was meant to establish a new city district, Lower Town, on the plain enclosed by the railway line connecting Zagreb and Vienna (1862) to the south and Medvednica mountain to the north. As the Lower Town was below the Gradec and Kaptol areas, the problem of fortifications in the case of Zagreb was not an issue. Minor interventions were sufficient to connect the old and the new modern parts of the city.[8] The regulatory plan introduced a pragmatic orthogonal grid of roads and city blocks (the so-called "closed" city building model), common in most Austro-Hungarian cities. It provided a simple subdivision of land plots and basic infrastructure – an economic solution to the network of streets, water supply and sewage systems. The focus of Milan Lenuci as a city architect was on sanitation technology and utility infrastructure, including the foundation of the first municipal utility company in charge of water supply (1878).[9] The experiences of a dozen European cities in Germany, France, Belgium and Great Britain had been considered through literature, participation at the international congresses and visits to international hygiene exhibitions.[10] The first of many, the *Ausstellung auf dem Gebiete der Hygiene und des Rettungswesens*, which took place in Berlin in 1883, was

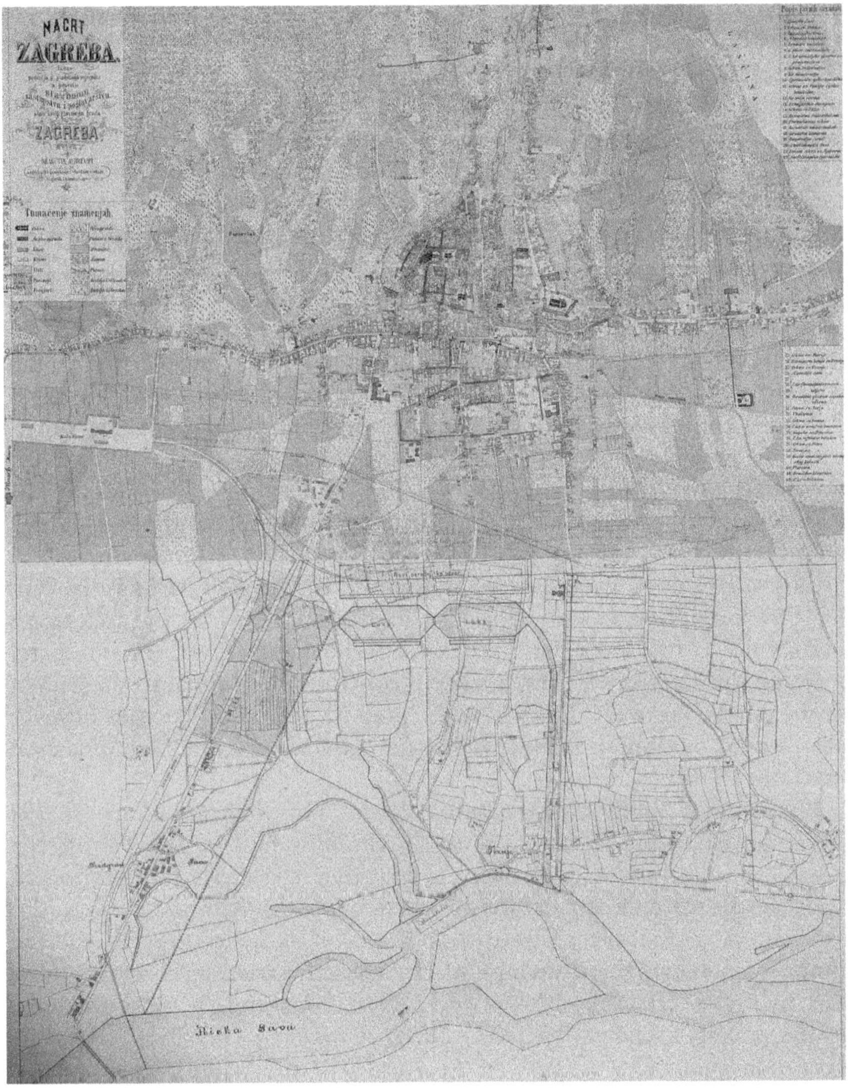

Figure 4.1 Zagreb Regulatory Plan, 1865.

Source: Muzej grada Zagreba, Collection of Plans and Regulatory Plans of the City of Zagreb, MGZ 5676; used with kind permission of Zagreb City Museum

attended by architect Janko J. Grahor, who also wrote about it in *Viesti društva inžinira i arhitekta*.[11] The Society's journal published several local and foreign articles on infrastructure and, after 1889, regularly featured excerpts from foreign "technical journals."[12]

The second plan, from 1887, was an extension of the first. Motivated by rapid city development, it provided Zagreb with its characteristic East Central European appearance (Figure 4.2). The so-called Zelena potkova (Green Horseshoe), a series of representative squares and parks with free-standing buildings for educational or cultural use – the Zagreb version of the Viennese Ringstrasse – was designed within the structure of the Lower Town by the previously mentioned Milan Lenuci. The architecture of the Horseshoe was influenced by Vienna, as well – directly, as Viennese architects such as Friedrich von Schmidt and Otto von Hofer were commissioned to design representative public buildings and private palaces, and indirectly, through the first generation of Zagreb-based architects, who were trained in Vienna and mostly designed the residential buildings.[13] The construction of the Horseshoe and the Lower Town was provided for by the newly established bourgeoisie, who, being at the same time investors and users, were able to tailor the city to their own needs. Primarily, the Horseshoe was a public space intended for the promotion of bourgeois social values and culture. Their desire for untouched nature was met in the northern hilly parts of the city, which were constructed according to the "open" city building model of country houses surrounded by greenery.[14] However, the Zagreb Regulatory Plan of 1887 did not neglect the workers' housing, planned for the area south of the railway line, because "in the cities, which truly represent and direct a nation, all the cultural branches will continue developing to the benefit of the whole nation."[15] Defined in the plan for the first time, the "closed" and "open" city building models became the standard that would be used until the 1930s.

Preoccupied with construction of the national pavilions at the Millennial Exhibition in Budapest in the first half of the 1890s, the Zagreb-based architects initiated a sequence of events that embodied their desire for emancipation and led to the establishment of a technical school. The Society published *Hrvatski građevni oblici* (*Croatian Building Forms*), the drawings of traditional Croatian rural architecture by architects Janko Holjac and Martin Pilar, and changed the name of the Society's journal to *Viesti Družtva inžinira i arhitekta u Hrvatskoj i Slavoniji* (*The Gazette of the Society of Engineers and Architects in Croatia and Slavonia*).[16] The first modernist generation of Croatian architects established itself at the beginning of the twentieth century against the background of the Croatian National Movement, which arose in opposition to the financial subordination of Croatia to Hungary. They were eager to emancipate the architectural profession and to establish a rule that competitions be held for the design of public facilities of national importance, seeing this as the only opportunity to implement their ideas around design and construction. Granted with commissions to construct buildings such as the National Library on the

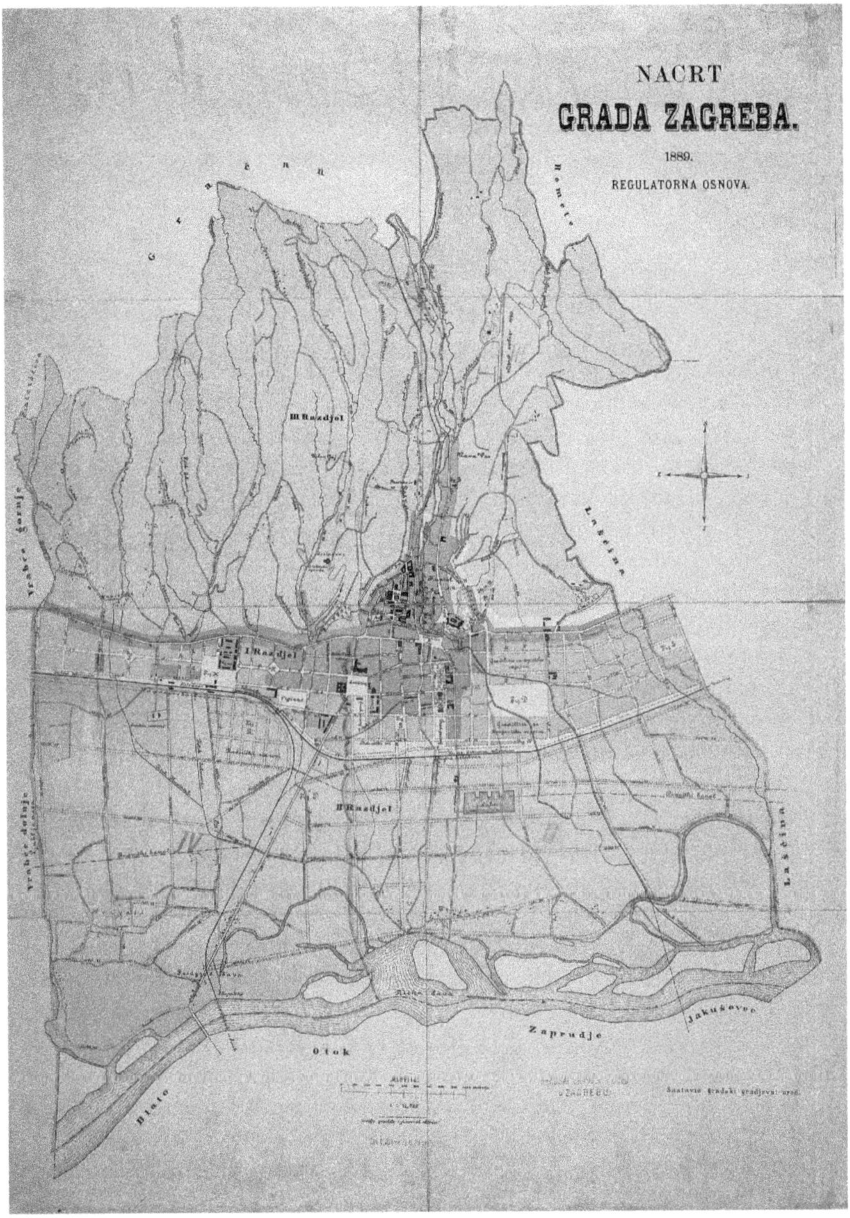

Figure 4.2 The so-called Green Horseshoe, Zagreb Plan, 1889.

Source: Nacionalna i sveučilišna knjižnica, Zbirka zemljovida i atlasa, Map Collection, 000237066 X-H-J-26); used with kind permission of the National and University Library in Zagreb

basis of the awarded competition design, they succeeded in interrupting plans to simply import a design from the capital.[17]

A Breakthrough – Stepping Out From the East Central European Architectural Circle

The first stage of intense industrialization occurred at the beginning of the twentieth century, in the golden years of the liberal economy. Zagreb was already beleaguered by problems of substandard workers' housing and inappropriately situated industrial facilities (Radnički dol and Tkalčićeva Street).[18] The implementation of regulatory plans became a question of vital importance, since "the mistakes that may occur when one builds without a plan sometimes cannot be repaired at all, or if they still can, it is beyond expensive."[19] Informed of the anomalies that the German cities (Berlin, Dresden, Leipzig) were suffering from – irregular development, unplanned construction of new urban areas and a high percentage of lot coverage at the cost of basic hygienic requirements and public interest – experts insisted on drawing up regulatory plans, considering it an important issue of the state's and cities' governments.[20] The first attempt to define a city planning discourse including theoretical and practical aspects was prompted by an order passed by the Provincial Government of Croatia and Slavonia in June 1902. All cities and larger towns, i.e. their building departments, were required to provide them. The plans were intended to define, "roughly, avoiding any detail," the major streets, the functional zones (residential, industrial, commercial, etc.), along with a city model ("closed" or "open"), the public spaces and buildings, etc.[21] Due to the lack of experts, Juraj Augustin (the head of the Building Department of the provincial government) turned to German urban planning theory and practice, along with those of the French, who were the European leaders in the field at the time, in order to provide general guidance. In 1903, when German urban planning theory and practice were demonstrated at the *Erste Städte-Ausstellung* in Dresden, Augustin published Cornelius Gurlitt's article "Pitanja o izgradnji gradova" ("The Questions of City Building"), taken from the Viennese *Neue Freie Presse* newspaper, in the *Viesti društva inžinira i arhitekta*.[22] On this occasion, the long-term collaboration between Zagreb and Dresden experts was initiated and continued up until the early 1930s.

Gurlitt's text theoretically formulated already established city building models. It is a polemic on finding the middle way in urban planning practice, between Josef Stübben's pragmatic functionalism and Camillo Sitte's romantic, "organic" planning, i.e. the orthogonal system of blocks and picturesque spaces of irregular streets and squares.[23] Gurlitt proposed a rational and coherent application of both models of city building, constantly keeping the image of the city in mind.[24] The rational construction in the city center, and residential areas with single-family houses built in the garden city manner, were upgraded with a fast traffic network. This was accepted as the template for the construction of Croatian cities, as formulated in a special report by the Building Department of the Provincial Government of Croatia and Slavonia. The report was drawn up and published by government engineers following a two-month study trip to Germany in December 1904 and January 1905. They dedicated it to the same target group – "the planners." In two chapters – "The overview of the city building experiences gathered during a study trip" and "Propositions" – they first listed the main characteristics of city building in Germany (from urban planning models, street networks and the creation of the city image, through public areas and city infrastructure, to the development and implementation of the regulatory plan, as well as the construction of department stores and workers' settlements), and then guidelines for the circumstances in Croatia in particular. They called for a rational application of the "new" model. By giving credit to its proponents – Camillo Sitte and Theodor Fischer, but also Gurlitt, they showed a thorough understanding of urban planning theory.[25] At that time, urban planning was considered entirely contemporary.

Aforementioned features were reiterated in Milan Lenuci's 1907 Zagreb regulatory plan for the eastern part of the city and the non-urbanized area between the railway line and the Sava River. In order to implement the plan of Zagreb, which was envisioned for the area between Medvednica mountain and Sava, two major interventions had to be made – the relocation of the railway line or raising it on top of columns and the regulation of the river.[26] Lenuci planned a new residential and business district along with an industrial zone. The district with larger built-up city blocks, a slightly curved new city avenue (the so-called Prachtstrasse), and radial boulevards and roundabouts is reminiscent of Haussmann's planning methods. At the same time, the residential areas were planned in the garden city manner, with family houses and picturesque streets full of greenery but lacking basic amenities and welfare facilities.[27] The garden city concept was presented to the Croatian community of experts in the following year, immediately preceding the completion of Letchworth.[28]

Lenuci's regulatory plan was not implemented because the state railways in Budapest did not agree with the proposed displacement of the railway line. In order to provoke action on the part of official institutions, the Association of Croatian Architects organized and published a public lecture by Cornelius Gurlitt, "Osnivanje gradova" ("The Foundation of Cities"), in September 1908, on the occasion of his visit to Zagreb.[29] The direct cause was the competition for the regulatory plan of Kaptol, one in a series of national competitions for detailed plans of city squares and promenades launched in the 1900s and characteristic of the *Gründerzeit*. Gurlitt's lecture went along the lines of his text dating back to 1903. The same year, a delegation of six architects from Zagreb attended the 8th International Congress of Architects held in Vienna. The image of the city, in the context of building codes (of Berlin, London, Paris, Rome and Vienna), was one of the discussed issues.[30]

The latest achievements of the Zagreb authorities, including Lenuci's regulatory plan along with water and sewer system plans, were presented at the Leipzig Internationale Baufach-Ausstellung (IBA) in 1913 to an international audience.[31] The main problem before World War I, as described by Juraj Augustin, was not actually the quality of plans but rather the general lack of experts, an insufficient number of specialists and inadequate organization within the Građevni odjel (City Building Department), which was in charge of drawing up the plans. Its task was "the biggest and most difficult" from both a professional and social-economic standpoint.[32] Evidently, another problem was the lack of academic expertise, i.e. an interdisciplinary approach to urban planning. The plan was to be designed by one man, although the task required a collaboration of engineers, architects and land surveyors.[33] There were no educated city planners, which was not a problem of Zagreb exclusively, but of the entire monarchy.[34] The first Croatian architect to take the "Science of Urban Planning" course was Stjepan Hribar, a student of Cornelius Gurlitt's at the Technical School in Dresden. Gurlitt's seminar on the foundation of cities, both theoretical and practical, was announced to Zagreb experts in 1911.[35] It was also Stjepan Hribar who was assigned with the task of providing Zagreb with a contemporary regulatory plan and a specialized department for the city – that is, to establish urban planning as a scientific discipline – in the late 1920s.

Years of Transition – From a Provincial Center to the "Croatian Capital"

In the 1920s, Zagreb, as the economic center of the Kingdom of Serbs, Croats and Slovenes, finally got an opportunity to open a technical school and to become a prominent center of a vibrant and growing architectural scene. For the first time, Croatian architects were granted an opportunity to export their knowledge to other parts of the new kingdom through competitions and the Zagreb-based section of the newly established Udruženje jugoslavenskih inženjera i arhitekta – UJIA (Association of Yugoslav Civil Engineers and Architects).[36] However, networking with Central and East Central Europe continued and even increased as new "hubs" of knowledge exchange appeared. Beside Prague, the most prominent were Berlin and Paris. Due to good political relations between Yugoslavia and France, the collaboration with the Paris architecture scene, characterized by new theoretical concepts that did not come into practice, intensified. In 1923, the *Hrvat* (*Croat*) daily newspaper wrote about Le Corbusier's *Voisin* plan – one of the visionary projects devised in the early twentieth century that aimed to provide cities with plenty of sun, fresh air and greenery – which Zagreb architects had the opportunity to see in the Pavillion de l'Esprit Nouveau at the International Exhibition of

Modern Decorative and Industrial Arts in Paris in 1925. However, it was some time before Le Corbusier's theory reached Zagreb, through German translations of the books *Vers une architecture* (*Kommende Baukunst*, 1926) and *Urbanisme* (*Städtebau*, 1929). The press wrote about other visionary projects as well, such as Henri Sauvage's ziggurats.[37]

Unfortunately, faced with constant population growth (almost doubling from the early 1920s to 1931) and a housing crisis resulting from the transformation of Zagreb into a metropolis, Zagreb authorities did not follow the good practices of Belgrade and Split. Both cities launched international competitions, a method popular in the 1900s, for new regulatory plans as early as 1921–1922 and 1924 in order to get the best possible city building model.[38] Zagreb-based architects insisted on a competition to come up with a new regulatory plan of Zagreb, and the introduction of quality social housing was elaborated upon in detail by Edo Schön for several reasons.[39] First, there were a number of huge, unprecedented, extremely complex and challenging social and urban planning problems; second, the City Building Department in charge of city planning and construction was incapable of solving them; third, there was an insufficient number of urban planners; and, finally, a slowing exchange of knowledge resulting from the foundation of the Technical School in Zagreb and difficult financial circumstances together with a reduction in the number of journals and decreased mobility.[40] The exchange of knowledge with Austria and Germany, the results of the housing policies of Red Vienna and the Weimar Republic, was further limited as dealing with issues of workers' housing was largely treated in Yugoslavia as communist propaganda. Therefore, public lectures of experts from Vienna, including Max Ermers, the city authorities' "consultant for small apartments and workers' housing settlements,"[41] in 1922, and Peter Behrens, a professor at the Academy of Fine Arts, in 1923, were crucial. The first lecture was organized by the Hrvatski radnički savez (Croatian Workers' Union) and supported by the Zagreb Architects' Section, which was in charge of the two lectures delivered by Behrens at the Technical Faculty.[42]

As well as arguing for established city building models, including garden cities on the outskirts of larger metropolises, the lecturers introduced several new issues – those of high-rise buildings, standardization and financing for social housing. While Behrens underlined typification and standardization in the construction of housing as the major precognition of cost-effectiveness,[43] Ermers called for the financing of worker's settlements through cooperatives supported by the state government.[44] The model was borrowed from agrarian reform. Like the peasants, who were provided with arable land, the workers, craftsmen and clerks should also be granted plots of land. Another model of social housing recommended by Ermers was that apartment buildings be constructed through cooperatives, which was not possible in Croatia due to the lack of a condominium system. Furthermore, Behrens lectured on the construction of city centers, primarily devoted to business and with high-rise buildings, distanced from residential areas. Examples of such centers in Germany and the United States often featured in Zagreb's daily newspapers and popular journals. The silhouette of high-rise buildings was becoming an important element in city planning, but the idea was discarded by local architects because of a prevailing attitude that such buildings were unacceptable in Zagreb. During Behrens' stay, the Zagreb Section organized a discussion on the regulatory plan of the city, including traffic and health issues, emphasizing once more the importance of the balance between technical and artistic aspects of urban planning. In order to impress the distinguished guest, Vjekoslav Heinzel, who served as mayor of Zagreb at the time, announced an international competition to welcome experts in the field, although he evidently had no intention of launching it.[45]

Disregarding both contemporary practices and socially vulnerable categories of citizens, he approved the City Building Department's plan, which was limited only to the northeastern part of the city and designed in the same year – 1923 (Figure 4.3).[46] Based on Lenuci's work prior

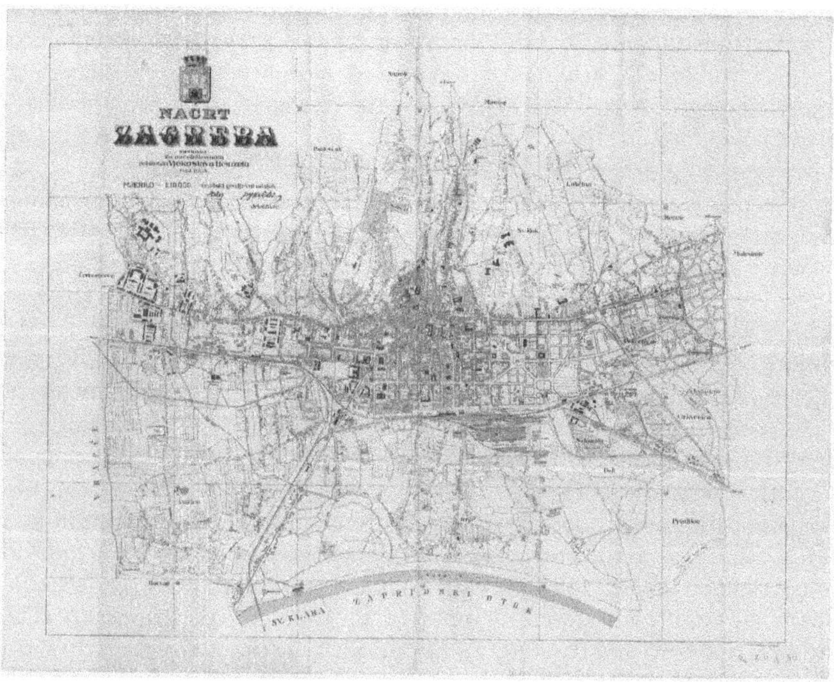

Figure 4.3 Zagreb Plan, 1923.

Source: Zagreb Plan, City Building Department, 1923 (Nacionalna i sveučilišna knjižnica, 000237071 X-H-J-30); used with kind permission of the National and University Library in Zagreb

to World War I, the plan, again drawn by a single man, still promoted nineteenth-century urban planning practices and models, having in mind Berlin and Paris, including Hausmann-like boulevards and the roundabout as the major novelty. The plan, which was actually a partial regulatory plan intended for a larger area, was marked by formalism, fewer public spaces and less greenery, as well as the segregation of the population. There is an obvious difference between elite residential quarters and rental apartment buildings for the lower middle class, who stood to be charged with extremely high rents.[47] The latter were located in the immediate vicinity of the railway line and industrial plants. Investors were not interested in good quality housing or representation, but in the placement of private capital with the aim of gaining the highest possible profit. This was possible due to the local governments who gave them an opportunity to exploit the land to its maximum capacity, with a disregard for future users.

Planned social workers' housing was not part of the city government's policy and, as a direct result of land speculation, overpriced rents and the absence of a condominium system, slums began to establish themselves.[48] Workers constructed houses without permits in the area between the railway line and the Sava River, where there was no water supply and no sewage system. In the early 1930s, a quarter of Zagreb's population (between 40,000 and 50,000 people) inhabited this area. As Zagreb was a kind of linear city squeezed in between the railroad to the south and Medvednica mountain to the north, the slums were constructed in the immediate vicinity of the city center. They became a major obstacle in the city's development and, already in the mid-1920s, the major social and urban planning issue typical of the interwar period (Figure 4.4).

The status quo was maintained until the mid-1920s, when it became even more evident that the city government had no control over the city's development. The expert community continued to join with the public to campaign for a new regulatory plan – the basic prerequisite for solving the problem of workers' housing, i.e. the reconstruction of the periphery. The movement gathered strength and, by 1927, a number of initiatives were in place, resulting in a shift in thinking about the role of urban planning and architecture.[49] The *Večer* (*Evening*) daily newspaper conducted a poll about living conditions which pointed to a great disproportion between the price of rent and the quality of apartments. Residents of the periphery founded the Komunalna organizacija za južni dio Zagreba (Municipal Organization for the South Part of Zagreb). Having exerted pressure on the city government, they secured temporary building permits for unplanned construction and continued their struggle for the construction of a sewage system, a water supply system and the introduction of public transportation.[50]

Criticized for the lack of transparency and design competitions, which were not even held for important municipal structures such as a city

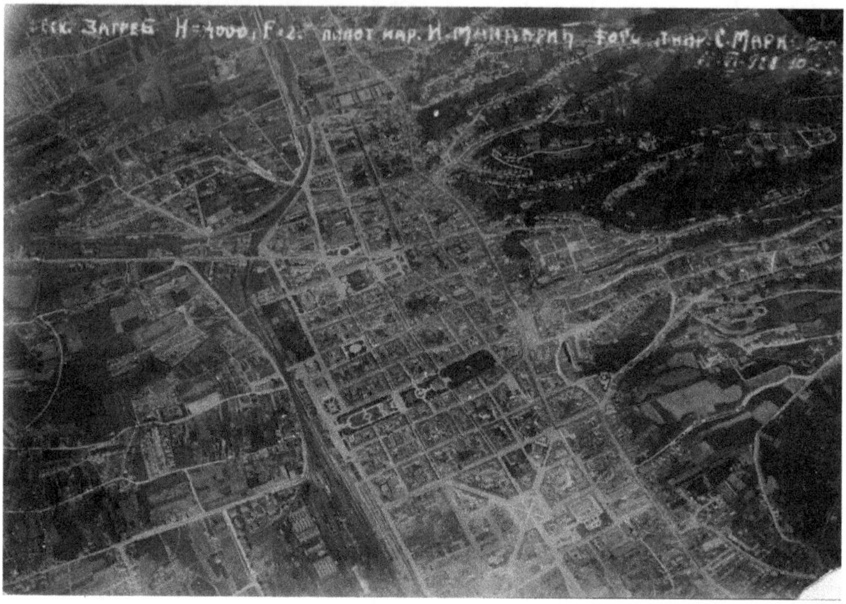

Figure 4.4 Zagreb aerial view, 1928.

Source: Muzej grada Zagreba, Photo Collections, MGZ fot-6422; used with kind permission of Zagreb City Museum

market and slaughterhouse, the city government accepted its share of the responsibility.[51] In February 1928, ten years following the end of World War I, eager to introduce the latest contemporary civilizational achievements, they announced a long desired international competition for the regulatory plan of Zagreb, which was to be launched in August of 1930.[52] At first, a special board was in charge of preparations, and, in August 1928, the Odsjek za regulaciju grada (Department for City Regulation) was founded – the first institution in Croatia exclusively dedicated to urban planning. The approach to urban planning was revolutionized. It was no longer in the hands of a single person. The employees were Stjepan Hribar, the head of department, and Josip Seissel, Antun Ulrich and Vladimir Antolić. Apart from Hribar, only Antolić was educated in urban planning, having attended Karl Heinrich Brunner's seminar at the Technical School in Vienna. Mayor Heinzel's resignation undoubtedly contributed to the significant change of urban policy.[53] Aware of growing discontent and the labor movement, the new city mayor Stjepan Srkulj addressed the public with his inaugural speech, saying that the municipal government "must serve the role of both mother and father to the socially and economically weakest citizens."[54] The slums started to be understood as a social problem, a disgrace for the city of Zagreb, a sign of social ignorance and backwardness. In place of workers' shacks, Srkulj wanted a new residential neighborhood – a functional, new model of city planning that would provide quality living, and economical and hygienic housing for many, as well as green areas, basic public services and an efficient and rational way of construction. All these aspects turned the regulatory plan into the most significant modernization project of interwar Zagreb and required a new approach to urban planning and architectural design, i.e. a change in the discourse, which had already been under way.[55] As state railway engineer Petar Senjanović claimed: "contemporary urban planners are not dealing with graphic design and land plots for future construction anymore; their job is now to solve major economic and social issues."[56] To achieve that, they adopted an academic, analytical, multidisciplinary approach, which included zoning, a "towers in the park" city model with stand-alone "slab" apartment buildings surrounded by greenery and, later on, typification, standardization and ultimately prefabrication. The use of new structures and materials, along with new approaches to design, inevitably resulted in a new kind of architecture – *Neues Bauen*. Falling behind on accepting *Neues Bauen*, the Zagreb Section of the UJIA organized in the spring of 1928 an exhibition of Czechoslovakian modern architecture, where the achievements of the fraternal Slavic nation were put on public display.[57]

In order to attract the most progressive foreign architects to take part in, and meet the conditions for, a successful competition, the quality of the competition brief and the selection of jury members were crucial, along with extremely attractive prizes. In drawing up the competition brief, experts from other fields were consulted, as were the briefs of the international competitions for the Belgrade, Split, Brno and Bratislava regulatory plans.[58] The competition brief for the Zagreb Plan included maps and a comprehensive publication providing insight into the contemporary circumstances, as well as detailed instructions for drawing up a plan of the construction, expansion and regulation of Zagreb, "with the expectation of a population increase to approximately 350,000."[59] The task was to provide a regional and city traffic network, to designate the main urban zones and the positioning of public spaces, and to produce a model of construction. Special attention was once more given to the regulatory plan of Kaptol and to three-dimensional city planning, instead of the usual two-dimensional planning, as well as to the implementation possibilities of the plan. To show what the particular areas of the city would look like, competitors were required to create prospective drawings and photomontages.

The jury chaired by the mayor had 15 members, 11 of whom were architects and engineers from the city government, Zagreb-based local and national institutions in charge of construction and urban planning and foreign associations of architects.[60] The initial plan was to invite three foreign experts into the jury – representatives of the Austrian, German and French associations of architects. This was a direct consequence of the professional connections established prior to World War I and current political circumstances. Inviting Swiss experts was also considered – architect Karl Moser and art historian and critic Peter Meyer from the Zürich ETH, with which Zagreb had long-standing connections.[61] In the end, only two foreigners were selected – Josef Gočar, as a result of the UJIA's politics of support and collaboration with Czechoslovak architects, and, not at all randomly, Paul Wolf, the Dresden city planning consultant.[62] The choice of the dean of the Prague Academy of Arts and a long-time practitioner once again confirmed the direction the plan was to take – a middle way between artistic and rational-functional principles of urban planning. Both foreign jury members came to Zagreb before the jury was due to meet in order to examine the "terrain" and all the proposals, even the eliminated ones. The selection process had two stages. Only local members of the jury participated in the first stage, drawing up a short list of the proposals.[63]

International Competition for the Regulatory Plan of Zagreb

German urban planners dominated the competition, providing 34 out of the 52 proposals – which was partially an effect of the 1929 economic crisis in Germany. The prizes were also won almost exclusively by architects based in Berlin and Dresden. There were nine entries from Yugoslavia, while proposals from Austria, Czechoslovakia, France, Hungary, Romania, Switzerland and even Spain were more of an exception.[64] According to the *Gradski vjesnik* (*City Herald*) published by the city council, proposals were sent by all the most renowned architects and urban planners, basically everybody capable of performing this task in Central Europe.[65] The competitors included professors of technical schools in Vienna, Dresden, Stuttgart, Berlin, and Zurich, as well as employees of Dresden and Hannover city planning departments: Leopold Bauer, Hans Bernoulli, Paul Bonatz, Otto Meffert, Adolf Muesmann, Hans Reichow and Hermann Ehlgötz, among others. There was a significant number of young German city planners, including collaborators of Hermann Jansen, Erich Mendelsohn and Hans Poelzig, as well as second prize winners Erich Kotzer, Ewald Liedecke and Peter Koller, along with Max Säume, Günther Hafemann and Hans Grosser, winners of the fourth prize.[66] Some of these men had been educated at the Stuttgart School, and were representatives of the long-lasting classicist tendency, led by Bonatz. The third prize was awarded to the

Croatian-German project by architect Zdenko Strižić, who was active in Berlin, and Hans Holzbauer.

As all the winning competition entries were by German architects, a shift toward German innovations in urban planning was inevitable. Besides, Germany had a significant body of theoretical work and, more importantly, it was successfully dealing with housing crises and land speculation by stimulating urban planning, implementing zoning and cooperative housing, providing social assistance programs for the lower income groups, and controlling and taxing land speculation.[67] Zagreb experts gained personal insight into the latest German achievements thanks to several exhibitions held in 1931, the year in which the selection process of the Zagreb Plan competition took place – *Internationale Hygiene-Ausstellung* (International Hygiene Exhibition) in Dresden, *Deutsche Bauausstellung* (German Building Exhibition) in Berlin, and the German Contemporary Art and Architecture in Zagreb and Belgrade under the auspices of the state authorities.[68] Max Taut wrote the text *Neues Bauen in Deutschland* (*New Construction in Germany*) for the bilingual catalog. He promoted economic and healthy housing that would meet the needs of contemporary life and would be available to everybody, regardless of social status. Therefore, among the exhibits were a dozen social housing settlements by Ernst May, Walter Gropius, Max Taut and Hans Scharoun in Frankfurt-am-Main, Berlin, Dessau and Karlsruhe, including Praunheim, Römerstadt, Törten, Siemens-Stadt and Britz, as well as several welfare facilities – public baths, primary schools, single-person homes, etc. These urban developments embodied the achievement of the Weimar Republic and sought to show the Yugoslav public, both professionals and politicians, that it was possible to provide working-class people with affordable, humane and healthy living space. Max Taut made it clear that this was, precisely, the architect's major task within contemporary society – to serve the well-being of the community.[69] The focus of architects and urban planners was no longer on the representation of the ruling class, rather on average citizens and their everyday needs.

All of these factors led to the discarding of nineteenth-century urban planning models, and of the traditional garden cities. The city blocks of apartment buildings were not an option due to hygienic reasons and the decreasing quality of living caused by the high percentage of lot coverage and lack of fresh air, sunlight and greenery. Furthermore, because the slums were located in the immediate vicinity of the city center, i.e. Lower Town, a higher level of urbanity was required. "Slab" apartment complexes, made up of several rows of apartment buildings with minimum subsistence dwellings, were an optimal solution. The idea of the "slab" apartment building had already been proposed at the 12th International Housing and City Planning Congress in Rome and the 2nd International Congress of Modern Architecture (CIAM) in Frankfurt-am-Main in 1929. The head of the Zagreb Municipal Building Department Ivan Zemljak participated in the former, and submitted a detailed report to his superiors, while Ernest Weissmann took part in the latter.[70] Working in Le Corbusier's studio from 1927–1930, Weissmann was the first to introduce the idea of constructing a city by using freestanding structures and roads raised on columns, opposing city blocks and leaving the ground to pedestrians. He presented these ideas in his competition entry for the Zakladni blok (Foundation Block) of Ban Jelačić Square, the main square of Zagreb, in early 1930.[71]

Second prize winners Erich Kotzer, Ewald Liedecke and Peter Koller were the most successful in meeting the previously mentioned demands. Highly implementable and functional, their proposal provided the basis for a new regulatory plan of Zagreb aimed at establishing an integrated flexible organism in which they successfully united different human activities – dwelling, work, traffic and leisure – and introduced the inversion of built and unbuilt spaces. Freestanding buildings were superimposed onto the "grounding" layer – a green surface covered with an orthogonal grid of streets surrounding the neighborhood units for 5,000–6,000 people. Each unit was provided with internal residential streets, terraced row houses, public spaces and facilities (playgrounds, a school, grocery stores, etc.). The north-south orientation of the buildings along its longer axis was designed to ensure the flow of fresh air from Medvednica mountain. While the grid of the streets, improved by the introduction of hierarchy (the separation of public and residential streets), was retained with respect to the nineteenth century urban model of the Lower Town, the city blocks of apartment buildings were dissolved. Transformed into a large "cassette," the traditional city block changed its usual form. It is important to note that, although the type of housing was changed, the spirit of grandeur was retained – the spirit of a modern metropolis, which also celebrated speed. The new representative public space was planned in the extension of the eastern part of the Green Horseshoe.

The winning project was somewhat modified.[72] Modifications were allowed due to a stipulation according to which competition organizers, who were most often also the investors, could do away with awarded entries as they saw fit, which included the possibility of compiling ideas from several projects. The employees of the Department for City Regulation, who had been introduced to contemporary urban planning and architectural production in Germany on the occasion of the study trip in the summer 1932,[73] compiled ideas taken from other award-winning entries and Nikolay Milytin's theoretical model of the linear city – Sotsgorod, advocated by Vladimir Antolić. He was acquainted with contemporary Soviet urban planning models, once again as a result of contact with German architects. The mediator between Arthur Korn, a Berlin-based leftist architect who visited the USSR in 1930, and Zagreb was Ernest Weissmann.[74] El Lissitzky's book *Russland. Die Rekonstruktion der Architektur in der Sowjetunion*, published in 1930 and available in Zagreb bookstores, had a crucial role as well. Similar to Milytin's Sotsgorod, the Zagreb Plan had clearly separated functional zones, aligned in a sequence from north to south. To the north, an exclusive residential area remained, which offered the best housing conditions.[75] The new residential area with apartment buildings and a green belt along the Sava River, which compensated for the higher urban density and the downsides of living in apartment buildings, was added in the area formerly occupied by the slums. The green belt was complete with sports and leisure facilities used for recreation and served as an intermediate area between the city and the countryside. Between two residential zones was the Lower Town, converted into a commercial-business zone with public facilities, "the City," as suggested by Behrens in his 1923 lecture, as well as Weissmann in his proposal for the Foundation Block. Placed in the center, the public facilities became available to all the social strata from both sides of the railway line. Relying on decentralization, the linear city model was significantly more democratic in a multitude of ways. It took into consideration the modernization of housing and public facilities in rural areas as well.[76]

With clearly defined zones (the city, residential areas, industrial zones), freestanding apartment buildings surrounded by greenery, a network of public and residential streets, as well as education, social and supply facilities, the regulatory plan of Zagreb, finished in the autumn of 1932, embodied most of the features of the "functional city" defined in the so-called Athens Charter at the Fourth CIAM Congress in Athens in 1933, where it was presented (Figure 4.5). The presentation was prepared by Vladimir Antolić and Josip Seissel. Antolić took part in the congress as a member of the CIAM national group for Yugoslavia, founded in 1932. The city of Zagreb funded his participation at the CIAM meetings and congresses until World War II.[77] With the plan finished and adopted, the circumstances radically changed – the financial crisis peaked, significantly reducing the personal collaboration between Zagreb architects and their foreign colleagues. Due to Hitler's rise to power, contacts with the German architecture scene broke off, while those with the Paris architectural circle centered around the journal *L'Architecture d'aujourd'hui* intensified, thanks to architect Ljubomir Ilić, who was based in Paris at the time.[78]

Post Scriptum

With regard to the import of knowledge in the field of urban planning from the mid-nineteenth century until the 1930s, the 1932 regulatory plan of Zagreb was the most comprehensive and most important achievement

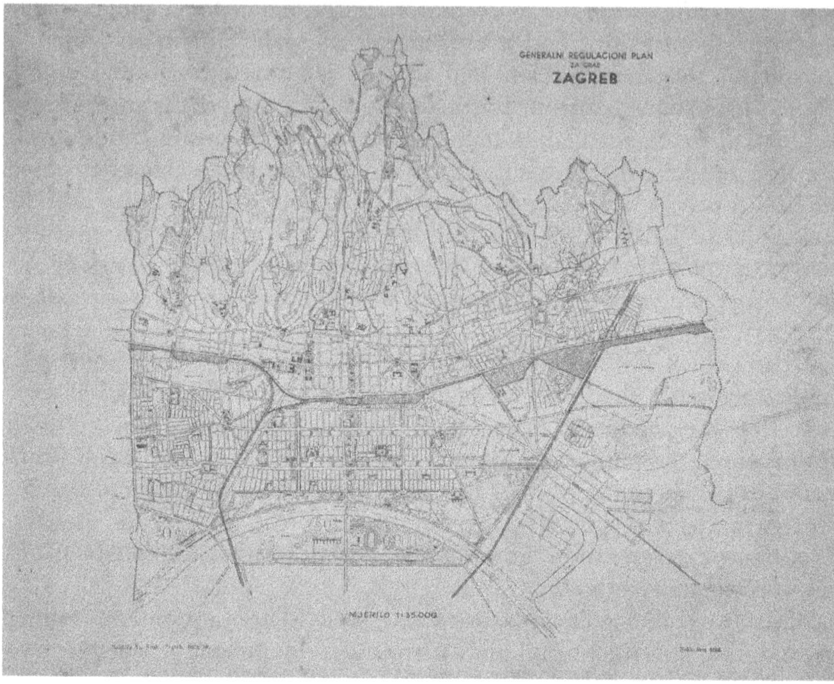

Figure 4.5 Zagreb Regulatory Plan, 1932.

Source: Hrvatska akademija znanosti i umjetnosti, Hrvatski muzej arhitekture – Map Collection; used with kind permission of the Croatian Academy of Sciences and Arts, Croatian Museum of Architecture

of this period in Croatia. Zagreb's urban development was based on imported principles (local architects relied on international practices and examples spanning, over time, the proto-urban, *Gründerzeit* and protomodern eras). In general, models were improved from one plan to another (1865, 1887, 1907 and 1923). The best-known and most luxurious international example to be adopted, was the Green Horseshoe – a series of public squares and parks – a local interpretation of Vienna's Ringstrasse. The international competition for the regulatory plan radically changed the usual modus operandi. The plan was not designed exclusively by Zagreb-based architects anymore, but rather by an international professional community. Introducing this approach, previously reserved almost exclusively for the wealthy capitals, Zagreb imported the most recent urban planning models and methodology, based on an analytical and scientific approach. This particular planning method was decisive for the future work of the Department for City Regulation, the first specialized urban planning institution responsible for the education of the first generation of modern urban planners. Furthermore, the plan embodied the radical change of social and planning discourse. The city was no longer understood as a place of bourgeois self-promotion but rather as a place of everyday life organized through neighborhoods and overseen by urban planners. Unfortunately, the so-called Bijeli Zagreb (White Zagreb), a district with plenty of sun, fresh air and greenery, which was planned to replace the neglected urban periphery, turned out to be a utopian project. Giving priority to public interest, instead of the extreme exploitation of land plots and rental buildings, it idealistically envisaged a better life for common people who did not own the land.[79] The city government knew exactly what it was looking for, but was not able to achieve it because it lacked the financial and legal means to do so. Despite the fact that it could not be carried out at this particular moment in history, the regulatory plan was important, both on the local and national levels. Besides contemporary urban planning models and science, it encouraged the foundation of urban planning institutions and educated the first generation of urban planners capable of independently tackling new challenges during the period after the World War II: post-war reconstruction and the construction of a new, socialist society at a time when collaboration and the exchange of knowledge among experts on the international level was not possible.

The regulatory plan itself, utterly schematic but flexible and economical, was the starting point of urban planning in Zagreb in the 1940s and 1950s. The 1948 directive regulatory plan by Vladimir Antolić, who became the head of the Zavod za urbanizam Narodnog odbora grada Zagreba (Urban Planning Bureau of the People's Committee of the City of Zagreb) in 1951, even borrowed some ideas from the 1930s competition entries of Paul Bonatz and Hans Reichhow, as well as from Hans Friedrich Hirsch – the new representative administrative center along Moskovska Street (later Beogradska Street and today Vukovarska Street) and the extension of the western part of the Green Horseshoe. Unfortunately, the reconstruction of workers' slums, which was envisioned in the period between two world wars, was too complex and too expensive even under socialism, when urban planners had the legal means to accomplish it. The plan was put on hold in the mid-1950s, when the Zagreb city government decided to construct Novi Zagreb (New Zagreb) on the southern bank of the Sava River.[80]

Notes

1. Renate Banik-Schweitzer, "Urban Visions, Plans and Projects, 1890–1937," in *Shaping the Great City: Modern Architecture in Central Europe, 1890–1937*, ed. Eve Blau and Monika Platzer (Munich, London and New York: Prestel, 1999), 58–72.
2. For example, Zagreb had Secession architecture as early as 1897 – the Rado Building by Ignjat Fischer at the Strossmayerov Square.

3. Austrian engineers paid a visit to Zagreb in 1882 and Hungarian engineers in 1895, on their way to Rijeka, Pula and Trieste. See in: Josip Dryak, "Društveni izlet u Beč i Prag," *Viesti družtva inžinira i arhitekta* 19, no. 8 (1898): 105–108; 20, no. 1 (1899): 6–7; 20, no. 2 (1899): 22–32; Josip Dryak, "Djelovanje kluba u drugoj polovici g. 1882.," *Viesti Kluba inžinira i arhitekta* 3, no. 2 (1882): 1; Josip Dryak, "Boravak ugarskih inžinira i arhitekta u Zagrebu dne 30. kolovoza 1895.," *Viesti družtva inžinira i arhitekta* 16, no. 6 (1895): 72–75.
4. *Congrès International des Architectes. Cinquième Session. Organisation, Compte rendu et notices* (Paris: Chaix, 1906).
5. "Družtvene viesti," *Viesti družtva inžinira i arhitekta* 6, no. 1–2 (1885): 14–16.
6. The list of journals for which abstracts were acquired and which were ordered for the Society's library changed over the years (Hrvatski državni arhiv [Croatian State Archives], HR-HDA-632: the list of books donated by the Zagreb Section of the UJIA to the Technical School in Zagreb).
7. The regulation of the northern part of the city was revised in 1911. See Darko Kahle, "Građevinski propisi grada Zagreba u razdoblju od 1850. do 1918.," *Prostor* 12, no. 28 (2005): 202–214; Snješka Knežević, *Zagrebačka Zelena potkova* (Zagreb: Školska knjiga, 1996).
8. In numerous Central European cities, such as Vienna and Pest, the outer line of fortification (defensive city walls) became a hindrance to the integration of the urban core into the suburbs and outlying villages. After becoming militarily obsolete, it was often restructured to be replaced with promenades and transportation facilities.
9. Milan Lenuci, "Kako napreduje u Zagrebu uvađanje vodovoda u kuće," *Viesti Kluba inžinira i arhitekta* 2, no. 1 (1881): 13–14.
10. Croatian architects participated in the 6th International Congress on Hygiene and Demography (1887) in Vienna and the 7th edition of the same congress in Budapest (1891). The magazine *Gesundheits-Ingenieur* was also in circulation. See Julio Stanisavljević, ed., *Spomen-knjiga na proslavu dvadesetipetgodišnjice opstanka Društva inžinira i arhitekta u Hrvatskoj i Slavoniji* (Zagreb: Društvo inžinira i arhitekta u Hrvatskoj i Slavoniji, 1903).
11. Janko J. Grahor, "Higienička izložba u Berlinu," *Viesti družtva inžinira i arhitekta* 5, no. 1 (1884): 4–6.
12. The journal did not publish the projects of the foreign architects.
13. Von Schmidt designed the palace of the Jugoslavenska akademija znanosti i umjetnosti (today Croatian Academy of Sciences and Arts) and Von Hofer Vranyczany Palace (today Modern Gallery). To learn more about Croatian students of Friedrich von Schmidt see Dragan Damjanović, *Bečka Akademija likovnih umjetnosti i hrvatska arhitektura historicizma. Hrvatski učenici Friedricha von Schmidta* (Zagreb: Hrvatska akademija znanosti i umjetnosti, 2011).
14. There was also the so-called "half-open" model, which combined the open and the closed models.
15. Valentin Lapaine, "Gradnja i razvitak gradova," *Viesti Družtva inžinira i arhitekta u Hrvatskoj i Slavoniji* 21, no. 5 (1900): 56; no. 6: 65–66.
16. The Society presented *Croatian Building Forms* at the Paris Exhibition 1900. Such publications were also common practice in German-speaking countries. See Ch., "Ustrojenje visoke tehničke škole u Zagrebu," *Viesti družtva inžinira i arhitekta* 19, no. 3 (1898): 46–48; Vesna Dubovečak, "Društvo inžinira i arhitekata i izdavanje atlasa Hrvatski građevni oblici," *Časopis za suvremenu povijest* 49, no. 1 (2017): 123–154.

17. The first competitions were launched in the late 1870s. They were almost exclusively for primary and secondary school buildings and churches, as education and religious affairs were under the authority of the Croatian and Slavonian governments.
18. The problem of workers' dwellings and the need to build working-class housing was emphasized by Josip Chvala at the end of the 1890s. See Josip Chvala, "Oskudica stanova u velikih gradovih i gradnja omanjih i jeftinih stanova," *Viesti družtva inžinira i arhitekta* 18, no. 7 (1897): 77–80.
19. Odjel za unutarnje poslove Visoke kr. zemaljske vlade, "Naredba visoke kr. zemaljske vlade odjela za unutarnje poslove od 17. lipnja 1902. br. 45967," *Viesti Družtva inžinira i arhitekta* 23, no. 5 (1902): 65–66, p. 65.
20. Chvala, "Oskudica stanova"; Valentin Lapaine, "O zdravstveno-tehničkim odnošajima grada Zagreba," *Viesti Hrvatskoga društva inžinira i arhitekta* 26, no. 4 (1905): 45–47.
21. "Naredba visoke kr. zemaljske vlade," 66.
22. Kornel Gurlitt, "Pitanja o izgradnji gradova," *Viesti Družtva inžinira i arhitekta* 24, no. 7 (1903): 95–100; Robert Freestone and Marco Amati, eds., *Exhibitions and the Development of Modern Planning Culture* (London: Routledge, 2014); Andrew Lees and Lynn Hollen Lees, *Cities and the Making of Modern Europe, 1750–1914* (Cambridge: Cambridge University Press, 2007).
23. At the beginning of the 1930s, Croatian architects still referred to Sitte and Stübben. Sitte's magazine *Der Städtebau* was available in Zagreb from the beginning of its publishing. See "Skica generalnog regulatornog plana za grad Zagreb," *Gradski vjesnik* 3, no. 18–20 (1932): 233–240.
24. The concept was represented through five chapters: "Straight or winding streets," "Broad or narrow streets," "Uphill, downhill," "Quiet and lively squares" and "Crossroads" (Gurlitt, "Pitanja o izgradnji").
25. Juraj Augustin, Josip Chvala and Gustav Hermann visited Berlin, Charlottenburg, Dresden, Fürth, Leipzig, Munich, Nuremberg, Stuttgart, Ulm, Prague and Vienna. The original report was supplemented with plans, brochures, etc. See Josip Chvala and Gustav Hermann, *Izvješće izaslanika građevnoga odsjeka kr. zemaljske vlade o poučnom putovanju po Njemačkoj u predmetu izgradnje gradova* (Zagreb: Građevni odsjek kr. zemaljske vlade, 1905).
26. The regulatory plan was preceded by a partial plan for the eastern part of the city from 1905, which was dismissed by the profession as it had not taken into consideration the city as a whole and it failed to define the building models. See Milan Lenuci, "Osnova za regulaciju iztočnoga diela kr. slob. i glavnoga grada Zagreba," *Viesti Hrvatskoga društva inžinira i arhitekta* 26, no. 3 (1905): 34–37 and att.
27. Snješka Knežević, "Regulatorna osnova Milana Lenucija za dio Zagreba od željezničke pruge do rijeke Save iz 1907.," *Radovi Instituta za povijest umjetnosti* 16, no. 16 (1992): 169–197.
28. Valentin Lapaine, "Vrtni gradovi," *Vijesti hrvatskoga društva inžinira i arhitekta u Zagrebu* 29, no. 3 (1908): 61.
29. The lecture was published as a separate publication. See Cornelius Gurlitt, *Osnivanje gradova* (Zagreb: Klub hrvatskih arhitekata, 1909).
30. The participants were Viktor Axmann, Julio Deutsch, Janko Grahor, Leo Hönigsberg, Martin Pilar and Josip Vancaš. See "VIII. Međunarodni kongres arhitekata," *Viesti Hrvatskoga društva inžinira i arhitekta* 29, no. 2 (1908): 36; "Zapisnik odborske sjednice od 4. svibnja 1908.," *Vijesti hrvatskoga društva inžinira i arhitekta u Zagrebu* 29, no. 4 (1908): 93–94.

31. Državni arhiv u Zagrebu (State Archives in Zagreb, further on HR-DAZG)-10 GPZ, GO, III-1, sign. 71: The list of plans to be exhibited at the Leipzig exhibition in 1913.
32. As early as 1905, Juraj Augustin suggested the founding of a contemporary office for the regulation of Zagreb. See Chvala and Hermann, *Izvješće izaslanika građevnoga odsjeka*, 46.
33. Vjekoslav Heinzel, "Regulatorne osnove za gradove," *Viesti Hrvatskoga družtva inžinira i arhitekta* 27, no. 3 (1906): 35.
34. Andrea I. Frank and Christopher Silver, eds., *Urban Planning Education. Beginnings, Global Movement and Future Prospects* (Cham: Springer International Publishing, 2018).
35. Hribar collaborated on the International Hygiene Exhibition in Dresden in 1911. See Anonymous, "Seminar u kralj. saskoj visokoj tehničkoj školi u Dresdenu za gradnju gradova," *Vijesti hrvatskoga društva inžinira i arhitekta u Zagrebu* 32, no. 6 (1911): 93–94; Hrvatska akademija znanosti i umjetnosti, Hrvatski muzej arhitekture (Croatian Academy of Science and Arts, Croatian Museum of Architecture, further on HAZU-HMA), Stjepan Hribar Archives (further Hribar): Stjepan Hribar to the City Council of Zagreb, 1933.
36. The collaboration with Serbian society was established already in the late nineteenth century. It intensified before World War I. See Upravni odbor Družtva inžinira i arhitekta u Zagrebu, "Zapisnik sjednice upravnog odbora družtva inžinira i arhitekta u Zagrebu obdržavane dne 13. svibnja t.g.," *Viesti družtva inžinira i arhitekta* 16, no. 3 (1895): 41; Odbor Hrvatskoga društva inžinira i arhitekta, "H.D.I.A. Zapisnik odborske sjednice od 28. svibnja 1912.," *Vijesti hrvatskoga društva inžinira i arhitekta u Zagrebu i Društva inženirjev v Ljubljani* 33, no. 7 (1912): 144–145.
37. "Budući velegrad," *Hrvat*, November 24, 1923; "Kako će izgledati veliki gradovi u budućnosti. Moderni arhitekti o razvoju gradova. 'Kolektivni neboderi', 'Zračne ceste', stambena kriza i prometne poteškoće. Pariški arhitekti Perret i Sauvage o Parizu," *Novosti*, November 18, 1928.
38. The preparation work for the Belgrade competition was presented in *Tehnički list* journal. Zagreb-based architects were familiar with the competitions for Vienna, Berlin, Düsseldorf, Lille and Paris. See Darovan Tušek, *Arhitektonski natječaji u Splitu 1918–1941* (Split: Društvo arhitekata Splita, 1994); Zlata Vuksanović-Macura, *San o gradu: Međunarodni konkurs za urbanističko uređenje Beograda 1921–1922* (Beograd: Orion Art, 2015).
39. Edo Šen, a professor at the Technical School, delivered a lecture and published an extensive article on the workers' housing. The workers' housing was one of the assignments of Šen's students. See Edo Schön, "O gradnji radničkih stanova," *Tehnički list* 1, no. 4 (1919): 39–42.
40. Participation at the international conferences and the visits to the world expositions were limited due to the "exchange rate circumstances." See Sekcija Zagreb Udruženja jugoslavenskih inženjera i arhitekta, "Zapisnik V. Glavne redovne skupštine Sekcije Zagreb UJIA, održane dne 17. februara 1924.," *Tehnički list* 6, no. 7 (1924): 92–96.
41. "Stručno predavanje o radničkim stanovima," *Obzor*, December 5, 1922; "Predavanje o gradnji radničkih stanova," *Obzor*, December 13, 1922.
42. The news about Behrens' professorship was announced in the daily newspaper *Obzor*. Juraj Neidhardt from Zagreb studied under Behrens from 1922. See "Peter Behrens ide u Beč," *Obzor*, January 21, 1922; "Budući projekat o izgradnji grada Zagreba. Predavanje o izgradnji modernih gradova," *Večer*, April 26, 1923.

43. Behrens visited the United States in 1912. See Nathan Harpaz, *Zionist Architecture and Town Planning. The Building of Tel Aviv (1919–1929)* (West Lafayette: Purdue University Press, 2013).
44. Social, hygienic and financial aspects of garden cities, accompanied by European, American and Australian examples, were presented in the lecture of Belgrade-based architect Jan Dubovy, published in sequels in *Tehnički list* journal. The last sequel considers the possibility of applying a model requiring the clearance of Belgrade's slums. The garden city model was still advocated even at the end of the 1920s. See Jan Dubovi, "Vrtarski gradovi. Predavanje, održano u UJIA, Sekcija Beograd," *Tehnički list* 7, no. 1 (1925): 7–11; no. 2 (1925): 19–24; no. 3 (1925): 42–46; "Moderna izgradnja gradova," *Novosti*, June 16, 1929.
45. "Diskusija o budućem projektu za izgradnju grada Zagreba," *Hrvat*, April 27, 1923.
46. The plan was merely a framework for the partial regulatory plans of the particular city areas.
47. The crisis reached both factory and intellectual workers.
48. The city government constructed only 1,210 substandard workers' dwellings. See Stjepan Hribar, "Razvitak grada Zagreba 1919/1929," in *Jugoslavija na tehničkom polju 1919. – 1929.*, ed. Rajko Kušević (Zagreb: Udruženje jugoslavenskih inženjera i arhitekta, 1930), 239–245.
49. That year, the Savez gradova Jugoslavije (Union of Cities of Yugoslavia) was founded, a platform for exchanging information on common utility challenges and experiences in solving them. The first Union congress was organized in Zagreb. See "Kongres saveza gradova u Zagrebu," *Novosti*, April 10, 1927.
50. In 1927, the city government provided building plots for about 200 smaller family houses without a utility infrastructure in the workers' district Trešnjevka. See Enes, "25.000 stanovnika Trešnjevke traže kanalizaciju i vodovod," *Novosti*, September 2, 1929; Stjepan Sterle, "O gradnji malih stanova na Selskoj cesti," *Večer*, March 10, 1927; "Anketa o stanbenom pitanju," *Večer*, May 2, 1931; "Građevne dozvole za južni dio grada izdane na 20 godina," *Novosti*, May 11, 1928.
51. The costs of the regulatory plan competition had already been planned for in the city's budget estimates in 1923, 1925 and 1926. See Minutes of the Session of the City Assembly, December 21, 1923, 130; "Što je sa regulatornom osnovom," *Večer*, April 26, 1926; "Natječaj za generalnu regulatornu osnovu za južni dio grada," *Novosti*, October 31, 1926; "Gdje je regulatorna osnova za grad Zagreb? Zagrebačka sekcija inženjera i arhitekta uputila je gradskom poglavarstvu memorandum tražeći da se raspiše natječaj za izradu regulatorne osnove," *Večer*, February 7, 1927.
52. At the same time, an international competition for the design of the Medical Center in Šalata was launched.
53. Heinzel even argued for two separate plans – one for the northern part of the city and the other for the area of slums.
54. "Dr. Srkulj izabran načelnikom," *Novosti*, November 21, 1928.
55. The importance of the city and the state government's contributions was highlighted by Petar Senjanović in his report from the *International Housing and Town Planning Congress* in Vienna in 1926. See Petar Senjanović, *Stambeno pitanje kao svjetski socijalni i državni problem* (Split: Hrvatska štamparija, 1926).
56. Anonymous, "Skica generalnog regulatornog plana za grad Zagreb," *Gradski vjesnik* 3, no. 18–20 (1932): 233–240, p. 233.

57. Another important event occurred that year: Peter Behrens completed the Stern building on the city's main square, the first modern structure in Zagreb in terms of design.
58. For competition briefs, see HR-DAZG-10 GPZ, GO, III-1, sign. 95.
59. The data was provided on existing structures, infrastructure, historical development, geographical placement, climate, traffic, economy, etc., and translated into German and French. The Institute of Cartography was hired to prepare the maps in the scales 1:25,000, 1:10,000, 1:5,500. See HR-DAZG-10 GPZ, GO, III-1, sign. 89*:* Raspis natječaja za izgradnju, proširenje i regulaciju grada Zagreba, Zagreb, 1930; *Natječaj za izradu generalne osnove za izgradnju, proširenje i regulaciju grada Zagreba. Podaci i smjernice*, Zagreb, 1930, 50.
60. Among them were representatives of UJIA and Zagreb Technical Faculty.
61. The ones taken into consideration were Cornelius Gurlitt, Franz Schumacher from Hamburg, Hermann Jansen and Werner Hagemann from Berlin, and Alois Dryák from Prague. Jansen was a jury member at the competition for the Split regulatory plan, and Gurlitt's first Ph.D. student Herman Muthesius was invited to evaluate competition designs for the Zagreb Stock Exchange Building and Esplanade Hotel. See HR-DAZG-10 GPZ, GO, III-1, sign. 89: Report on the meeting of the board in charge of the competition, September 21, 1929.
62. Another Dresden-based architect, Wilhelm Kreis, was the member of the jury in charge of the medical center (Zakladna i klinička bolnica) in Šalata. See Tamara Bjažić Klarin. "Međunarodni natječaj za Zakladnu i kliničku bolnicu u Zagrebu 1930–1931," *Prostor* 20, no. 44 (2012): 282–295.
63. Before the arrival of foreign jury members, two rounds of selection had already taken place. See HR-DAZG-10 GPZ, GO, III-1, sign. 99: Reports on meetings of the board in charge of the competition preparation, September 21, 1930 and October 4, 1930.
64. HR-DAZG-10 GPZ, GO, III-1, sign. 88: List of architects requesting competition briefs.
65. The journal was founded that year and dedicated to the utility politics and the problems of city building.
66. The first prize was not given because "a large number of submitted entries deserved an award, and no particular one stood out from the others." The second *ex aequo* award was given to Hans Lübke, Edi Reissner, and Willy Schöne. The entries by Richard Haffner and Hannes Mayer, Paul Bonatz, Otto Meffert and associates, Max Arlt, Otto Schubert and Velimir Stiasni and Adolf Muesmann were given honorary mentions. Entries by Hans Reichow, Hans Friedrich Hirsch, and Otto Czekelius from Madrid were praised. See "Rezultat natječaja za generalnu regulatornu osnovu za grad Zagreb," *Gradski vjesnik* 2, no. 20–21 (1931): 346–347.
67. An article published in *Gradski vjesnik* dealt with the housing issues in Germany. See John Robert Mullin, "City Planning in Frankfurt, Germany, 1925–1932: A Study in Practical Utopianism," *Journal of Urban History* 4, no. 1 (1977): 3–28; Anonymous, "Rad njemačkih gradova na popravljanju stambenih prilika," *Gradski vjesnik* 1, no. 6 (1930): 9–10.
68. The exhibition held in Zagreb and Belgrade was prepared by the Deutschen Kunstgesellschaft E.V. Berlin. The curator was Alfred Kuhn. Stjepan Hribar and city mayor Srkulj visited Berlin and Dresden exhibitions. See *Nemačka savremena likovna umetnost i arhitektura. Beograd – Zagreb. Deutsche zeitgenössische Bildende Kunst und Architektur* (Zagreb: Deutschen Kunstgesellschaft Berlin, 1931); HAZU-HMA-Hribar: Payment order.

69. Max Taut, "Neues Bauen in Deutschland / Novo neimarstvo u Nemačkoj," in *Nemačka savremena likovna umetnost i arhitektura. Beograd – Zagreb. Deutsche zeitgenössische Bildende Kunst und Architektur* (Zagreb: Deutschen Kunstgesellschaft Berlin, 1931), 39–43.
70. HR-DAZG-10 GPZ, GO, III-1, sign. 71: Ivan Zemljak, Report on Congress, 1929.
71. For more on Weissmann's work in Le Corbusier's studio and the competition for the design of the Foundation Block, the multifunctional facility on the main square of Zagreb, see Tamara Bjažić Klarin, *Ernest Weissmann – društveno angažirana arhitektura, 1926. – 1939. / Ernest Weissmann – Socially Engaged Architecture, 1926–1939* (Zagreb: HAZU, 2015).
72. The competition entry *Jelačić* was deposited in the State Archives in Zagreb. See HR-DAZG-10 GPZ, GO, III-1, sign. 105.
73. Antolić and Seissel visited Frankfurt-am-Main, Stuttgart and Berlin. During their trip, they met Ewald Liedecke. See HAZU-HMA-Hribar: Vladimir Antolić and Josip Seissel, Postcards to Stjepan Hribar, 1932.
74. Korn lived in Zagreb from 1935–1937 and collaborated with Vladimir Antolić.
75. "Kako će izgledati Zagreb u budućnosti. Pitanje regulatorne osnove i željezničko pitanje," *Novosti*, November 17, 1928.
76. Antolić explained Milytin's linear city in his lecture and article *Grad i društvo* (*City and Society*). See Vladimir Antolić, "Grad i društvo," *Arhitektura* 3, no. 3–4 (1933): 42–46.
77. The group was established by Weissmann. He published CIAM's *La Sarraz Declaration* in the book *Problemi savremene arhitekture* (*Problems of Contemporary Architecture*), an overview of work of Zagreb-based architects who advocated the *Neues Bauen* in early 1932. They had already gathered in 1931 on the occasion of the exhibition of the Udruženje umjetnika Zemlja (Association of Artists Zemlja), which was devoted to social goals, as well. Antolić attended the Fifth CIAM Congress in Paris (1937) and CIRPAC meetings in Amsterdam (1935) and Zurich (1939). For more, see Bjažić Klarin, Ernest Weissmann; Eric Mumford, *The CIAM Discourse on Urbanism, 1928–1960* (Cambridge, MA: MIT Press, 2000); Van Es, Evelien et al., eds., *Atlas of the Functional City: CIAM 4 and Comparative Urban Analysis* (Bussum and Zurich: Thoth Publishers and gta Verlag, 2014).
78. On collaboration between Croatian and French architects, see Tamara Bjažić Klarin, "*Le Corbusier, s'il vous plâit? – Oui, mais . . .* Inter-War Architecture Between Zagreb and Paris," in *French Artistic Culture and Central-East European Modern Art*, ed. Ljiljana Kolešnik and Tamara Bjažić Klarin (Zagreb: Institut za povijest umjetnosti, 2017), 124–142.
79. Franjo Brozović, "Budući Zagreb. Generalna regulatorna osnova grada Zagreba," *Jutarnji List*, January 10, 1932.
80. Hans Reichow and Hans Friedrich Hirsch, whose entry triggered particular interest among Croatian architects, envisaged the new city squares and parks on the south bank of the Sava River.

Part II

Aiming at the Healthy City

Experiments With Best Practices

5 Learning From Smaller Cities

Moscow in the International Urban Networks, 1870–1910

Anna Mazanik

In 1881, the Moscow City Council invited a famous German engineer James Hobrecht to prepare a plan for a sewage system for Moscow. One of the municipal deputies at the council's meeting advocated the need to invite a foreign expert with the following arguments:

> Although we have our local authorities, we concluded that they need to be checked by inviting a European authority who can say whether what we have done is good or bad and who can grade us. Mr. Hobrecht, a recognized authority, said that our technicians had worked a lot on this issue but they did not have enough experience for us to rely on their solutions, so we should not miss the chance to reach the level that Hobrecht shows to us.[1]

This quote, one of many quotes of a similar kind, reveals two important assumptions behind Moscow's municipal reforms at the turn of the 1880s. First is the idea of European modernity as "the golden standard" that needs to be followed. Second is the image of Moscow as a pupil and a backward city that requires foreign help and guidance to become a "modern" and a "European" city.

Such vision and problematization of urban reforms by the municipal authorities reminds one of a familiar model of spreading knowledge, especially modern scientific and technological innovations, as a linear, one-directional process "from the West to the rest." In recent decades, this model of monolithic and progressive diffusion of Western science has been challenged from standpoints of post-colonial studies and the renewed interest in the local practices of science. The revisionist interpretations favored a less hierarchical idea of the universal circulation of knowledge and emphasized that urban modernity as such was a product of the constant international exchange of ideas, people, technologies and commodities. Historians revealed that colonial and peripheral cities, which had previously been imagined to be the passive receivers of innovations, in fact acted as laboratories of modernity where planners and engineers had more freedom to experiment. At the same time, more attention has been paid to the processes of domestication of borrowed innovations, which were not only adapted to the local contexts, but also sometimes received a new meaning and form.[2]

Although there exists a substantial amount of historical scholarship on infrastructural reforms in late-imperial Moscow, those are rarely put in the context of global urban change, transnational municipalism and the circulation of science and technologies.[3] This is partly due to the weak traditions of comparative history in Russia,[4] partly to the (often unreflected) assumptions of Russia's exceptionalism. Recent studies in the intellectual history of Russian science have attempted to "normalize" Russian modernity and (re-)integrate it into a wider European or Western context,[5] and urban history of science and technology can also benefit from this approach. A close look at Moscow's reforms at the turn of the twentieth century reveals that the city was thoroughly integrated in the formal and informal scientific networks of the Western world. However, we know very little about the foreign models that influenced Russian reformers, the routes along which new ideas and practices travelled or how and why innovations were introduced, adapted and justified, and how relevant Russian experience was for other cities.

These were the questions that inspired the present chapter. It is based on my previous research in the history of Moscow's public health and focuses primarily on sanitary reforms and engineering. The urban change in imperial Moscow was by no means limited to this sphere alone (the city government also devoted substantial attention to the reform of schooling, transportation, maternal and psychiatric care, and various artistic endeavors). Yet, this was a very dynamic sphere that required major investments, reshaped urban space, affected the entire urban population and played an important role in the representation of the city. In the following pages, I will reconstruct the network of Moscow's foreign models and reveal the forms, processes and mechanisms of the circulation of knowledge. The revisionist interpretations in the history of science and technology also call for the critical analysis of the nineteenth-century debates on urban innovation and self-perceptions of municipal reformers. This chapter will also explore how the image of Moscow's backwardness was constructed and overcome and which role international transfers played in this process.

Constructing Moscow's Backwardness

The narrative of "backwardness" is a familiar trope in Russian history. Yanni Kotsonis has argued that in the Russian Empire "backwardness" emerged as a self-contained framework of explanation and a kind of ideology in its own right. The educated public agreed that Russia was backward and undeveloped, and this claim could be used to explain practically any phenomena.[6]

In 1885, when the Moscow City Council discussed sanitary reforms, one of the municipal deputies exclaimed:

> [W]e see the examples of municipal expenses in such beautiful cities as London, Paris and especially Vienna. We are spoiled by the life in these beautiful cities, but we should not forget how those countries are much wealthier and more productive than ours, how much more valuable the labor is there and how much better the work.[7]

The vision of Moscow as a "backward" city that needs to "learn" from Europe seems to fit into this longer pattern in Russian history, but it also had an important international dimension. In the second half of the nineteenth century, local elites in many other cities across Central, Eastern and Southern Europe were striving to make their cities cleaner and healthier and urgently bridge the perceived gap between their own and more "advanced" Western societies. Those ideas of urban transformation and catching up with a "European standard" often merged with ideas of a more general political change.[8]

In Moscow, the discussion about sanitation and pollution, health and disease, had a deep political meaning and, importantly, was activated only in the time of the major political transformation connected to the liberal reforms of Alexander II, especially the abolition of serfdom and the empowerment of the elected local governments.

Before that, it seems, Muscovites did not consider themselves particularly backward. As Alexander Martin has argued, in the first half of the nineteenth century, Moscow, with its small houses and abundant gardens, cultivated the myth of being a healthy and harmonious place and enjoyed a sense of superiority over the Western European cities that suffered from overcrowding and social conflict. Although the Moscow public was aware of dirt and fetid odors, they did not invoke any images of decay or danger, but rather those of closeness to nature, patriarchal mores and social harmony. In Martin's interpretation, the silence of the Russian public about the everyday filth and stench of Moscow was a way of affirming the *ancien régime* values and vitality of the country's social order.[9]

In the second half of the century, after the disaster of the Crimean War, after the Great Reforms and the later conservative turn in Russia's internal policy, the earlier visions of social harmony in the eyes of many yielded to the loss of public faith in the political regime. They gave way to the deepening sense of Moscow's "backwardness," when the growing number of accounts on the city's filth, pollution and anti-sanitary conditions reflected not only the physical reality, but also the demand for political changes and modernization among those who were writing and reading them. Moreover, the post-Reform accounts described Moscow's pollution and dirt not as a new development, but, on the contrary, as a historic or even "primeval" practice, and drew a connection between pollution and the underdevelopment of Russia's civil society.[10]

Although looking westward was not necessarily crucial to the construction of backwardness, it certainly played a role in the imagination of Moscow's municipal leaders. The Moscow reformers did not fail to make comparisons with other big cities; all available sources of information confirmed their conviction that Moscow was far behind "European cities." Growing sets of statistical data, especially mortality statistics, played an important role (not without grounds) in backing that claim:

> In public, in the City Council, and in the press we hear complaints about the exceptionally high mortality rates in Moscow. It is said that the rate is 39 out of every 1,000, and that there is no other place with such a high mortality rate, either in the small towns, or in the big cities of Western Europe. Indeed, our mortality rates are very high, and it is the responsibility of the municipality to reduce them, but how can it reach this goal?[11]

European experience was interpreted and misinterpreted to confirm the backwardness of Moscow, which was sometimes declared to be several centuries behind its role models. For example, when in 1885 the city council was considering the construction of a new public slaughterhouse, the entire discussion was embedded in the narrative of Moscow's perceived "backwardness" compared to Western cities. The speakers invoked Moscow's "universal pollution," "anti-sanitary conditions," infection, disease and poverty to call upon the council to "make a step toward the accomplishment of the city so that it may resemble a European one." Quite illustratively, one municipal deputy referenced the English law of 1486 prohibiting the organization of slaughterhouses in the cities to claim that Moscow was 400 years behind in resolving this issue – although the city of London did not ban private slaughterhouses until 1927, and throughout the nineteenth century, British butchers successfully opposed the introduction of public abattoirs.[12]

Overcoming that "backwardness" and turning "more European" was presented as "public good." The "public good" of urban reforms in Moscow rhetorically referred to the formula of "serving the people," which had dominated the circles of the Russian intelligentsia since the 1860s. "Service to the people" was combined with the promotion of scientific knowledge that was meant to reorganize urban life according to new rational principles and make it "less backward."

In Moscow, the narrative of "backwardness" served as a powerful justification of radical intervention in the life of the city and its residents. The practical mechanism of overcoming "backwardness" and achieving "public good" was seen in municipalization, which in the 1880s became the basis for the city policy in the sphere of infrastructural reforms and sanitation. Both the city council deputies and invited experts regarded the municipal government as the key guardian of public interest and health.[13] The process of municipalization, and the expansion of the city activities and jurisdiction, was by no means peculiarly Russian – it was a phenomenon known to the whole Western world in the nineteenth century. In many European and American cities municipalization was a response to the failure of market forces to cope with the complex problems of urban life, such as transportation, health and welfare.[14]

However, in Russia the municipalization arguably had a particular symbolic value and was a part of some specifically Russian discussions. The claim of being the mouthpiece of certain social groups or of "the people" was typical for all participants of the political debate, in Russia and elsewhere, yet in the autocratic tsarist Russia, only municipalities and *zemstvos* (rural administration), which were the only elected governing bodies, could legitimize this right in legal terms. The Moscow municipal elites presented themselves as the only legitimate representatives of the city population, as acting on behalf and for the benefit of the urban community because of their unique elected status.[15] Dominated by active entrepreneurs and professionals, the municipality juxtaposed itself both to the imperial administration, to private service-providers and to "the people," whom it claimed to serve and who it wanted to educate, discipline and civilize. According to this rhetoric, only municipal institutions were responsible, competent and efficient suppliers of urban services and only the public government could lead Moscow from "backwardness" to "Europeanness."

The narrative of backwardness created a sense of utmost urgency for urban transformation and allowed the municipality to mobilize resources for urban reforms, not only from the city budget but also through imperial loans and preferences and huge private donations from the Moscow elites. Municipal deputies and the mayors themselves provided their own private capital for the construction of hospitals, schools and welfare institutions.[16]

In a sense, the idea of Moscow's backwardness was constructed to be overcome. Failure at the beginning was stressed in order to highlight the speed and the scale of progress. On the eve of World War I, urban elites successfully promoted Moscow as the city that had managed to become "European" with the help of an elected government, public engagement and openness to foreign experience, implicitly asserting these values for the modernization of the entire empire.

Foreign Inspirations and the Circulation of Knowledge

Urban modernity was very much about the circulation of ideas, people and artifacts across cities, countries and continents. This circulation happened through a variety of institutions and practices, such as international congresses, societies and exhibitions, formal and informal study trips, professional journals and especially through traveling experts.[17] Which of these mechanisms were important for Moscow in the last decades of the nineteenth century? How did the city participate in the global circulation of knowledge?

From the late 1870s, the official journal of the Moscow City Council, *Izvestiia Moskovskoi Gorodskoi Dumy*, regularly published articles and reports on the urban development in other European cities, thus introducing and shaping the ideas about the innovations that Moscow needed, the models it should follow, and the cities whose experience could be of use. The mechanisms and directions of such transfers were, however, very diverse.

One option – in fact, a relatively rare one – was to invite foreign experts who had already gained recognition abroad. In the 1880s, when the Moscow municipality was preparing to re-develop water and sanitary infrastructure in the city, two internationally known experts were consulted: German engineer James Hobrecht was invited to design a sewage system and English engineer William Lindley was asked to prepare a project for the introduction of a new water supply. At that point, the Moscow municipality was inexperienced in large infrastructural projects, so the motivation behind inviting foreign experts who had built sanitary amenities in several European cities was both pragmatic and symbolic. On the one hand, it could compensate for the lack of experience of the Moscow municipality and Russian engineers with such complex infrastructure. On the other, it was meant to highlight the "Europeanness" of the planned urban innovations and to ensure Moscow's parity with other European cities. The insistence of municipal leaders on inviting foreign experts reflects their initial belief in the superiority of Western European knowledge, experience and technology. In practice, however, the projects of both Hobrecht and Lindley were found to be problematic as they failed to consider Moscow's peculiar climatic and social conditions and were eventually rejected in favor of local designs.[18]

Unlike in some other cities and towns in Eastern and Central Europe,[19] in Moscow nationalist rhetoric did not play a significant role in the choice of experts and technologies. On the contrary, the use of the most advanced foreign technologies was presented as the best way to serve one's city and country (sometimes bordering on self-deprecation). The belief in the value of the foreign expertise and experience seemed to outweigh the questions of national pride. In 1881, answering to one of the very few deputies who suggested that Russian engineers should be commissioned when possible, the retired mayor Prince Shcherbatov referred to the case of Pavel Yablochkov, a Russian electrical engineer who developed a commercially viable electric carbon arc lamp ("Yablochkov candle") used for the illumination of the Paris World Fair in 1878:

> I admit that I do not understand such patriotism. In the given case, I understand only one type of patriotism – to provide the city of Moscow, which we ought to serve, with the conditions for healthy life. . . . It is secondary to me whether the engineer will be Russian or non-Russian. In Paris, when they wanted to introduce new illumination, they invited Yablochkov without asking whether he was French or Russian. I believe that in such questions the references to nationality have nothing to do with the matter.[20]

Although as a rule, the infrastructural projects in Moscow were implemented by Russian engineers and architects, the minutes of municipal discussions did not preserve any evidence that such choices were motivated by national pride and generally did not invoke the question of nationality.

Another way of knowledge circulation was the employment of young European specialists who made their career in Russia. Hygienist Friedrich Erismann (1842–1915), one of the founders of community medicine in Russia, can be a good example of such a scenario. Erismann was born in Switzerland and graduated from the University of Zurich, specializing in ophthalmology. In 1869, he moved to Russia following his Russian wife Nadezhda Suslova, where he soon abandoned his private practice in eye diseases and became interested in public hygiene. His Russian-language works on hygiene, *Rukovodstvo k gigiene* and *Obshchestvennaia gigiena*, were translated into German, Dutch, Hungarian and Finnish. In 1882, Erismann received a chair in hygiene at Moscow University and from then on actively cooperated with the Moscow municipal government as an expert and consultant. He was involved in the development of sanitary inspection, food control, school hygiene, outpatient medical care, investigations into the living conditions of the working classes, waste treatment, slaughterhouse reform and the construction of new water pipes and sewers.[21] Thanks to Erismann's personal connections with scholars in various countries, the Moscow municipality had the opportunity to receive informal consultations with foreign experts, for example, with a famous German hygienist Max von Pettenkofer.[22] In 1896, because of the political conflict with the Ministry of Public Instruction, Erismann left Russia and settled in Switzerland. In 1902, he was elected a member of the Zurich City Council from the Social Democratic Party and used his 27 years of Russian experience to inform his work on sanitary reforms in the city, including the construction of a hospital and a slaughterhouse, disinfection and school hygiene.

Naturally, not only did foreigners travel to Moscow, but Moscow specialists also went abroad. Municipal study trips to investigate foreign experience were a norm in Europe and the United States in the nineteenth century, and Moscow also joined that trend. Most major urban projects in Moscow were preceded by at least one trip to Europe to study how similar problems were tackled elsewhere.

Usually such trips had multiple destinations, enabling Moscow experts and reformers to compare various solutions. In fact, building infrastructure according to only one foreign model was uncommon. The norm was a combination of several foreign models and a kind of creative synthesis from their experience. What was borrowed, however, was ideas and plans, while their implementation and production remained in Russian hands. The construction of the public slaughterhouse in Moscow (1886–1888) can provide a good illustration. The entire idea of the centralized public abattoir appeared in France; from there, it had spread to many European cities, including St. Petersburg, which was an important example for Moscow. The Moscow abattoir was built according to the French system, where each function of slaughter was performed in a separate building. However, in line with the German influence, the abattoir in Moscow had a scientific laboratory and a strong veterinary organization. The sterilization machines from the Moscow abattoir were invented in Belgium and refrigerators were built according to the model of the Hamburg slaughterhouse, while the local sewage system was English. However, the project itself was designed by Russian engineers and architects, waste treatment facilities with filtration fields were organized by a Moscow University professor, Anatoly Faddeiev, and all equipment was produced at Russian factories.[23]

International experience and knowledge were important not only at the stage of creating innovative infrastructure. After the innovative projects had been introduced, there was ongoing active cooperation between relevant organizations and foreign experience continued to be monitored. Moscow municipal institutions were subscribed to international professional journals, took part in congresses and exhibitions, and regularly sent their employees to internships abroad at municipal expense. For example, when in 1910 Paul Ehrlich created the first effective treatment for syphilis, Salvarsan-606, two physicians of the Myasnitskaya municipal hospital for workers were immediately sent to Germany to Ehrlich's laboratory to study that new medicine. Salvarsan-606 was first used at a Moscow municipal hospital already in August 1910; that is, only several months after its official presentation.[24]

The geography of Moscow's foreign models was very diverse. Urban historians have traditionally focused on the importance of the big metropolises, such as London, Paris, Vienna and Berlin, as the donors of knowledge. Yet, in Moscow, many innovative practices and technologies came not from the familiar metropolitan models but from "less iconic" cities and towns. Throughout the nineteenth century, Moscow remained one of Europe's largest cities, but it often had to borrow from urban centers that were significantly smaller in size. For example, the new Moscow slaughterhouse used the experience of Brussels, Antwerp, Hannover and Hamburg; the new waterpipe combined water filtration systems from Zurich, Bristol and other British cities; the reconstruction of the city roads involved study trips to Baku, Finland and Sweden.[25]

Rhetorically, Moscow competed with and aspired to be like major European metropolises, such as Paris, London and Berlin; those traditional role models were important to problematize the need for specific innovations. However, the exact technologies that had been implemented in Paris or London decades earlier had often become somewhat outdated by the 1880s and could not be borrowed. In a way, to be like Paris or London – that is, modern, scientific, innovative, cutting-edge and "European" – one had to borrow from other emerging cities, often of a smaller size and not necessarily in Europe, because this was where innovations were developed and tested. In the last section of my chapter, I would come back to the history of the Moscow sewage system to discuss how the experience of smaller cities was used and adapted to create metropolitan infrastructure.

Learning From Smaller Cities: The Case of the Moscow Sewage System

However indispensable the sewage system seems to us today, it was only in the nineteenth century that it became an inherent part of urban infrastructure. Throughout most of the nineteenth century, it was the miasmatic theory that provided the background and rationale for developing the technologies of sanitation. The miasmatic theory assumed that disease originates from decomposing organic waste and is spread through its emanation. The depositories of "filth," including cesspools, dumps and waterways, were believed to be the main sources of contamination. The prompt removal of the decaying organic materials and preventing the spread of their rotting smells and environmental sanitation were considered essential for fighting epidemics. In the 1850s through the 1870s, the belief in the connection between disease and filth and in the health value of flushing away household wastes prompted many cities across Europe and America to build or expand their sewers.[26] In the last decades of the nineteenth century, the "bacteriological revolution" replaced filth, miasma and foul odors with germs as the causes of disease, but the commitment to develop wastewater infrastructure persisted.

The Russian Empire was rather late in introducing these types of sanitary infrastructure. St. Petersburg, the imperial capital, never received a sewage system – it was not until the Soviet era that one was constructed. Moscow was among the very few large cities of the Russian Empire that built a sewage system. The Moscow sewage system was launched in 1898; it was not only the biggest and the most expensive project of the Moscow municipality, but also the one that took the longest to complete.

In the 1870s and early 1880s, the Moscow municipality considered several potential projects for the sewage system. As previously mentioned, one of those projects was designed by the invited engineer James Hobrecht, whose international fame was supposed to enhance the symbolism of the new Moscow infrastructural achievement as a mark of "Europeanness." All of the early projects, including that of Hobrecht, proposed the combined single-pipe systems – a standard design functioning in many European cities – that carried rainwater and human waste together to the filtration fields.

However, in 1887, preference was eventually given to the project of a municipal engineer, Vsevolod Kastalsky. Kastalsky designed a separate system that dealt with anthropogenic wastes only and let the precipitation run directly into the surface waters.[27] Today, the separate system is believed to have a general sanitary advantage over the combined one, due to the frequency of combined sewer overflows during periods of heavy rain or snowmelt, when the system becomes overloaded and releases untreated waste directly into surface waters, posing environmental and health risks.[28]

In the nineteenth century, the separate system was an innovative project, although not exactly Kastalsky's own. He received the idea from the city of Memphis, United States, where American engineer Colonel George Waring Jr. constructed a separate sewage system in 1881.

The idea of separate sewers originated in Europe in the 1840s. Famous British sanitarian Edwick Chadwick advocated them in the belief that human wastes could be conveniently used as agricultural fertilizer and that such use would make sewage system self-financing – assumptions that were soon proven wrong. When the city of London finally constructed a sewage system in 1858, the choice was made in favor of a combined system, setting an influential precedent for the design of sewers in many European and American cities for the following decades.[29]

It was not until the turn of the 1880s that the designs of George Waring brought the separate system back to the table. In 1875–1876, he constructed a separate system in the small Massachusetts resort town of Lenox, but it was his work in Memphis that made him and his design famous. In the 1870s, Memphis was struck by two devastating yellow fever epidemics and was notorious for its poor sanitation. At the request of the city's officials, the National Board of Health appointed a special commission for sanitary improvement. Among several plans for the sewerage of Memphis, the commission chose Waring's design of a separate system (probably because of its low costs), which was then built within several months. The construction of the Memphis separate sewer system and the considerable sanitary improvements it caused in a nearly bankrupt city stimulated a great debate in the engineering circles and press. In his influential 1881 report on combined and separate sewers, American engineer Rudolf Hering attempted to resolve the controversy by concluding that neither system has a sanitary advantage. He recommended a combined system for large, densely populated cities, and a separate system for smaller cities primarily concerned with household wastes, and until the early twentieth century, American practice followed these guidelines.[30]

It was probably during the debates of the early 1880s that the separate system caught the attention of Vsevolod Kastalsky in Moscow. Moscow, however, was no Memphis. The dramatic difference in size, climate and geographical conditions of the two cities meant that Waring's initial design had to be transformed beyond recognition to fit Moscow's needs. In the early 1880s, Memphis was a city with approximately 40,000 inhabitants and covered 10 square km (4 square miles). Moscow had a population of 750,000 and an area of more than 72 square km (63 square versts).[31]

Both Waring and Kastalsky praised the separate system for its low construction and maintenance costs. Although the combined system, which handled household wastes and stormwater in a single pipe, functioned well in many European cities, there were significant differences in climate and precipitation between Western Europe and the United States or Central Russia. The projects devised for the separate system proposed by Waring and Kastalasky excluded the provisions for dealing with volatile levels of precipitation and only needed to discharge human waste – the supply of which remained relatively stable in all seasons – allowing them to reduce the size of the pipes.

However, the main justification for the sewage system was the improvement of urban health, and in this matter, Memphis and Moscow relied on very different medical-sanitary views. Waring was a major advocate of the miasmatic theory of disease and strongly believed in the idea that the "sewer gas" produced by the decomposing wastes was the primary source of infectious disease. The sanitary rationale for his system was based on tightly fitting pipes that would protect the households from the "poisonous air."[32]

In Moscow, on the contrary, the final argument in favor of the separate system was bacteriological. The new discoveries in bacteriology connected infectious disease to specific microbes and showed that water sources, contaminated with the feces of the sick (for example, as a result of combined sewer overflows), could play a key role in spreading epidemics such as cholera and typhoid.

When the Moscow City Council discussed the competing sewer designs in 1887, the outcome of the debate was decided by the statement of architect Vladimir Shervud, who called the combined system "the perfect laboratory for bacteria" and scolded it for spreading infectious disease:

> There is one serious hygienic question that should be considered – that the excrement of people sick with typhoid, cholera and so on do not get into the river. That would inevitably be a disaster. . . . I compared those systems several times, but I have to repeat that the main question is in the dilution of wastes. Does the dilution really eliminate the bacteria? This is the question. Pasteur, for example, proves that it does not. At the recent Hygiene Congress in Austria, Dr. Brouardel argued that infection is transmitted not so much through the air, not so much from the laundry of the sick, but through the water polluted with excrement of those suffering from typhoid and other contagious diseases.[33]

Historians have reminded us that science turns into policy only when scientific conclusions correspond to the more general political and socio-economic goals of the decision makers.[34] The potential sanitary advantage of the separate system in light of the bacteriological discoveries was a timely and convincing point and also fitted well in the agenda of the Moscow municipality. Taking up the bacteriological argumentation allowed the Moscow authorities to continue with municipalization, to reject the rivaling combined system design proposed by a private concessionaire and to choose the cheapest project while appearing to support the newest scientific ideas.[35]

The construction of the separate system in Moscow was finished in 1898. By that time, the population of Moscow was approaching 1 million. The sewage system is a good example of how such a big emerging city could learn from smaller "peripheral" cities. Although in line with established patterns, at the stage of project implementation, the municipality organized study trips to Warsaw, Berlin, Oxford and Hitchin, the main inspiration for Moscow's separate sewage system came from Memphis. However, not only did that initial design have to be rescaled and adjusted to Moscow's conditions, as well as to include a waste treatment plant absent in Waring's project, but also the entire scientific rationale behind that separate system changed to the opposite – from anti-contagionism to contagionism, from miasma to bacteria, from the sewer gas to the untreated waste released in the waterways.

In this respect, the Moscow sewage system, inspired by the example of a much smaller city of Memphis, designed and constructed by Kastalsky in the era of paradigmatic changes in medicine and sanitary engineering, was a part of the global process of validation and establishment of the new bacteriological theory of disease. On the other hand, it was a kind of international experiment, a test for a new technological system which became a norm in the twentieth century.

Conclusion

Foreign experience and constant interaction with other cities and scientific centers were very important for Moscow's urban reforms and played a fundamental role in shaping its image as a "modern" and "advanced" European metropolis. It is impossible to single out one dominant national tradition (for example, German) as the main donor. On the contrary, the norm was a combination of several models, often both "traditional" and "emerging." The geography of interconnections was very broad and included not only big European metropolises, but also smaller cities and towns.

The circulation of knowledge was not linear and hierarchical (from Western Europe to the rest, from center to periphery, from the "emerged" to the "emerging," from a big city to a small town), but rather was multi-level and multi-directional. It also implied a lot of horizontal connections among institutions and specific experts. Although Western European metropolises helped articulate the need for certain technologies, the most innovative designs could come from the periphery. Emerging and "peripheral" cities could also successfully borrow from each other – even if the utmost goal was to catch up or compete with the larger metropolises.

Because of the "belated" start, the sanitary reforms in Moscow were carried out in the era of a paradigmatic shift in the understanding, prevention and treatment of disease and urban sanitation. This rapid change partially devalued the practices of sanitation in "older" European metropolises and increased the relevance of "emerging" cities as the donors and testers of new technologies. In this context, Moscow's sanitary reforms were a part of a global process of validation of the germ theory of disease as the dominant one, and also a testing ground for new preventive and therapeutic practices and technological solutions.

Notes

1. *Izvestiia Moskovskoi Gorodskoi Dumy* [IMGD] 9 (1881): 993.
2. Mikael Hård and Thomas J. Misa, eds., *Urban Machinery: Inside Modern European Cities* (Cambridge, MA: MIT Press, 2008); David Arnold, *Science, Technology and Medicine in Colonial India* (Cambridge: Cambridge University Press, 2000), 1–18.
3. There are exceptions to this trend, for example: Blair Ruble, *Second Metropolis: Pragmatic Pluralism in Gilded Age Chicago, Silver Age Moscow, and Meiji Osaka* (Cambridge: Cambridge University Press, 2001); Jan C. Behrends and Martin Kohlrausch, eds., *Races to Modernity: Metropolitan Aspirations in Eastern Europe*, 1890–1940 (Budapest: Central European University Press, 2014), but none of them focuses specifically on scientific and technological innovations in the urban context.
4. I have provided a detailed discussion of the post-Soviet historiography of urban history in Russia in two articles: Anna Mazanik, "Research in Urban History: New Research Trends in Doctoral Dissertations in Russia Since 2000," *Urban History* 42, no. 3 (2017): 509–520; Anna Mazanik,

"Kul'turnyi povorot i rossiiskaia istoricheskaia urbanistika," in *Proshlyi vek*, ed. Alexei Miller (Moscow: INION RAN, 2012).

5. Marina Mogilner, *Homo Imperii: A History of Physical Anthropology in Russia* (Lincoln and London: University of Nebraska Press, 2013); Daniel Beer, *Renovating Russia: The Human Sciences and the Fate of Liberal Modernity, 1880–1930* (Ithaca and London: Cornell University Press, 2008).
6. Yanni Kotsonis, *Making Peasants Backward: Agricultural Cooperatives and the Agrarian Question in Russia, 1861–1914* (Houndmills, Basingstoke and Hampshire: Palgrave Macmillan, 1999), 1–8.
7. *IMGD* 10 (1885): 1109.
8. Jan Behrends and Martin Kohlrausch discuss it in their introduction to *Races to Modernity*, 1–19; see also Peter Hanak, *The Garden and the Workshop: Essays on the Cultural History of Vienna and Budapest* (Princeton: Princeton University Press, 1998). The other chapters in the current volume should also provide a good comparative context.
9. Alexander M. Martin, "Sewage and the City: Filth, Smell, and Representations of Urban Life in Moscow, 1770–1880," *The Russian Review* 67 (April 2008): 243–274.
10. Anna Mazanik, "Sanitation, Urban Environment and the Politics of Public Health in Late Imperial Moscow" (Ph.D. Thesis, Central European University, Budapest, 2015), 1–6, 48.
11. *IMGD* 9 (1881): 994.
12. I have analyzed the history of the Moscow public slaughterhouse and its place in the debates on modernization and "Europeanness" in my article " 'Shiny Shoes' for the City: The Public Abattoir and the Reform of Meat Supply in Imperial Moscow," *Urban History* 45, no. 2 (2018): 214–232. The persistence of private slaughterhouses in London is discussed in Ian Maclachlan, "A Bloody Offal Nuisance: The Persistence of Private Slaughter-Houses in Nineteenth-Century London," *Urban History* 34, no. 2 (2007): 227–254.
13. See, for instance, discussions of sanitary reforms in *IMGD* 7 (1885): 779–788; Central State Archive of Moscow (TsGA Moskvy), 179:58:44:17–18.
14. Robert Morris, "Governance: Two Centuries of Urban Growth," in *Urban Governance: Britain and Beyond Since 1750*, ed. Robert Morris and Richard H. Trainor (Aldershot: Ashgate, 2000).
15. *IMGD* 10 (1885): 1113.
16. L.F. Pisar'kova, *Gorodskiye reformy v Rossii i Moskovskaya Duma* (Moscow: Novy khronograph, 2010), 274–275.
17. Mikael Hård and Thomas J. Misa, "Modernizing European Cities: Technological Uniformity and Cultural Distinction," in Hård and Misa, eds., *Urban Machinery*, 10–12.
18. "Zhurnaly zasedaniya Komissii po rassmotreniyu proyektov kanalizatsii Moskvy, sostavlennykh gg. Gobrechtom i Popovym," in *Trudy III (Stroitel'nogo) otdela Imperatorskogo Russkogo tekhnucheskogo obshchestva, 1880–1884* (St. Petersburg: Tipografiya Panteleyevykh, 1884), 51–68, 131–153, 193–231, 273–280; E.S. Fyodorov, *Po povodu trudov Komissii pri Russkom Teckhnicheskom obshchestve po rassmotreniyu voprosov ob ochistke gorodov* (Kazan: Tipogrfiia Okr. Shtaba, 1885), 4–15.
19. See, for example, Chapter 6 by Heidi Hein-Kircher in the current volume.
20. *IMGD* 9 (1881): 1005.
21. N. Mikhailov, *Pamiati professora F.F. Erismana* (Moscow: Tipo-litogragiya T-va I.I. Kushnerev i Ko, 1915).
22. *Zhurnaly Komissii po nadzoru za ustroystvom novogo vodoprovoda i kanalizatsii v Moskve [1892–1893]* (S.l: S.n., 1894), 50, 139–144; I.A. Verner, ed.,

Sovremennoie khoziaistvo goroda Moskvy (Moscow: Gorodskaia tipografiia, 1913), 350.
23. Mazanik, *Sanitation*, 144–145.
24. Ibid., 118.
25. S.A. Poderni, *Tekhnicheskoye opisanie moskovskikh tsentral'nykh gorodskikh boien* (Moscow: S.n., 1896), 25, 55, 126–137; Verner, ed., *Sovremennoie khoziaistvo goroda Moskvy*, 359–376, 555.
26. "Doklad N 55 po vorposu o kanalizatsii Moskvy," *IMGD* 10 (1879): 4–12; Martin Melosi, *The Sanitary City: Urban Infrastructure in America from Colonial Times to the Present* (Baltimore: Johns Hopkins University Press, 2000), 93.
27. V.D. Kastalsky, *O razdel'noy sisteme splavnoy kanalizatsii gorodov* (Moscow: Gorodskaya Tipografiya, 1889).
28. David Butler and John Davies, *Urban Drainage* (New York: Spon Press, 2011), 20–26.
29. Joel A. Tarr, "The Separate vs. Combined Sewer Problem: A Case Study in Urban Technology Design Choice," *Journal of Urban History* 5, no. 3 (1979): 313–314.
30. Ibid.; Melosi, *The Sanitary City*, 153–159.
31. *Sovremennoie khoziaistvo goroda Moskvy*, 4.
32. Melosi, *The Sanitary City*, 155.
33. *IMGD* 10 (1887): 864, 867–868.
34. This argument has been famously elaborated in Richard J. Evans, *Death in Hamburg: Society and Politics in the Cholera Years 1830–1910* (Oxford: Clarendon Press, 1987).
35. Mazanik, *Sanitation*, 202–206.

6 Best Practices From a Polish Perspective

Improving Health Conditions in Lviv Around 1900

Heidi Hein-Kircher

"Lviv is not healthy for everyone" ("*Lwów – nie każdemu zdrow*") is an old saying that alluded to the poor health and hygiene conditions in the city.[1] Referring to that proverb in 1881, the young but well-known professor of the Polytechnic University in Lviv, Juljan Zacharewicz, pointed out that "today one could say, that [the city] has become putrid and unhealthy for everyone."[2] He alluded to the fact that Lviv, with an average of 35 deaths per 1,000 inhabitants, had one of the highest rates of mortality in the Habsburg monarchy. Referencing a number of further comparisons in regard to the city's public health conditions, for example relating to water usage, Zacharewicz designed three interdependent targets for Lviv's urban development: first, the improvement of public health; second, provisions for the satisfaction of everyday needs; and third, facilities to ensure a pleasant stay in the city so that even wealthier populations would choose to remain living there. The public address he gave showed not only that public health issues were one of the most urgent tasks facing the local government in Lviv (as in every city) at that time, but also that the changes and innovations he was proposing derived from an observation of other cities and from a handful of assumed best practices that were to be adapted to the specific conditions in Lviv.[3] Furthermore, public health issues were quite tightly interwoven with the urbanization processes and with the general pursuit to improve the urban fabric according to the zeitgeist,[4] to which the local politicians regularly referred, and to streamline it in order to create a modern Polish city. The lecturer emphasized that this deployment would only be possible through extensive knowledge exchange and transfer, because – quite paradigmatically – Zacharewicz[5] had mainly completed his training as an architect at the Polytechnic Institute in Vienna and through study trips around Austria and Germany so that he profited from the respective networks of knowledge exchange.

The case of Lviv is not an isolated one – we can find quite similar processes in every Eastern European city at that time, though the starting point and the solutions undertaken during the processes were often different. This was a phenomenon that Western European cities had already experienced: "Each city responded differently to the urban problems which they shared in common."[6] Since the advent of the first scientific and medical findings, relating to the emergence and spread of epidemics, "public health" had become a central theme in all major European cities and was mainly connected with the prevention and containment of epidemics that threatened the whole society and with a general belief in progress.[7] In addition, in Eastern European cities, urban development in general, as well as the development of public health infrastructures in the urban fabric in particular, had an impact on nationalizing processes, and vice versa. Local actors aiming at modernizing "their" cities used this (self-proclaimed) task as an argument to demonstrate that they were capable of modernizing the whole nation and to show that their nation was as competent as every European nation in general.[8] The local actors tended to be strongly ambitious and operated very deliberately in this. Discourses on these goals and the practices implemented to accomplish them is hence of central importance when we look at the interplay of nationalizing discourses.

In Eastern European cities, it was often the perception of being backward compared to Western European cities that provided the initial impulse for urban innovation and development. In general, the great Western metropolises of Paris and London, and possibly Berlin, Brussels and Vienna, were perceived as role models of city development. One reason for this way of thinking was that the Eastern cities were mainly situated in rural surroundings, and on the peripheries of the Empires' territories. This perception led to a strong feeling of needing to catch up. Another reason was that the actors acknowledged that the poor health conditions endangered the whole society within "their city" because of epidemics. The resulting process of catching up and the modernizing strategies and practices were strongly characterized by knowledge transfer and adapting and applying knowledge by orientating toward best practices.

In the case of public health issues in the cities of Eastern Europe, we can observe a twofold knowledge transfer. First, medical and biological findings were transferred into applied sciences, for example in the context of urban medical services. Second, local actors developed their own (practical) knowledge through applying practices and technical solutions to combat epidemics and with regard to hygienic food production. Hereby, scientific findings not only from microbiology and medicine, but also from the rapidly developing field of civil engineering, were combined with new technical innovations and implemented through the adaptation of best practice solutions from other cities, according to the particular local needs. As a consequence, these actors in Eastern European cities often discovered breakthroughs, or at least solutions that were frequently more modern than those developed in the Western metropolises, where the infrastructures had been set up years before according to what was now outdated knowledge.

Generally, this twofold knowledge transfer in the cities found its expression in the slogan of "public health," which became a political topic concentrated on the containment of infectious diseases around 1900. The discourse on "public health" – and in particular "hygiene" – developed in the last third of the nineteenth century, and these became central concepts in the debates on social reform and city modernization. To my mind, they are a consequence of the rise of "social security" as a societal value and norm in modern societies. "Public health" debates and measures were thus closely tied in with technical infrastructures, as well as urban planning, so that the implementation of such measures provoked a rearrangement of the urban landscape, too. Public health was, therefore, next to nationalization the leading issue driving the transformation of the cityscape and legitimate measures in urban planning, for example, the restoration of whole districts.

So, applied knowledge played a crucial role in developments in urban planning and thus in local politics, which aimed to modernize and nationalize Eastern European cities. In the following, I will explain and expand on this phenomenon through the example of Lviv, but, in order to comprehend the interplay with nationalizing discourses, it is first necessary to briefly outline the population structure of Lviv and its status within the imperial frame. Second, I have to consider the extensive discourses on the "healthy city" of Lviv. Third, I want to present three examples of the implementation of applied knowledge and to show how the actors achieved this. My considerations are based, on the one hand, on a recently finished book project on the question of how local politicians tried to polonize the city[9] and, on the other hand, on the concept of emerging cites developed in collaboration with Eszter Gantner.[10] Therefore, my considerations mainly refer to local official sources published on behalf of the local government or the crownland government, like the semi-official *Gazeta Lwowska* (*Lviv's Journal*).

Lviv's Status and Population in the Late Habsburg Empire

Lviv was the capital of both the greatest and the poorest crownland of the Habsburg monarchy. Its rule over Galicia and Lviv was not generally questioned from 1870 until World War I. As all over Eastern Europe, a very typical problem was the multi-ethnic and multi-denominational structure of the population, so that Lviv was also a highly multi-ethnic and a multi-cultural city whose population consisted 1910 of about 51 percent of Polish, 28 percent of Jewish and about 18 percent of Ruthenian ethnicity.[11] As a prime example for the multi-ethnic cities of East

Central Europe, the social and denominational strata of Lviv's population was more or less determined by nationality, so that the Polish population mainly formed the middle and upper classes, while most of the Jews and Ruthenians belonged to the lower classes.

When the first part of the new crownland of Galicia and Lodomeria was annexed in 1772, Lviv was quite run-down. From that time on, due to the city's new status as a crownland capital, the population began to grow and the general cityscape was developed.[12] Even though public life was Germanized, the local Polish upper classes in particular – mainly the upper bourgeoisie – were able to regain power in local government during the revolution of 1848–1849, in which the nationality conflict with the Ruthenians arose for the first time. Lviv experienced a certain, but not really spectacular degree of urban growth, which increased at the turn of the twentieth century because of migration from the surrounding Eastern Galician countryside.[13]

In general, the empire strongly influenced the development of the cities. This was because of the Imperial Local Law (Reichsgemeindegesetz) of 1862, which defined fields of (only) local interests. The crownland capitals and bigger, more important cities were granted the right to have their own laws (a statute), giving them autonomy particularly in the areas of urban planning and development, charity, culture and lower education. The local government only achieved an autonomous status in 1870. But during a period of about ten years, when the statute as the fundamental law for this status was discussed, the Polish actors successfully established Polish as the official local language and were able to assert their influence over local issues, too, because of election regulations favoring the Polish bourgeoisie. Most of the 100 aldermen were Polish, while only a handful Ruthenians were elected up until the first decade of the twentieth century, after which no Ruthenian representatives were elected at all. The city council could include, at most, 20 Jewish aldermen – though this rate was never achieved. To put it sharply: from the 1860s onwards, the city council (and because of that, the whole local government) was mainly a Polish arena, and was defended as such until World War I. Local government issues were hence interpreted as Polish issues. However, Lviv's local government was loyal toward the Habsburgian dynasty – just as the Polish elites in general never acted disloyal toward the monarch – and never questioned the affiliation to the Habsburg Empire. As a result, the local authorities were quite free to pursue their own agenda of establishing a Polish town and an (unofficial) Polish spare capital.

As Lviv only experienced some progress in small-scale industries, the social question was not solved at all. Unskilled, unemployed or day laborers often migrated from the rural provinces into the city where they made up the lower demographic strata of the population. The increased poverty caused by this was a main reason for the poor public health conditions. Other reasons could be found in local infrastructures, particularly the insufficient sewage system and poor water supply from wells that were in contact with ground and surface water. Hence, in the early 1880s, Lviv had, alongside Pest (40.0) and Trieste (35.5), the highest annual mortality rate within the Habsburg monarchy of 35 per 1,000 inhabitants, while this rate was only 23.7 in London and 24.3 in Brussels, while Paris stood at 25.1 and Berlin at 31.4.[14] A significant contribution to the rate in Lviv came from various epidemics such as cholera, which last broke out in the city in 1894, as well as tuberculosis, typhoid, etc., which are mainly the result of unhygienic, unhealthy and impoverished living conditions.

The Local Political Discourse in Lviv of the Modern "Healthy City"

The starting point for a Polish-Galician modernization discourse was the perceived backwardness of the Habsburg crownland of Galicia and its capital Lviv. In 1888, Stanisław Szczepanowski, a member of the Galician Diet, strikingly described Galician poverty by using the slogan "Galician misery"[15] in his work on the region's economy. This perception of backwardness and poverty was not new at all, but it had become more and more clear in the 1880s. Attentive local actors repeatedly referred to the imperial statistics on health conditions during political debates in the city council and recognized that there was an urgent need to develop the city. However, because it was necessary to borrow several million imperial Guldens in order to improve urban living conditions, it was only at the turn of the 1890s, when a new generation of councilors gained power in the city council, that progress could finally be made. The vision for the city was epitomized in the slogan of "beautiful Lviv" ("*piękny Lwów*"), which quickly developed into a code of practice for all political activity in the city.[16] Here, "beauty" did not only mean embellishing Lviv by creating a modern cityscape with boulevards (like the *Wały hetmańskie*/Hetman's dam [Figure 6.1] and the less important Ulica Akademicka/Academic Street [Figure 6.2]), but also by accomplishing order through the creation of hygienic living conditions in "tidied up" residential districts and by increasing the general wealth of the city.[17] This master plan reflected the aspiration for Lviv to become not only a regional metropolis, but also to operate as an (unofficial) Polish capital. The master plan of "beautiful Lviv" was launched and immediately progressed at the beginning of the 1890s, because preparations were already underway for the General Crownland Exposition, which was to take place in 1894. An important argument for this acceleration was that the visitors coming from the crownland, the empire and abroad should get the "best impressions" of the city.[18]

A main reason for organizing the exposition was the objective to economically develop the country and its capital. During the planning phase, which involved more or less all the regional elites, the local politicians

Figure 6.1 Hetman's dam/Waly hetmanskie, postcard 1915.

Source: Private collection of Heidi Hein-Kircher

Figure 6.2 Academic Street/Ulica Akademicka, postcard 1917.

Source: Private collection of Heidi Hein-Kircher

recognized how important Lviv's modernization was for the city itself and the whole country. This insight led to the vision of creating a "metropolitan character"[19] and providing Lviv with the "importance of a metropolis" ("*wielkomiejskiego znaczenia*"), which could not be realized without basic urban development.[20] During the planning phase, the organizers expanded their objectives: The exposition was to function as a showcase of the Galician economy on the one hand, and, on the other hand, it should present important regional achievements in (small) industries, handicrafts and public health in order to influence the further development of Lviv and Galicia. A third aim of the event, also with regard to influencing provincial progress, was to exhibit up-to-date technical achievements from outside the country that offered solutions for actual problems. The (privately financed) pavilion of William Lindley[21] was set up with this in mind, even though he appeared to be promoting himself.[22]

Within this frame, we can observe that the discourse of the "healthy city"[23] only emerged in connection with the developing discourse around modernization and "beautification." For all members of the local government and for the local (Polish) social and political elites, it went without saying that the "beautiful" and "modern" and hence "tidied up" and "healthy" Lviv should only be Polish. For example, the 1912 annual report of the local beautification society (Towarzystwo rozwoju i upiększenia miasta Lwowa), an association in which political and civil actors collaborated on initiatives to modernize the city, pointed out that all new buildings should be explicitly modern and, at the same time, have a national, i.e. Polish, character.[24] In this way, the local actors wanted to position themselves and their city as the unofficial Polish capital instead of the "unfree" Warsaw, which was at that time being subjected to strict Russification politics. Accordingly, the idea was for Lviv to have a "really European style"[25] and to part of the mainstream of European urban development, even though it was situated on the periphery of the Habsburg Empire. The topos of Europeanness[26] as a vision of city development is – as in every Eastern European national movement – a part of the national consciousness, because the connection with (Western) European modernity was considered as proof of Polish national capabilities. Catching up with the advances in urban development in other cities was the overall political aim and the demonstration of local (Polish) performances was an important part of this vision in the eyes of the local politicians.[27]

Therefore, Lviv's development in all spheres of local life was interpreted as a Polish performance, and it was not considered convenient at all to characterize the initial processes of city development and of urbanization, and hence the prioritization and adaptation of modern knowledge for these developments, as supranational processes. On account of this, it becomes clear that knowledge transfer, especially into applied knowledge convenient to the local conditions, was intrinsically connected with the efforts to position Lviv as the Galician and Polish capital at the turn of the twentieth century. As a consequence, improving the conditions of public health was the main challenge for the political actors in demonstrating that they could catch up with (Western) European standards.

Networks of Knowledge Transfer

Urban development was particularly understood in terms of sanitation and of making the city "healthier."[28] Sanitation was closely linked to "public health" and therefore became a local political issue and part of a politically formulated catalog of measures; the "city's hygiene" should:

> consider the community as single entity regardless of any difference in class, because in fact the benefits of sanitation work . . . are for everyone, and the neglect of one part of the community is at the same time a threat to the health of all the other parts.[29]

In regard to public health, the living conditions in Lviv were quite poor. As previously mentioned, the mortality rate here was higher than in Western European metropolises and in most other larger Habsburgian cities, and was particularly impacted by epidemics like cholera, typhus and measles. In the eyes of the local physicians, Lviv was even the "capital of tuberculosis" ("*stolica gruźlicy*").[30] To put it shortly: Improving the public health conditions was one of the main challenges in the modernization process, not least because the city itself was quite poor and could not afford to implement new, large-scale developments. In order to understand how this problem was overcome, we have to look closer at the decision-making processes in the local government.

A prerequisite of the discourse was for actors to engage in an international exchange of knowledge, like visiting the German Cities' Exhibition in 1903[31] or the Dresden Hygiene Exposition in 1911 and sending delegations of city council members and the public health officers to the major cities of the German Empire and the Habsburg Monarchy to investigate local solutions and best practices to be adopted in Lviv.[32] Such findings and proposals were often taken on in the wake of the cholera or other epidemics, but also as a response to the high mortality rate and the high rate of tuberculosis within the city.

Securitizing discourses also played an important role here. The perception of "healthy" versus "annoying"/"unhealthy" or "poor" was connected with the perception of "secure" as opposed to "unsafe"/"threatening."[33] Thus, local actors acknowledged and responded to the close reciprocal relationship between "making order" ("*uporządkowanie*"), "cleaning up" i.e. cleanliness, and "beautification," which together constituted the face of modernization. "Cleaning up" meant that the cleaning of public spaces, and garbage and sewage disposal were determined by the city's own urban regulations. The health threats of epidemics distressed the urban society and its political elites and exacerbated the existing social destabilization and insecurity that already existed because of socio-economic and political change and, in particular, the growing conflict between nationalities. Arguments based on environmental conditions and natural phenomena were therefore used as a means to legitimizing political-ethnic objectives and attitudes. However, this uncertainty was not projected onto the Ruthenian, but mostly onto the Jewish population, especially since they tended to live, unlike the Ruthenians, in spatially cramped neighborhoods.[34]

As we can see, the actors linked the city's supposed backwardness with the social and particularly multi-ethnic make up of its population. Especially in the discourses on cholera, a link was made between outbreaks of the disease and the Jewish population. This was particularly clear in the debate on the defense against cholera in 1892, where cholera was closely associated with the "worst disorder" of the Jewish quarter. In this context, "disorder" referred to dirty sewers or very cramped housing and poor living conditions. Discussions often revolved around religious aspects, but it became clear that problems were in fact rooted in social and urban environmental problems – and these discourses always outweighed the "Jewish" question. Thus, the cramped Cheder schools (*chadorim*) were considered as a symbol of Jewish backwardness. In fact, they were rather the result of overcrowding and bad health conditions in the poor Jewish neighborhoods, which resulted in outbreaks, for example, of scarlet fever around 1900. Thus, the focus of debates over health was skewed by anti-Semitic resentments, especially the idea that Jewish districts, as "breeding grounds" for epidemics, posed a danger to the "intelligent" – that is, more educated and wealthier – population in the city. The 1908 report of the Municipal Health Council, for example, emphasized that the inhabitants of Jewish quarters, in particular the III. (Żółkiew) district, constituted a "major source of epidemics," which, in turn, had a significant impact on health conditions throughout the city and led to further consequences for the whole country.[35] One councilor in 1914 even identified this district as an "evil" of the city and proposed that it be demolished in order to eradicate the "source of disease."[36] The councilor argued that, as long as "we" [the council] did not come together to bring this neighborhood to order, "we are sitting on a powder keg."[37] Thus, the spread of epidemics, which was a major threat to the urban population, was seen to be the result of the lack of public hygiene, which was reinforced by poverty. However, the reasons given were not based on social status, but on ethno-denominational grounds, which included perceiving the Jews as a "danger" to the city due to the social and sanitary security risk they were seen to represent. Anti-Semitic attitudes thus became more entrenched. However, the data for tuberculosis deaths shows that such statements on the sanitary conditions were influenced by anti-Jewish resentments, because there were significantly more reports of Christians dying than Jews.[38] These discourses formed the background of modernization discourses in regard to the implementation of certain decisions and practices. During the period of municipal autonomy, the measures for the "recovery" ("*uzdrowienia*") of the city developed into central objectives, but the local government could not solve the underlying social problems at all.

To catch up with (Western) European standards and living conditions, it was necessary to undertake initiatives to improve every area of public life. At the turn of the nineteenth and twentieth centuries, the innovations being introduced in smaller cities were at the forefront of European urban development. For example, in some metropolises like London, expensive urban sewage systems had been installed decades before and, though they originally represented the most modern advances in technical and hygienic knowledge, they had become quite outdated by the end of the century. In contrast, minor German cities, where the latest engineering innovations were being developed in the area of urban services, were considered the forerunners in the field. Frederic C. Howe pointed out from an American perspective in 1913:

> But there are cities that justify hope, cities . . . that consciously promote comfort, convenience, happiness, life. Such cities are to be found in Germany, and to a lesser s degree in the other countries of Europe as well. . . . The German city is an experiment-station for all of us.[39]

For this reason, city expositions like the one in Dresden in 1903[40] and the exhibition for Western Prussian lands in Düsseldorf in 1912 were generally important meeting places where information about the latest innovations in the field of public health innovations could be shared. Being nodes in the network of knowledge exchange, it was perhaps more important to see the realization of technical solutions in the cities themselves. For this reason, the local government in Lviv decided not only to send out delegations – for example, to the hygiene exposition in Berlin in 1883 and to Dresden in 1911 – but also, before deciding on measures, it sent delegations of councilors and leading urban employees to various cities to investigate the local solutions in operation, as examples of best practices. Coming back, the delegation would not only report to the city council, but often wrote and published treatises combining descriptions of the various services and innovations in the cities with reflections on the conditions and possibilities of applying these solutions in Lviv.[41]

The scientific findings in regard to bacteriology and the routes of infection made it clear to the actors that it was not only the poor but also the social and political elites who were threatened by disease. They recognized that one main problem causing catastrophic health conditions was the lack of technical infrastructures in the city. Consequently, the improvement of these infrastructures became an important political topic, so that during local election campaigns in the 1890s, for example, the interest group of (local) engineers (Komitet Techników) was quite successful. Expertise and political engagement were thus quite closely interwoven. Technical knowledge came to have a direct impact on political decisions, which were enforced by the more and more professionalizing local administration (magistrate). It is important to remember that, in contrast to other emerging cities, Lviv's city council engaged its own experts and selected examples of best practices itself. In doing this, the councilors wanted to demonstrate in each major project that the home-grown, i.e. Polish, experts were well connected and capable.[42]

Thanks to the progress in biological and medical research, the contamination of the water pipes had been identified as a major reason for the unhealthy living conditions in Lviv. Thus, improving the sewage system and the fresh water supply were considered to be the most crucial challenges facing the city.[43] Particularly the renovation and construction of the sewage system as an alluvial system was central to the creation of improved local health conditions, particularly as it would eliminate the problem of feces in the city streets. Local experts had recognized that the Poltva river was not only the "main fabric of perfume,"[44] i.e. the main source of smells, but also contributed significantly to the spread of epidemics. As the local gazette *Gazeta Lwowska* pointed out, there was an urgent need to upgrade the city's sewage system in order to combat the spread of malaria. The sewage system still consisted of partly leaky wooden pipes built in the eighteenth century, so the councilors regarded the canalization of the Poltva river, including its inflowing streams and the surrounding marches that were used for sewage treatment until the 1890s, as a priority in improving the local health conditions. Particularly between 1883 and 1905, the sewage system was modernized. A number of other streams, springs and ponds were drained, filled and removed, too, while a separate system was installed. In contrast to other cities, where sewage systems had been built some years before, it was possible to use modern concrete pipes. Apart from improving public health, the canalization of the Poltva water system as the main feature of the new sewage system had consequences in the area of urban planning, too. Because its source was located in the town center, the connections between districts were interrupted by the river and the associated swamps. At the end of the city council's session, the mayor stated proudly that even the Viennese council was looking at adopting similar measures to improve public health there; in their plans to canalize the small Wien River, the Lviv solution was assessed to be the most suitable ("*najodpowiedniejsze*") compared to solutions in other cities.[45] This example demonstrates that, particularly when it came to technical infrastructures, the best practice solutions were not necessarily developed within the major metropolises.

The canalization of the Poltva river resulted in a number of new spaces opening up within the city, such as the Jesuit Gardens, which acted as small "green lungs" in the urban landscape.[46] This in particular provided the local government with an important opportunity to open up the city to modern planning ideas. Thus, in 1890, in an article on the construction progress, the *Gazeta Lwowska* enthusiastically reported that:

> with each passing year our city [Lviv] continues to change its old physiognomy – it is expanding, rising up and becoming beautified. . . . already today Lviv is beginning, in its outward appearance, to resemble the major European capitals.[47]

These words show that the modernization of the urban landscape and of public health were dependent on each other. The inclusion of the Poltva river into the underground sewer system, which was initiated primarily due to sanitary reasons, led to the creation of a "new center," with the *Wały Hetmańskie*/Hetman's Dam as its main boulevard, leading from the Municipal Theater, inaugurated in 1901, to St. Mary's Place Square. Public buildings, hotels, coffee houses and restaurants lined the street. But, even before the construction of the theater and the other buildings had started in 1897, this area was hailed as the "most metropolitan vision" of the city: the impressive boulevard *Wały Hetmańskie* should thus find a duly urbanistic bargain.[48] This clearly shows the interconnection between public health measures – carried out due to a perceived social threat through bad hygienic conditions – and urban landscaping, which was a phenomenon that characterized all modernizing cities in the nineteenth century.

The city council ascertained that the fresh water supply was inadequate for both private and public use. Thus, establishing a fresh water supply was another major challenge in terms of public health. Being situated on the European watershed, Lviv had a general water supply problem anyway, due to topography, but this was exacerbated by a growing population. Thus, the council noted with concern in September 1899 that typhoid fever and malaria would probably be transmitted through water pipes and that, in this way, not only the poor, but also the "intelligentsia," would be affected.[49]

It was necessary to supply the growing city with "healthy water" from fresh, clear springs outside the city and not with water from fountains within the city, which were constantly threatened by bacteriological contaminations.[50] Even if local wells were cleaned several times a year, neither the well water nor the surface groundwater, which was also often used, was healthy. That is why, from the beginning of the 1890s, the provision of spring water became a priority for the city of Lviv. The council carried out some feasibility analyses and, in the late 1890s, decided to build a technically elaborate waterworks system[51] 30 km in length.

Right from the start of the planning phase, physicians and engineers worked closely and energetically together to promote the realization of the project between 1899 and 1901.[52] For this purpose, four German experts were invited to Lviv in 1896 to share their expertise, because Juliusz Hochberger, the magistrate engineer responsible for the works, looked to Berlin for solutions, for which he was blamed by critics who felt that he should have been focusing on engaging local experts. Rather than commissioning Galician firms, he brought in German firms to construct the waterworks systems.[53]

It was not until the end of the first decade of the twentieth century that the new water supply system finally met the demands of the city. This was because industrialization and a rising urban population had significantly increased the rate of water consumption.

As in other cities, the building code reflected the current scientific knowledge of "healthy" housing, which was intended to be affordable for the poorest section of the population.[54] In addition, a key area of responsibility for "public health" was the "cleanup" and "regulating" of neighborhoods and, thus, of the densely populated residential areas. In 1890, 60.6 percent of all dwellings in Lviv had no more than two rooms. As in other cities, a significant problem was the quality of the apartments: In 26.4 percent of these homes, there lived between six and 11 people, and another 2.2 percent housed between 12 and 20 people, which was due not only to the poverty of the urban lower classes, but also the problem of rising rents as a result of high construction costs.[55] The number of people per apartment continued to increase, which significantly worsened public health conditions. Of particular importance for the creation of "healthy" housing conditions in Lviv were the building regulations, which were meant to ensure that the latest scientific findings in regard to well-lit and well-ventilated housing, would be implemented. Unlike in other major cities, an overall concept and a regulatory plan failed to be designed until the outbreak of World War I. Nonetheless, because there was an emerging consensus among scholars (and politicians) that health conditions were closely linked to housing conditions. It was understood, for example, that the fight against tuberculosis needed bright and well aired apartments. But how to achieve this proved to be another major problem for the councilors in their search for best practice solutions.

Adaptation of Best Practice Solutions

Everywhere in Europe, building regulations were considered of particular importance in the creation of "healthy" housing conditions, which we will discuss as a second example of how best practice solutions were adapted to local conditions. Building codes were a major instrument through which to apply scientific knowledge and use it for practical regulations:

they reflected the current scientific knowledge about "healthy" housing, which it was believed should be affordable for even the poorest parts of the population.[56] They decreed, for example, that new houses had to provide all apartments with enough sunlight and fresh air to fight tuberculosis and other illnesses resulting from cramped living conditions, and that they should be connected to the local sewage and water supply systems.[57] The designers of building regulations generally tried not only to implement recent scientific achievements, but also to orientate their designs toward regulations in other cities, for example, in regard to building lines. In 1892, a draft for an intended revision of the building code in Lviv formulated this task, for instance, by pointing at the "zeitgeist."[58]

Therefore, in Lviv's building code of 1885, cellar dwellings, except for souterrain on slopes, and loft apartments, except for those with steep roofs on palaces, were forbidden in newly constructed buildings, while sewer drains were mandatory. The building regulations from 1885 became obsolete a few years later, but only a minimal revision took place in 1909. As the changes only concerned new buildings, the old ones could conserve the status quo, because a general sanitation plan was not decreed.[59]

This was because of the political implications. Since the proposed measures significantly infringed on the rights of homeowners, who were also the city council's voters, only a minimal level of consensus was ultimately reached. Apart from the respect for the voters' interests, a further major reason lay in the fact that, according to the magistrate's records of 1914, a cadastral register, which was necessary for an appropriate excess planning of the urban area, was lacking. This also makes clear that it was the city council that failed to make the official structures efficient enough, especially in technical fields, and thus they failed to lay the necessary foundations for a well-planned and efficient urban development. This example shows clearly the limits of concrete knowledge application.

Conclusion

Lviv developed in the last third of nineteenth century into a modern city with a rapid, but not dramatic, rate of growth. Predominantly, the public health infrastructures that were implemented here concerned the improvement of public health. The reason for that was, on the one hand, recent findings that the spread of epidemics was not limited to the lower social strata and the "other" ethnic group – mainly Ruthenians and poor Jews – but concerned the whole population. The local actors adopted modern knowledge through best practices in order to make the city "European" and "modern." Within this process, the General Crownland Exposition of 1894 functioned as a catalyst, because of the necessity to present the city at its best to all visitors. The master plan of the city's embellishment comprised mainly the implementation of modern infrastructures, from the "dernier cri" – an electric tramway – to modern boulevards and up-to-date sewage systems. As we can see from these measures, including the exposition itself, public health issues played a key role in these advancements.

In the case of Lviv around 1900, city modernization was not thinkable without recourse to Western best practice solutions in technical infrastructures and urban planning. The aldermen and the officials oriented themselves particularly toward German solutions, which were at this time leading in regard to technical urban innovations. Knowledge was thus transferred in the form of best practice solutions – in a way that was quite comfortable for the local decision makers. As in other emerging cities in East Central Europe, the local government could also select applications that they considered to be the best fit for local conditions rather than operating according to a trial and error principle.

But the case of Lviv also shows the limits of such knowledge application, which lay beyond financial questions: The practical and technical applications of the latest scientific knowledge in urban development, which we have explored here, show clearly that, in spite of the good will of local functionaries and engineers, the application and orientation toward best practices was ultimately based on a nationalizing impetus. What this meant in the case of Lviv was that, in the eyes of the aldermen, engineers, technicians, etc., any modernization measures should "be and think Polish," and promote Polish engineers, firms etc. The actors did not only want to make the city "healthier"; they wanted to make it modern and Polish at the same time.

In this regard, we can observe that the practices and strategies that were adopted were in many ways complementary: the ostensible aim of making the city "healthier" and more "beautiful" was legitimized by making the city "modern" – moreover, with regard to city development, these adjectives were used nearly as synonyms. To catch up with the latest trends was hence an aim in the not explicitly, but implicitly, palpable race between every regional city that was emerging at this time as a provincial capital and/or a regional metropolis. The underlying argument was to "Europeanize" the city, to give it a pan-European "face" with local characteristics. Being modern without being European was not conceivable at all. Through this process, the local politicians could demonstrate how efficient they were. For our question, it is also important to acknowledge that these strategies and their realization in the cityscape "up-dated" these cities that were perceived as backward, replacing this feeling with the experience of being highly modern. To demonstrate this was to attempt a virtual shift – from the periphery of the Habsburg Empire into the middle of Europe. At the same time, the modernizing process and this demonstration constituted a realization of nationalizing concepts, too.

This objective encouraged efficiency among the local political elites – the Poles – and legitimized their rule and their polonizing measures. Furthermore, through these politics they fulfilled "their" civilizing mission: bringing "European modernity" (and hence culture and knowledge) into the rural Galician province. As we can see through the example of Lviv, in Eastern European multi-ethnic regions the overlaying concept was that of nationality, which shaped even technical and infrastructural modernization. These processes were only possible because of multi-directional knowledge transfer(s) and the practice(s) of using current knowledge in emerging cities where it could be applied as local best practices. Lviv was hence no longer a provincial, peripheral city, but a regional center on a par with other European metropolises.

Notes

1. As the author is part of the collaborative project "Dynamics of Security" (SFB/TRR 138) of the German Research Association, the article is influenced by the conceptional work on "securitization": The discursive perception and aiming at producing security for one society. Using Lviv's name is quite complicated: Although the Habsburgian denomination was "Lemberg," "Lwów" was used for the interwar period (and early modern times) under Polish rule, and Ukrainian "L'viv" refers to its belonging to Ukraine since 1945, I use the English version ("Lviv"), but I refer to the Ukrainian population with the Habsburgian denomination "Ruthenians."
2. That is, "*to dziś powiedziśby można, że wszystkim niezdrówź*," *Gazeta Lwowska*, March 10, 1881.
3. Ibid.
4. That is, "*duch czasu*," e.g. *Gazeta Lwowska*, November 19, 1910.
5. B. Tscherkes, "Julian Sacharijewytsch und der Einfluss österreichischer Architekturvorbilder in Galizien," in *Bürgerliche Selbstdarstellung. Städtebau, Architektur, Denkmäler*, ed. Hanns Haas and Hannes Stekl (Wien: Böhlau, 1995), 129–144; P. Czartoryski-Sziler, "Wielce zapomniani. Julian i Alfred Zachariewiczowie – sławni architekci Lwowa," *Nasz Dziennik*, www.lwow.com.pl/naszdziennik/zachariewiczowie.html, accessed January 14, 2020.
6. Asa Briggs, *Victorian Cities* (Harmondsworth: Penguin Books, 1975), 33–34.
7. Dieter Schott, *Europäische Urbanisierung (1000–2000). Eine umwelthistorische Einführung* (Köln: Böhlau, 2014), 230.
8. Jan C. Behrends and Martin Kohlrausch, "Introduction," in *Races to Modernity: Metropolitan Aspirations in Eastern Europe 1890–1940*, ed. Jan C. Behrends and Martin Kohlrausch (Budapest: Central European University, 2014), 1–20, p. 3.
9. Heidi Hein-Kircher, *Lembergs 'polnischen Charakter' sichern. Kommunalpolitik in einer multiethnischen Stadt der Habsburgermonarchie zwischen 1861/62 und 1914* (Stuttgart: Steiner, 2020).
10. Eszter Gantner and Heidi Hein-Kircher, "'Introduction, Emerging Cities': Knowledge and Urbanization in Europe's Borderlands 1880–1945," *Journal of Urban History* 43, no. 4 (2017): 575–586.
11. Hein-Kircher, *Lembergs 'polnischen Charakter' sichern*, 15.

12. Overview: Yaroslav Hrytsak, "L'viv: A Multicultural History Through the Centuries," in *L'viv: A City in the Crosscurrents of Culture*, ed. Johan Czaplicka (Cambridge, MA: Harvard University Press, 2005), 45–75.
13. In 1850/1851, the population of Lviv was around 69,000, in 1869 it was 87,000, in 1880 it was 103,500, in 1890 it was 119,400, in 1900 it was 195,800 and in 1913 it was 212,000. See *Kurzgefasste Zusammenstellung statistischer Daten über die königl. Hauptstadt Lemberg im Kronlande Galizien* (Lviv, 1851), 10–11; Ewa Callahan, "Struktura wyznaniowa i narodowościowa Lwowa w latach 1857–1931," *Literatura Ludowa* 59, no. 4–5 (1995): 57–70.
14. *Gazeta Lwowska*, March 10, 1881.
15. Stanisław Szczepanowski, *Nędza Galicji w cyfrach i program energicznego rozwoju gospodarstwa krajowego* (Lwów: Gubrynowicz & Schmidt, 1888).
16. *Gazeta Lwowska*, November 16, 1862.
17. Teofil Merunowicz, *Rozwój miasta Lwowa* (Lwów: Nakładem Wł. Bełzem, 1877), 5.
18. *Gazeta Lwowska*, November 16, 1892. As this was generally an important issue in all expositions at this time, it was of particular importance for the organizers.
19. Nathaniel Wood, *Becoming Metropolitan: Urban Selfhood and the Making of Modern Cracow* (DeKalb: Northern Illinois University Press, 2010).
20. Zakład Narodowy im. Ossolińskich, *Papiery Rutowskiego*, 13405/III, 72; *Sprawozdanie wydziału Towarzystwa dla Upiększenia* (Lwów: Towarzystwo dla Upiększenia Miasta Lwowa, 1912), 14.
21. The Englishman William Lindley (1808–1900) is one of the most important urban planners in the second half of nineteenth century, particularly with regard to sewage and water treatment and to railway systems. Lindley was involved into the urban planning of Hamburg, Frankfurt-am-Main, and also Warsaw (filter system), Prague, Budapest, St. Petersburg and Moscow. The reasons why Lindley financed his own pavilion, are not clear, but I would suppose that he tried to "advertise" himself.
22. *Katalog Powszechnej Wystawy Krajowej we Lwowie roku 1894* (Lwów: Piller, 1894).
23. On important milestones in the European discourses on "public health," see Alfred Grotjahn, *Die hygienische Kultur im 19. Jahrhundert* (Berlin: Aufklärung, 1902); Alfred Grotjahn, "Vorwort," *Jahresbericht über die Fortschritte und Leistungen auf dem Gebiete der Sozialen Hygiene und Demographie* 3 (1904): III–XV.
24. *Sprawozdanie*, 14.
25. "*W stylu prawdziwie europejskim*"; Merunowicz, *Rozwój*, 96.
26. Nathaniel D. Wood, "Not Just the National: Modernity and the Myth of Europe in the Capital Cities of Central and Southeastern Europe," in *Capital Cities in the Aftermath of Empires: Planning in Central and Southeastern Europe*, ed. Emily Gunzburger Makas and Tanja Damljanovic-Conley (London: Routledge, 2010), 258–269.
27. Teofil Merunowicz, "Rozwój Lwowa w okresie samorządu," in *Ilustrowany Przewodnik po Lwowie i powszechnej Wystawie Krajowej* (Lwów, 1894), 91–97, p. 91.
28. Attilio Rella, "Die Assanirung der Städte in Oesterreich-Ungarn 1848–1898," *Zeitschrift des Oesterr. Ingenieur- und Architekten-Vereins* 51, no. 17 (1899): 273–282.
29. Ibid., 273.

30. Berner Włodzimierz, "Stan sanitarny, ochrona zdrowia i sytuacja epidemiologiczna chorób zakaźnych we Lwowie w okresie autonomii galicyjskiej (lata 60./70. XIX w. – do 1914 r.)," *Przegląd epidemiologiczny* 61, no. 4 (2007): 815–825, pp. 818–820.
31. Kazimierz Bruchnalski, *Szkolnictwo Ludowe na Wystawie Niemieckich Miast w Dreźnie w r. 1903* (Lwów: Towarzystwo dla Upiększenia Miasta Lwowa, 1904), in State Archive of the Lviv Region (Deržavnyj Archiv L'vivs'koï Oblasti, DALO, fond (f.) 3, opis (op.) 1, sprava (spr.) 4898, 1–16.
32. Sending delegations to expositions or to explore best practices in other European cities through study tours were quite popular practices; see Marjata Hietala, *Services and Urbanization at the Turn of the Century* (Helsinki: Suomen Historiallinen Seura, 1987), 355–381.
33. Hein-Kircher, *Lembergs 'polnischen Charakter' sichern*, 190–191.
34. Ibid., 210–215.
35. *Korespondencja ratuszowa*, in DALO, f. 3, op. 1, spr. 5418, 84, October 19, 1908.
36. *Gazeta Lwowska*, April 25, 1914, see too: Korespondencja Ratuszowa, DALO, f. 3, op. 1, spr. 5418, 136–138, 150–151.
37. Ibid.
38. Wiadomości Statystyczne o Stosunkach Krajowych 15, 1912–1922, 39–41.
39. Frederic C. Howe, *European Cities at Work* (London: Leipsic, 1913), VIII.
40. Hietala, *Services*, 23–24.
41. For example, Bruchnalski, *Szkolnictwo Ludowe na Wystawie Niemieckich Miast w Dreźnie w r. 1903*, in DALO, f. 3, op. 1, spr. 4898, 1–16.
42. *Gazeta Lwowska*, March 20, 1896 (criticizing the works of the Habsburgs architects Fellner & Helmer), and March 27, 1904. See also *Sprawozdanie*.
43. *Gazeta Lwowska*, March 10, 1881, May 19, 1881, April 26, 1893.
44. *Gazeta Lwowska*, July 11, 1891.
45. *Gazeta Lwowska*, April 26, 1893.
46. See Angela Schwarz, *Der Park in der Metropole. Urbanes Wachstum und städtische Parks im 19. Jahrhundert* (Bielefeld: Transcript, 2005).
47. *Gazeta Lwowska*, August 8, 1890; see also: Mykola Bevz, "Urbanistychni transformatsiyi tsentralnoyi chastyny mista Lvova u XIX-XX st.," in *Arkhitektura Halychyny Architectura Halyčchyny XIX–XX st. Vybrani materialy mizhnarodnoho sympoziumu, prysvyachenoho 150-richchyu zasnuvannya Derzhavnoho universytetu L'vivs'ka politekhnika*, ed. Bohdan Cherkes (L'viv: Akademia Politechnycza, 1999), 362–377.
48. *Gazeta Lwowska*, December 28, 1892.
49. *Gazeta Lwowska*, September 28, 1899. Mieczysław Dunin-Wąsowicz, *Woda do picia we Lwowie. Rozbiory wód wodociągowych i studziennych* (Lwów: Miasto Lwów, 1894).
50. This question was discussed by the city council without any allusion to solutions in other cities like Paris or Vienna, but generally a lot of cities found such solutions for their water supply problems, because pumping facilities were improved and the water supply in the growing cities too short.
51. Józef Tuszyński, *Kilka uwag technicznych w sprawie nowo założonego wodociągu wulecki* (Lwów: Miasto Lwów, 1886).
52. *Sprawozdanie komisyi Rady miejskiej o wodociągach dla miasta Lwowa* (Lwów: Miasto Lwów, 1898); Stanisław Aleksandrowicz, *Wodociąg lwowski* (Lwów: Miasto Lwów 1902).
53. *Gazeta Lwowska,* March 5, 1896, February 7, 1896, March 16, 1899.
54. Hein-Kircher, *Lembergs 'polnischen Charakter' sichern*, 165–166.
55. Berner, "Stan," 816.

56. Hein-Kircher, *Lembergs 'polnischen Charakter' sichern,* 165–166.
57. Antoni Pawlikowski, "Stosunki zdrowotne," in *Miasto Lwów w okresie samorządu 1870–1895* (Lviv, 1896), 265–282, p. 269.
58. CDIAL, Bibliothek, *Szkic projektu ustawy budowniczej dla krol. stoł. miasta Lwowa*; generally: Peter-Heinz Marauschek, "Graz. Strukturwandel einer Stadt im Lichte ihrer Bauvorschriften (1856–1968)" (Ph.D. Diss., University of Graz, 2010).
59. Landes-Gesetz- und Verordnungsblatt für das Königreich Galizien und Lodomerien sammt dem Großherzogthume Krakau No. 31/1885 and No. 111/1909.

7 Improving Health in a Mediterranean City

Barcelona and the European Network (1931–1937)

Celia Miralles Buil

Introduction

In April 1937, in the midst of the Spanish Civil War, the Tuberculosis Dispensary was inaugurated in Barcelona. According to the conservative newspaper *La Vanguardia*, this "new sanitary institution established for the service of the people [was] in line with the best of its kind in the world."[1]

Indeed, the building, planned in 1934 by the Generalitat de Catalunya,[2] combined all the most innovative ideas in terms of public health and hospital architecture of that time. The aim was to promote the most modern medicine for the benefit of the Catalonian population. Moreover, as the dispensary was entrusted to prestigious architects, it also represented architectural modernity and an important urban transformation.

Why was a dispensary, with such innovative and prestigious characteristics, built in Barcelona? How could this project go ahead, given the financial and political constraints of the time? What was at stake for the public authorities and which reasons drove them to entrust the project to expensive architects? Why did they choose to build this healthcare establishment in a neighborhood with poor hygiene standards situated in the heart of the city? Who were the key groups and individuals directly involved in its construction? How did the implemented measures fit into an international context?

Drawing on the dispensary's construction as a case study, this chapter aims to analyze the measures planned or taken to improve urban health in Barcelona. It takes into special account this interaction between local practices and international networks.

Beyond this purpose, the chapter also aims to contribute to the historiographical field specifically focused on the circulation of ideas about health in cities. Historians have studied the dissemination of ideas around public health in interurban networks.[3] They have stressed the importance of international networks – through correspondence, study travels and various international events – in the shaping of public policies at the local level.[4]

International networks have been the subject of particular attention, considering the attempts to establish “an international health order,”[5] especially during the interwar years.[6]

What was the place of Spain in these networks? From 1921 onwards, the League of Nations Health Organization, helped by the Rockefeller Foundation, tried to federate health initiatives around the world.[7] The League began to publish statistical reports about the state of health in various European countries,[8] including Spain. These reports showed that Spain remained far behind other European countries in terms of life expectancy, due to mortality caused by infectious diseases.

For Spanish doctors and hygienists, this discrepancy could be explained by a backwardness in terms of sanitation and hygiene and the lack of a global scheme for public health.

The Spanish backwardness argument is common in Spanish medical historiography and is usually related to the assumption that little to no scientific innovation took place in Spain during that period. For instance, the historian Ricardo Campos wrote:

> Spain was not a country that produced original scientific ideas, but a peripheral center that received and reworked ideas from abroad, adapting them to its own circumstances. But this work, no matter how obscure it may be presented, was fundamental in the modernization of Spanish medicine and society and deserves to be historicized.[9]

Thus, Spain has been considered as a mere recipient of ideas coming from elsewhere, and its integration into the European modern network has been analyzed in terms of scientific transfers from a center (France, Britain or Germany) to the periphery (here Spain). Following this logic, the conditions of these transfers and their practical implementation by specific agents have been the subject of a number of studies. For instance, Isabelle Renaudet analyzed the role of medical elites in transferring scientific knowledge from France to Spain.[10]

Focusing on the Barcelonan republican context, this chapter aims to demonstrate that, in addition to the adaptation of models from elsewhere, the strategies actors developed in order to be included in international networks also involved developing their own original models.

It argues that this articulation between adaptation and innovation can be understood by observing the rhetoric of modernity in the discourses. Furthermore, the study of such discourses allows us to question the core binary division of center-periphery, frequently used by historians. There are at least two reasons for taking this approach. On the one hand, for the actors, the (so-called) “modernity” could come from anywhere, including medium-sized cities or Southern and Eastern European cities. On the other hand, the actors at that time did not use this concept to define or measure the difference or distance between their city and the rest of the world.

To carry out this analysis, the chapter focuses on a number of Barcelonan public actors who participated in the construction of the new dispensary. Indeed, in building this modern healthcare establishment, two types of professionals were particularly involved: physicians and architects, who had been charged, in more general ways, to improve health conditions in republican Barcelona. They proposed different kinds of urban measures with a view to, first, bringing medicine into the center of the city and, second, properly sanitizing the urban environment by acting directly on urban space. These two kinds of measures were combined in the designing of the dispensary. The first part of this chapter will be focused on the solutions implemented by physicians, particularly Lluís Sayé, heading the fight against tuberculosis, to bring modern medicine closer to the population. It will explain how he followed the example of European cities and adapted their actions within the specific context of Barcelona. The second part will be focused on the models used by the architects and, more precisely, by the GATCPAC (Group of Catalan Artists and Technicians for the Progress of Contemporary Architecture), a group of modern architects who designed the dispensary. Finally, the chapter will expose the strategies used by all these actors to position themselves as major players in the European modern network.

Central Discourses and Peripheral Practices to Bring Health and Medicine Into the City

This first part explains how and why the fight against tuberculosis in Barcelona took into account models from elsewhere, focusing on one major historical actor, the physician Lluís Sayé (1888–1975). It aims to show that, short of a knowledge transfer from center to periphery (which related to a search for European legitimacy), an exchange network of practices between the "peripheral" cities[11] was implemented instead.

In 1931, a proclamation of the Second Spanish Republic sanctioned a decentralized model based on "autonomies" (regional powers). This new organizational system led to a double transfer of powers to the new Generalitat de Catalunya: from the state and from the provinces.[12] This institutional and political strengthening incited the new autonomous government to rebuild the organization of social and medical care.[13] Among the many projects started, one of the most important was the establishment of a global organization in the fight against tuberculosis (which was still a major concern at the time) by Lluís Sayé, a physician who specialized in the study and treatment of tuberculosis.

Lluís Sayé can be considered one of the most influential physicians from Catalonia. In studying his biographies, it is possible to identify three phases in his medical career.[14] During the first phase, he became one of the most recognized physicians in the Catalan and European context. He studied medicine in Barcelona and specialized in tuberculosis. He worked as a private practitioner, in public hospitals and in a public tuberculosis dispensary located in Radas Street in Poble Sec, a popular neighborhood near the old center of Barcelona (see Figure 7.2) in 1921. He also taught medicine (specializing in tuberculosis) at the University of Barcelona. During this time, he published a lot of scientific works, from very specialized articles about specific medical techniques to more generalized medical books about the organization of the fight against tuberculosis.

In 1919, he was put in charge of a regional service for the treatment and prevention of tuberculosis set up by the Mancomunitat de Catalunya[15] and continued working in this prestigious role during the republican years. The second phase of his career began with the Spanish Civil War, and in 1937 he went into exile, first in France and then in Buenos Aires. He continued his work on fighting tuberculosis there until 1951. In the last part of his career, Sayé returned to Barcelona, where, despite his non-involvement with the Civil War, he was never allowed to assume the same responsibilities as he had before the war. Nevertheless, he continued working on tuberculosis, but the profession had changed a lot due to the development of new medication. Even though he fell from grace during the dictatorship, today he is still considered a pioneer in the fight against tuberculosis.[16]

During his time as head of the regional tuberculosis service, Lluís Sayé was asked by the Catalan government to propose an innovative plan to aid the fight against tuberculosis in Catalonia (1919). For this purpose, he began to study the disease in detail in order to understand how it grew and spread. He first used the data collected by the Catalan dispensaries, in particular the Central Dispensary in Radas Street where he was working.[17] This data allowed him to demonstrate that the danger of being contaminated was increased by geographical and physical proximity over an extended period of time. Sharing a house or, even worse, a bed with a contagious patient was proven to be the biggest danger. In such circumstances, the attention of healthcare authorities needed to be focused on the individual and private house or, to a lesser extent, other confined spaces such as small factories, bars, etc., while the preoccupation with streets and large public spaces was considered secondary. This focus on private spaces was in keeping with the times and could be explained by the bacteriological theory, which now became hegemonic in international medical networks. As Koch's bacillus (discovered in 1882) was considered by Lluís Sayé as the major causative agent of tuberculosis, spaces where these germs were present were considered the most dangerous. The measures taken had to be focused on the bacillus, and on people who carried it. In other words, more than focusing on the patient, Lluís Sayé was interested in the germ, and the places where it grew. In addition to his concern for private spaces, Lluís Sayé developed a theory about how the disease spread in the city.

> When tuberculosis spreads massively in a city, the first victims are children, adolescents, then women and, finally, men of all ages. The disease spreads most virulently in the poorest neighborhoods of the city, then extends to the wealthier areas, and, when the whole city is tuberculized, it spreads to the nearest rural environment.[18]

Consequently, it was decided that efforts to prevent the disease should be focused on the central and poorest neighborhood of Barcelona, which was also the nucleus of contamination.

In order to find the most efficient system for Catalonia, Lluís Sayé also learned a lot about how other countries, particularly European countries, were organizing their fight against tuberculosis.

The information gathered on health systems, hospitals and methods abroad came from numerous European contacts. According to Jacint Corbella, Lluís Sayé had connections with international medical networks at a much higher level than any other Catalan physician of his time.[19] He cites numerous trips, the first being a study trip to Hamburg just prior World War I in 1914, which enabled him to learn alongside recognized specialists (p. 144). In 1927, he visited Latin America (Córdoba, Rio de Janeiro, La Habana) and then the United States (New York), hosted by the Rockefeller Foundation. This trip enabled him to discover and develop material that would prove important for his Catalan mission. In these interwar years, he also went on many shorter trips to Paris. Lluís Sayé also participated in congresses of specialized medicine in Spain and elsewhere in Europe. For instance, in 1926, he traveled to Paris to speak at "La société médicale des hôpitaux de Paris."[20] Finally, Sayé collected many articles, from scientific as well as general press, that were sent to him by colleagues or that he found in Barcelona.[21]

A first approximation of Lluís Sayé's work leads us to think that he looked to France and French cities in the search for examples to follow. Jacint Corbella explains that the German bibliography from Sayé's first student work was quickly superseded by French scientific literature. Indeed, among the documents that helped him build his plan for Catalonia, held in the National Archive of Catalonia (ANC), we can find many clippings from the French press and French scientific papers.[22] Moreover, according to the shortened version of his speeches, the Catalan fight against tuberculosis had to be guided by the French method because it was the most suitable for the circumstances there.[23]

According to Sayé, there were in fact three models for combating tuberculosis currently being implemented in Europe, any of which could be followed by Catalonia. The British model was based on dispensaries and health education; the German model gave preference to sanatoria and the French model was a combination of the two systems, dispensaries and hospital-sanatoria.[24] He was very interested in the experiments carried out in the first two models, for example, in Framingham, United Kingdom, where the authorities decided, with good results according to Sayé, to focus their efforts on health education instead of medical care.[25] Even though the German and British experiments were interesting, Sayé thought that the French model seemed to be more flexible and adaptable to the Catalan context.

This proximity to the French system can also be explained by his integration into the European medical networks, and, in this case, into the Institut Pasteur in Paris, with which he worked increasingly from the 1920s on. Albert Calmette was one of his friends, and this friendship did much to build a strong connection between the Catalan capital and the Institut Pasteur. In 1927, for example, Calmette and Guérin were welcomed by the Catalan physicians in the public dispensary to present their BCG vaccine.

This vaccine, discovered in 1924, was the central point of Lluís Sayé's proposition, and was indeed one of the biggest investments of the Generalitat's public health policies after 1934. Lluís Sayé used the vaccine as a tool to position himself within the international network. This helped him to secure his decision-making role in the Catalan context and justified his proposals which were then in line with the common idea of "modern medicine" disseminated by the advocates of the "medical orthodoxy."[26]

However, it would be wrong to think that this "medical modernity," in the sense understood by contemporaries, was found only in France, the United Kingdom or Germany. In addition to his strategy of referring to the French model to legitimize his position, the physician also used models from other cities of Europe. As he was seeking the best system for Catalonia, Lluís Sayé carried out a substantial investigation of the characteristics of tuberculosis control in European countries. In *Las nuevas orientaciones de la lucha antituberculosa y su aplicación en España*, published in 1933,[27] Sayé used statistics and data from countries such as Brazil, Poland, Yugoslavia and New Zealand. He also listed examples of methods of combating tuberculosis developed in Sweden, Denmark, Belgium and Italy, as well as examples from small and medium-sized French, English and German cities. Therefore, his network seems to have extended further than we might imagine.

Rather than strictly following models from abroad, Lluís Sayé's objective was to adapt them to Catalonia. Sometimes, the measures and methods that he considered the most innovative and/or suitable came from countries other than France, the United Kingdom or Germany.

The case of the dispensary is, in this respect, very representative, as it was the major achievement of the regional tuberculosis service.

Under Lluís Sayé, the public fight against tuberculosis was organized around the dispensary. His primary aim was to build a network, connecting all the agents involved in fighting tuberculosis, from both the public and private sectors, in order to federate initiatives. To rationalize medical aid, links needed to be created between healthcare establishments and the dispensaries were of primary importance in achieving this. They served to establish diagnostics, provide the initial treatments and, finally, send patients to a sanatorium or hospital, depending on their medical needs. The hospital's purpose was to receive patients who required a surgical intervention. The sanatorium was a destination for those who were less affected and only needed some rest and a lower level of treatment.

While dispensaries served local populations, corresponding to neighborhoods, the other establishments had a wider and more diffuse area of influence (see Figure 7.1). The dispensary, in the mind of the physician, was therefore the heart of the system: "these dispensaries represent the nucleus of the fight against TB in the city."[28] Because it formed the center of the system, it was believed that the public authorities should control this step. Indeed, the Central Dispensary, as it was planned, had a larger area of influence compared to other dispensaries.

For this reason, the dispensary also had to be located in the center of the city, in a well-connected area. To justify his choice of focusing on the local work of the dispensary instead of treatments in hospitals, Lluís Sayé referred to examples and data from cities such as New York and countries like the United Kingdom, but also to Italy, which had implemented these policies earlier.[29]

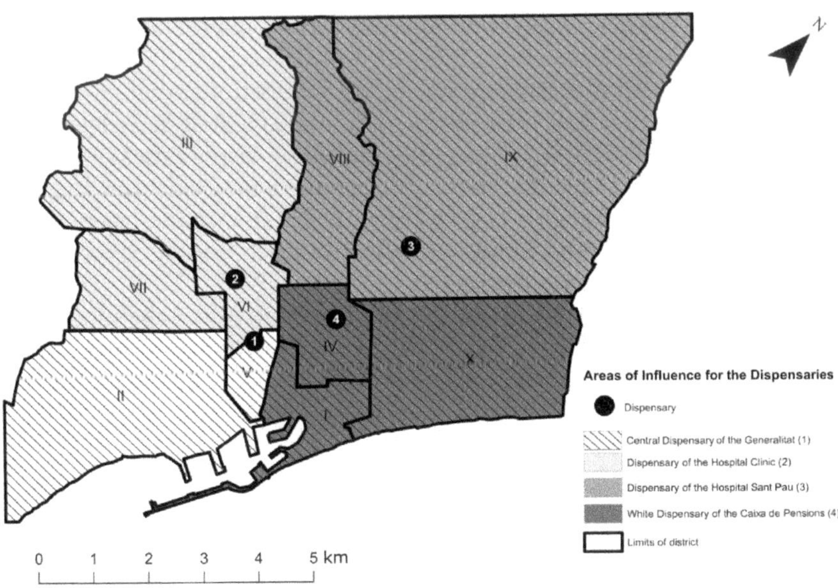

Figure 7.1 Area of influence for the tuberculosis dispensaries in Barcelona, 1930.

Source: Created by Celia Miralles Buil

Although the tuberculosis dispensary model initially appeared in Northern Europe,[30] Lluís Sayé was more interested in initiatives from the so-called peripheral countries of Europe to adapt that model. For him, the traditional functions of epidemiological investigation, diagnostics and the distribution of patients, which characterized the dispensaries in France, Germany and the United Kingdom, was inadequate in countries with a shortage of hospital beds.[31]

The new dispensary had to allow outpatient treatment, as was the case at the dispensary founded in Madrid in 1901.[32] The investment in outpatient treatment can be observed in a lot of countries, but the model proposed by the dispensary in Madrid was more radical. This Spanish initiative was then followed by other European countries, particularly Italy and France, according to him. Thus, Sayé showed that medicine practiced in places considered to be less modernized was more suited to current problems, and also more innovative.

Even though Sayé related his general proposals to models from Northern Europe, when he had to propose tangible solutions, his search for models better suited to the Catalan city drove him to consider recent projects in Southern Europe or in European countries with geographical and social conditions similar to those in Barcelona. In this way, when planning the construction of the new Central Dispensary, Lluís Sayé visited several healthcare institutions across Europe. He was very interested in the new sanatorium Benito Mussolini inaugurated in Rome in 1934. This new building followed all the modern recommendations in terms of healthcare-related architecture and the facility offered an innovative vision of treatments.

Finally, Sayé also suggested increasing the number of ambulant dispensaries like those that had been successfully implemented in Sweden and Italy. Ambulant dispensaries, also called sidewalk dispensaries or trucks, were driven around the city streets, distributing medicine and hygiene recommendations. The goal was to bring medicine into the heart of the most precarious neighborhoods in order to reach people who would never go to the dispensary themselves.

This idea, while heavily criticized, subsequently received the support of Josep Dencàs, Counselor of Public Health,[33] who compared it to Soviet initiatives, thereby attributing a political dimension to a public health program.[34]

From the Soviet Union to the Mediterranean Sea: Models for a Healthy City

The second part of this chapter analyzes how models from abroad were used by the architects of GATCPAC and political authorities to improve health conditions in Barcelona. It demonstrates that some of the models were used in a political way, to increase the actors' legitimacy.

GATCPAC was founded in 1929 in Barcelona and prefigured the Spanish group, called GATEPAC, which was established in 1930. It comprised of a group of Catalan architects, who were part of the Modern Movement and strongly connected to Le Corbusier. These architects were very aware of hygiene issues and the need to improve health conditions in cities.[35] The integration of social and public health issues into their vision of modern architecture led the Catalan government to entrust them with several construction projects. They were particularly involved in the Generalitat's project to construct workers' housing. Though a number of the buildings they designed were never realized, one of them, known as "Casa Bloc," was built in Barcelona between 1932 and 1936. In addition, three architects participated in the realization of the Central Dispensary: Josep Lluís Sert, Josep Torres Clavé and Joan Baptista Subirana.

Located in the heart of the city, in the neighborhood of El Raval, the construction of the dispensary drew criticism from some doctors and political opponents of the Catalan government at that time. Indeed, when the authorities announced the construction in 1934, it was deemed too expensive and unnecessary. Moreover, on another level, the inhabitants of El Raval were worried about the danger posed by the establishment of a healthcare center where all the contagious patients from around the city would be gathered in one place.[36]

Nevertheless, for the public authorities and the architects, the creation of a healthcare establishment was particularly justified in El Raval due to the very high number of tuberculosis patients there. Indeed, this poor and run-down neighborhood had the highest death rate of the city, and consequently represented the most dangerous area in terms of contagion (see Figure 7.2).[37]

Therefore, the dispensary's role was to decontaminate the area, promoting public health through the ambulant dispensaries but also by its mere presence. Due to its modern architectural features, the dispensary brought air and sunlight to the district at the same time as the medical services (see Figure 7.3).[38]

More generally, the construction of the dispensary must be understood in the context of larger projects that aimed to purify the city, and in particular the historic center.[39] Thus, the dispensary was situated near the projected main road through El Raval. This avenue, envisioned in the Cerdà Plan in 1860, was updated by successive plans such as the Darder Plan in 1918 and the Vilaseca Plan in 1932.[40]

The construction of the dispensary should also be linked to the plan to sanitize the historic center (*Pla de sanejament del casc antic*), which was proposed by the architects of the GATCPAC in 1934.[41]

These architects proposed "urban surgery,"[42] which would involve replacing the most derelict and unhealthy areas with public facilities, green and public spaces, and the dispensary itself.

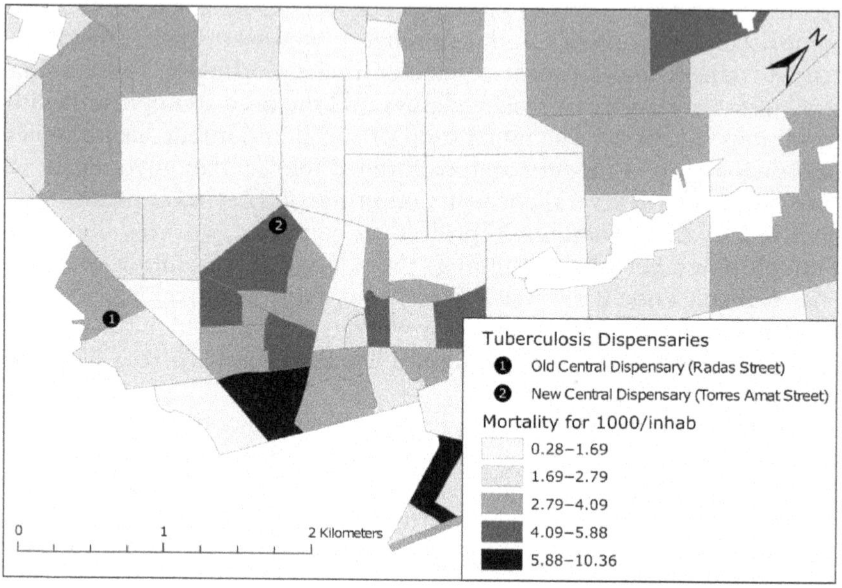

Figure 7.2 Locations of tuberculosis dispensaries and mortality rates, 1924.
Source: Created by Celia Miralles Buil

Figure 7.3 The Central Dispensary of Barcelona, 2014.
Source: Photo by Diego Miralles Buil

The opponents of the dispensary project also criticized another urban aspect of the project: the system of ambulant dispensaries. Josep Dencàs defended himself in the face of these criticisms by directly aligning his project with the Soviet Union, which had, according to him, put into practice measures of this kind. This explicit link to the "parentage" of the Soviet model aligned with the political interests of the councilor and, on a higher level, of the Catalan government and the ERC party. They were anxious to demonstrate their commitment to social justice by reducing social inequality and improving living conditions.

Finally, the most ferocious criticism against the dispensary was economic. The Generalitat was accused of spending too much on building modern structures in a context of sanitary urgency. Some physicians suggested that the money be better spent on increasing the number of beds in hospitals or improving old healthcare establishments.[43] To counter this criticism, the councilor argued that the old dispensaries were not up to the level needed, and that it was urgent to build a new one. Furthermore, because it prioritized social justice and promoted rationality, modern architecture was well suited to the project.

Indeed, the architects of GATCPAC built the dispensary in close consultation with the services of the Generalitat and the head of tuberculosis control, Lluís Sayé. Sometimes, the Central Dispensary is merely considered as an implementation of the theories of Le Corbusier.[44] On the contrary, it concentrated all the principles of modern architecture as set out by the GATCPAC in their writings. A major pillar of the GATCPAC's philosophy was that architecture should be at the service of science and health.[45] Thus, the dispensary followed all the recommendations of hygienists and physicians, as well as the motto of modern architecture: "sun, air and light." It was also influenced by the architects' previous experience, and by ideas formed during their study travels in Europe.[46]

The main designer of the dispensary was Joan Baptista Subirana, who, following Javier Heredero's Ph.D. dissertation, was deeply influenced by German architecture.[47] Indeed, Subirana studied architecture in Berlin, and during this period visited several buildings designed by the German rationalist school. This experience inspired his design for the dispensary but also other similar projects that would not see the light of day.[48] In terms of construction, Joan Subirana was inspired by the use of metal structures, which he had seen in German designs.[49] This technique, widely used by modern architects, facilitated the construction and the following reproduction of public buildings. Furthermore, it was less expensive than other methods.

Boris Berenguer Allaert also argues that the construction of the dispensary required new techniques and materials (steel and glass). These innovative techniques were first implemented in Belgium, France and

Germany, but in Barcelona they were adapted to the local context, making use of Catalan expertise.[50] In more general ways, as Julie Rolland explains, the GATCPAC and GATEPAC were influenced by international architecture and tried to break away from the national style.[51] But at the same time, these models and architectural theories had to be adapted to the specific context.[52]

From a broader perspective, just like other GATCPAC constructions, the dispensary project was part of a commitment to standardization, rationalization and universalization in modern architecture. References to the USSR, and to the implementation of construction programs, are very present in the writings of the group of Catalan architects,[53] as well as in the ideas of other modern European architects, such as Le Corbusier.[54] It was the purity of form and functionality, but also the idea of social justice promoted by this model, that interested these architects. It reminds us of Josep Dencàs' strong interest in the projects of the Soviet Union, as well as the inclusion of artists, intellectuals and scientists in a political project.[55]

The influence of the USSR was very present in another unachieved project of the GATCPAC: "La Ciutat de Repòs i Vacances" (The City of Rest and Holidays). This project aimed to provide a recreation area for Barcelona's inhabitants on the coast south of the city. It clearly had an objective of regeneration[56] aiming to improve peoples' health through fresh air and rest.[57] According to Julie Roland, the project was largely based on the Green City of Moscow and the projects of the Soviet Disurbanists.[58]

However, as explained by authors who have worked on the subject, this claimed affiliation with the Soviet Union was primarily a political manifesto. It was based on concepts and on an abstract idea. Julie Roland speaks of "disillusionment" when, in 1934, the group traveled to Moscow and was largely disappointed by the materials used in the buildings.[59] Therefore, according to her, the architects turned to Mediterranean architecture in order to provide a continuity for their modern architecture.[60]

In a more general way, in speeches given by members of GATCPAC, we can detect clear opposition to the building models of Northern Europe, especially the Haussmann model, which they described as unsanitary and unsuited to modern life. Faced with these complex and bourgeois forms, the simplicity of the vernacular/popular architecture was highlighted because it permitted and enhanced people's well-being and health. Mediterranean architecture (from Greek antiquity to the popular buildings of the Balearic Islands) thus appeared to be a suitable model, both for healthy housing and public health buildings.[61] Looking beyond the context of Barcelona, we can also see how Mediterranean architecture began to be promoted as a model for modern architecture in general.

Finding a "New Way" for a Modern European City

> Modern architecture, technically, is largely a discovery of the Nordic countries, but spiritually it is Mediterranean architecture without style that influences this new architecture. Modern architecture is a return to the pure and traditional form of the Mediterranean. This is another victory for the Latin sea![62]

In their magazine *AC* (*Documents of Contemporary Activity*), the architects of GATCPAC clearly explained the reasons why, according to them, international modern architecture partly derived from the Spanish vernacular tradition. Incidentally, they claimed that a continuity existed between their projects and the Mediterranean model, just as Marcelo Piacentini did in Italy while he was seeking to move away from the domination of Northern Europe in order to define Italian architecture.[63]

Julie Roland has observed that a tension existed in GATCPAC between the declaration of internationalism and regionalism. According to her, when they returned to the Mediterranean, the architects of GATCPAC did not revert to classic models, but rather proposed an evolution of the concept. The Mediterranean was conceived as "a cultural melting pot with an international vocation."[64]

For these agents, it was through "vernacular art," typically Mediterranean, that it was possible to reach the universality of architecture. Moreover, the architects explained, German architecture found its founding principles in Mediterranean vernacular architecture.[65] The reference to the Mediterranean was dramatically amplified after the "disenchantment" of the study trip to the USSR and, consequently, the rise of totalitarian regimes in the former "model" countries of Germany and Italy.[66]

Thus, these architects turned back to the Mediterranean models, for their own projects in Catalonia but also for the European architecture in general. As they came from the Mediterranean area, this re-centering allowed them to justify their position in the international network. In this sense, the Mediterranean model, like the Russian model before it, also seemed to represent quite a political standpoint and a rhetorical device.

Furthermore, for the public authorities who financed these projects, the Spanish and Catalan positions were strengthened: these constructions helped reinforce their legitimacy at the European level, demonstrating the uniqueness of their geographical space. As previously mentioned, in 1934, when the decision of the Generalitat to call on renowned architects to build an expensive dispensary was criticized, Josep Dencàs justified the move by referring to the skills of the GATCPAC, arguing that this building should not only house patients, but would also contribute to the decontamination of the entire city. The aim of the Generalitat was not to propose an emergency solution to the problem of tuberculosis in the city, but rather to make "something new" and to propose a sustainable solution. By choosing a structural solution instead of a short-term one, the agents of Generalitat also positioned themselves on the political spectrum. They wanted to reform society and deeply change the city. The construction of such a prestigious building could also be explained by the desire to show to the world the action and the commitment of the Generalitat in the fight against diseases and social segregation.[67]

In this way, the various health agents in Barcelona were able to gain access to the European network, positioning themselves as major players whose ideas and proposals could in turn become examples to follow. They actively took part in the story, contributing to the rise of modern medicine and offering innovative solutions instead of just applying models from elsewhere. Evidence of this ambition can be found in the work of Dr. Sayé even before the organization of tuberculosis control. Sayé was very present on the international stage, not only as a renowned practitioner whose work was an inspiration to many others, but also as a legitimate representative and a pioneer of medical modernity. Jacint Corbella explains that he published a lot in French, in scientific journals and with prestigious publishers.[68] In 1930, he became a "Chevalier de la Légion d'Honneur" (Knight of the Legion of Honor) in France, a prestigious distinction.[69] Lluís Sayé was a distinguished researcher and practitioner. He was invited to international conferences in Europe to discuss the innovative solutions offered in his services in Barcelona, such as the use of chrysotherapy.[70] In that sense, Sayé was recognized as an official promoter of the newest ideas in medicine.

But it was through the vaccine that Lluís Sayé distinguished himself on the French and international stages, especially after the Lübeck disaster. In 1930, the BCG vaccine developed by Calmette and Guérin was administered to babies in the German town of Lübeck. After 72 children died, a lawsuit was launched against Calmette and his vaccine. In this context, Lluís Sayé took up the cause in support of his friend and colleague and in favor of the vaccine. As a practitioner and researcher, he demonstrated that the vaccine, administered correctly, was safe.[71] In doing so, the physician showed that he was not only a proponent of the vaccine, but he also contributed to its improvement and further development through its diffusion in medical practice.

The work carried out by the dispensary in managing the control of tuberculosis did not just involve identifying the best system for Catalonia; it also aimed at developing a whole new system, the likes of which had never been seen before. Thus, Sayé's proposal of outpatient treatment in the dispensary went further than what he had been observing elsewhere in Europe. For example, he planned to practice phrenicectomy (ablation of a part of the phrenic nerve). As Sayé himself wrote: "It is an excellent opportunity to practice in a new way, specifically based in the work of the dispensary."[72] His vision was for Barcelona to become a leading center in terms of the fight against tuberculosis, not only at the national level, with the introduction of BCG, but also internationally through its new organization.

In light of these events, the classical concept of center-periphery used to describe the relationship between Northern and Southern Europe may be challenged.[73] All these projects had the objective to improve urban health because the city's situation was considered intolerable. There may have been a gap between Barcelona and other European cities, although the actors did not expand very much on the matter at this stage, but it was not described using the term "periphery." Indeed, neither Lluís Sayé nor the architects ever employed this term to describe Barcelona or Catalonia. Rather, they spoke of a "delay" vis-à-vis modernity. More precisely, Lluís Sayé spoke of different "phases of tuberculization" experienced by cities that were connected with their phases of urbanization and industrialization. Thus, the high mortality rate experienced by some cities could be explained by the fact that they were situated in a different stage of modernization. Lluís Sayé ascribed to a linear vision of history and did not particularly develop a spatial approach (in the sense implied by the term "periphery").

His challenge was to enter into modernity and to participate in its advancement by proposing new models developed from the local context.

Conclusion

This chapter has focused on the discourses and practices adopted by architects and physicians in their efforts to improve public health in Barcelona during the republican period. To lower mortality rates and build a healthier city, a number of different solutions were proposed: to adapt models successfully implemented elsewhere and to innovate, producing "something new." The models used to improve the public health conditions of Barcelona were not limited to those used in projects carried out in cities of Northern Europe. The local experts and agents also chose examples from many other countries situated in the so-called "European periphery." We have seen how Dr. Lluís Sayé, in charge of organizing the fight against tuberculosis, connected his proposals to French projects. However, these models seemed to be mainly used to legitimize his actions and his influence both at local and international level. In practice, the models followed and adapted to the Barcelonan situation often came from the "periphery," in particular when it was a question of tangible buildings.

Similarly, when the architects of GATCPAC proposed projects to improve the quality of Barcelona's urban space, they first relied on Soviet examples, and then highlighted Mediterranean rather than French or German architecture. These choices had contextual reasons (socialist influence and disenchantment), but were also due to a shared conviction that these models were more suited to the characteristics of Barcelona. Indeed, the spread of urban innovations was not always a vertical process: in his work about the diffusion of modern hygiene in France and Europe, Stéphane Frioux explained that, sometimes, small and medium-sized French cities were experienced in modern hygiene ideas even before systems were set up in larger cities.[74] Similarly, the agents from Barcelona tried to show that innovation could come from countries other than France, the United Kingdom and Germany. Innovation could also come from Barcelona. This chapter has also demonstrated the actor's strategies to be major players in the European and international network. The new focalization on the Mediterranean context for architectural models, recommended by the architects of GATCPAC, helped to reinforce their role in the international context. Lluís Sayé used his connections with the Institut Pasteur and the BCG vaccine as tools to become a major player on the international stage. The objective of the Central Dispensary was to propose a "new way" in terms of medicine and architecture that would ensure and promote public health.

Furthermore, adaptation and innovation were not opposed in the discourses; on the contrary, they were part of the same process to be included in the modern European network. Indeed, the rhetoric of modernity could be considered as essential to understand the actors' propositions. Instead of analyzing the gap between Barcelona and other European cities using the concept of center-periphery, they rather spoke of "delay" in terms of modernization.

Following this logic and the various discourses, the Central Dispensary promoted the most modern medicine for Barcelona's inhabitants. It brought new standards of public health into the unsanitary neighborhoods of Barcelona and offered services and facilities that had previously been lacking in number and quality in Catalonia. But the building was also intended to have an influence beyond Catalan borders. By promoting modern medicine from a new dispensary built by prestigious modern architects, this facility and the building it was housed in was an innovative model to be admired and emulated around the world.

Ultimately, however, these projects and ambitions failed to have important repercussions. With the beginning of the Civil War and the change of political regime under the Francoist dictatorship, these innovations were abandoned because they also integrated a political vision that was opposed to Francoist ideas. During the dictatorship, the Central Dispensary lost its leading role in controlling the fight against tuberculosis. It remained a simple dispensary, while the new Anti-Tuberculosis National Board,[75] located in Madrid, emphasized a system based on sanatoria. However, the protagonists of our story remained actively involved in international networks. Lluís Sayé helped to improve healthcare systems in Latin America. Josep Lluís Sert went into exile in the United States, where he became an important figure of modern architecture. Joan

Baptista Subirana remained in Barcelona and continued his practice on a more modest level due to difficulties with the political authorities. He realized some projects related to his commitment to modern architecture and social questions.[76] The dispensary achieved posterity in some respects; today it is considered to be one of the most accomplished works of GATCPAC and represents modern Catalan architecture.

Acknowledgments

This chapter was written with the support of the project VISLIS (PTDC/IVC-HFC/3122/2014) of the *Fundação para a Ciência e a Tecnologia* (Portugal). I would like to thank Joy Blackmore for the formal corrections.

Notes

1. "Una nueva institución sanitaria puesta al servicio del pueblo . . . está situada a la altura de las mejores del mundo en su clase," *La Vanguardia*, April 28, 1937, 3.
2. The Catalan autonomous government re-established in Republican Spain during 1931.
3. Stéphane Frioux, *Les batailles de l'hygiène: Villes et environnement, de Pasteur aux Trente Glorieuses* (Paris: PUF, 2013).
4. Anne Rasmussen, "Jalon pour une histoire des congrès nationaux au XIXe siècle," *Relations internationales* no. 62 (1986): 115–133.
5. Paillette Céline, "Épidémies, santé et ordre mondial. Le rôle des organisations sanitaires internationales, 1903–1923," *Monde(s)*, no. 2 (February 2012): 235–256.
6. Iris Borowy, *Coming to Terms with World Health, the League of Nations Health Organisation 1921–1946* (Frankfurt-am-Main: Peter Lang, 2009).
7. Ibid.
8. Josep L. Barona and Josep Bernabeu Mestre, *La salud y el Estado. El movimiento sanitario internacional y la administración española (1851–1945)* (Valencia: Universitat de València, 2008).
9. "España no fue un país productor de ideas científicas originales, sino un centro periférico que las recibía, reelaboraba y adaptaba a su realidad. Pero esa labor, por oscura que se nos presente, por poco lustrosa que parezca, fue fundamental en la modernización de la medicina y la sociedad española y merece ser historiada" Ricardo Campos Marín, "Monlau Giné. Curar y Gobernar. Medicina y liberalismo en la España del siglo XIX," *Nivola*, coll. Novatores no. 16 (2003): 16 (my translation).
10. Isabelle Renaudet, "Eveilleurs de conscience, passeurs de savoirs: élites culturelles, élites médicales, Espagne, XIXe–XXe siècles. Acteurs, savoirs, pratiques" (Habilitation Thesis, Université Aix-Marseille 1, 2010).
11. By using the concepts of "center" and "periphery," I refer to the "classical works" such as the quote of Ricardo Campos in introduction.
12. The Generalitat de Catalunya is the political organization of the autonomous Catalan regime. It existed during medieval and modern times but was suppressed by Felipe V in 1716. It was restored in August 1931, suppressed by the Francoist regime in 1939 and finally restored in 1980.
13. Carles Hervás i Puyal, "Sanitat a Catalunya durant la República i la Guerra Civil: política i organització sanitàries: l'impacte del conflicte bèlic" (Ph.D.

Diss., Universitat Pompeu Fabra, Institut Universitari d'Història Jaume Vicens Vives, 2004).

14. Jacint Corbella, "L'obra científica del doctor Lluís Sayé i Sempere (Barcelona, 1888–1975)," *Gimbernat* 20 (1993): 143–163.
15. The Mancomunitat de Catalunya was an administrative and political institution aimed at federating the four Catalan provinces. It was authorized by royal decree in 1913. It is considered to be the first step towards a recognition of Catalan autonomy. It was active between 1914 and 1925, when it was abolished by the dictator Primo de Rivera.
16. Corbella, "L'obra científica," 143–163.
17. Arxiu Nacional de Catalunya (ANC) / collection ANC1–372 Dispensari Dr. Lluís Sayé (Dispensari antituberculós).
18. That is, "*Cuando la tuberculosis se difunde masivamente en una ciudad, las primeras víctimas son los niños, los adolescentes, la mujer y después los hombres de todas edades. Constituido así el foco más virulento en los barrios más pobres de la ciudad se extiende a los más ricos, y cuando toda la ciudad está tuberculizada, se difunde al medio rural más próximo.*" Lluís Sayé i Sempere, *Las nuevas orientaciones de la lucha antituberculosa y su aplicación en España* (Madrid: Escuela Nacional de Sanidad, 1933), 5.
19. Corbella, "L'obra científica," 143–163.
20. Ibid.
21. ANC1–372 Dispensari Dr. Lluís Sayé (Dispensari antituberculós).
22. Ibid.
23. "El método francés es el que creo más adaptable a nuestra situación." Lluís Sayé i Sempere, *Profilaxis de la tuberculosis* (Barcelona: Oliva de Vilanova, 1924).
24. Ibid.
25. About Framingham: Marjaana Niemi, *Public Health and Municipal Policy Making: Britain and Sweden, 1900–1940* (Farnham: Ashgate, 2007).
26. About this notion: See the work of Jorge Molero Mesa, "Historia Social de la Tuberculosis en España, 1889–1936" (Ph.D. Diss., Universidad de Granada, 1989).
27. Sayé, *Las nuevas orientaciones*, 20.
28. Ibid, 16. That is, "*Estos Dispensarios representan el núcleo director de la lucha antituberculosa en la ciudad.*"
29. Ibid.
30. In 1887 Robert William Philip founded the Victoria Dispensary for Consumption and Diseases of the Chest, in Edinburgh.
31. Sayé, *Las nuevas orientaciones*, 21.
32. Dispensary "María Cristina" founded in 1901: José Verdes Montenegro, *Deficiencias de nuestra organización antituberculosa. Discurso de recepción leído en la RANM el 3 de febrero de 1935* (Madrid: Augusto Boué, 1935), 57.
33. Josep Dencàs i Puigdollers (1900–1965), physician and politician, member of ERC (Republican Left of Catalonia).
34. "El Dr. Dencàs fa manifestacions sobre la nostra enquesta," *La Publicitat*, April 14, 1933, 3.
35. Antonio Pizza and Josep María Rovira, *GATCPAC. Una nova arquitectura per a una nova Ciutat 1929–1939* (Barcelona: COAC Publicacions, 2007); Julie Roland, "Les identités du mouvement moderne en Espagne, dans le GATEPAC (1930–1937)" (Ph.D. Diss., Université Paris IV, 2011).
36. "Protesta contra el emplazamiento de un dispensario antituberculoso," *La Vanguardia*, June 22, 1933.

37. Sayé, *Profilaxis de la tuberculosis.*
38. Celia Miralles Buil, "L'architecture au service de la santé: l'exemple du dispensaire antituberculeux de Barcelone (1934–1936)," *Carnets du LARHRA* (2016): 131–149.
39. Alfons Zarzoso and José Pardo-Tomás, "Anatomy of an Urban Underworld: A Medical Geography of the Barrio Chino," in *Barcelona: An Urban History of Science and Modernity 1888–1929*, ed. Oliver Hochadel and Agustí Nieto-Galan (London and New York: Routledge, 2016), 158–178.
40. Mercè Tatjer, "Las intervenciones urbanísticas en el centro histórico de Barcelona: de la Via Laietana a los nuevos programas de rehabilitación," in *Oportunidades de desarrollo sostenible para los conjuntos urbanos históricos. III Jornadas de Geografía Urbana (Burgos, 18 a 21 de mayo de 1998)*, ed. Begoña Bernal Santa Olalla (Burgos: Servicio de Publicaciones de la Universidad de Burgos, 2000), 18.
41. GATCPAC, "Pla de sanejament del casc antic." *AC Review*, no. 25 (Barcelona, 1937), 28.
42. Ibid.
43. "Que penseu dels projectes sanitaris del Dr. Dencàs?" *La Publicitat*, April 14–16, 1933.
44. About the influence of Le Corbusier in GATCPAC: Roger Sauquet, "¿Existe un urbanismo del GATCPAC sin Le Corbusier?" *Revista Proyecto Progreso Arquitectura*, no. 11, *Arquitectura en común* (2014): 16–25.
45. Pizza and Rovira, *GATCPAC. Una nova arquitectura.*
46. See the travels in the USSR, Greece or in Andalusia: Javier López Rivera, "La fotografía en el viaje de arquitectura: Margaret Michaelis y el GATEPAC, Grecia y la URSS," *ZARCH: Journal of interdisciplinary studies in Architecture and Urbanism*, no. 1 (2013): 244–257.
47. Javier Heredero, "Subirana, la conexión alemana del GATCPAC" (Ph.D. Diss, Universitat Politècnica de Catalunya, 2015).
48. See Revista AC (Documents d'Activitat Contemporània).
49. Heredero, "Subirana," 45.
50. Boris Berenguer Allaert, "Estudis de dos edificis: Dispensari central antituberculós i Casa Bloc" (Master Thesis, Universitat Politècnica de Catalunya, 2011).
51. Roland, "Les identités du mouvement moderne," 34.
52. Ibid., 18.
53. See other examples in Julie Roland's PhD. Dissertation, 103.
54. J.-L. Cohen, "Le Corbusier and the Mystique of the U. S. S. R.," *Oppositions* 23 (1981): 84–121.
55. About the Soviet influence on intellectuals and artists in Spain: Allison Taillot, "El modelo soviético en los años 1930: los viajes de María Teresa León y Rafael Alberti a Moscú," *Cahiers de civilisation espagnole contemporaine*, no. 9 (2012), http://journals.openedition.org/ccec/4259; https://doi.org/10.4000/ccec.4259.
56. For the concept of "regeneracionismo," see Isabel Jiménez Lucena, "La cuestión del regeneracionismo sanitario y su debate durante la Segunda República: elementos de clase e ideología," *Dynamis*, no. 18 (1998): 285–314.
57. Julie Roland, "La Ciutat de Repòs i Vacances," *Mélanges de la Casa de Velázquez* 39, no. 2 (2009); Roger Joan Sauquet Llonch, "Recolección de ideas para la ciudad de reposo y vacaciones. Aportaciones extranjeras al proyecto del GATCPAC," in *Viajes en la transición de la arquitectura española hacia la modernidad* (Pamplona: Editions Universidad de Navarra, 2010), 311–318.

58. Roland, "Les identités du mouvement moderne," 195. About disurbanists' projects: Alla Vronskaya, "The Utopia of Personality: Moisei Ginzburg's Project for the Moscow Park of Culture and Leisure," *Quastio Rossica,* no. 4 (2015): 40–56.
59. Roland, "Les identités du mouvement moderne," 196.
60. Ibid., 206.
61. Carmen Rábano Faci, "GATCPAC, GATEPAC y mediterraneidad," in *El Mediterráneo y el Arte Español: Actas del XI Congreso del CEHA*, ed. Joaquín Bérchez, Mercedes Gómez-Ferrer Lozano, and Amadeo Serra Desfilis (Valencia: Comité Español de Historia del Arte, 1998), 282–286.
62. That is, "*La arquitectura moderna, técnicamente, es en gran parte un descubrimiento de los países nórdicos, pero espiritualmente es la arquitectura mediterránea sin estilo la que influye esta nueva arquitectura. La arquitectura moderna es un retorno a las formar puras, tradicionales, del Mediterráneo. ¡Es una victoria más del mar latino!*" "*Mediterranean roots of the modern architecture*", *AC*, 18, 1935. Cited by Roland, "Les identités du mouvement moderne," 217.
63. Ibid., 216.
64. That is, "*un creuset culturel à vocation internationaliste.*" Roland, "Les identités du mouvement moderne," 208.
65. That is, "*Raíces mediterráneas de la arquitectura moderna,*" *AC*, no. 18, 31–33, cited by Roland, "Les identités du mouvement moderne," 211.
66. Ibid., 197.
67. Miralles Buil, "L'architecture au service de la santé."
68. For instance: Lluís Sayé i Sempere, *Pneumolyse intrapleurale* (Paris: Masson, 1932).
69. Corbella, "L'obra científica."
70. Lluís Sayé i Sempere, *Goldbehandlung der Tuberkulose* (Amsterdam: VIII International Conference About Tuberculosis, 1932).
71. See all the articles published in *La revue de la tuberculose* during the 1930s.
72. That is, "*se nos ofrece una ocasión excelente para hacer una obra en cierto modo nueva, basándola especialmente en la acción del dispensario*"; Sayé, *Las nuevas orientaciones*, 68.
73. See the quote of Ricardo Campos-Marín in the Introduction.
74. Frioux, *Les batailles de l'hygiène.*
75. "Patronato Nacional Antituberculoso," created in December 1936 in Francoist Spain. After the Civil War, it integrated all the Tuberculosis public establishments.
76. For instance, a project of a private clinic in Barcelona in 1944. The third architect, Josep Torres Clavé, was killed at the end of the Civil War.

Part III

The New Urban Space

Experiences and Institutions

8 A Discourse of Modernity?

Warsaw's Press on Urban Poverty (1880s–1910s)

Clara Maddalena Frysztacka

> Warsaw is the biggest Polish city. Warsaw is the only truly big Polish city. Warsaw ranks sixth in the list of the biggest European cities. It is bigger than the capitals of Italy, Belgium or Spain. . . . Its population has grown constantly over the last 50 years . . . people have not stopped moving to Warsaw during this whole period. Lesseps predicted a great future for Warsaw: in the 20th century, it will become the biggest European city. Such a city will not be able to maintain a purely Polish character. In a certain way, it has to become cosmopolitan. We can already feel this transformation taking place. . . . Of all Polish cities, Warsaw has the best hygienic conditions – except maybe for Poznań. It has a very good sewer system and water pipelines, a hundred times better then Cracow and Lviv, which, however, thanks to their political autonomy, could see greater development in other fields of urban culture. . . . The city can boast of historical districts which arouse great admiration, as well as new neighborhoods displaying modern architecture, full of modern comfort. And it even has urban areas planned for the future, which will inaugurate a new era of progress in the coming years.[1]

This enthusiastic statement about the demographic and architectural development of Warsaw opens the last part of a long reportage with the title "The Development of Polish Cities," published in 1912 in the Warsaw illustrated magazine *Świat* (*The World*). One after the other, the reportage analyzes the five main urban centers of the Polish partitions, Cracow, Lviv, Poznań and Łódź, ending with the capital of the former (and future) Polish state. What is particularly interesting in this paragraph is the three-tiered discursive framing of the city: national, European and modern. Through the depiction of inexorable urban expansion and improvement, the author, A. Pawłowski, locates Warsaw on the mental map of a national territory which did not yet politically exist, or no longer politically existed, while being represented on an equally imagined map of the European metropolises and by a diachronic narrative of modernity and progress. In each of the article's three frameworks, Warsaw takes a position which can be defined as being in between or as an incomplete centrality. On the national level, Pawłowski affirms its absolute supremacy over the other Polish cities, while also admitting that this supremacy can potentially result in cosmopolitanism and therefore denationalization. On the European level, he explicitly presents Warsaw as topping Rome or Madrid but implicitly declares it inferior to London, Paris and Berlin. Finally, the modern development of Warsaw appears as an unfinished process which the author partially identifies in the present, partially projects into the future and which, due to the situation of political dependence on the Russian Empire, reveals delays in comparison to Cracow or Lviv in "other fields of urban culture."

This chapter points paradigmatically to the ambivalent entanglements between the categories of nation, modernity and (urban) Europe as the main horizon of references which shapes the self-understanding and discursive self-construction of Warsaw as an Eastern European city on the eve of the twentieth century. These three categories constitute the central view for an historiographical analysis of the urban experience in the nineteenth and early twentieth centuries: the majority of the manifold processes the historians normally label as "nation building," "modernization" and "Europeanization," with a higher or lower degree of normativity and teleology, are linked to urban space. In the case of Eastern Europe, however, some scholars attest that nation building tends to be the predominant plot, whereas questions on modernity (and Europeanness) mostly imply a narrative of real or (self-) attributed delay and peripherality.[2] This applies especially to urban space: on the one hand, Eastern European cities are presented as the cradle of the national idea as well as the centers of imagined national space and national symbols. On the other hand, their modernization patterns constantly fall under suspicion of representing a mere imitation and reproduction of their Western European counterparts and functioning as triggers for (post-)colonial paradigms of national/Eastern European dependence and backwardness compared to metropolitan centers like London or Paris. Critics of such a narrative emphasize an interurban level of discursive references and transfers, where both Western and Eastern municipalities were embedded, and the transnational, joint Eastern European urban aspirations to Europe as a *locus* of modernity. For instance, Jan Behrends and Martin Kohlrausch understand the "genesis of Eastern European cities"[3] not as a mimicry but as a process "sui generis"; Nathaniel Wood stresses their "becoming metropolitan"[4] and the importance of the "myth of Europe"[5] for the Eastern European urban elites, whereas the editors of this volume coined the concept of "emerging cities." From their perspective, the analysis of Eastern European cities enables the highlighting of a counter-narrative of alternative autochthonous Eastern European progress or belonging to a non-national globalized modernity which has been largely overlooked by researchers until now.

This chapter explores the construction and interactions between these two narratives of Eastern European cities – the narrative of modernity and Europe on the one hand, and that of nation and peripherality on the other hand – analyzing the Polish-speaking Varsovian press from the 1890s to the outbreak of World War I. As demonstrated by Wood for Cracow or Peter Fritzsche for Berlin, the relatively new mass periodicals and newspapers were central actors in modern urban life and key producers of images of urban modernity.[6] Unlike these two scholars, however, I want to focus on a particular discourse of the Polish-speaking illustrated magazines; namely, the discourse on poverty. Here, I use poverty as an analytical concept to define differing socially, architecturally, hygienically, sanitarian, educationally and "morally" precarious or problematic statuses mostly linked with the poor, such as material indigence, criminality, urban overcrowding, cheap housing, disease, infant mortality, illiteracy, prostitution or the emergence of slums. Although none of these phenomena are genuine features of the cities or a new challenge of the modern era,[7] the studies of Alan Mayne and Angela Schwarz on the slums of London, Birmingham, Sydney and San Francisco have given rise to the potential for a greater focus on discourses of poverty in investigating the urban narratives of modernity.[8] These studies show how the concentration, visibility and new forms of social hardship represented a crucial experience of modern urban space and a topic of great interest in different periods on an interurban level. Transformed into objects of "curiosity," "entertainment," "drama" and "othering" by the press, the poor became an integral part of modern urban self-understanding and self-fashioning and the "reportage from the slum" an interurban circulating press format. What does not represent the main focus of interest of Mayne and Schwarz, due to the "Western" character of their case studies (as is my hypothesis), is the question of the national or non-national coding of the problem of the poor as well as the question of the potentially Janus-faced connotation of the experience of poverty in a context of an (self-)attributed delay of modernization. Through the analysis of the ways in which the Varsovian magazines dealt with the topic of poverty, this chapter therefore aims to reconstruct the modern self-understanding of Warsaw on the one hand, while addressing both the category of the national and the paradigm of peripherality on the other.

Discussing the Ambivalences of the National, the Peripheral and the Modern in the Constellation of Warsaw at the Turn of the Twentieth Century

After the third partition was established in 1795, the Polish state ceased to exist until the end of World War I. In its stead there emerged separated territorial units (the Polish partitions), divided between three different imperial formations: Russia, Austria (from 1867, Austria-Hungary) and Prussia (from 1871, the German Empire). Despite this territorial fragmentation and its inclusion in three different imperial frames, the nation plays a crucial role in Polish intellectual history and in the history of the Polish political ideas of the nineteenth century. Historians not only consider the nation a central idea for all the main Polish thought-currents of that period – romanticism, positivism, neo-romanticism, the conservativism of the Cracow historiographical school, integral nationalism of the National Democracy and even socialism – but they also highlight the "modernization" of this idea throughout the century in a process of inclusion/exclusion of different territories (the "Piast" vs. the "Jagiellonian" concept), ethnic groups (Ukrainians, Lithuanians, Germans and Jews) and social classes (the shift from the aristocratic nation to the *Volksnation*).[9]

The importance historiography attributes to the nation should, however, not allow us to forget that the nation was not the only (and also not always the most important) point of reference: Europe and its empires played a crucial role in the self-understanding and self-location of Polish-speaking society.[10] The borders, administrative status, degree of autonomy and even imperial allocations of the three Polish partitions changed more than once over time. Nevertheless, they shared an ambivalent position within Europe and within their empires throughout the nineteenth century. From a post-colonial perspective, the definition of this positionality as peripheral may be justified by several factors: the lack of state autonomy, the consequent exclusion from key phenomena of European modernity such as the colonial enterprises and the (self-) attributed delay or incompleteness concerning those social and economic transformations which could be categorized as tenets of modernization. Certain specific elements of the Russian partition, and in particular of Warsaw at the end of the nineteenth century, reinforce the thesis of peripherality in the imperial context. After the two uprisings of 1831 and 1863, the city experienced strong militarization, the suppression of education in the Polish language and the institution of strict censorship, while access to administrative positions for local elites was severely curtailed. Many studies of Warsaw in the second half of the nineteenth century highlight the lack of career opportunities for members of the intelligentsia and indicate the cultural, economic and political marginalization of this group on an imperial level as a trigger for political activism and national self-identification.[11]

However, defining the Polish partitions as peripheral can be also highly misleading. Steven Tötösy de Zepetnek identifies two main features of the Eastern European post-colonial configuration in comparison with the extra-European colonial spaces. On the one hand, the Eastern European "peripheries" experience simultaneous dependence on several centers – the imperial economic-political capitals of Vienna, St. Petersburg or Berlin and the Western European global cultural-economic metropolises of

London and Paris, whereas, on the other hand, they show a certain degree of "self-referentiality," namely of understanding themselves as cultural centers.[12] The concept of "inbetween peripherality," which Tötösy de Zepetnek coins to describe this configuration, accentuates how the Eastern European cities do not really fit the binary scheme of center/periphery. Surely this applies to Warsaw: in the case of Warsaw, we can observe a clear non-coincidence between the center of political decision-making, St. Petersburg, and the orientation toward the Western European modernity model of the Warsaw positivist (but also integrally national) intellectual elites.[13] Authors such as Christoph Mick and Malte Rolf highlight that, from an economic and cultural point of view, Warsaw was definitely a center in the Russian empire and that even the Russian elites considered their provincial capital Warsaw as belonging to the Western European civilization.[14]

These considerations draw our attention to the fact that the main Polish cities in the period of the partitions played the role of centers not only in national terms, but also as modern urban spaces, and also in this regard, it is possible to observe certain ambivalences. Indeed, on the one hand, in the territories of former Poland, the period of the partitions coincided with the abolition of serfdom and thus with rapid demographic growth, a mass exodus from the countryside, industrialization and urbanization. On the other hand, the imperial framings and the distinct economic and political positions of the Polish lands within each empire deeply affected the patterns, rhythms and results of these phenomena. Socio-economic "modernization" processes were particularly swift and virulent in the Kingdom of Poland,[15] and were especially visible in its two main urban centers, Warsaw and Łódź. Despite being able to hark back to a much longer urban tradition than the comparably new city of Łódź, the old capital Warsaw had also undergone dramatic changes. In the last three decades of the nineteenth century, the city's population grew by 131% (from 383,000 to 885,000).[16] The construction of railway connections and bridges, as well as both industrial and commercial development, contributed to the creation of an image of Warsaw as a modern European metropolis.[17]

The rising number of rural immigrants in the city's industrial center placed topics such as homelessness, housing shortages and unsightly hygienic conditions in the urban outskirts at the forefront of the agenda of public discourse. Patrice Dabrowski estimates that "in the years 1868 to 1891 the housing stock nearly doubled" and remarks that "these constructions were generally of poor quality."[18] It was precisely the political situation of dependence that created peculiar conditions for city governance and the urban groups aspiring to promote the modernization of Warsaw and solve the new problems linked to rapid urbanization. Most notably, due to the suppression that followed the national uprising of 1863, the local administration had no autonomy to invest in local infrastructures, whereas St. Petersburg concentrated much more on the pacification of the rebel province than on projects of urban improvement.[19] The same political logic transformed Warsaw into a fortified city. The citadel, which had already been constructed by the Russian authorities after the first uprising in 1831 and was largely used for the imprisonment of political prisoners and the stationing of Russian troops, impeded Warsaw's urban expansion toward the north and exacerbated the overcrowding in the city.[20] In this situation, Warsaw's modernization and the fight against modern social hardships were primarily in the hands of private philanthropic initiatives. In fact, single exponents of the wealthiest social classes promoted the construction of the Warsaw Philharmonic, of hospitals, schools, cheap housing for the working class and the establishment of a hygienic society.[21] Private initiative could therefore be interpreted as an alternative, specifically Varsovian, route toward modernity.

The Press and the Discourse on Warsaw's Modernity

The analysis of Warsaw's popular weekly press at the turn of the century allows for a reconstruction of the strong impressions made by rapid urbanization on its inhabitants. The existence and circulation of affordable Polish-speaking newspapers, be they illustrated tabloids, periodicals for women or modern press for "the people,"[22] can in fact be considered a manifestation of the formation of a new modern urban society. This new mass circulation press, which developed in Warsaw between the 1860s and the first decade of the 1900s, accompanied the emergence of the intelligentsia and of the proletariat as core urban social groups, as well as a decrease in illiteracy rates.[23] In contrast to previous press-formats, their "modernity" was determined by a policy of profit maximization (visible by the increasing number of printed copies or by the presence of advertisements), the abundance of illustrations (and later photographs) and the orientation toward a differentiated literate public which was far broader than the intellectual elites of the first half of the century.[24]

The *Tygodnik Ilustrowany* (*Weekly Illustrated*), one of the main sources of this chapter, is paradigmatic of this phenomenon. Founded in 1859 by Józef Ungar and purchased by one of the more technological innovative and capitalist-organized Varsovian publishing companies, Gebethner & Wolff, in 1882, the *Tygodnik* was one of the oldest and most important media outlets of the Polish-speaking intelligentsia (also circulating in the two other partitions). Furthermore, it sold the biggest number of copies among Varsovian magazines (20,000 copies on the eve of the twentieth century), using modern technologies of printing, graphics and the reproduction of illustrations. *Świat*, the second most important source for this chapter, quoted already at the very beginning, also counts among the most "modern" printed products on the Varsovian market. Founded in

1906 as part of a wave press liberalization after the revolution of 1905, it became famous for being the first Varsovian magazine to make extensive use of photography, while explicitly interpreting its role as addressing the modern zeitgeist of the city.[25]

Popular weekly magazines were not only products of "modernization" processes: they also represented a central medium for the transmission of knowledge on these processes for the growing urban population. *Tygodnik* and *Świat* depicted Warsaw's urban space for their readership, with its buildings, streets and monuments, as well as urban life, while commenting on socio-economic changes in the city and discussing the modern experiences of other cities in the Russian Empire or in Europe. The reception of different topics from the foreign press and the adoption of innovative, "modern" formats, similar to those emerging all over Europe, give rise to an understanding of these Varsovian magazines as part of the "interurban matrix of words and images describing the modern world"[26] which Wood theorizes in his studies on Cracow. According to Wood, this matrix is based on the circulation of journalistic genres and content through mutual percipience and transfers between different magazines across national and state borders, creating a common narrative on urban modernity.[27]

However, *Tygodnik* and *Świat* were not just propagators of transnational discourses on modernity, but also key producers of Warsaw as a modern city. We can agree with Mayne, who offered a critique of the English-speaking press during the same period:

> Journalism did not simply mirror cities, . . . [it] helped to create cities in popular imagination. Urban scale – the magnitude of population, the geographical dimension of settlement, the pace of change – had left personal experience and personal knowledge insufficient as information sources about modern society. City journalism helped to meet that need.[28]

One could therefore conclude that the magazines contributed decisively to the creation and formation of the idea of the Warsaw's modernity.

The Polish-speaking press also played a crucial role in the national discourse. As highlighted by many studies, especially in the Russian partition, periodicals saw the development of national consciousness as their most important duty in the absence of legal Polish educational and political institutions.[29] The mere fact of publishing in the Polish language represented a way to comply with this duty. Moreover, in *Tygodnik* and *Świat* we can find biographies of successful exponents of Polish society (doctors, intellectuals, journalists); re-printings of famous Polish novels, poems and paintings; and articles on Polish history and literature, as well as regular reports from the main cities of the other partitions. In keeping with the previous discourse on modernity, we should not look at these magazines as merely popularizing elitist national culture to the wider public, but as central actors in the discursive construction of the Polish nation. The reception of a Polish-speaking press and the circulation of information across the partitions´ borders played an intrinsic role in the establishment of the idea of Polish space and society for an ever-expanding population.[30]

In terms of a discussion on the Varsovian magazines in the context of this chapter, the last aspect to consider is the question of peripherality. The strong preventive and repressive censorship of the Russian authorities not only intervened in the contents of the articles before and after their publishing, but also restricted the creation of new newspapers and magazines.[31] Censorship functioned, therefore, as a limitation both of the modern and the national characters of the press in the Kingdom of Poland, casting the shadow of political imperial dependence and backwardness on it.

The ambivalence between the modern, national and imperial-peripheral can be discerned in the articles on Warsaw between the 1890s and 1914. The specific discourse on the modernity of Warsaw in the press is based on images of a radical break with the past, of stunning urban expansion and the Europeanization of urban space, which was due to improvements in infrastructure, architecture and public health. An article in the *Tygodnik Ilustrowny* from 1903 includes one of these images:

> The appearance of Warsaw, which at the beginning of the last century counted some ten thousand people and now comes close to one million, has changed and is still changing beyond all recognition, assuming the characteristic of an enormous city. . . . At the same time, this also changes the spiritual physiognomy of its inhabitants, who are losing their typical features and acquiring a universal template, common to all the masses of people of the biggest cities on the European continent.[32]

Similar to the article in *Świat* quoted at the beginning of this chapter, a paradigmatic example of the narrative on Warsaw's newly achieved modern appearance can be observed in its ambivalent interactions with the national discourse. Alexander Kraushar, a well-known historian, publicist and author of the article, expresses his astonishment about the evolution of the city on the one hand, while on the other, he somehow regrets the unavoidable development from a specifically national past into a universal Europeanized present implied in this evolution. An analogous mix of feelings concerning the modernity of Warsaw is also present in another article in *Świat* published in 1908. The anonymous author states and applauds the new status of Warsaw as a modern city in accordance with European standards, but he laments the fact that, with the rise of modern Warsaw, the Old Town, as a symbol of the national identity, has completely been forgotten.[33] Through the construction of a Varsovian modernity, such examples highlight the ways in which the press relocated Warsaw from the heart of Polishness to a denationalized and standardized European urban space.

However, the interaction between nation and modernity cannot be reduced to declaring the emergence of the latter to be at the expense of the former. Writing in 1910, an anonymous author of the *Tygodnik Ilustrowany* referred to the discursive construction of the former Polish capital as the vanguard for the modernization of the whole nation, as he explained to his readers that writing on the modern development of the city meant that "day after day we do not only write the story of Warsaw but also our own story. The story of Polish spirit and Polish culture."[34] Therefore and as the *Świat* article shows, the press discourse on Varsovian modernity was also a discourse on the nation, redeemed from a backward past and guided by Warsaw into a modern present, re-affirming the centrality of the city in the national space and among other Polish cities. In fact, through the depiction of Warsaw as the most modern city, the periodicals were able to compensate for the paradigm of backwardness, deriving from its inclusion in the Russian Empire and the strong limitation of national life in comparison to Cracow or even Poznań, instead presenting the development of Warsaw as a pattern which the other Polish urban centers would follow in the future.

Finally, yet importantly, by attributing an urban modern character to Warsaw, the magazines analyzed here not only defined the relationship between the "only Polish metropolis" and the imagined Polish national context. The discourse also allowed for a re-negotiation of the Varsovian position in the context of the "interurban matrix" of urban points of references and comparison, to which both Polish and (Western) European cities belonged, as well as the urban centers of the Russian Empire. The issues of urban hygiene and hygienic activism seem to be of particular relevance in this regard. Three major hygiene exhibitions had been organized in Warsaw even before World War I. Commenting on the exhibition of 1896, the *Tygodnik Ilustrowany* highlighted that the first exhibition of the year 1887 had also been one of the first of its kind in Europe, and that Warsaw had achieved a notably progressive standing in this young and modern science, thanks to such exhibitions.[35] The article then introduced the Warsaw Hygiene Society, orchestrator of the exhibition, showing how the self-organized social system embodied a successful Polish pattern of modern urban development and positioning Warsaw at the heart of the European modernity. Further articles reported on philanthropic models in Western countries[36] and the efficiency and modern hygienic standards of those in Warsaw,[37] constructing as well hygiene and philanthropy as a field of modern urban European culture, where the former Polish capital could claim to be on the same level with the major European metropolises. The hygienic measures represented at the same time also a framework for proving one's own modernity as regards the imperial center. In 1908, for example, the *Tygodnik* sought to reassure its readers with regard to the recent cholera outbreak, arguing that cholera was far less dangerous for a city like Warsaw than it was for St. Petersburg, due to Warsaw's developed and functioning sewer system.[38] In this article, the supposedly peripheral Warsaw appeared more European, advanced and centrally located than the imperial capital.

The Press on Urban Poverty Between Self-Attributed Backwardness and National Duties

As we have seen, most articles focused on the new developments in urban space with a mix of positive and negative connotations, but the alleged loss of the distinctive national character was not the only reason for these ambiguous depictions. For instance, *Świat* published a series of articles in 1906 under the title of "Warsaw's Dreams." The main topic of the series was the planning of a new Warsaw with monumental public spaces in a classicistic style, with modern private buildings, grand avenues, large department stores for the centralized sale of colonial or textile products and with an immense pavilion canteen to alleviate the working class from the problem of daily alimentation.[39] The word "dreams," however, highlighted the unrealistic character of these plans: indeed, the author admits in the first part of the series that the citadel, a symbol of Russian domination, makes the realization of such radical modernization practically impossible. On the one hand, the changes in Warsaw transformed its urban space into a scenario for utopic architectonic and social visions, while on the other hand, the contemporary conditions of political dependence postponed these visions and rendered them an idealized future. The author contrasted the utopia with current modernity, comparing contemporary Warsaw to a big version of Łódź.[40] During this period, Łódź, called the "Polish Manchester," symbolized industry, uncontrolled urban explosion, architectural ugliness and the terrible smell emanating from the factories. Analogously, the author attributed chaotic urban growth to modern Warsaw, characterized by extreme population density along with a lack of green areas and representative buildings.

An article written in a similar vein appeared in the same magazine a number of years later. Discussing the necessity for a new bridge across the Vistula, the anonymous author defined modern Warsaw as the "ugliest" and "most disgusting" city, lacking any semblance of harmonious architectural development.[41] In both examples, as in many other press articles on Warsaw, the inscription of a "dark" side of urban modernity can be observed. This dark side rested on the concept that urbanization triggered forms of social, spatial, moral or biological degeneration, labeled in most cases as different but specific urban dimensions of poverty/misery. Indeed, the Varsovian press complained about the shortage of cheap housing for the working class, the narrowness or poor hygienic conditions of these houses, and the dirty air and extreme overcrowding in many of the city's districts.[42] Some authors placed a specific focus on the spatial dimension, reporting on the uncontrolled spread of suburban neighborhoods. For example, the district of Wola was described as a huge slum, lacking supplies for the most basic living standards, a hive of criminality and therefore an unofficial no-go area for the rest of society.[43] Other authors rather highlighted the immaterial aspect of this poverty, criticizing the low level of education of the urban working classes, the decline in morality and the ignorance of basic standards of hygiene.[44] The discourse on the modern evolution of the city was a double-edged sword: one side was linked to the positive teleology implied in the notions of progress and modernity, while the negative side attested to the fact that the concrete realization of this progress in Warsaw also signified the emergence of a wide range of forms of urban poverty.

The misery of urban space and urban life was often presented as evidence for the peculiar political, social and/or economic peripherality which came to characterize the Polish partitions at the end of the nineteenth century. For example, in *Tygodnik*, Aleksander Rembowski blamed incredibly high illiteracy rates among the Warsaw population in comparison with London on the substandard education system, hence accusing the Russian educational policy of being responsible for the cultural poverty of the urban Polish population.[45] Similarly, in an article published by *Świat*, Henryk Mierzejewski indicated the lack of social housing and public transport as the main causes of poverty and overcrowding in Warsaw's working class districts. In this regard, he compared the disadvantaged situation of Polish workers, completely neglected by the Russian government, to their British counterparts, where the working class enjoyed remarkably higher living standards thanks to state investments on infrastructure.[46] Finally, the aforementioned anonymous article in *Świat* on the necessity of a new bridge attributes "neither the same financial resources nor the same elegance as Paris" to Warsaw, which would explain its ugliness in comparison with the French capital.[47]

All three articles interpret the different manifestations of urban poverty in Warsaw as specific forms of a local/national delay of Polish civilization, evident through the comparisons with developments in Britain or France. Moreover, they identify (directly or mostly indirectly, due to censorship) the political dependence on a backward empire as the origin of the delay in comparison with Western Europe. It is no coincidence that *Świat* again warned against the unprecedented rise of the cost of living in Warsaw after the revolution of 1905–1906, and against the resulting spread of urban poverty. The increasing phenomenon of urban poverty represented a clear indicator for the author of the city's alarming shift away from Westernization and toward Orientalization and Russification.[48] In other words, urban poverty was viewed as a symptom of Polish "inbetween"-peripheral backwardness between East and West.

In the Kingdom, the positivist movement, which dominated the intellectual life of Warsaw between the late 1860s and 1890s and continued to influence public debate until War World I, had a great tradition of framing the fight against poverty in categories of Polish national duty. After the disaster of the January uprising in 1863, the positivists advocated a pragmatic approach to the national struggle, known as "organic work." This term referred to different ways of self-organization which would have to fill the absence of state institutions in the economic, social and educational realms. Organic work aimed to prioritize Polish self-modernization, intended as the key to the survival and further development of the Polish nation, over the unrealistic and counterproductive uprising strategy. In 1889, the positivist Adolf Suligowski published one of the first long studies on the catastrophic living conditions in the poor districts of Warsaw, in which he argued for the implementation of English and French urban policies to solve the problem.[49] Starting out from the positivist idea of the nation as a biological body based on the functioning of its organs, he saw the possibility to restore the health of Polish society as a whole through the alleviation of urban poverty. Several authors in the Varsovian press shared this position. They considered the improvement of urban space in the former capital a crucial national task for every Pole.[50] In particular, some highlighted the need for private philanthropic initiatives in the absence of state policies to tackle the varying aspects of urban poverty and produce a narrative of the material and spiritual emancipation of the poorest urban classes, intended as a national core interest which would go beyond any social division.[51] "We should not neglect our responsibility for the moral situation of the working class. . . . Each inhuman crime taking place among the lowest social classes is a slap in the face of our consciousness as [Polish] citizens."[52] Such rhetoric transformed the question of urban poverty into a perceived national struggle and the urban poor into the target of an agenda which considered them an important component of the nation.

The key concept of this agenda was the idea of *lud*, which may be translated as "folk" or "people." As mentioned in the Introduction, the Polish national idea was based on aristocracy before the partitions and was very closely linked to the notion of Sarmatism. Sarmatism postulated the (cultural, ethnic) difference of the Polish nobility, the *szlachta*, from the other social groups (peasants, urban population, Jews), thus legitimizing the exclusive political supremacy of this class in the republican system of the Polish-Lithuanian Commonwealth.[53] Since the partitions put the sarmatic worldview under the accusation of being the main cause of the disintegration of the state, the *szlachta* began to lose its central position in the Polish national idea in favor of the *lud*.[54] During the Romantic era, the *lud* was imagined as the peasantry, which embodied original positive Polish national values and traditions and was opposed to the egoism and the corrupt customs of the aristocracy. After the failed uprisings, the Polish intelligentsia identified the lack of mobilization in the countryside as the reason for this failure and sought greater inclusion of the peasantry in the national discourse.[55] At that time, a series of ethnologic studies appeared in which the depiction of the rural population fluctuated between an idealization of peasant folklore and a very realistic view of their dramatic misery, especially in the Galician countryside. Thus, the material and moral emancipation of the peasants became a part of a necessary national emancipation.[56]

The narrative of the necessity of addressing urban poverty as a national duty cannot be separated from the narrative of the peasants and should be understood as a continuation of it, to a degree. Some articles considered the rural origins of the urban poor, framing both groups under the common concept of *lud* and making no distinction between the fight against poverty in the city or in the countryside.[57] Others considered the urban manifestation of the two forms of poverty to be much more dramatic than its rural counterpart, supporting a more urgent need for national mobilization in the cities.[58] In both cases, the topic of urban poverty was nationalized and considered a form of national backwardness on the one hand and a reaction to the latter as a national duty on the other. These articles agreed in considering (national) education as the key to overcoming Polish backwardness caused by mass poverty, and also as a tool to include the poor in the imagined nation.

Urban Poverty as Part of the Modernity Discourse: Nation vs. Class?

National delay and imperial peripherality were not the only (and not the main) interpreted frameworks of the Varsovian press when it came to urban poverty. I have already demonstrated that, through topics such as disease and hygiene, the press affirmed Polish modernity within Europe and toward their own imperial center. In a lengthy, two-piece article on the cholera epidemic in 1892, *Prawda*, another Varsovian popular magazine and voice of the liberal intelligentsia, went even further and depicted cholera as a typical disease of Western urbanity.[59] The author of the article explained that the city's slums constituted the perfect environment for different bacteria in comparison to the countryside. Without exception, this phenomenon concerned every modern urban conglomerate, including wealthier and more advanced metropolises like London and Paris. According to the author, the picane of cholera was thus no indication of a specific Varsovian backwardness, but was rather a global manifestation of the modern process of urbanization, which generally gave rise to poor, overcrowded districts afflicted by hygiene issues. Moreover, the author highlighted that disease did not affect all levels of urban society but only the poorest part of the city's population. In this article, cholera therefore represented a discursive tool to negotiate Warsaw's belonging to a global urban modernity on the one hand and the social hierarchies within local urban space on the other.

Similarly, the previously cited article on cholera published in *Tygodnik Ilustrowany* in 1908 identifies the disease as a marker both for urban modernity and social differences. The author makes a mockery of the mass hysteria triggered by the outbreak, arguing that cholera exclusively affects "the poor chaps and the paupers, the hungry and the devastated, [it] is an epidemic of the dirty basements and garrets."[60] Instead, the "intelligent," "reasonable" and "materially/financially well-off" part of the urban population – thus, the average reader of the magazine – had nothing to fear. Furthermore, in this case, the narrative about cholera created both economic and moral gaps between Warsaw's upper-middle and working classes, emphasizing not only the material and spiritual misery of the latter but also the rationality and bourgeois character of the former as a direct contrast. The poor undergo a denationalization process, transforming from the national *lud* into the social "other," a mirror image of the modernity of the rest of Varsovian society. Linked to the figure of the poor, the philanthropy narrative in the article also shifted from that of the aspired national inclusion of the working class through their emancipation to a demarcation line of their exclusion and otherness. Indeed, although the author motivated his readers to undertake actions in solidarity with potential cholera victims, he consequently failed to describe the epidemic and the initiatives against it from a national perspective of collective shame and duty. On the contrary, he called the epidemic a welcome lesson for the poor to improve their hygienic standards and viewed the solidarity initiatives as mere acts of goodwill, giving expression to the highly civilized nature of the wealthy and modern half of Warsaw's inhabitants.

We can find a further example of this shift in a report published in 1896 concerning another philanthropic initiative from members of the Varsovian upper class, labeled by the *Tygodnik Ilustrowany* as an institute of "moral hygiene" for the children of the working class. Marian Gawalewicz presented his aims and goals as follows:

> This [institution] should be a kind of disinfection room for underage vagabonds who drift along the city's pavements, grow up in the fumes of the various sewers of depravity, wandering around the rubbish of the proletariat.[61]

In the words of Gawalewicz, philanthropic activity had no emancipatory character, but instead resembled medical treatment to cure a somewhat infectious plague. Similarly, the young descendants of the poor urban class certainly did not embody the backward section of the imagined nation deserving emancipation, even from a paternalistic perspective. He portrayed them with disregard as byproducts of modern urbanization which should be "disinfected," so as not to contaminate the remaining urban space. From this point of view, they already constitute a part of the urban landscape of modern Warsaw; namely, the negative one.

Articles aiming to demonize the poor increased after 1905. The revolution of the same year can be viewed as a watershed in the development of Polish national thinking.[62] While Warsaw's intelligentsia initially welcomed the revolution with sympathy as a new chapter in the national uprising of the nineteenth century, it rapidly became clear that social issues dominated the revolutionary mobilization as opposed to concerns at the national level. Unabashed patriots like Bolesław Prus completely distanced themselves from it. Intimidated by the strikes and the violence, the Polish upper classes almost resorted to requesting Russian intervention. In the same period, a new post-positivist generation emerged called the *niepokorny*, convinced of the need for renewed action and divided between a socialist and a nationalist wing. All of these phenomena coincided to place the working class in a new social light and to introduce modern imperialist, anti-Semitic, racial, biological/evolutionist and nationalist rhetoric into the public Polish debate on poverty.[63]

As a result, imperialistic, racial, ethnic or biological/evolutionistic categories were employed to demarcate social difference. For instance, in its weekly comment on local occurrences in 1905, the *Tygodnik Ilustrowany* published an invective against criminality in Wola, at that time the biggest industrial suburb on the western outskirts of the city. The author stigmatized the violence in the peripheral district as being suitable for the "wildest inhabitants of Polynesia" and considered it unacceptable that such conditions could exist "at the gates of a civilized city in the twentieth century."[64] The analogy between the Polish working class and non-European "primitive" people as the object of colonial discourses indicates the exclusion of Warsaw's poor from the urban community, no longer defined by nationality but by its belonging to a universal, modern civilization. The article translates here the social difference within the Polish society as an ethnic, even racial difference, thus making it much more comprehensible for the public and simultaneously more absolute. Moreover, despite the author's criticism of the situation in Wola, using adjectives such as "intolerable," he did not question the modern character of Warsaw in general. The ethnic and racial marker of the otherness of the poor, the civilization gap and the bourgeois aversion to savageness/barbarism actually represented classical elements of the narrative of modernity of the West and indicated the colonial rather than national aspirations of Warsaw's intelligentsia toward its working class.

Nevertheless, in an era of strong nationalistic thinking, such social exclusion and racialization of the poor did not mean the disappearance of the national element from the discourse on poverty but rather implied new patterns of integrating the poor into the imagined national society. A good example of this can be found in a short series of reportages published by the *Tygodnik* in 1906 under the title "Among Warsaw's Miserables." The author, Remigiusz Kwiatkowski, visited a number of Warsaw's philanthropic structures which sought to take care of the poor, such as dormitories, public canteens and "earning houses," places where the unemployed could undertake simple day jobs and receive a small wage. This series is a genuine Varsovian manifestation of the format of the "reportage from the slums," analyzed by Mayne and Schwarz in their studies. Simply put, the existence of this genre not only indicates the belonging of the Varsovian periodicals to a Western discourse on urban modernity based on the othering of the lower classes, but also to an inter-urban press network. Kwiatkowski enacted his first visit to the dormitory as an encounter between two completely separate worlds: the journalist representing the respectable, well-dressed, hygiene-aware, morally impeccable part of Warsaw was looking, both fascinated and disgusted, down at the dirty, smelly, and unhealthy other half of the city.[65] The author´s praise for the dormitory's management presented the philanthropic institution as a proof of Warsaw's modernity, successfully tackling and controlling the endemic poverty produced by modern urban space.

Interestingly, the dormitory contained two groups of people. One group, sleeping on the dirtier and more stifling ground floor, was composed of apathetic, passive, lazy drunkards who refused all communication and whose physical proximity drew the journalist's disgust. The second group on the fresher and brighter first floor mostly consisted of young newspaper street vendors. Kwiatkowski could interact with them and learned with sympathy of their entrepreneurial character, interest in news and frequent incarceration in the citadel for their illegal press distribution. Whereas the first group represented the "other," the opposite of bourgeois industriousness, the second, thanks to their economic activity and national consciousness, embodied the perfect target for inclusion into the nation. Further articles, such as a second reportage by Kwiatkowski on the earning houses and a depiction of different elements of Warsaw's working class published by *Świat* some years later, stressed the willingness, or lack thereof, to be economically active as the defining factor in the social inclusion or exclusion of members of the working class, while also serving as an encapsulation of the question of the modernity of national society itself.[66] Both characterizations of the poor as being lazy or industrious especially contributed to the construction of the nation as no longer backward and in need of catching up with the modernization of Western Europe, but as already being genuinely modern. These articles propagated an image of Warsaw as a city ruled by modern bourgeois values and confirmed the crucial role of the middle class in urban space and the imagined nation. Work ethic now assumed the role of education as the most important component of modern Polish society, and the poor represented the social figure which confirmed this work ethic through its ability or inability to adopt it.

A second integration pattern for the poor in the modern nation concerned ethnicity. An article published in *Świat* in 1912 by Zofia Daszyńska-Golińska, economist, socialist and feminist activist, which commented on a study on the physical characteristics of the Warsaw proletariat, shows this paradigmatically.[67] The author welcomed the study as a demonstration of the leading Polish position in a very new discipline, the "anthropology of the poor," which aimed to provide an adequate response to the question of whether the poor were living in misery due to their long history of being exploited or their biological inferiority. Reminiscent of the studies of Cesare Lombroso on the physiognomy of criminals published a few decades earlier, this biologist approach clearly supported a vision of the urban poor as being racially different from the rest of Polish society. The study demonstrated that the average body of Warsaw's proletarians was shorter and thinner than their aristocratic and bourgeois counterparts. In her comment, Daszyńska-Golińska actually considered the influence of social factors like malnutrition or mothers working during and shortly after pregnancy as causes for these results. Nevertheless, the undertaking and enthusiastic publication of such a study alone is itself symptomatic of the spread of an image of poverty that went far beyond the idea of a mere social gap and instead sought to construct the racial distinction of the poor, thus reaffirming the biological superiority of the Warsaw upper-middle classes in modern rather than national terms. However, the study also contained the possibility of the nationalization of the poor. Indeed, the measurements not only concerned Warsaw's working class in general but distinguished between the Jewish and the Polish proletariat, showing that the former was physically weaker than the latter, or rather that the Polish proletariat was somewhat sturdy in physical terms in comparison with other ethnic groups; in particular, their Jewish counterparts. Therefore, while on the one hand the study reinforced the Western-colonial self-identity of Warsaw's upper classes, on the other hand, it included the Polish poor in a national society which was primarily imagined in ethnic and even racial terms. As soon as ethnicity and race became the central categories of national definition, the poor could therefore represent both the ethical-racial other, as well as the Polish ethnic-racial self, to define the ethical-racial otherness of other groups.

Conclusion

The analysis of Warsaw's Polish press at the turn of the century shows that the issue of poverty was framed along two lines of discourse: the first concerning the imagined nation, and the second concerning global Western modernity. On the one hand, the various spatial, physical and spiritual manifestations of poverty in Warsaw represented an indicator for the Polish delay in comparison with Western Europe due to political dependence on the backward Russian Empire; following the captivity of the nation, the eradication of poverty was presented as a task for the national emancipation. On the other hand, poverty constituted an important element for the discursive construction of Warsaw as a modern metropolis and for the self-assurance of the magazine's target audience as a modern Western bourgeoisie. From this perspective, urban poverty can be considered a progressive poverty intrinsically linked with the discourse of modernity. However, in light of the last examples, we also have to conclude that it is not possible to present a clear divide between a narrative of social or racial othering of the poor which enables an affirmation of belonging for the rest of Warsaw to Europe and modernity, and a national framing of poverty which implies a discourse on urban delay and peripherality. On the contrary, the discourse on the poor paradigmatically shows the complex entanglements between the categories of nation, Europe and modernity, as well as the manifold patterns of the self-location of Warsaw at the turn of the century in the direction of these categories. Through the topic of poverty, the Varsovian magazines simultaneously negotiated the position of Warsaw in relationship to other (Western) European cities and its belonging to an urban (Western) European modernity, as well as the core and the borders of the modern Polish nation. Addressing urban poverty, the Varsovian press discerned between the national and/or modern self and the social or ethnic other, and reproduced an ambivalent self-consciousness of Warsaw as a modern city.

Acknowledgments

This publication was supported by the Viadrina Institute for European Studies of the European University Viadrina.

Notes

1. A. Pawłowski, "Rozwój miast polskich: Rozwój Warszawy," *Świat*, September 7, 1912, 11.
2. See for example: Nathaniel D. Wood, "Not Just the National: Modernity and the Myth of Europe in the Capital Cities of Central and Southeastern Europe," in *Capital Cities in the Aftermath of Empires, Planning in Central and Southeastern Europe*, ed. Emily Gunzburger Makaš and Tanja Damljanovic Conley (London: Routledge, 2009), 258–269.
3. Jan C. Behrends and Martin Kohlrausch, "Races to Modernity: Metropolitan Aspirations in Eastern Europe, 1890–1940," in *Races to Modernity: Metropolitan Aspirations in Eastern Europe, 1890–1940*, ed. Jan C. Behrends and Martin Kohlrausch (Budapest: Central European University Press, 2014), 1–20, p. 2.

4. Nathaniel D. Wood, *Becoming Metropolitan: Urban Selfhood and the Making of Modern Cracow* (DeKalb: Northern Illinois University Press, 2010), 12.
5. Wood, "Not Just the National," 259.
6. Peter Fritzsche, *Reading Berlin 1900* (Cambridge, MA: Harvard University Press, 1998).
7. For a historical perspective on politics and poverty in Europe, see for example S.J. Woolf, *The Poor in Western Europe in the Eighteenth and Nineteenth Centuries* (London: Methuen, 1986); Frauke Sassnick, *Armenpolitik zwischen Helfen und Strafen: Das Problem der Armut in Winterthur vom Ancien Régime zum 19. Jahrhundert* (Winterthur: Stadtbibliothek, 1989); Lutz Raphael, ed., *Zwischen Ausschluss und Solidarität: Modi der Inklusion / Exklusion von Fremden und Armen in Europa seit der Spätantike* (Frankfurt-am-Main: Lang, 2008).
8. Alan Mayne, *The Imagined Slum: Newspaper Representation in Three Cities, 1870–1914* (Leicester: Leicester University Press, 1993); Angela Schwarz, " 'East Enders': Zur Konstruktion des neugierigen Blicks auf die städtischen Unterschichten in der Illustrated London News," in *Illustrierte Zeitschriften um 1900: Mediale Eigenlogik, Multimodalität und Metaisierung*, ed. Natalia Igl and Julia Menzel (Bielefeld: Transcript, 2016), 281–307.
9. Andrzej Walicki, *Poland Between East and West: The Controversies Over Self-Definition and Modernization in Partitioned Poland: The August Zaleski Lectures, 18–22 April 1994* (Cambridge: Harvard Ukrainian Research Institute, 1994); Brian Porter, *When Nationalism Began to Hate: Imagining Modern Politics in Nineteenth Century Poland* (Oxford: Oxford University Press, 2000); Tomasz Kizwalter, *Über die Modernität der Nation: Der Fall Polen* (Osnabrück: Fibre, 2013).
10. Historians such as Tara Zahra and Peter Judson coined for the Habsburg context the concept of "national indifference" to highlight the multiple identities and loyalties of imperial subjects in Central-Eastern Europe. See Tara Zahra, "Imagined Noncommunities: National Indifference as a Category of Analysis," *Slavic Review* 69, no. 1 (2010): 93–119; Pieter M. Judson and Tara Zahra, "Introduction," *Austrian History Yearbook* 43 (2012): 21–27.
11. Porter, *When Nationalism Began to Hate*, 75–81.
12. Steven Tötösy de Zepetnek, "Configurations of Postcoloniality and National Identity: Inbetween Peripherality and Narratives of Change," *The Comparatist: Journal of the Southern Comparative Literature* 23 (May 1999): 89–110.
13. Walicki, *Poland Between East and West*.
14. Malte Rolf, *Imperiale Herrschaft im Weichselland: Das Königreich Polen im Russischen Imperium (1864–1915)* (München: Oldenbourg Wissenschaftsverlag, 2014), 431–437; Christoph Mick, "Colonialism in the Polish Eastern Borderlands 1919–1939," in *The Shadow of Colonialism on Europe's Modern Past*, ed. Róisín Healy and Enrico Dal Lago (Basingstoke: Palgrave Macmillan, 2014), 126–141, p. 127.
15. The term Kingdom of Poland refers to the western part of the Russian partition with Warsaw as its capital. Although this name is actually anachronistic for the Russian administrative nomenclature of the end of the century, both the Polish press of the time and scholars today use this expression to define the region until World War I.
16. All this data is approximated. The data on the different partitions is taken from different studies, inter alia: Maria Nietyksza, *Ludność Warszawy na przełomie XIX i XX wieku* (Warszawa: Państwowe Wydawnictwo Naukowe, 1971); Jerzy Myśliński, "Prasa polska w Galicji w dobie autonomicznej:

(1867–1918)," in *Prasa polska w latach 1864–1918*, ed. Jerzy Łojek (Warszawa: Państwowe Wydawnictwo Naukowe, 1976), 114–176; Porter, *When Nationalism Began to Hate*; Anna Bitner-Nowak, "Wohnungspolitik und Wohnverhältnisse in Posen in den Jahren 1900–1939," in *Wohnen in der Großstadt 1900–1939: Wohnsituation und Modernisierung im europäischen Vergleich*, ed. Alena Janatková and Hanna Kozińska-Witt (Stuttgart: Franz Steiner, 2006), 151–178.

17. Nietyksza, *Ludność*, 50–59.
18. Patrice M. Dabrowski, "Cracow and Warsaw," in Makaš and Conley, eds., *Capital Cities*, 201–202.
19. See Rolf, *Imperiale Herrschaft im Weichselland*, 234.
20. Martin Kohlrausch, "Warszawa funkcjonalna: Radical Urbanism and the International Discourse on Planning in the Interwar Period," in Behrends and Kohlrausch, eds., *Races to Modernity*, 205–231, p. 209.
21. See Rolf, *Imperiale Herrschaft im Weichselland*, chap. 10; Ute Caumanns, "Mietskasernen und 'Gläserne Häuser': Soziales Wohnen in Warschau zwischen Philanthropie und Genossenschaft 1900–1939," in Janatková and Kozińska-Witt, eds., *Wohnen in der Großstadt 1900–1939*, 205–224, pp. 209–212. In this chapter, Malte Rolf highlights the necessity of cooperation with the Russian authorities to realize philanthropic initiatives and therefore Russian participation in the modernization of Warsaw.
22. By the term "press for the people," here I translate the Polish term *pisma / prasa dla ludu* which the Polish-speaking historiography of the media uses to indicate those magazines written for the rural population or the urban working class. See Janusz Kostecki and Zofia Byczkowska, "Czytelnictwo czasopism ludowych w Królestwie Polskim w drugiej połowie XIX wieku," *Przegląd Humanistyczny* 22, no. 10 (1978): 107–127; Grażyna Gzella, "Główne Trendy w rozwoju prasy dla ludu w XIX wieku," in *Książka i prasa w systemie komunikacji społecznej: Przeszłość, dzień dzisiejszy, perspektywy*, ed. Maria Juda (Lublin: Wydawn. Uniwersytetu Marii Curie-Skłodowskiej, 2002), 119–128.
23. Despite the fact that many authors highlight the rapid decrease in illiteracy in the Russian partition, it is not easy to find quantifications of this phenomenon. In this regard, Brian Porter estimates that in 1883 57% of male Varsovians could read and that illiteracy decreased further to 30% in 1914, while remaining at 80% in rural areas. Porter, *When Nationalism Began to Hate*, 77.
24. For the emergence of new literate Polish-speaking social groups see e. g.: Anna Żarnowska, ed., *Workers, Women, and Social Change in Poland, 1870–1939* (Aldershot: Ashgate, 2004).
25. On this regard, see the opening article of the magazine: Anonymous, "Powitanie," *Świat*, January 1, 1906, 1–2, p. 1.
26. Wood, *Becoming Metropolitan*, 51.
27. On the circulation of formats and contents through the genre of popular weekly magazines on a European level, see Clara Frysztacka et al., "Kolumbus Transnational: Verflochtene Geschichtskulturen und europäische Medienlandschaften im Kontext des 400. Jubiläums der Entdeckung Amerikas 1892," *Journal of Modern European History* 15, no. 3 (2017): 418–447.
28. Mayne, *The Imagined Slum*, 6–7.
29. See, for example: Marek Chamot, *Entuzjazm i zwątpienie: Obraz własny Polaków w wybranej publicystyce prasowej trzech zaborów w latach 1864–1914* (Toruń: Wydawn. Uniwersytetu Mikołaja Kopernika, 2003), 7–14.
30. On the crucial role of the press in the creation of the nation, see Benedict Anderson, *Imagined Communities: Reflections on the Origin and Spread of Nationalism* (London: Verso, 1990), 37–40.

31. For an overview on the censorship rules valid in Warsaw after 1863 and their consequences on the Varsovian public see Rolf, *Imperiale Herrschaft im Weichselland*, 125–154.
32. Alexander Kraushar, "Typy i oryginały warszawskie z odległejszej i mniej odległej przeszłości," *Tygodnik Ilustrowany*, March 29, 1903, 296.
33. See also "Ze starej Warszawy," *Świat*, April 18, 1908, 22–23.
34. J. Cz, "Nowa Warszawa," *Tygodnik Ilustrowany*, December 10, 1910, 1019–1020, p. 1020.
35. See W. Sz, "II-ga wystawa hygeniczna w Warszawie," *Tygodnik Ilustrowany*, May 2, 1896, 345–348.
36. See for example Anonymous, "Jedni dla drugich: Z dziejów miłosierdzia," *Biesiada Literacka,* August 1, 1890, 68–70; M. Bukowińska, "Domy zarobkowy dla dzieci," *Tygodnik Ilustrowany*, June 18, 1898, 482–483.
37. See for example St. Gr., "Kropla mleka w Łodzi," *Tygodnik Ilustrowany*, October 28, 1905, 801.
38. See Anonymous, "Wobec cholery," *Tygodnik Ilustrowany*, October 3, 1908, 812–813.
39. See A. Lange, "Marzenia Warszawskie," *Świat*, January 20, 1906, 12–13.
40. Ibid., 40–41, p. 40.
41. S. Dzik, "Przyszła Warszawa," *Świat*, February 12, 1910, 9–11.
42. See e. g. also: Stanisław Kozłowski, "Warszawa dzisiejsza a dawna," *Świat*, February 29, 1908, 2–3; Henryk Mierzejewski, "Nasz przemysł a kwestya robotnicza," *Świat*, November 19, 1910, 6–8.
43. See J.O., "Z tygodnia na tydzień: Czy jeście nie dosycz?" *Tygodnik Ilustrowany*, May 27, 1905, 385–386; Z.D., "Okolice Warszawy," *Tygodnik Ilustrowany*, October 8, 1910, 827.
44. See Aleksander Rembowski, "Miasto Analfabetów," *Tygodnik Ilustrowany*, August 5, 1905, 570–571.
45. See Rembowski, "Miasto."
46. See Mierzejewski, "Nasz przemysł."
47. S. Dzik., "Przyszła Warszawa," 9.
48. See Kozłowski, "Warszawa."
49. Adolf Suligowski, *Kwestia mieszkań* (Warschau, 1889).
50. See Lange, "Marzenia"; Z.D., "Dla Warszawy," *Tygodnik Ilustrowany*, May 14, 1910, 395.
51. See S.P., "Działalność prywatna a potrzeby ogólne," *Tygodnik Ilustrowany*, March 5, 1898, 182.
52. Gryf, "Smutna staystyka," *Tygodnik Ilustrowany*, January 14, 1899, 42.
53. For the sarmatic idea, see Kizwalter, *Über die Modernität der Nation*, 77–89.
54. Ibid., 310–322.
55. See Keely Stauter-Halsted, *The Nation in the Village: The Genesis of Peasant National Identity in Austrian Poland, 1848–1914* (Ithaca: Cornell University Press, 2001), 97–99.
56. See Stauter-Halsted, *Nation*, 99–112.
57. See J.K., "Co robić można i co robić trzeba," *Tygodnik Ilustrowany*, April 22, 1899, 322.
58. See E. Jankowski, "Chleb i ziemi," *Tygodnik Ilustrowany*, March 3, 1906, 146.
59. See Zen Piet., "Życie społeczne: Zdrowotność miast," *Prawda*, August 13, 1892, 391; Zen Piet., "Życie społeczne: Zdrowotność miast (Donończenie)," *Prawda*, August 20, 1892, 403–404.
60. Anonymous, "Wobec Cholery," 813.
61. Quis. [pseudonym for Marian Gawalewicz], "Z tygodnia na tydzień," *Tygodnik Ilustrowany*, April 4, 1896, 263–264, p. 264.

62. See Magdalena Micińska, *Inteligencja na rozdrożach* (Warszawa: Instytut Historii PAN, Wydawn. Neriton, 2008), 138–150; Scott Ury, *Barricades and Banners: The Revolution of 1905 and the Transformation of Warsaw Jewry* (Stanford, CA: Stanford University Press, 2012).
63. See Porter, *When Nationalism Began to Hate*, 176–188.
64. J.O., "Z tygodnia na tydzień," 385.
65. See Remigiusz Kwiatkowski, "Wśród nędzy Warszawy," *Tygodnik Ilustrowany*, April 14, 1906, 281–282.
66. See Remigiusz Kwiatkowski, "Wśród nędzy warszawskiej," *Tygodnik Ilustrowany*, August 18, 1906, 645–646; Anonymous, "Z życia proletaryatu warszawskiego: Parę obrazków," *Świat*, November 19, 1912, 3–4.
67. See Zofia Emilia Daszyńska-Golińska, "Proletaryat Warszawy," *Świat*, November 19, 1912, 1–3.

9 Going East

Gustave Loisel and the Networks of Exchange Between Zoological Gardens Before 1914

Oliver Hochadel

A Parisian in Budapest

In April 1907, the Budapest newspaper *Pester Lloyd* announced the visit of "the Professor from the Sorbonne in Paris, Dr. Gustav [sic!] Loisel." The article reported that:

> On behalf of the French Ministry of Culture he intends to gather experiences at the Hungarian Ornithological Center that might be instrumental for the establishment of a similar institute in France. Dr. Loisel spent an entire morning studying the organization of the headquarters and the means used to make birds artificially autochthonous. Then the scholar went on to Margaret Island and inspected the birds' shelters and the nest caves. Dr. Loisel expressed the greatest appreciation with respect to the experiences he had had. He announced that, in the autumn, another French scholar would visit Budapest in order to gather practical experience in the Ornithological Center.[1]

The great interest of a French scholar in a scientific institution in Budapest in the early twentieth century might at first appear surprising. Maybe even more astonishing is the fact that Loisel was on an official mission by a French ministry actively searching for best practices (in this case, in ornithology and wildlife management) in Eastern Europe in order to import them back to France. We are used to knowledge traveling in the opposite direction: Around 1900, scholars from allegedly peripheral countries would go to France, Germany or Great Britain in order to study and to learn the most advanced scientific practices. In terms of scientific excellence, we tacitly assume, Budapest could hardly hold a candle to Paris. Yet the visit of Loisel to Budapest in April 1907 might be a good starting point to question this hierarchical and unidirectional relationship. This article will analyze Loisel's journeys through Europe. Between 1906 and 1910, he visited a large number of zoological gardens and other institutions that kept wild animals for different purposes such as display, breeding, research and hunting.

In order to reconstruct this interurban zoological matrix, we will first have to briefly sketch the rise of the modern zoo in the second half of the nineteenth century and its close relationship with the urban sphere. We will then go on to describe not only the aim of Loisel's zoological journeys, but also his methods. He was able to gather and process an enormous wealth of information of different kinds in his publications, in particular his three *Rapports sur une Mission Scientifique dans les Jardins et Établissements Zoologiques Publics et Privés* (1907/1908)[2] and the third volume of his *Histoire des ménageries de l'Antiquité à nos jours* (1912).[3] In order to question the traditional epistemological hierarchy between metropolis and "periphery," this chapter will look in particular at four zoological institutions in Northern and Eastern Europe that Loisel found exemplary and worthy of emulation. The hypothesis is to conceive of the zoological garden as an interurban and transnational institution in which best practices were intensely discussed and exchanged around 1900. Gustave Loisel was one of its most vocal explorers and discussants.

The Zoo and the City in the Nineteenth Century

The nineteenth century witnessed the birth of the modern zoo, an institution guided by scientific principles and at the same time – at least in principle – open to visit for everybody. There were three zoological gardens by 1830, seven by 1840, ten by 1850, 16 by 1860, 29 by 1870, 41 by 1880, 54 by 1890 and 69 by 1900.[4] The large majority of these were located in Europe and around 15 of them on German territory (from 1871 on, the German Empire). Yet, already by the late nineteenth century, zoos existed on all continents; quite quickly, it had become a truly global institution. Nevertheless, zoos came in many different forms. They varied widely, for example, with respect to their organizational structures. Most were run by associations such as zoological societies in the form of a stock company. Then there were zoos run by the state, by the municipality or even by individuals.[5] Also, the agenda of the zoos could vary considerably, wavering between entertainment, instruction, research and mere commerce. In fact, a mix of often conflicting aims was most characteristic for the late nineteenth century zoo, an issue that Loisel would directly address, as we shall see ahead.

The history of the zoological gardens in the nineteenth and early twentieth centuries has been told in a number of ways: as a transition from the princely collection of animals to the "bourgeois" zoo and, by extension, as part of a cultural history in which the zoo manifests the emerging bourgeois self-confidence and the political aspirations of this class; as the symbolic appropriation of the exotic through acclimatization in the context of colonial history; as an attempt to create a space for zoological research (taxonomy, ethology *avant la lettre*, breeding); and as an example of one of the earliest cultural public institutions and thus of mass culture. With respect to the latter, historians have tried to reconstruct the experiences of zoo visitors while also pointing to the zoos' educational and disciplinary agenda.[6] All these approaches have shown what a rewarding object of study the zoological garden might provide in this long nineteenth century up to World War I.

In Europe and beyond, the zoo evolved into a typical urban cultural institution just like the natural history museum, the park or the opera. It had become an object of civic pride. A "modern" city needed a zoo, as its proponents invariably argued when they were canvassing for such an institution in their city. This relationship has been the starting point for a number of publications that have demonstrated how the zoological garden transforms the urban space.[7] Ayako Sakurai, for example, showed how closely the rise of the Frankfurt liberal urban middle class and the foundation of the zoo in the "Westend" were connected in the 1850s and 1860s.[8] Donna Mehos made a similar case for Amsterdam and its Artis zoo.[9] To understand the early history of the London zoo, founded in 1828, its location in Regent's Park, an upper-class neighborhood in the making, was crucial.[10] In Vienna, thousands of visitors flocked every weekend to the Schönbrunn Menagerie (at the time still outside the city limits), transforming Hietzing, the village nearby, into a thriving amusement center.[11]

Yet the close relationship between urban space and the zoo goes even further, as Christina Wessely demonstrated. She pointed to striking parallels between department stores and zoological gardens, with regard to the architecture and the way they presented their objects. The merchandise in a department store and the animals in the zoo were both offered for visual consumption in galleries. Wessely also argued that the zoo was presented as "ordered" nature, while the rapidly growing city around 1900 seemed more and more like an impenetrable and "unreadable" jungle.[12]

So, while historians have studied the intrinsic liaison between zoological gardens and cities of the nineteenth century, the relationship *between* zoos (and thus between different urban spaces) has not been studied in great detail. In this chapter, we will call this network between zoological gardens the "interurban zoological matrix," adapting the concept of the "interurban matrix" coined by Nathan Wood.[13] Just like the city-dwellers reading in newspapers about other urbanites, zoo directors and other actors concerned with zoos were highly aware of developments in other zoological gardens, even those located thousands of kilometers away.

In the introduction of this volume, we discussed the concept of interurban knowledge transfer. Study trips abroad were a crucial feature of gathering best practices. These "fact-finding missions" were mostly dedicated to questions of urban planning, public health and architecture. Yet the rise of specific urban cultural institutions such as museums or zoos also required an internationally oriented search for examples to follow, or rather, to adapt.[14]

Omnipresent as they were to be in the second half of the nineteenth century in the European city, zoological gardens thus also became one of the destinations for this traveling circus of experts darting across the continent in order to visit the corresponding institutions in other cities. Just as with respect to sewage systems, tramways or tuberculosis clinics, these envoys had been commissioned by town halls or ministries to gather information and practical advice that could be instrumental back home. The aim of this chapter is thus to investigate the intersection between urban history and the history of zoological gardens, which has not yet been touched upon, either by urban scholars or zoo historians.

Zoo Voyages Before Loisel

Zoo experts were explorers of a particular kind. They traveled to see exotic animals, yet without having to leave civilization. What did they learn on their journeys? How did the knowledge they acquire travel back to where they came from? Was it implemented in the zoos back home? What does "best practices" mean in this context? This chapter will not be able to answer all these questions. The idea is rather to formulate a research program by looking at the journeys of Gustave Loisel.

The first person to resume the activities of these zoo travelers was none other than Loisel himself. In the introduction of his first *Rapport*, he gave a succinct overview of a handful of zoologists (mostly zoo directors) who had embarked on a reconnaissance mission to other zoos. This critical summary served to construct a point of departure for Loisel's own *Rapports* – which went well beyond the accounts of his predecessors, as we shall see.

Leopold Philipp Martin (1815–1885) is the first to be mentioned by Loisel. Today's historians do indeed consider the German naturalist and conservationist to be one of the first zoo reformers. Martin's opus magnum are the three volumes of *Praxis der Naturgeschichte*. The third volume, entitled *Naturstudien* and published in 1878, deals with 27 zoological gardens mainly in Germany (but also London, Paris, Amsterdam, Antwerp, Brussels and Basel) and is the fruit of an extensive journey undertaken the previous summer. In *Naturstudien*, Martin first describes the zoos he visited and then lays out his idea of an ideal zoo, departing from the taxonomic representation of animals toward a more holistic vision. Martin was one of the first to suggest that animals be grouped according to climatic zones and he was a protagonist of what Lynn Nyhart labeled the "German reform movement in natural history." This movement had its strong base outside academia and placed the focus on the living animal.[15]

Philip Lutley Sclater (1829–1913) was at the time a famous zoologist (in particular, an ornithologist) with a global network. According to

Loisel, Sclater traveled each year between 1863 and 1900 to visit zoos in continental Europe but also in Africa. Sclater published his observations in individual articles that appeared in *Proceedings of the Zoological Society of London* – and not in an "étude complete," as Loisel laments.[16]

Next, Loisel mentions *The Zoological Gardens of Europe* by Charles Peel, also a member of the Zoological Society of London (ZSL), the society that still runs the zoo in the Regent's Park in London. Peel had visited 36 zoos in Western Europe around 1900, yet Loisel criticizes imprecision, mistakes and the lack of systematics in his report.[17] Clearly, Loisel studied these zoo journeys intensely. He even asked the ZSL to provide him with the unpublished report by R.J. Pocock. In 1904, Pocock had been sent by the ZSL to visit zoos in Germany, Belgium and the Netherlands in order to gather useful information for a reform of the London Zoo.

Arguably, Loisel's most important interlocutor was British naturalist Stanley Flower (1871–1946), director of the zoo in Giza near Cairo, Egypt, since 1898. Flower lists 80 zoos worldwide, of which he visited 31; two in Africa, two in Asia and 27 in Europe (ten in Germany).[18] Later, Flower read Loisel and commented on his *Rapports*.[19]

The accounts of these zoological journeys take on different forms, as this little overview shows, ranging from shorter articles in newspapers and illustrated magazines to articles in more specialist journals to fully-fledged monographs but also unpublished manuscripts. It is a regular feature of these zoo voyages not only to report on the status quo of zoological gardens, but also to both criticize the existing zoos and elaborate on the criteria of how an "ideal" or "modern" zoo should look (both adjectives are actors' categories).

Loisel's focus is on the very recently produced reports by Peel, Pocock and Flower, all connected with the ZSL. These reports date from 1903, 1904 and 1905, respectively, and thus indicate that the ZSL – just like the ones responsible for the Paris zoo – felt that their zoo was in need of reform. Loisel knew that he, Martin and the other experts visiting the English zoo shared a common intellectual project: studying other zoos in order to come up with new solutions. Yet, outside of Great Britain, Martin, Sclater, Peel, Pocock and Flower mainly visited zoos in Western Europe, principally in Germany, France, Belgium and the Netherlands. Zoos in Southern and Eastern Europe or in North and South America hardly featured in their reports. In a sense, these accounts represented the foil against which Loisel tried to distinguish himself. He visited many more zoos than any of his predecessors, and his *Rapports* would turn out to be considerably more extensive, precise and systematic, with a geographical scope extending well beyond Western Europe. Before we turn to Loisel's zoo travels, we must sketch his professional background in order to understand what his reform plans were aiming at.

The Career of Gustave Loisel

Gustave Loisel is a household name in the history of zoological gardens. The three volumes of his *Histoire des ménageries de l'Antiquité à nos jours*, totaling 1,274 pages, are arguably the most comprehensive history of the zoo ever written.[20] The *Histoire* represents a treasure of information and it is difficult *not* to cite Loisel even today.[21] There was a small peak of interest to commemorate the centenary of the publication of the *Histoire* in 2012.[22] Yet, generally, historians have used his opus magnum merely as a mine of information on individual zoos. They have hardly paid any attention to the underlying reform project, which led Loisel to write the *Histoire*. If Loisel receives any personal mention by scholars at all, it is usually as the disciple of a much better-known French biologist, Alfred Giard (1846–1908).[23]

Gustave Antoine Armand Loisel (1864–1933) obtained Ph.D.s both in medicine (1893) and natural sciences (1896). He was a professor at the Sorbonne University, or, as the *Pester Lloyd* more precisely reported, an assistant professor. In 1905, he became the director of the Laboratoire d'embryologie générale et expérimentale.[24] His letterhead featured the image of a turtle creeping out of its shell (Figure 9.1).

"His scientific interest covered nearly all fields of medicine and biology. From cell physiology to the hereditary problems of ducks and from the study of the human and animal spermatogenesis to the defensive strategies of the sponges."[25] So, unlike many of the other zoo travelers he cited, Loisel himself never worked at a zoo, either before or after his reconnaissance missions and publications on the zoo. However, also in 1905, with the death of Émile Oustalet, the chair for mammalogy at the Muséum National d'Histoire Naturelle (MNHN) in Paris had become vacant. This chair included the directorship of the adjacent zoo in the Jardin des Plantes.[26] This was in all likelihood the reason why Loisel's interests turned to the zoo and its reform.[27] Yet he did not simply long for a more prestigious position. Dedicated to the study of living animals, Loisel looked at the zoo with his professional background. What he saw

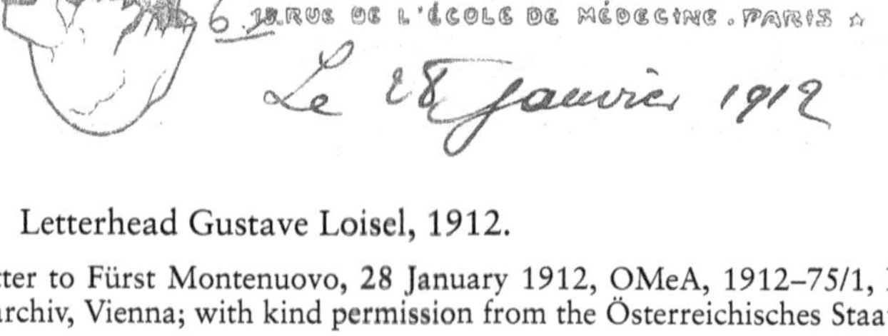

Figure 9.1 Letterhead Gustave Loisel, 1912.

Source: Letter to Fürst Montenuovo, 28 January 1912, OMeA, 1912–75/1, Haus-, Hof- und Staatsarchiv, Vienna; with kind permission from the Österreichisches Staatsarchiv

was an opportunity for research, an opportunity that so far had been largely missed out on. We may think of Loisel as a representative of the modern experimental sciences in biology as opposed to traditional natural history (collecting, taxonomy, comparative anatomy). He advocated a laboratory-based approach in the study of living beings. This explicitly included observation and experiments in order to study the behavior of animals. In 1906 and 1907, he published several papers that stressed the need for reform of the MNHN in general and its zoo in the Jardin des Plantes in particular. He highlighted the opportunities for research that the zoo might provide.[28]

For a long time, it was a commonplace argument of contemporaries, and later of historians, that French natural history went into some sort of decline in the second half of the nineteenth century. Its leading role in the late eighteenth and the first decades of the nineteenth centuries, marked by scholars such as Buffon, Lamarck, Georges Cuvier and Isidore Geoffroy Saint-Hilaire, was lost to British and German naturalists. Historians of science nowadays tend to draw a more complex and nuanced picture.[29] Yet, around 1900, many French naturalists were convinced that the zoological sciences were in urgent need of reform.[30]

The Jardin des Plantes was – according to Loisel but also to many others – the mother of all modern zoos.[31] Founded in 1793 at the height of the French Revolution, it belonged (and still belongs) to the MNHN. However, well over a century after its foundation, contemporaries considered the zoo in the heart of Paris to be an institution of the past. The Jardin was "overcrowded," the mortality rate of the animals was high, the buildings were old and inappropriate for animal keeping, and the personnel lacked proper training.[32]

Strategically, Loisel lamented the dismal state of the zoo in the Jardin des Plantes and published pleas for reform. He could thus convince the Ministère de l'Instruction Publique et des Beaux-Arts to send him on a reconnaissance mission through Europe and later on North America "to realize a reorganization and a more comprehensive use of our old national menagerie."[33] So, in 1906 and 1907, Loisel undertook three *Missions Scientifiques* that were soon afterwards published in three *Rapports*. The first *Rapport* details his visit to Great Britain, the Netherlands and Belgium, the second one to Germany, Denmark, Switzerland and Austria-Hungary and the third one to the United States and Canada. In total, he visited 87(!) zoological institutions, most of them zoos but also aquariums, natural history museums, nature preserves and what we would today call biological research institutes.

In the summer of 1910, he undertook a fourth voyage to Eastern and Northern Europe, inspecting zoos and other animal-keeping institutions in the East of the German Empire (today Poland), the Russian Empire and Scandinavia.[34] This time, the journey was under the auspices of the Société d'Acclimatation de France. Loisel may even have traveled as part of a group. Only his visit to the open-air museum in Skansen near Stockholm was published separately.[35] The results of this last zoo journey are to be found in volumes 2 and 3 of the *Histoire* published in 1912. His thinking about how to reform the zoo of the present ignited his interest for the history of keeping exotic animals going back to antiquity.

It is also significant which countries Loisel did not include in his zoological journeys. It seems that he had a clear idea of where to look for information that he and his French superiors could use in order to reform their own institutions. Loisel had very little to say about zoos and other animal institutions in Southern Europe, not least because there were actually very few zoos there. Spain only had two zoos around 1900, both of seemingly little significance, in Madrid and Barcelona.[36] The Lisbon zoo, founded in 1883, might have merited a visit. Due to its direct colonial connection, it boasted a considerable number and steady supply of interesting exotic animals. Loisel was aware of this, but had to rely on second-hand information.[37] In Italy, too, zoos were scarce and founded late compared to the other side of the Alps, and hence Loisel had little to report about the brand new zoo in Rome, opened in 1910, and the one that was supposed to be founded in Milan at the time.[38] We might suspect that Loisel did not expect to learn much from a trip to the Mediterranean. His interurban network included Eastern Europe, North America and even Buenos Aires, but not the Iberian Peninsula or Italy. In fact, none of the zoological travelers mentioned in this chapter went to Southern Europe. Eastern and Northern Europe was a different matter. In line with the research program of this volume, I will present four "models" of zoological institutions from Loisel's writings that are situated in Breslau, Budapest, Stockholm and Pilawin.

Model 1: Zoologischer Garten Breslau

Loisel dedicates over 15 pages in his second *Rapport* and another ten pages in his *Histoire* to the zoo in Breslau (present-day Wrocław; today the zoo is called Ogród Zoologiczny we Wrocławiu), a city at the time located in the southeast of the German Empire.[39]

His account of the Breslau zoo is typical for the *Rapport* in its all-encompassing scope and matter-of-fact tone: a brief history of the zoo, its budget, number of employees and their salaries and lists of animal food are followed by a minute description of the layout and architecture of the zoo. Loisel's account includes plans of the monkey house, the elephant house, the deer house and the small-bird house ("sparrow house"). He details how the architectural and technical features of the enclosures contribute to the well-being of the animals in terms of control of temperature, feeding, managing their social life and so on.

The "deer house" was modeled after the one at the Berliner Zoologische Garten. It was built in 1905 at the relatively modest cost of 20,000 marks, as Loisel remarks – and could thus serve as a model for other zoos.[40] It was not (only) the architecture that was seen as worth imitating, but also the economical way of constructing a specific enclosure for animals. The lion house of the Breslau zoo became in turn the model for the one in the zoo of Buenos Aires, yet "on a larger and grander scale."[41]

Another claim to fame of the Breslau zoo is the longevity of its gorilla, who lived for over seven years (1897–1904) in the zoo on the banks of the Oder. As Loisel knew very well, apes had an extremely low life expectancy in zoos, the record before had been only 18 months! He made sure to include a photo of a statue of the gorilla (Figure 9.2) in his *Rapport*.

Model 2: Magyar Ornithologiai Központ, Budapest

The *Pester Lloyd* did not exaggerate if we compare the newspaper article cited at the beginning of this chapter with Loisel's enthusiastic account of

Figure 9.2 Statue of the famous gorilla of the Breslau Zoo, 1907.

Source: From Gustave Loisel, Rapport sur une Mission Scientifique dans les Jardins et Établissements Zoologiques Publics et Privés de l'Allemagne, de l'Autriche-Hongrie, de la Suisse et du Danemarck. Paris: Imprimerie Nationale, 1907; after p. 192. Public domain: Bibliothèque Nationale de France, département Collections numérisées, 2012–132614

the Hungarian Ornithological Center, published the same year in his second *Rapport*; "there is no other institution like this one in Europe." He dedicates five pages of his account on the Center in Budapest, detailing the work done at Magyar Ornithologiai Központ (MOK), including – once more – the salaries of the institute's personnel.[42] And just as the newspaper had reported, Loisel did indeed urge the French ministry to create an analogous institute back home.[43] The director of the MOK, founded in 1893, at the time was the renowned Hungarian naturalist Ottó Herman (1835–1914).[44] He had organized the second Ornithological Congress in Budapest in 1891, and had thus become an important actor in ornithology on an international level. Yet the idea for the Hungarian Ornithological Center goes even further back to the first Ornithological Congress held in Vienna in 1884, as Loisel explains. He also highlights the support from the Hungarian state and its ministries in this venture. The MOK started off studying the migration patterns of birds – purely with a focus on research, and very much dependent on international collaboration, amassing huge amounts of observational data from different locations. In the meantime, the MOK also pursued a more applied agenda, i.e. identifying "useful" and "harmful" birds, to use Herman's terminology. How the former could be protected and the latter eliminated was one of the central research questions. This mixture of pure and applied research, the support received by the state, but also the mission of the MOK to educate and train people, both professionals and lay people (foresters, hunters, amateur ornithologists, collectors and so on), was very much in tune with Loisel's vision of how modern biological research should be pursued; that is, as a collaborative enterprise.

Loisel's sober and at the same time very positive account of the MOK was reciprocated in the notice published in *Aguila*, the journal of the institute. The MOK was very pleased to host "the famous scholar" on his official mission.[45] Loisel was clearly selective in his visits. The city of Budapest had had a zoological garden since 1866, but in 1907, this zoo was in transition from private to public ownership. Loisel was not impressed, and only mentioned it briefly.[46]

Model 3: Skansen Friluftsmuseum, Stockholm

On his fourth zoological journey in the summer of 1910, Loisel also visited Stockholm. He was member of a delegation of the Société d'Acclimatation de France on its travels to eastern regions. In a speech delivered to the Society the following year, he reported on their visit to Skansen, just outside Stockholm. Founded in 1891, Skansen was the world's first open-air museum and not primarily a zoo. It focused on Swedish rural life, including displays and even performances showcasing Swedish architecture, customs, dress and so on; in short, a romanticization ethnography of the Swedish people. Yet the vision of Artur Hazelius

(1833–1901), the founder of Skansen, was holistic and the open-air museum thus also included Swedish flora and fauna. Loisel even claims that Hazelius realized ideas first formulated by Buffon, the great champion of French natural history of the late eighteenth century. In his speech to the *Société*, Loisel touches upon a number of issues that he felt French acclimatizers should take to heart, including a focus on conserving indigenous species, investigating how to breed them and possibly reintroduce them in the wild; a pedagogical agenda in order to instill an interest and love for (French) nature in school children; and a plea for a French institute for acclimatization research to be founded, including a huge nature reserve. Sweden, and also the United States, Argentina and Switzerland, were well ahead of France in these respects, and Loisel admonishes his French audience, appealing to their national pride and calling for action.[47]

Model 4: The Nature Reserve of Pilawin, Volhynia, Russia

On the same journey in the summer of 1910, Loisel also visited the Park of Pilawin, founded in 1901 by the Polish count Joseph Potocki. Pilawin is located in the Volhynia region, which nowadays mostly belongs to the Ukraine. Before World War I, it was part of the Russian Empire. Loisel dedicates four pages of his *Histoire* to Pilawin, and also mentions the park in his Skansen report. The enclosure is enormous, with an area of 6,800 hectares. Loisel writes:

> The idea of the noble Pole had been, first of all, to reestablish and encourage the original fauna of his country with the help of his nature reserve . . . Count Potocki then wished to use his reserve for experiments in order to acclimatize species imported from the Asian part of Russia.[48]

A total of 285 animals representing 15 different species had been transferred to Pilawin, among them bears, bison, eland and different kinds of deer.

We find similar ideas as in Loisel's speech about Skansen: the breeding and conservation of "indigenous" species that are threatened and the pursuit of "applied" acclimatization research. Loisel was impressed with this "grandiose work": Pilawin "is currently unique with respect to the number and variety of introduced animal species it harbors."[49] Pilawin was both a nature reserve and a hunting ground for the Polish aristocrat and his invitees. What might seem like a strange mixture to us was by no means uncommon at the time, as Loisel knew very well. He cites similar parks run by owners of large estates in England, the Netherlands and Russia.[50] Again, models for nature reserves could be found in different parts of Europe.

Loisel was not the first to note the exemplary character of the four institutions mentioned in this section. In a sense, he picked up on hints made by earlier zoo travelers such as Peel and Flower. Both had already praised the well-designed animal houses of the Breslau Zoo, as well as the longevity of the gorilla.[51] Yet while Flower's remarks are cursory, Loisel is much more detailed. The plans he provided for animal houses were able to serve as a direct model for another zoo. Loisel was also not the only one impressed by the efforts of Count Potocki. The highly renowned British naturalist and biogeographer Richard Lydekker had already visited Pilawin in 1906 at the invitation of Potocki and published an entire booklet on it.[52] Skansen, too, had become internationally known well before Loisel's visit. In other words, Loisel did not venture into an unknown territory when he traveled east and north. There were already established networks of exchange between zoos and in the fields of ornithology and acclimatization research and he followed their connections. The four examples given here also clearly show that Loisel was not only interested in zoos, but in all kinds of zoological (or biological) institutions and not always located in a city, a point to which we will return ahead.

The Interurban Zoological Matrix

Around 1900, zoological gardens worldwide (and not only in Europe) were clearly aware of one another. They exchanged information through publications in specialized journals, and also through the daily press, personal networks (correspondence and visits) and contact with animal dealers.[53] They also traded animals. For Loisel, they represented one large community. The hundreds and hundreds of pages of the *Rapports* and of the *Histoire* bear a clear testimony to the genuine interest and scholarly respect Loisel had for zoos and similar institutions elsewhere. He asked himself continuously what could be learned from them. Not every single one had something to teach, but many did. For example, the zoological gardens in Vienna (Schönbrunn), Copenhagen and Buenos Aires had succeeded in the difficult task of elephant breeding. With respect to the rearing of smaller monkeys, the zoos in Philadelphia, Amsterdam, Halle, Manchester, Münster and Copenhagen were exemplary.[54] Ram Brahma Sanyal (1858–1908), the long-time director of the Calcutta zoo, had published in 1892 a *Handbook of the Management of Animals in Captivity*, which was still held in high esteem by many zoo directors.[55] It might be true that, in mere quantitative terms, Loisel names mostly zoos in Germany, Great Britain, Belgium and the Netherlands as exemplary. Yet, he does this always with respect to specific issues, be they exemplary zoo architecture, the successful handling of specific species or an innovative research focus. Loisel was interested in virtually all aspects of building and running a zoo. Some Eastern

European institutions he considered exemplary, too, as we have seen. Loisel conceived of Eastern Europe neither as a particularly innovative zone nor as a particularly "backward" one. "Eastern Europe" is not even a concept he uses. Loisel was simply looking for best practice models that might serve French zoology and his vision of modern biological research institutes dedicated to the living animal. His approach is deliberately eclectic; models worthy of emulation might be literally found in many parts of the world.

Take, for example, his reflections about the different ways to study the nutrition of exotic animals, one of the most serious challenges of the zoo. He mentions three complementary methods: (1) the "direct observation" in the wild of what the animals were eating as practiced by the "experimental stations" in the United States; (2) the study of the stomachs of animals killed in the wild, as practiced by the Hungarian Ornithological Center in Budapest, "observational stations" in the United States and some amateurs in England and France; and (3) the regular weighing of the animals and study of their feces, as it was done in the zoo of Buenos Aires.[56]

Loisel sees a geographically and institutionally very diverse community working on the nutrition question, including zoos, research stations (some of them in the countryside) and amateurs. Clearly, in principle, any institution (or even individuals) may serve as a source of best practices to be taken up by other actors in this zoological matrix.

Zoo architecture – for Loisel a major feature – provides us with a number of surprising interurban connections. Reading through the *Histoire* we may discern an "architectural dialogue" between zoos. Thanks to his first-hand knowledge, Loisel could identify the transfer of models for animal houses – and the adaptations made by the "recipient" zoo, as we have already seen in the case of the Breslau zoo, connected with the zoos in Berlin and in Buenos Aires. Concepts such as center and periphery lose their meaning in these interurban and, on occasion, even transcontinental exchanges.

Rather, what Loisel's focus brings to light is the shift of zoological research from the urban zoo to research stations far away from the noisy and crowded city centers. Around 1900, Loisel was by no means the only biologist pondering a relocation of zoological, and in particular ethological, research.[57] The argument of the naturalists: many zoos have become fully commercialized. Their main aim is – for economic reasons – to attract and entertain the paying public. Research is hardly possible anymore with the visitors being a massive disturbing factor. American zoologist Charles Otis Whitman demanded in 1902 "above all, complete isolation from the public" for serious biological research. Loisel opts for reform rather than complete separation. He writes: "Theoretically, a zoological garden should be located far away from the great agglomerations."[58] But a well-conceived and equipped zoo might still be an excellent place to study animals and remain in the city. People should still be able to flock to the zoo, Loisel argues. But the emphasis should be on education – the original mission of the zoo – and not mere entertainment. This is Loisel's answer to the conflicting agendas of the zoo around 1900. After all, his task was to come up with a reform plan for the zoo in the heart of Paris.

Loisel the Information Broker

Already in 1914, in a lengthy and appreciative review of the *Histoire*, Louis Davillé highlighted among other qualities the enormous scholarship that went into the work. Loisel's opus magnum displayed profound knowledge, both scientific and historical. The reviewer also extolled the meticulous handling of the details, which made it nearly impossible to find a spelling mistake in the three hefty volumes.[59] More than a century later, one is still very much inclined to subscribe to this praise.[60]

As this chapter is interested in the circulation of knowledge about zoos, we should try to reconstruct how Loisel actually gathered this wealth of information. Visiting more than 100 institutions is no small feat. How were all these best practices identified and described? Travels, reading and correspondence fed into Loisel's work. His correspondence was enormous, as we can reconstruct from his publications and archival material. Linguistic barriers seem not to have been a major problem. He must have been able to read (and probably to converse in) English, German and possibly more languages, although the letters he wrote to announce his visits or to ask for information seem to have all been in French. And the institutions responded to him mostly in French, occasionally in English or German.[61]

Systematically, Loisel contacted the institutions he wanted to visit in advance. He would explain the purpose of his journey and ask for assistance. Being on an official mission on behalf of the French Ministry of Education surely helped to open doors. Yet, on occasion, some of the commercial zoos, for example in northern Germany, did not respond to Loisel's letters.[62] Loisel also lets the reader know that his technique of gleaning information did not always work, as in the case of the zoo in Rome.[63] Other zoos Loisel did not visit (we may assume for lack of time or other logistical obstacles). In these cases, he reported the written information he had gathered.[64]

When he planned to visit a zoo, an aquarium or a zoological research institute, he meant serious business. In some cases (Berlin, London, New York), he stayed longer than a week at the local zoo to pursue all the questions he was interested in.[65] He was also demanding, paying extensive visits, asking for plans, sketches, photographs and information of all sorts. His hosts from the MOK in Budapest reported admiringly that

Loisel informed himself "with a thoroughness that extended to the smallest details" and that "he visited the many and extensive collections with untiring attention."[66]

Apart from his personal visits, he tried to get hold of all kinds of other information; for example, books, magazines and also newspapers. A well-documented case is his "in depth visit" – as the Austrian administration put it – of the Menagerie Schönbrunn, the zoo of the Austrian emperor in Vienna in the spring of 1907.[67] In this case, we do not only have the corresponding accounts in the *Rapport* and in the *Histoire*, but also a number of letters that he exchanged with the Austrian officials.[68] After his return to Paris, he asked in a letter for exact plans of the new monkey house that had been built the same year. Loisel thought this might be innovative, and thus wanted to document it, including some critique, as well.[69] The construction of monkey houses was a seminal issue at the time, given the extremely high mortality (and zoological value) of monkeys and in particular of apes. How to provide proper conditions – in particular, apt temperatures for the tropical creatures – and how to avoid chilly drafts, as well as the contagion of tuberculosis brought by visitors, were literally vital questions much discussed in zoological circles at the time.[70]

A couple of years later, when preparing the *Histoire* in 1911/1912, he asked for plans of the Schönbrunn Menagerie from the time of Maria Theresia, from 1907 and from the present. In both cases, he was duly served by the Austrian imperial administration.

Loisel was scrupulous also in the elaboration of his writings. As we know in the case of the Schönbrunn Menagerie, he sent the corresponding passages about the Viennese zoo of both his *Rapports* (in 1907) and of his *Histoire* (in 1912) before they went to print to the Viennese authorities to be checked for accuracy, asking them to strike out anything that the Austrian authorities might deem unfit.[71] At least for the Viennese case, we know that he also took photographs, which he did not, however, use for his publications. Both the *Rapports* and the *Histoire* contain a considerable number of photographs of zoological gardens, as well as drawn plans. As far as we can tell, the institutions he visited provided him with the illustrations.

His growing historical interest also led him to hunt for information in libraries. In the second volume of the *Histoire*, which dealt with animal keeping in the seventeenth and eighteenth centuries, he included a chapter on "The menageries of the Slavic and Scandinavian countries." To gather material for this chapter he even studied historical documents in the Imperial Public Library in St. Petersburg, looking at the initiatives of the Radziwiłł family.[72] A hundred years later, Piotr Daszkiewicz was able to use the *Histoire* to compile information about "Polish" zoos when Poland did not exist as an independent state.[73]

Conclusions

In this article, we wanted to reconstruct the interurban zoological matrix that existed in Europe at the beginning of the twentieth century. Loisel's *Rapports*, the *Histoire* and some of his articles have proven to be rich sources in this respect. In his search for best practices, Loisel was simply curious and thus very eclectic. Whether the institution he described was Russian, Swedish, Hungarian or Argentinian mattered little to him. Hierarchical spatial concepts such as "periphery" and "center" are hard to find in the *Rapports* or the *Histoire* despite the fact that the professor of the Sorbonne, Gustave Loisel, was, at least nominally, a representative of the metropolis of Paris and its scientific establishment. Rather, what emerges in his vision is one large space with an increasing number of nodes that are connected with each other. To be sure, this space was not uniform in Loisel's work. The majority of nodes were still to be found in Western Europe, but Eastern Europe and North America certainly featured prominently, while Latin America (Buenos Aires) and India (Calcutta) were on Loisel's map, too.

Ideas on how to run a zoo, how to display animals and guarantee their well-being, how to house them properly, how to do research on living animals and how to acclimatize them circulated through different channels. Zoological journeys such as Loisel's travels were crucial. In his account, the existing models of zoological gardens were imitated and adapted in a non-linear way, depending on a variety of factors: available resources (finances, space, expertise) and the commitment of the corresponding institution (the state, the city council, a wealthy aristocrat, etc.).[74]

Most of the animal-keeping facilities that Loisel analyzed were located in or very near to a city: first and foremost, zoological gardens, but also aquariums, natural history museums and research institutes working with living animals. A small number of the sites were located well outside the urban space, such as the Pilawin Park and the large nature reserves in the United States.

Yet the urban space as such did not feature much at all in Loisel's writings. He would provide the location of the zoo, either central or on the outskirts, comment on ownership issues and little else. In the perception of Loisel and many other research-oriented biologists, the city – or more specifically, its inhabitants – featured as a disruptive factor. However, as we have seen, Loisel did not advocate a complete withdrawal of zoos and similar facilities from the public sphere. Despite the obvious tension between increasingly commercialized zoos and their masses of visitors on the one hand, and the need of modern biological research for seclusion on the other hand, Loisel did not want to give up the original idea of the nineteenth-century zoo, combining leisure, instruction, research and even acclimatization. Yet, while the general idea of combining all these different functions was not new, his reflections dealt in more concrete terms with the question of what a "modern," i.e. scientific, zoo should look like, in terms of its organizational structure, its architecture and the handling of animals.

The modern zoo is, in a sense, a very urban space, peopled by "artificial animals," as Christina Wessely put it. It represents a form of exotic nature in the midst of the urban jungle that could be controlled, ordered, visually consumed and researched. Like the modern city around 1900, the zoo was a European and also a global phenomenon – plagued with practical problems, yet full of promise. Claiming to be "modern" was part and parcel of its identity. This included negotiating and disputing the very meaning of this omnipresent yet elusive term "modern." This discussion formed part of an international discourse on how to run zoos and even more fundamentally what they were for, the "masses," science, preservation or the economy (acclimatization). The forum of this discussion was an interurban matrix, highly tangible in the work of Gustave Loisel.

Loisel's suggestions for the reform of the zoo in the Jardin des Plantes and the creation of a scientifically oriented zoo in Paris or better even outside the city limits did not materialize. The outbreak of World War I has been cited as an obvious reason.[75] Loisel himself had to serve in the French army during the war and even returned to Eastern Europe: he spent some time in Serbia in 1915.[76] But the story is more complicated than this. The plans for a new zoo in Paris and the question of what this institution should actually accomplish were hotly contested among French scholars – for decades. It was not until 1934 that the new zoo opened its doors in the Bois de Vincennes, featuring at least some of the elements that Loisel had demanded decades earlier.[77] Loisel had died the year before, in 1933, but had already been frustrated about the little impact his reform ideas had had. In the 1920s, he found comfort in translating the *Meditations* of the Roman emperor-philosopher Marcus Aurelius from Ancient Greek.[78]

Acknowledgments

Maddalena Cataldi, Piotr Daszkiewicz, Raf De Bont, Eszter Gantner, Heidi Hein-Kircher, Gerhard Heindl, Jonas Livet, Jan Surman and Marion Thomas helped me in different ways: to access sources and secondary literature difficult to obtain or to understand (Hungarian and Polish), as well as with their constructive criticism and comments. Research for this chapter was supported by the project "Ciencia y Ciudad. Historia Natural, Biología y Biopolítica en la Urbe Dividida. Barcelona frente a Buenos Aires (1868–1936) (HAR2013–48065-C2–1-P, Ministerio de Economía y Competitividad)," the Proyecto intramural especial "¿Ciencia en la periferia? La cultura científica de ciudades en el Sur y el Este de Europa alrededor de 1900: paralelismos, contextos y redes" (201510I030, Consejo Superior de Investigaciones Científicas) and the Grup de recerca consolidat i finançat (2017 SGR 1138, AGAUR-Generalitat de Catalunya).

Notes

1. Gustave Loisel, "Studien eines französischen Gelehrten in Budapest," *Pester Lloyd*, April 17, 1907, p. 2. Loisel's visit is reported in greater detail in "Látogatások / Besuche," *Aquila a Magyar Ornithologiai Központ Folyóirata* 14 (1907): 357–361, pp. 357–358. All translations from German and French are mine.
2. Gustave Loisel, *Rapport sur une Mission Scientifique dans les Jardins et Établissements Zoologiques Publics et Privés du Royaume-Uni, de la Belgique et des Pays-Bas* (Paris: Imprimerie Nationale, 1907); Gustave Loisel, *Rapport sur une Mission Scientifique dans les Jardins et Établissements Zoologiques Publics et Privés de l'Allemagne, de l'Autriche-Hongrie, de la Suisse et du Danemarck* (Paris: Imprimerie Nationale, 1907); Gustave Loisel, *Rapport sur une Mission Scientifique dans les Jardins et Établissements Zoologiques Publics et Privés des États-Unis et du Canada, et conclusions générales sur les jardins zoologiques* (Paris: Imprimerie Nationale, 1908).
3. Gustave Loisel, *Histoire des ménageries de l'Antiquité à nos jours, 3 vols.* (Paris: Doin, 1912).
4. "Liste zoologischer Gärten und Aquarien nach Gründungsjahr," https://de.wikipedia.org/wiki/Liste_zoologischer_Gärten_und_Aquarien_nach_Gründungsjahr#19._Jahrhundert, accessed July 19, 2019.
5. Loisel was highly aware of these different kinds of zoos, as they provide the ordering principle for the third volume of his *Histoire*, which deals with the zoo of the present.
6. The literature is far too vast to cite here. To mention but a few more recent and innovative books: Nigel Rothfels, *Savages and Beasts: The Birth of the Modern Zoo* (Baltimore and London: Johns Hopkins University Press, 2002); Mitchell G. Ash, ed., *Mensch, Tier und Zoo. Der Tiergarten Schönbrunn im internationalen Vergleich vom 18. Jahrhundert bis heute* (Wien: Böhlau, 2008); Helen Cowie, *Exhibiting Animals in Nineteenth-Century Britain: Empathy, Education, Entertainment* (Basingstoke: Palgrave Macmillan, 2014); Takashi Ito, *London Zoo and the Victorians, 1828–1859* (Woodbridge: Boydell, 2014).
7. Annelore Rieke-Müller and Lothar Dittrich, *Der Löwe brüllt nebenan. Die Gründung Zoologischer Gärten im deutschsprachigen Raum 1833–1869* (Wien, Köln and Weimar: Böhlau, 1998).
8. Ayako Sakurai, *Science and Societies in Frankfurt am Main* (London: Pickering & Chatto, 2013), chap. 3.
9. Donna C. Mehos, *Science and Culture for Members Only: The Amsterdam Zoo Artis in the Nineteenth Century* (Amsterdam: Amsterdam University Press, 2006).
10. Ito, *London Zoo.*
11. Christina Wessely, *Künstliche Tiere. Zoologische Gärten und urbane Moderne* (Berlin: Kadmos, 2008), 124–125.
12. Ibid., 103–114.
13. See Nathaniel Wood, "Urban Self-Identification in East Central Europe Before the Great War: The Case of Cracow," *East Central Europe/ECE* 33 (2006): 11–31, pp. 20, 28, 31; also Nathaniel Wood, "The 'Polish Mecca',

the 'Little Vienna on the Vistula' or 'Big-City Cracow'? Imagining Cracow Before the Great War," *Urban History* 40 (2013): 226–246.

14. For reconnaissance missions to museums of technology, see Jaume Sastre Juan, "Pilgrimages to the Museums of the New Age: Appropriating European Industrial Museums in New York City (1927–1937)," *Science Museum Group Journal* (2016), doi:10.15180/160606/001, and the article of Elena Canadelli in this volume on the journeys of Guido Ucelli.
15. Philipp Leopold Martin, *Naturstudien. Die botanischen, zoologischen und Akklimatisationsgärten, Menagerien, Aquarien und Terrarien in ihrer gegenwärtigen Entwickelung, nebst Vorschlägen und Entwürfen für die Anlegung von Naturgärten in kleineren Verhältnissen und grösserer Centralgärten für Natur- und Völkerkunde: Praxis der Naturgeschichte*, vol. 3/1 (Weimar: Voigt, 1878); Lynn K. Nyhart, *Modern Nature: The Rise of the Biological Perspective in Germany* (Chicago and London: The University of Chicago Press, 2009); in particular pp. 92–107 provides a compelling summary of Martin's vision of a modern zoo. For a new biography see Uwe Albrecht, *Bilder aus dem Tierleben: Philipp Leopold Martin (1815–1885) und die Popularisierung der Naturkunde im 19.* Jahrhundert (Baden-Baden: Tectum Wissenschaftsverlag, 2018).
16. Loisel, *Histoire, I*, 2.
17. C.V.A. Peel, *The Zoological Gardens of Europe: Their History and Chief Features* (London: F.E Robinson, 1903); reprint 2012.
18. Stanley S. Flower, *Report on Mission to Europe* (Cairo: National Printing Department, 1905).
19. Stanley S. Flower, "Miscellaneous Notes on Zoological Institutions Recently Visited in Europe," *The Zoologist* (1911): 281ff; referring to Loisel e.g. on p. 425.
20. Only fragments of Loisel's works have been translated, e.g. the first *Rapport* in an abridged version in English: Gustave Loisel, "The Zoological Gardens and Establishments of Great Britain, Belgium, and the Netherlands," *Smithsonian Institution. Annual Report . . . for the Year Ending June 30, 1907* (1908): 407–448. A recent translation into German is: Gustave Loisel, "Architektur für wilde Tiere. Idealplan einer Menagerie," in *Architektur und Zoologie. Quellentexte zur Zooarchitektur*, ed. Natascha Meuser (Berlin: DOM Publishers, 2017), 35–45. For other recent attempts to translate Loisel's *Histoire* see Leszek Solski, "Loisel, Who? – Or the Centennial of 'Histoire des Ménageries'," *International Zoo News* 59 (2012): 467–476, p. 474.
21. Due to the increased interest in the history of zoos in the last two decades or so, Loisel has been quoted numerous times; see already Solski, "Loisel, Who?" 471.
22. Jonas Livet, "Einführung in die 'Geschichte der Menagerien von der Antike bis zum heutigen Tage' von Gustave Loisel (1912)," *Der Zoologische Garten* 81 (2012): 260–263; Solski, "Loisel, Who?"
23. François Bouyssi, *Alfred Giard (1846–1908) et ses élèves: Un cenacle de 'philosophes biologistes': Aux origines du scientisme?* (Paris: École Pratique des Hautes Études, 1998); Raf De Bont, "Organisms in Their Milieu: Alfred Giard, His Pupils, and Early Ethology, 1870–1930," *Isis* 101 (2010): 1–29, pp. 26–27.
24. For a kind of CV of Loisel, see Bouyssi, *Alfred Giard (1846–1908) et ses élèves*, 171–174; also see Solski, "Loisel, Who?" 467–468.
25. Solski, "Loisel, Who?" 467. For his early work, see his own bibliography: Gustave Loisel, *Gustave Loisel, Exposé des titres et des travaux scientifiques (1892–1905)* (Paris: De Lahure, 1906).

26. Bouyssi, *Alfred Giard (1846–1908) et ses élèves*, 643.
27. De Bont, "Organisms in Their Milieu," 27. Also see Raf De Bont, *Stations in the Field: A History of Place-Based Animal Research, 1870–1930* (Chicago: The University of Chicago Press, 2015), 113–114.
28. Gustave Loisel, "Projet de réorganisation de la Ménagerie du Muséum," *Revue internationale de l'enseignement supérieur* 51 (1906): 63–68; Gustave Loisel, "Études diverses. La Ménagerie du Museum et la Zoologie expérimentale," *Revue scientifique. Revue rose illustrée* 24 (1906): 778–787; Gustave Loisel, "Projets et études sur la réorganisation et l'utilisation de la ménagerie du Jardin des Plantes," *Revue des idées* 24 (1907): 9–14.
29. Claude Schnitter, "Le développement du Muséum national d'histoire naturelle de Paris au cours de la seconde moitié du XIX siècle: 'se transformer ou périr'. The Development of the Paris Muséum national d'histoire naturelle During the Second Half of the Nineteenth Century: Either Adapt or Perish'," *Revue d'histoire des sciences* 49 (1996): 53–98.
30. Loisel, "Études diverses," 779, citing Alphonse Milne-Edwards and other French zoologists from the 1890s; also see Eric Baratay and Elisabeth Hardouin-Fugier, *Zoos: Histoire des jardins zoologiques en Occident (XVIe–XXe siècle)* (Paris: Éditions La Découverte, 1998), 165.
31. Loisel, *Rapport, I*, 1.
32. Maryvonne Leclerc-Cassan, Dominique Pinon, and Isabelle Warmoes, *Le Parc zoologique de Paris des origines à la rénovation* (Paris: Muséum National d'Histoire naturelle, 2014), 20–21.
33. Loisel, *Histoire, I*, 1.
34. Loisel, *Histoire, I*, 1.
35. Gustave Loisel, "Sur la Ménagerie de Skansen (Stockholm) et le rôle des ménageries dans les sciences zoologiques," *Bulletin de la Société nationale d'Acclimatation de France* 58 (1911): 479–492.
36. Loisel, *Histoire, III*, 110.
37. Ibid., 294–295.
38. Ibid., 295–300.
39. Loisel, *Rapport, II*, 186–202.
40. Ibid., 198; Loisel, *Histoire, III*, 248.
41. Loisel, *Histoire, III*, 117.
42. Loisel, *Rapport, II*, 256–260.
43. Virtually all the literature on the institute is in Hungarian; Lilla Vönöczky, "A Magyar Ornithológiai Központ története 1893–1944" (Ph.D. Diss., ELTE Budapest, 2009).
44. One of his most important publications was translated into German: Otto Herman, *Nutzen und Schaden der Vögel*, trans. J.C. Rösler (Gera-Untermhaus: Fr. Eugen Köhler, 1903).
45. "Látogatások/Besuche," 357.
46. Loisel, *Histoire, III*, 249.
47. Loisel, "Skansen."
48. Loisel, *Histoire, III*, 82–85; Loisel, "Skansen," 491.
49. Loisel, *Histoire, III*, 83.
50. Loisel, "Skansen," 491.
51. Peel, *The Zoological Gardens*, 136, 138; Flower, *Report on Mission*, 17.
52. Richard Lydekker, *A Trip to Pilawin, the Deer-Park of Count J. Potocki in Volhynia, Russia: With Illustrations, and a Preface by Count J. Potocki* (London: Rowland Ward, 1908). Loisel mentions it explicitly: *Histoire, III*, 82, note 4.
53. In the case of German speaking territories the journal *Der Zoologische Garten* (later on called *Der Zoologische Beobachter*), founded in 1859, was the

"central organ" of the zoos, running to several hundred pages each year, providing a wealth of information on zoos in Germany but also abroad; see Nyhart, *Modern Nature*, 108–109. Loisel used it as a source, e.g. Loisel, *Rapport, II*, 155.

54. Loisel, *Histoire, III*, 332.
55. Ibid., 22.
56. Ibid., 119, 382.
57. Loisel, *Rapport, III*, 133.
58. Charles Otis Whitman, "A Biological Farm: For the Experimental Investigation of Heredity, Variation and Evolution and for the Study of Life-Histories, Habits, Instincts and Intelligence," *The Biological Bulletin* 3 (1902): 214–224, p. 221; see already Richard W. Burkhardt, "Ethology, Natural History, the Life Sciences, and the Problem of Place," *Journal of the History of Biology* 32 (1999): 489–508, p. 496; Oliver Hochadel, "Watching Exotic Animals Next Door: 'Scientific' Observations at the Zoo (ca. 1870–1910)," *Science in Context* 24 (2011): 183–214, p. 206.
59. Louis Davillé, "Compte-rendu critique G. Loisel Histoire des ménageries de l'antiquité à nos jours," *Revue Historique* 115 (1914): 141–148, p. 146.
60. Piotr Daszkiewicz, "Polskie zwierzyńce i ogrody zoologiczne w 'Histoire des ménageries de l'Antiquité à nos jours' Gustawa Loisela," *Kwartalnik historii nauki i techniki* 49 (2004): 119–128, p. 128; Solski, "Loisel, Who?" 468; Livet, "Einführung," 263.
61. See the letters to Loisel: Archive of the Muséum National d'Histoire naturelle, Paris, Ms 2152; Archives Nationales de France, Paris, F/17/17276; the letters from the Imperial Menagerie of Schönbrunn are also in French: OMeA, 1912–75/10, Prot. Nr. 1384, Haus-, Hof- und Staatsarchiv, Vienna (HHStA).
62. Loisel, *Rapport, II*, 226.
63. Loisel, *Histoire, III*, 295.
64. For example, Posen/Poznań: Loisel, *Rapport, II*, 223.
65. Ibid., 130.
66. "Látogatások/Besuche," 357.
67. OMeA, 1907–75/13, Z. 836, HHStA.
68. Loisel, *Rapport, II*, 231–249; Loisel, *Histoire, II*, 68–73; Loisel, *Histoire, III*, 46–57.
69. Loisel, *Rapport, II*, before 244; Loisel, *Histoire, III*, 54.
70. With respect to the threat of tuberculosis e.g. for the Philadelphia zoo, see Elizabeth Anne Hanson, *Animal Attractions: Nature on Display in American Zoos* (Princeton: Princeton University Press, 2002), 228; for the London zoo, Ito, *London Zoo*, 98.
71. Letter Gustave Loisel to Fürst Montenuovo, January 28, 1912, OMeA, 1912–75/1, HHStA.
72. Loisel, *Histoire, II*, 74–90, 77. See already Daszkiewicz, "Polskie zwierzyńce," 122.
73. Daszkiewicz, "Polskie zwierzyńce."
74. As it turned out, by far the most influential model for the display of animals and zoo design was created by the Hamburg animal dealer and entrepreneur Carl Hagenbeck. Loisel is well aware of the importance of Hagenbeck's zoo in Stellingen just outside Hamburg, opened in 1907, the year of Loisel's first *Rapports*.
75. Livet, "Einführung," 263; Solski, "Loisel, Who?" 472; Meuser, *Architektur und Zoologie*, 34.
76. Bouyssi, *Alfred Giard (1846–1908) et ses élèves*, 172.

77. Ibid., 643; Leclerc-Cassan, Pinon, and Warmoes, *Le Parc zoologique*; Marion Thomas, "Between Biomedical and Psychological Experiments: The Unexpected Connections Between the Pasteur Institutes and the Study of Animal Mind in the Second Quarter of Twentieth Century France," *Studies in History and Philosophy of Biological and Biomedical Sciences* 55 (2016): 29–40.
78. Marcus Aurelius, *À Moi-même, Manuel de vie stoïcienne écrit par l'Empereur Marc-Aurèle Antonin pour lui-même*, trans. Gustave Loisel (Paris: Presses universitaires de France, 1926); Gustave Loisel, "L'ouvrage de Marc-Aurèle de la mort de l'empereur à nos jours," *Bulletin de l'Association Guillaume Budé* 15 (1927): 18–27; Albert Rivaud, "Review of Gustave Loisel, Marc-Aurèle," *Revue des Études Grecques* 42, no. 195–196 (1929): 207; De Bont, "Organisms in Their Milieu," 27; De Bont, *Stations in the Field*, 114.

10 Architectural Conversations Across Europe's Borderlands

Transnational Exchanges Between Barcelona and Bucharest in the 1920s

Lucila Mallart

Introduction

Transnational intellectual relationships have been addressed from a variety of angles in recent years. On the one hand, historians have recognized the need to transcend the nation-state as a unit of analysis.[1] History does not take place in different spaces that may occasionally interact, or which may be the object of comparative analysis. History occurs across those different spaces, and some developments can only be fully apprehended if we take that spatial leap. It is, indeed, a matter of spatiality. What are the spaces of transnational history? In a recent article, Ángel Alcaide argued that when using transnational history as a methodological perspective, the very notion of space needs to be reformulated, since space is always historically constructed, just like time.[2] If transnational history occurs across different spaces, we need to conceptualize what those spaces are. Intellectual history offers a privileged viewpoint to identify such transnational spaces: international congresses, gatherings of experts, publications and journals formed, in the nineteenth and early twentieth centuries, what Rodogno, Struck and Vogel named the "transnational sphere."[3] The transnational sphere also has an invisible counterpart: those international meetings, publications and journals formed "invisible colleges."[4] Informal, flexible and, on many occasions, personal relationships shaped the advancement of scholarly research, prompted paradigm shifts and were crucial to the integration of international developments into local academies.

The present chapter adopts these methodological perspectives in order to study intellectual exchanges between Barcelona and Bucharest in the interwar period. The two principle nodes of this "invisible college" were the Catalan architect, politician and art historian Josep Puig i Cadafalch (1867–1956) and the Romanian historian and politician Nicolae Iorga (1871–1940). The network also extended onto other secondary actors such as the Catalan medievalist Antoni Rubió i Lluch (1856–1937) and the Romanian architect Petre Antonescu (1873–1965). The contacts took place in eminently transnational spaces: formal gatherings such as the First Congress of Byzantine Studies celebrated in Bucharest in 1924, archival visits to Barcelona and study trips to Romania, but also personal visits and sightseeing, all of which resulted in diverse kinds of publications. None of these constituted formal research networks, and yet the impact of these exchanges was prominent in the intellectual production of the actors involved.

Focusing on Barcelona and Bucharest also allows us to reformulate historical space in additional ways. Most research on transnational intellectual exchanges on the Iberian Peninsula has looked at connections with cultural and academic centers such as France, Germany and Britain.[5] There have been a few approaches to relationships with Europe's borderlands, such as Alison Sinclair's study of Spanish exchanges with Russian intellectuals.[6] Still, Sinclair focuses on Madrid-based institutions and Spanish-language media, such as the academic residence Residencia de Estudiantes and the journal *Revista de Occidente*. Looking at alternative cultural nodes in Spain such as Barcelona does not only expand and complicate the map of intellectual dynamics in the Iberian world, but also informs and benefits from transnational history as a methodological approach. Indeed, "second" cities (as Maiken Umbach called them)[7] seem to be absent from intellectual histories that adhere to the nation-state as a frame of reference. Thus, these second cities arguably provide a privileged viewpoint from which to analyze the constructed character of historical space and to reformulate the role of spatiality in transnational history.

Additionally, discussing intellectual exchanges between Catalonia and Romania raises questions about transnational dynamics from periphery to periphery. The "creativity" of peripheries has recently emerged as an area of scholarly interest. From a post-colonial perspective, Walter Mignolo called for research into how borders contribute to the world's system of knowledge.[8] Pascale Casanova suggested that writers at the margins of Europe were more receptive to innovation, and Nygård and Strang have argued that peripheries are more open to creative eclecticism, while actors in cultural centers regard local ideas as universal.[9] Yet the role of cultural peripheries in the generation and transfer of knowledge to other borderlands is still unclear. The present chapter contributes to this debate by analyzing academic relations during the 1920s and 1930s, a period in which intellectual transnationalism experienced a significant development due to the impact of World War I, according to Gisèle Sapiro.[10]

The present chapter sheds new light on these debates through a study of several academic and professional exchanges between Barcelona and Bucharest. The text first describes the origins of the exchanges between Puig, Iorga and other scholars around the study of the expansion of the medieval Crown of Aragon in the Eastern Mediterranean, as well as Puig's researches on Romanian historical architecture. Next it analyzes

Puig's interaction with Romanian architects such as Petre Antonescu, paying particular attention to their discussions on modern urban planning and the tensions between tradition and modernity in contemporary architectural practices. It then moves to Iorga's travels in Catalonia and his reflections on Barcelona as a capital city. Finally, it discusses the influence of Puig's work on Iorga's urban thinking, as well as of the latter's changing attitudes toward Catalan nationalism.

Transnational Historiographies

Josep Puig i Cadafalch and Nicolae Iorga had parallel careers traversing scholarly research, cultural activism and politics. Puig was a renowned *Modernista* architect and president of the Mancomunitat, a federation of Catalan provinces, from 1917 to 1923. He was also a leading archeologist, restorer of historical monuments and art historian.[11] In turn, Iorga is considered to be one of the most influential Romanian historians of the twentieth century and, according to Marius Turda, it was he who "successfully provided Romanian nationalism with the essential notions of historical continuity and cultural unity."[12] In 1910, he founded the conservative Democratic Nationalist Party (PND), and he held several positions in the parliament and Romanian government until he became prime minister in 1931–1932.[13]

Puig had connections with academics and professionals from around the world. Out of a total of 1,000 single correspondents, half were international, with a clear predominance of French ones.[14] France was Puig's most important intellectual reference throughout his life, and it also played a crucial role in the dissemination of his work on the history of Romanesque art and architecture.[15] He also had numerous exchanges with North American art historians, such as Walter W.S. Cook (1888–1962) and Arthur Kingsley Porter (1883–1933), as well as others of German, Italian and British origin. Next to those, the number of correspondents from Romania stands out, especially if we compare it to other "peripheral" countries. While Puig only had less than a handful of contacts in countries such as Norway, Sweden and Greece, he had as many as 13 Romanian correspondents. These were part of a complex research network that was sparked by the initial contact between Puig and Iorga and extended to their adherents, colleagues, and other subject specialists. Together, they constituted a transnational academic network characterized by "multi-stranded relations."[16]

Initially, contacts between Catalonia and Romania emerged around a shared interest in the history of the Crown of Aragon (to which the Catalan counties belonged in the Middle Ages) in the Eastern Mediterranean. Nicolae Iorga's student Constantin Marinescu (1891–1970) visited Barcelona in the 1920s with the aim of studying the archives of the Crown of Aragon.[17] While working in Barcelona, Marinescu may have met the medievalist Antoni Rubió i Lluch, with whom he shared research interests and methodologies.[18] Rubió published several compilations of archival materials on Catalan medieval literature and history, which Marinescu then used for his research. For instance, in 1921, Rubió began to work on a compilation of sources on the diplomatic relations of the Kings of Aragon in the East during the fourteenth century.[19] Marinescu's contribution to the First Congress of Byzantine Studies also analyzed documentation on the same topic, in particular a series of letters written by the Byzantine Emperor Manuel II Palaiologos (r. 1391–1425) to the Aragonese Crown.[20] Marinescu's research on the Crown of Aragon is still positively regarded today.[21]

Rubió i Lluch was invited to participate in the Bucharest congress together with Puig i Cadafalch, but only Puig made it in the end.[22] The visit sparked a multiplicity of contributions from Romanian scholars on the history of medieval Aragon, and of Catalan studies on Romania's historical architecture. Marinescu continued to publish on the history of Aragonese kings such as Alphonse V the Magnanimous (1396–1458), as well as about the chivalric novel *Tirant lo blanch* (1490), which narrates the adventures of a Valencian knight who aids the Byzantine Emperor in fighting the Turks.[23] Iorga also researched Catalan medieval literature, in particular the anonymous short novel *Història de Jacob Xalabín* (written around 1404), a series of love and battle stories inspired in Yakub Çelebi, a son of the Ottoman Emperor Murad I (r. 1362–1389).[24] He was also interested in the chronicle (1325–1328) of Ramon Muntaner (1265–1336), a Catalan commander who participated in the expansion of the Crown of Aragon in the Eastern Mediterranean.[25] The two works appeared in a single volume in 1927, with the title of *Contributions catalanes à l'histoire byzantine* (*Catalan Contributions to Byzantine History*).[26] In turn, Puig carried out extensive studies on the painted monasteries and churches of Moldavia, in northeastern Romania. He was fascinated by the evolution of style in these fifteenth- and sixteenth-century churches, as he saw a parallel with the evolution of early Romanesque art in Southwestern Europe in the eleventh century. To that end, he published a series of articles that he discussed in conferences in Bucharest (1924), Belgrade (1927) and Oslo (1928), and which also appeared as the final chapter of his major work *La geografia i els orígens del primer art romànic* (*Geography and the Origins of Early Romanesque Art*), published in 1939.[27]

Shared Architectures

Parallel to his research on Moldavian painted churches, Puig also engaged with several Romanian architects, with whom he exchanged publications and thoughts on modern architectural practices.

Puig was a pivotal figure in the renovation of Barcelona's Old Town in the early twentieth century. He was very critical of the nineteenth-century plan for the urban expansion of the city, designed by the engineer Ildefons Cerdà (1815–1876) in 1859. Nowadays, the Cerdà Plan is considered a masterpiece of modern urban planning,[28] but Puig perceived it as a "geometrical eruption" that "spread infinitely."[29] Cerdà's project was characterized by a uniform grid that, in line with the engineer's social thinking, reduced hierarchies and homogenized the city's urban space. Puig's aversion for the Cerdà Plan was notorious. In 1891, he criticized it for "[embodying] little more than a spirit of uniformity," and in the winter of 1900–1901, he published three articles in favor of an amendment of Cerdà's Eixample – the new town – as it resembled the horrors of "corny" South American cities.[30]

In the mid-1910s, Puig began to envision a new "Plaça de Catalunya," Barcelona's central square, which linked the old and the new towns. He worked on a series of drafts during the next decade, which never fully materialized. In 1927, Puig committed the project to paper and published a booklet, *La Plaça de Catalunya*, which contained reflections, models and the unrealized plans (see Figure 10.1). The preface is clear on the architect's intentions: Puig intended to bring singularity to the center of Barcelona, challenging Cerdà who, "instead of a square, had projected streets and plots of land where houses like any other could be built."[31] Puig's earlier interventions in the Eixample have also been seen as a way to overcome Cerdà's uniform grid, which, as Umbach wrote, "failed to

Figure 10.1 Plaça de Catalunya, project by Josep Puig i Cadafalch, 1927.

Source: Barcelona: Llibreria Catalònia, 1927, Làm. XLVIII. Dipòsit Digital de Documents de la UAB, Universitat Autònoma de Barcelona, open access

connect with the discourse of Catalan separatism" as "the grid was a universal, not a culturally specific shape."[32]

La Plaça de Catalunya is the publication that Puig sent to the largest number of international contacts. Puig was generous in exchanging works with international colleagues, but he tailored the contents to the correspondent's interests to a great extent, and thus he rarely sent the same book or article more than once or twice. Conversely, archive records show evidence of at least seven international shipments of *La Plaça de Catalunya*: to Belgium, Switzerland, the United States, Serbia and, on as many as three occasions, to Romania. *La Plaça de Catalunya* was published in Catalan, but this did not restrain Puig from sending it abroad; while he published regularly in French, he often sent his Catalan publications to his international contacts.

In Romania, the recipients of the book were the aforementioned architect Petre Antonescu and two female adherents of his, Marica Cotescu and Maria Irineu. Antonescu was one of the main representatives of Romania's "national style," and has been considered "the most complete [Romanian] architect of his time."[33] Antonescu's national architecture drew on the style developed under the rule of Constantin Brâncoveanu (1654–1714), a Prince of Wallachia who favored Romanian culture, arts and language during Ottoman rule. He was beheaded by the Sublime Porte in 1714, which turned him into one of Romania's most important national heroes. Brâncoveanu's (and Antonescu's) architecture fused Ottoman motives with Venetian loggias.[34] This approach, which favored Wallachia's material culture over that of Moldova or Transylvania (the other two constituents of the modern Romanian state), was reflected in significant buildings such as Bucharest's Triumphal Arch (1922–1935) and the Municipal Hall, projected by Antonescu between 1906 and 1910 (see Figure 10.2). Just like Puig, Antonescu also added urban planning and monument restoration to his professional activities.

Antonescu's reaction to *La Plaça de Catalunya* was discrete: he simply praised it for its contribution to "Catalan science."[35] However, the words of Cotescu and Irineu provide a richer insight on the reception of Puig's architectural ideas in Romania. Marica Cotescu is considered one of the first Romanian female architects. Her theoretical contributions, for example for the magazine *Simetria*, were especially significant.[36] Cotescu's letters suggest an intense dialogue with Puig on the role of modern architecture vis-à-vis vernacular traditions, which run parallel to their discussion of the origin and significance of Moldavia's painted churches. Thus, Cotescu praised Spain's and Puig's architectural taste for "ancient tradition," through which they could escape "the ugliness of the 'reinforced concrete' style." In Romania, she regretted, "the total absence of old secular monuments and of a national school of architecture have caused a mixture of the styles."[37]

Figure 10.2 Bucharest City Hall, 2019.
Source: Photograph by the author

Cotescu was also interested in Puig's research on Romanian churches, and the correspondence suggests that she may have attended his talk at the Bucharest congress. She was surprised by the similarity of styles between early-modern Moldavian churches and eleventh-century Mediterranean ones, and enquired:

> How is it that the exterior ornamentation of the Catalan churches is so similar to the ornamentation of our Moldavian churches? Would Lombardy really be a common source of inspiration? But how did the influence spread in Catalonia – [and] in Romania?[38]

Puig would later argue that the parallel evolution of the styles was due to both following a "universal law," rather than to shared influences.[39]

In turn, Maria Irineu had a more positive view of the interplay between architectural traditions and modernity than Cotescu's. In a letter to Puig, she foresaw Catalonia (which she longed to visit) as the "happy country where modern architecture is harmoniously linked to ancient traditions." She also referred to Puig as "master" and claimed that the reproductions of his works gave her "courage and impetus."[40]

Unlike Irineu, Nicolae Iorga did have the chance to see Catalonia in person twice, in 1927 and 1929. Even though he did not explicitly discuss Puig's work on Barcelona, his words echo Puig's architectural cosmology, all the while projecting his own interests and Romanian agenda onto his reading of the city.

In spring 1927, Iorga went on a ten-day tour of Spain that brought him to the Basque Country, Castile, Madrid, Andalusia, and Catalonia, including the counties in the Roussillon, in the south of France.[41] He intended to meet Puig in Barcelona, as a telegram dated 1 March 1927 shows, but the meeting did not take place, for unknown reasons.[42] Upon his return to Romania, he narrated the experience in a series of lectures at the National Theatre and in a book, *Câteva zile prin Spania* (*A Few Days in Spain*).[43] This book has received considerable attention in Spanish-language milieus in recent years. Mircea Anghelescu has underlined that, in line with previous Romanian travelers in Spain, Iorga highlighted the similarities between the two countries. In fact, many of his statements on Spain were matched by references to Romania, including historical episodes, national heroes, or regional landscapes.[44] Thus, passages on the Spanish "Reconquista" (the Christian conquest of Al-Andalus between the eighth and the fifteenth centuries) were used to build a narrative of historical continuity in present-day Romania. Iorga drew a parallel between the "Reconquista" and the medieval expansion of Wallachians and Moldovans into Transylvania, which had just been incorporated into the modern Romanian State after centuries of Hungarian, Ottoman and Austrian rule. His description of the unity of Spain, which he called a "secular national unification," also served the purpose of advocating the unity of the Romanian principalities after World War I.[45] Deepening this line of thought, Iorga also claimed that Catalonia did not appear to be different to the rest of Spain. He stated that Catalonia had had a different historical evolution due to the fact that the Catalan counties emerged under the Carolingian Empire, but argued that "the land is the same as in the rest of the Peninsula."[46] He went on to say that Barcelona had:

> streets without personality, which even imitate, without any sense, Arab ornaments. Red streetcars roam them. The same carriages with high wheels. A very motley crowd, in which all different types can be distinguished. No sign of any difference in the costumes, which are the usual ones.[47]

Incidentally, the "Arab ornaments" Iorga complained about may have actually been made by Puig, who built several houses in the Eixample with an eclectic mixture of decorative styles. Puig's ornamentations often stem from Catalan Gothic or Renaissance motifs, reimagined in order to echo the plasticity and intricacy of Arabesques.[48] This is visible, for instance, in the Casa Macaya, the Casa Amatller and the Palau del Baró de Quadras. Iorga then added that Catalonia's "long historical development" had not yet been "represented in monuments" which, together with the previously mentioned lack of singularity, made, according to him, the claim for a Catalan autonomy weak.[49]

Even though he did not see Catalonia's built environment as culturally specific, he thought differently about Catalonia's language and literature. Thus, he contended that a "sweet language, closer to Provençal than to Castilian" was spoken in Catalonia and that it had produced "remarkable works" in prose and verse, including, of course, Muntaner's chronicle, on which Iorga had published that same year of 1927. The Catalan nationalist movement had thus resulted in "the renaissance of a literature" from which the whole of humanity could benefit.[50]

Iorga's discourse changed slightly two years later, when he revisited Barcelona on the occasion of the 1929 Barcelona International Exhibition. The Exhibition was originally designed by Puig during the 1910s, but his project did not fully materialize due to Primo de Rivera's coup d'état in 1923.[51] Iorga told his friend about his intention of visiting the Exhibition several months in advance, in a letter and a postcard that he sent from Fontenay-aux-Roses, close to Paris, and home of a research center known as the Romanian School.[52] He later shared his impressions on the trip in another book, *O mică ţară latină: Catalonia şi exposiţia din 1929. Note de drum şi conferinţe*, published in 1930. The title may be translated as *A Small Latin Country: Catalonia and the 1929 Exposition. Travel Notes and Lectures.* There, he described Barcelona and other Catalan towns, such as Terrassa, Sant Cugat, Tarragona, Vic, and Ripoll, all of which played an important role in Catalonia's architectural history and especially in Puig's works. Yet, Puig seems to have accompanied Iorga only on his visit to the last two.[53] The book consists of the travel diaries, two lectures on Catalan "Literature" and "Art," and a selection of "samples" of Catalan poetry, divided into "Popular," "Medieval" and "Modern."[54]

In this work, Iorga changed his political discourse on Catalonia and his appreciation of Catalonia's singularity within the context of the Spanish state. Thus, he argued that there was indeed a "Catalan nationality, different to the nationality that conforms [to the] Spanish nationality" and that this should not "disturb anyone."[55] In Catalonia, he wrote, there used to be "a great autonomy, larger than that of the abolished Mancomunitat."[56] The Mancomunitat was a federation of Catalan provinces that existed between 1914 and 1925, over which Puig presided in the period 1917–1923. When Puig attended the First Congress of Byzantine Studies in Bucharest, in April 1924, he presented himself as the president of a "suspended" "Catalan provincial union" in an interview with the Romanian newspaper

Dimineata.[57] However, he had left office a few months earlier, and there was a new president designated by General Primo de Rivera, Alfons Sala (1863–1945), whom apparently Puig did not recognize as such.

Iorga's account of his visit to Barcelona echoes Puig's thinking on the city to a large extent, even though there is no evidence of Puig accompanying him. Puig played a key role in the re-urbanization and restoration of the Old Town in the early 1900s, when a new avenue, known as Via Laietana, was built with the aim of sanitizing the historic neighborhoods and bringing them closer to the look of European capitals.[58] One of Puig's main concerns was the intertwining of old and new urban fabrics. In the Via Laietana, he combined the opening of large and functional streets with the creation of new perspectives onto the cathedral's façade and the preservation of the city's historic landmarks, such as the Palace of the Kings of Aragon.[59] Arguably, this entailed a combination of Camillo Sitte's (1843–1903) embellishment principles (through his famous *Der Städtebau nach seinen künstlerischen Grundsätzen*, first published in 1889) with the technological approach of authors such as Josef Stüben (1845–1936), author of *Der Städtebau* (1890), who also corresponded with Puig.[60]

Iorga's concern for the contrast between Barcelona's old and new towns is evident in the text. "One of the weird characteristics of many cities," he says, "is this duality between the Middle Ages – narrow, dark, full of hidden beauties – and the present day that displays, proclaims, shouts everything."[61] In Barcelona, he adds, "the new and large streets cut through the confusing shadow of the old districts."[62] Modern interventions had reached those neighborhoods, but in Iorga's view, these interventions had been respectful with the medieval past. "The care of modernism," he writes, "has reached it [the Gothic quarter] . . . , a modernism that is not afraid of the colored glass with Madonna's face."[63] The "Gothic style" of the churches of Santa Maria del Mar and Sant Pau del Camp, he adds, "has been changed to a minor extent by contemporary interventions."[64] In another part of the text he complains that restorers have "taken away" the "element of mystery" of the cathedral's façade which, he says, was "restored a long time ago."[65] In fact, the façade had been built, not restored, in neo-Gothic style between 1887 and 1912.[66]

Iorga offers an idealized view of Barcelona in which huge industrial crowds move "from here to there" without causing disturbance, "so easily following the indications of traffic agents."[67] "Merchants," he adds, "are not calling, not inviting, not discussing; they are just announcing briefly the prices of their merchandise."[68] He uses this account of an apparently perfectly functioning modern town to compare it to the situation in his homeland Romania, just as he had done in his 1927 book. In Barcelona, he says, "there is no . . . Calea Victoriei [Bucharest's main avenue], where the police and the army can hardly discipline the lazy *flânerie*."[69] Despite these present-day differences, historic Romania and

Catalonia did have things in common. Just like Aragonese kings, medieval Romanian rulers also came "from the mountain . . . to the sea"; for instance, the Princes or Voivodes of Moldavia Roman I (whom he calls "Roman-Voda") and Alexander I ("Alexandru cel Bun"), who reigned in the 1390s and early 1400s, respectively.[70] In this narrative, Iorga makes an analogy between Barcelona, which he insistently refers to as a port city, and Cetatea Albă, a medieval Moldavian fortress located on the Black Sea, in present-day Ukraine, which marked the territorial expansion of the aforementioned princes.[71]

The transnational historiographies developed by Catalans and Romanians in the early 1920s also appear in Iorga's account of this trip to Barcelona. He accurately recalls an encounter with Rubió i Lluch, whom he describes as a "great historian and poet":

> I found him in the supreme solitude of his home, where everything reminds him of his life companion, who he has recently lost. Every time he mentions her, tears well up and his eyes are full of pain, eyes that he offered to science – small, white, yet still strong at over 70 years old. This historian, who studied the Catalan expansion to the countries and the seas of the Byzantine Orient, shows [me] the numerous cover books in which copies of Aragonese-Catalan documents are waiting to be published.[72]

There are also traces of Puig's research on Romanesque architecture. Echoing his argument on the similarity between Catalan and Moldavian churches, Iorga argues that, on the way to Barcelona, he saw, from the train, "[a] heavy tower with long, narrow windows, similar to the Wallachian churches from the 17th century." "Over seas and countries," he states that he encountered "the lines from our lands, on their long way from Asia, to reach the Iberian Sierra," once again echoing Puig's view on the dissemination of artistic forms in the medieval period.[73]

Conclusions

Josep Puig i Cadafalch, Antoni Rubió i Lluch, Nicolae Iorga, Constantin Marinescu and Petre Antonescu were part of an informal research network built through events and meetings held in Barcelona and Bucharest during the 1920s. These included formal academic activities, such as Marinescu's visits to the archives of the Crown of Aragon in Barcelona, and the Bucharest Congress of Byzantine Studies. But other meetings had a leisurely character or were shaped by personal relationships, such as Iorga's visits to Catalonia in 1927 and 1929, or Puig's correspondence with Antonescu and his disciples Marica Cotescu and Maria Irineu. The interplay between those diverse gatherings and the letters and texts that were exchanged, reviewed and published created a transnational space across Barcelona and Bucharest, enabling a series of intellectual outcomes that were also eminently transnational in nature. Puig and Rubió contributed to the history and art history of medieval Romania, while Iorga and Marinescu researched and published on the Oriental campaigns of the medieval Crown of Aragon. These national histories were in fact transnational: embedded in the political struggles of early-twentieth-century Catalonia and Romania, and yet produced across the two edges of Southern Europe.

Contacts between Catalan and Romanian intellectuals in the interwar period are an example of transnational processes not only because they occurred across different national frameworks, but also because they transcended the conceptual limits of the nation-state. While acknowledging the importance of Barcelona, Sinclair accords Madrid a central position in the transfer of culture in early-twentieth-century Spain.[74] Conversely, Christophe Charle has argued that Barcelona was an exception in Europe's cultural space as, unlike other regional centers such as Lyon or Lille in France, it was able to "compete in intellectual terms with the political capital, Madrid."[75] Was Barcelona really an exception, or is the pre-eminence of the nation-state as a unit of analysis a burden for the study of intellectual history in early twentieth-century Europe? Puig's and Rubió's engagement with scholars in Romania was not mediated by Madrid institutions, individuals or cultural spheres. The use of Catalan posed no constraint to this internationalization – Puig repeatedly sent *La Plaça de Catalunya*, written in that language, to his Romanian colleagues, and Iorga and Marinescu learned Catalan in order to visit archives and translate poetry into Romanian. This echoes Jo Labanyi's assumption that Catalonia developed a cultural sphere separate from the central Spanish, Castilian-speaking one.[76] The international language Puig, Iorga and their colleagues used was French, and Paris was the cultural center they both looked to. Undoubtedly, academic exchanges between Catalonia and Romania were not independent from Paris' sphere of influence. Puig and Iorga first met at a conference held there in 1921,[77] and they continued to use French as a language and French-speaking milieus to discuss and publish their work. At the same time, the historical and architectural knowledge they produced was created and to some extent validated between the two peripheries. Cotescu and Irineu regarded Puig as a "master," and Iorga integrated, to some extent, Puig's perspective on the urban development of Barcelona when he visited the city in 1929.

As Alcalde argues, transnational history is not a discipline, but a methodological approach.[78] In this chapter, it has brought to light a series of cross-national historical and architectural productions that, especially in the case of Catalonia, challenge the validity of the nation-state as a point of departure for the study of intellectual exchanges in interwar Europe. This transnational perspective has also shown the vivacity of knowledge exchanges between cities traditionally considered to be "peripheral" or "secondary," and therefore dependent upon more "central" hubs such as Madrid. Indeed, new knowledge on medieval history, art history and architecture was produced through the transit of ideas and scholars between Barcelona and Bucharest. Knowledge was an interurban product: it was the outcome of reciprocal visits to the two cities, and of integrating the other's material and historical realities into one's own research practices.

Acknowledgments

Research for this article was supported by a Fritz Thyssen Stiftung Travel Subsidy, which allowed me to carry out a three-week research stay in Bucharest, Romania, in the summer of 2019. I am grateful to the New Europe College, Institute of Advanced Study of Bucharest, for facilitating my stay. Dr. Ada Hajdu offered me key support and guidance; she tragically passed away shortly before this article was finished, and I am most indebted to her. This research is also part of the project AEI/FEDER, UE-PGC2018-098348-A-I00.

Notes

1. Pierre-Yves Saunier, *Transnational History* (Basingstoke: Palgrave Macmillan, 2013).
2. Ángel Alcalde, "Spatializing Transnational History: European Spaces and Territories," *European Review of History: Revue Européenne d'histoire* 25, no. 3–4 (2018): 553–567, p. 555.
3. Davide Rodogno, Bernhard Struck, and Jakob Vogel, eds., *Shaping the Transnational Sphere: Experts, Networks and Issues from the 1840s to the 1930s* (New York: Berghahn Books, 2015); cited in Alcalde, "Spatializing Transnational History," 557.
4. The term was in use since the 1970s among historians of science, for example in David Elliston Allen, ed., *The Naturalist in Britain: A Social History* (Princeton: Princeton University Press, 1976). More recently, Margarita Díaz-Andreu applied the term to the history of the humanities in Margarita Díaz-Andreu, "Revisiting the 'Invisible College': José Ramón Mélida in Early-Twentieth-Century Spain," in *Histories of Archaeology: Archives, Ancestors, Practices*, ed. N. Schlanger and J. Nordbladh (Oxford: Berghahn Books, 2008), 121–129.
5. A few recent examples from a variety of disciplines can be found in: David Jiménez Torres, *Ramiro de Maeztu and England: Imaginaries, Realities and Repercussions of a Cultural Encounter* (Woodbridge: Tamesis, 2016); Raquel Sánchez García, "Circulación de ideas y transferencias culturales: España y Europa en el siglo XIX. Presentación," *Hispania Nova. Primera Revista de Historia Contemporánea on-line en castellano. Segunda Época* 14 (2016): 265–268; Margarita Díaz-Andreu, *Archaeological Encounters: Building Networks of Spanish and British Archaeologists in the 20th Century* (Newcastle upon Tyne: Cambridge Scholars Publishing, 2012).
6. Alison Sinclair, *Trafficking Knowledge in Early Twentieth-Century Spain: Centres of Exchange and Cultural Imaginaries* (Woodbridge: Tamesis, 2009).
7. Maiken Umbach, "A Tale of Second Cities: Autonomy, Culture, and Law in Hamburg and Barcelona in the Late Nineteenth Century," *The American Historical Review* 110, no. 3 (2005): 659–692.

8. Walter Mignolo, *Local Histories/Global Designs: Coloniality, Subaltern Knowledges, and Border Thinking* (Princeton: Princeton University Press, 2000).
9. Stefan Nygård and Johan Strang, "Facing Asymmetry – Nordic Intellectuals and Center-Periphery Dynamics in European Cultural Space," *Journal of the History of Ideas* 77, no. 1 (2016): 75–98. For Casanova, also cited in Nygård and Strang's article, see Pascale Casanova, *La république mondiale des lettres* (Paris: Editions du Seuil, 1999), 73–74. Translated into English in Pascale Casanova, *The World Republic of Letters* (Cambridge, MA: Harvard University Press, 2004).
10. Gisèle Sapiro, "Introduction," in *L'espace intellectuel en Europe: de la formation des états-nations à la mondialisation, XIXe–XXIe siècle*, ed. Gisèle Sapiro (Paris: Découverte, 2009), 5–25.
11. For an overview of Puig's activities, see Lucila Mallart, ed., *Josep Puig i Cadafalch: Vision, Identities, Cosmopolitism* (Mataró: Museu de Mataró, 2018); Albert Balcells, ed., *Puig i Cadafalch i la Catalunya contemporània* (Barcelona: Institut d'Estudis Catalans, 2003); Xavier Barral i Altet, ed., *Josep Puig i Cadafalch: escrits d'arquitectura, art i política* (Barcelona: Institut d'Estudis Catalans, 2003); Judith Rohrer and Ignasi de Solà-Morales, eds., *Josep Puig i Cadafalch: la arquitectura entre la casa y la ciudad* (Barcelona: Fundación Caja de Pensiones: Colegio de Arquitectos de Cataluña, 1990).
12. Marius Turda, "Historical Writing in the Balkans," in *The Oxford History of Historical Writing: Volume 4: 1800–1945*, ed. Stuart Macintyre, Juan Maiguascha, and Attila Pók (Oxford: Oxford University Press, 2011), 349–368, p. 352; see also Corina Teacă, "In Search of National Traditions: Art History in Romania," in *Art History and Visual Studies in Europe: Transnational Discourses and National Frameworks*, ed. Matthew Rampley, Thierry Lenain, and Hubert Locher (Leiden: Brill, 2012), 451–460, p. 455.
13. For a complete biographical account, see Nicholas M. Nagy-Talavera, *Nicolae Iorga: A Biography* (Iaşi: Center for Romanian Studies, 1998).
14. Mallart, *Josep Puig i Cadafalch*, 110–125.
15. Olivier Poisson, "La 'carrera francesa' de Josep Puig i Cadafalch," in *1907: el paper de l'IEC en la història de l'art i en la restauració de monuments medievals a Catalunya i Europa*, ed. Raquel Lacuesta Contreras (Barcelona: Diputació de Barcelona, 2009), 15–25; Antoni Pladevall i Font, "Puig i Cadafalch i la difusió de la coneixença de l'art romànic a Europa," in *Puig i Cadafalch i la Catalunya contemporània*, ed. Albert Balcells (Barcelona: Institut d'Estudis Catalans, 2003), 69–74.
16. Margarita Díaz-Andreu, "Transnationalism and Archaeology: The Connecting Origins of the Main Institutions Dealing with Prehistoric Archaeology in Western Europe: The IPH, the CIPP and the CRPU (1910–1914)," in *150 anni di Preistoria e Protostoria in Italia*, ed. A. Guidi (Florence: IIPP, 2014), 163–177, p. 164.
17. Constantin Marinescu, *Compte-rendu du premier Congrès international des études byzantines: Bucharest, 1924* (Bucharest, 1925), 28.
18. On Rubió's work, see Albert Balcells, "Introducció: Antoni Rubió i Lluch i els estudis sobre els catalans a la Mediterrània oriental," in *Els catalans a la Mediterrània oriental a l'edat mitjana*, ed. Maria Teresa Ferrer i Mallol (Barcelona: Institut d'Estudis Catalans, 2003), 17–20; Albert Balcells, "Antoni Rubió i Lluch, historiador i primer president de l'Institut d'Estudis Catalans," in *Documents per a la història de la cultura catalana medieval*, by Antoni Rubió i Lluch (Barcelona: Institut d'Estudis Catalans, 2000), 5–46.

19. Rubió signed a contract to publish this work with the Institut d'Estudis Catalans in 1921, although the extension of the research and, later on, the Spanish Civil War and its aftermath, delayed its publication until the 1940s. See Antoni Rubió i Lluch, *Diplomatari de l'Orient Català 1301–1409: col·lecció de documents per a la història de l'expedició catalana a Orient i dels ducats d'Atenes i Neopàtria* (Barcelona: Institut d'Estudis Catalans, 1947). The book was reedited with an introductory study by Maria Teresa Ferrer i Mallol in 2001. See Antoni Rubió i Lluch, *Diplomatari de l'Orient català (1301–1409): col·leció de documents per a la història de l'expedició catalana a Orient i dels ducats d'Atenes i Neopàtria* (Barcelona: Institut d'Estudis Catalans, 2001).
20. "Commentaire sur quatre lettres inédites en latin, expédiées par la chancellerie byzantine en Aragon au temps de Manuel II Paléologue," published as Constantin Marinescu, "Manuel II, paléologue et les rois d'Aragon: commentaire sur quatre lettres inédites en latin, expédiées par la chancellerie byzantine," *Académie Roumaine, Bulletin de la Section Historique* 11 (1924): 192–206.
21. See, for example, Daniel Duran Duelt, "Diplomacia de cruzada. Las misiones de Manuel II Paleólogo a la Península Ibérica y la recaudación de subsidios," in *Cataluña y Navarra en la Baja Edad Media*, ed. Eloísa Ramírez Vaquero and Roser Salicrú i Lluch (Pamplona: Universidad Pública de Navarra, 2010), 53–110, p. 53.
22. Marinescu, *Compte-rendu du premier Congrès international des études byzantines*, 66.
23. Constantin Marinescu, "Notes sur le faste a la cour d'Alphonse V d'Aragon, roi de Naples," *Mélanges d'Histoire Générale* I (1927): 133–146; Constantin Marinescu, "Les affaires commerciales en Flandre d'Alphonse V d'Aragon, Roi de Naples (1416–1458)," *Revue Historique* V (1939): 33–48; Constantin Marinescu, "Alphonse le Magnanime, protecteur d'un rival du commerce catalan: Jacques Coeur. Pourquoi?" *Estudios de Historia Moderna* III (1953): 27–63; Constantin Marinescu, "Jacques Coeur et la Catalogne," *Butlletí de la Societat Catalana d'Estudis Històrics* 3–4 (1963): 41; Constantin Marinescu, "Nouvelles recherches sur 'Tirant lo Blanc'," *Estudis universitaris catalans* 23 (1979): 402–421.
24. On the Catalan original, see Antoni Comas, Joaquim Molas, and Martí de Riquer, eds., "Una novel·la oriental: la Història de Jacob Xalabín," in *Història de la Literatura Catalana*, vol. 3 (Barcelona: Editorial Ariel, 1985), 243–248.
25. Muntaner's is one of the "four great chronicles" that narrate the history of the Crown of Aragon during the thirteenth and fourteenth centuries. On this topic, see Jaume Aurell, *Authoring the Past: History, Autobiography, and Politics in Medieval Catalonia* (Chicago and London: University of Chicago Press, 2012); Jaume Aurell, "From Genealogies to Chronicles: The Power of the Form in Medieval Catalan Historiography," *Viator* 36 (2005): 235–264. English version of Muntaner's chronicle in Ramon Muntaner, *The Chronicle of Muntaner*, trans. Anna Kinsky Goodenough (London: The Hakluyt Society, 1920).
26. Nicolae Iorga, *Contributions catalanes à l'histoire byzantine* (Paris: Librairie J. Gamber, 1927). The book was published in Catalan in 1961. See Nicolae Iorga, *Ramon Muntaner i l'Imperi bizantí* (Barcelona: Rafel Dalmau, 1961).
27. Josep Puig i Cadafalch, "Les églises de Moldavie: contribution à l'étude des origines de leur forme décorative, une école parallèle pendant le XIe siècle dans l'Europe Occidentale," *Académie Roumaine. Bulletin de la Section*

Historique. Congrès de Byzantiologie de Bucharest. Mémoires 11 (1924): 76–89; Josep Puig i Cadafalch, "Les périodes successives de l'influence byzantine en Occident. Premier art roman. Architecture Mudéjar. Églises de Moldavie," in *Mélanges Charles Diehl. Études sur l'histoire et sur l'art de Byzance*, vol. 2, 2 vols. (Paris: Librairie Ernest Leroux, 1931), 161–169; Josep Puig i Cadafalch, *La geografia i els orígens del primer art romànic* (Barcelona: Institut d'Estudis Catalans, 1930), 525–532.

28. See, for instance, Thomas Hall, "Introduction," in *Planning Europe's Capital Cities: Aspects of Nineteenth-Century Urban Development* (London: E & FN Spon, 1997), 2.
29. The Catalan term Puig uses is "*erupció*," which relates to both a volcanic "eruption" and a medical "rash." Here the context emphasizes the medical meaning of the word. Josep Puig i Cadafalch, "A votar per l'Exposició Universal," *La Veu de Catalunya*, November 11, 1905, 3.
30. Lluís Quintana i Trias, "Joan Maragall, el Pla Jaussely i la Reforma de 1908 a la ciutat de Barcelona," *Zeitschrift für Katalanistik* 20 (2007): 149–165, p. 150.
31. Josep Puig i Cadafalch, *La Plaça de Catalunya. Comentaris, Projectes, Làminas* (Barcelona: Llibreria Catalònia, 1927), 11. All translations are mine.
32. Maiken Umbach, "The Modernist Imagination of Place and the Politics of Regionalism: The Case of Puig i Cadafalch and Early Twentieth Century Barcelona," in *The Re-Enchantment of the World: Secular Magic in a Rational Age*, ed. Joshua Landy and Michael T. Saler (Stanford, CA: Stanford University Press, 2009), 81–101, p. 93.
33. Carmen Popescu, *Le style national roumain: construire une nation à travers l'architecture (1881–1945)* (Rennes and Bucharest: Presses Universitaires de Rennes; Simetria, 2004), 187.
34. Even though he does not directly discuss Brâncoveanu's style, Cosmin Minea's article is a good introduction to the use of historical architectural in the making of the modern Romanian nation. See Cosmin Minea, "The Monastery of Curtea de Argeş and Romanian Architectural Heritage in the Late 19th Century," *Studii de Istoria Şi Teoria Arhitecturii* 4 (2016): 181–201.
35. "[Letter from Petre Antonescu to Josep Puig i Cadafalch]," January 20, 1931, UC 1092, ANC. Fons Puig i Cadafalch.
36. Luminita Machedon and Ernie Scoffham, *Romanian Modernism: The Architecture of Bucharest, 1920–1940* (Cambridge, MA: MIT Press, 1999), 64, 165.
37. "[Letter from Marica Cotescu to Josep Puig i Cadafalch]," September 10, 1924, UC 1246, ANC. Fons Puig i Cadafalch. In the archive Cotescu's name appears as "Cotesen."
38. Ibid.
39. Puig i Cadafalch, "Les périodes successives de l'influence byzantine en Occident", p. 169.
40. "[Letter from Maria Irineu to Josep Puig i Cadafalch]," August 18, 1929, UC 1415, ANC. Fons Puig i Cadafalch.
41. Juan José Ortega Román, "Nicolae Iorga: viajero por España," *Revista de Filología Románica* 20 (2003): 151–162, p. 152.
42. "[Telegram from Nicolae Iorga to Josep Puig i Cadafalch]," March 1, 1927, UC 1414, ANC. Fons Puig i Cadafalch; Nicolae Iorga, *Cîteva zile prin Spania* (Bucharest: Editura Casei Şcoalelor, 1927), 77; cited in Ortega Román, "Nicolae Iorga," 158.
43. Lourdes Sánchez Rodrigo, "Las relaciones literarias entre Cataluña y Rumanía," *Revista de lenguas y literaturas catalana, gallega y vasca* 19 (2014): 99–108, p. 104. The lectures were also published. See Nicolae Iorga,

Trei conferințe la Teatrul Național din București, despre Spania (Bucharest: Editura Casei Școalelor, 1927).
44. Mircea Anghelescu, "Viajeros rumanos en España, en busca de las raíces comunes," *Revista de Filología Románica* IV (2006): 277–284, pp. 282–283.
45. Ortega Román, "Nicolae Iorga," 157.
46. Iorga, *Cîteva zile prin Spania*, 75; translated into Spanish and cited in Ortega Román, "Nicolae Iorga," 157.
47. Iorga, *Cîteva zile prin Spania*, 77; translated into Spanish and cited in Ortega Román, "Nicolae Iorga," 158.
48. Daniel Pifarré, "Josep Puig i Cadafalch and the Sgraffito Technique: Influence and Adoption of Motifs from Gothic Art," in *Josep Puig i Cadafalch. Vision, Identities, Cosmopolitism*, ed. Lucila Mallart (Mataró: Ajuntament de Mataró, Direcció de Cultura, 2018), 235–242.
49. Iorga, *Cîteva zile prin Spania*, 77; translated into Spanish and cited in Ortega Román, "Nicolae Iorga," 158.
50. Iorga, *Cîteva zile prin Spania*, 77–78; translated into Spanish and cited in Ortega Román, "Nicolae Iorga," 158.
51. Lucila Mallart, "From Electricity to the Photo Archive: National Identity and the Planning of the 1929 Barcelona International Exhibition," in *Urban Histories of Science: Making Knowledge in the City, 1820–1940*, ed. Oliver Hochadel and Agustí Nieto-Galan (London: Routledge, 2018), 208–226.
52. "[Letter from Nicolae Iorga to Josep Puig i Cadafalch]," September 2, 1929, UC 1414, ANC. Fons Puig i Cadafalch; "[Postcard from Nicolae Iorga to Josep Puig i Cadafalch]," 1929, UC 1414, ANC. Fons Puig i Cadafalch.
53. Nicolae Iorga, *O mică țară latină: Catalonia și expoziția din 1929. Note de drum și conferințe* (Bucharest: Editura Casei Școalelor, 1930), 38. I would like to thank Xavier Montoliu for sharing his copy of the book with me.
54. Xavier Montoliu, "Notícia sobre Joan Maragall, traduït en romanès (II)," *Haidé. Estudis Maragallians. Butlletí de l'Arxiu Joan Maragall* 2 (2013): 115–134, pp. 126–127.
55. Iorga, *O mică țară latină*, 51; translated into Catalan and cited in Xavier Montoliu and Diana Moțoc, "Quatre apunts sobre les relacions entre la literatura romanesa i la catalana," *Visat* 15 (2013): n.p.
56. Iorga, *O mică țară latină*, 14. I am grateful to Liliana Iuga for her help in the translation of the text from Romanian into English.
57. "De vorbă cu d. Puig i Cadafalc, președintele Uniunei provinciale catalane," *Dimineata*, April 23, 1924, UC 2542, ANC. Fons Puig i Cadafalch.
58. Joan Fuster Sobrepere, Antoni Nicolau i Martí, and Daniel Venteo, eds., *La construcció de la gran Barcelona: l'obertura de la Via Laietana 1908–1958* (Barcelona: Museu d'Història de la Ciutat, Institut de Cultura de Barcelona, Ajuntament de Barcelona, 2001).
59. Lucila Mallart, "Illustrated Media, the Built Environment and Identity Politics in Fin-de-Siècle Catalonia: Printing Images, Making the Nation," *Cultural History* 4, no. 2 (2015): 113–135, pp. 118–123.
60. For a discussion of architectural debates in Germany at the time, see Rainer Schützeichel, "Die räumliche Ordnung der modernen Stadt. Karl Henricis Beitrag zum städtebaulichen Raumdiskurs des ausgehenden 19. Jahrhunderts," in *Die Stadt als Raumentwurf. Theorien und Projekte im Städtebau seit dem Ende des 19. Jahrhunderts*, ed. Vittorio Magnago Lampugnani (Berlin and München: Deutscher Kunstverlag, 2017), 111–127.
61. Iorga, *O mică țară latină*, 15.
62. Ibid, 11.

63. Ibid., 14.
64. Ibid.
65. Ibid., 13.
66. Agustín Cócola Gant, *El Barrio Gótico de Barcelona: planificación del pasado e imagen de marca* (Barcelona: Edicions Madroño, 2011), 20.
67. Iorga, *O mică ţară latină*, 12.
68. Ibid., 12.
69. Ibid., 11.
70. Ibid., 13.
71. Ibid., 13.
72. Ibid., 15–16.
73. Ibid., 10.
74. Sinclair, *Trafficking Knowledge in Early Twentieth-Century Spain*, 1.
75. Christophe Charle, *Les intellectuels en Europe au XIXe siècle: essai d'histoire comparée* (Paris: Seuil, 2001), 161.
76. Labanyi does not directly discuss a separate Catalan-speaking public sphere, but she argues that the late nineteenth-century Spanish novel – which she calls a "national novel" – contributed to "bind the nation together – provided that [readers] are speakers of Castilian" and that "Oller's novels, written in Catalan, would perform the same function for Catalonia." See Jo Labanyi, "Relocating Difference: Cultural History and Modernity in Late Nineteenth-Century Spain," in *Spain Beyond Spain: Modernity, Literary History, and National Identity*, ed. Brad Epps and Luis Fernández Cifuentes (Lewisburg: Bucknell University Press, 2005), 168–186, p. 172.
77. The Congress of Art History. See *Actes du Congrès d'histoire de l'art, organisé par la Société de l'histoire de l'art français, Paris, 26 septembre–5 octobre 1921* (Paris: Presses universitaires de France, 1923), 235–236.
78. Alcalde, "Spatializing Transnational History," 554.

11 In the Driver's Seat of Modern Urbanization

A Case Study of Automotive Development in the Emerging City of Barcelona, c. 1900–1950

Barry L. Stiefel

Between 1900 and 1950, the automotive industry developed within the "secondary" and "peripheral" cities of Southern Europe (henceforth to be called "emerging cities"), where substantial population and economic growth was taking place. The automobile is also the transportation technology that would come to define the twentieth century (and beyond), most significantly the design of urban areas and city living. The budding automotive science and technology of the emerging cities had an inverted relationship in the transferal of knowledge and influence from peripheral cities to central metropolises. This intersection of automobiles and urban develop gives us a unique opportunity to apply the actor network theory (ANT) to people and cars, as postulated by Michel Callon, Bruno Latour and John Law.[1] ANT is a social theory that uses a "material-semiotic" method of analysis, where objects of material culture, such as automobiles, are treated as part of social networks. Therefore, what roles did automobiles play in the dissemination of urban culture and design in places like Barcelona, as well as related technological knowledge across time and places? This case study supports Dorothee Brantz's hypothesis that cities can be considered agents of change, and that cities are sometimes more than the sum of their components.[2] For this study, I argue that during the first half of the twentieth century, urban manufacture and use of automobiles both physically as well as symbolically served as vehicles for the spread of the idea of an idealized urban future, which every developing country desired. This case study will explain some of the socio-spatial complexities of urban processes and the historical contingencies of network relations among actors. While there were automotive manufacturers in the central metropolises of Paris, London and Vienna,[3] emerging cities in France, the United Kingdom and Austria played a disproportionately large role for their size in the production of automobiles. When considering how automobiles have shaped the built environment and culture, acknowledging the contributions of emerging cities like Barcelona is significant in order to better understand the directions and channels through which knowledge was created and disseminated in these interurban networks.

Previous Scholarship on Spain's Early Automotive History

Most scholars of Spain's automotive manufacturing history gloss over the early decades of the twentieth century. The historical emphasis is on 1950 and after, which coincides with the state-founded company Sociedad Española de Automóviles de Turismo, better known as SEAT, presently the most significant Spanish automotive manufacturer.[4] Two exceptions of scholars who have studied Spain's early automobile industry are Salvador Estapé-Triay and Ángel Calvo Calvo. Estapé-Triay comments that it is difficult to access original materials from the small number of important automotive industry companies in Spain before 1950.[5] Since Spain did not have a domestic automotive mass producer until the mid-twentieth century, and none of the early companies survived after 1940, Estapé-Triay claimed in 2000 that scholars of Spanish automotive history have written off this period as having been a failure. Preceding him is Calvo, whose article from 1985 on the beginnings of Barcelona's automobile industry was a pioneering exploration. Calvo identifies that the material demands of World War I were a catalyst for industrial development.[6] Both Estapé-Triay and Calvo concentrate on the history of automobile manufacturing firms of Spanish origin, giving little attention to foreign companies, such as those from France, Italy and the United States who were very active in Spain. The dearth of attention to foreign automotive companies in Barcelona – or to Spanish companies operating abroad – is an extension of Estapé-Triay's frustrations with the lack of access to records. There are records on automotive development not physically located in Spain. These records are located outside of the country where the various actors played their roles within the proposed network's framework. The foreign automobile companies that operated in Spain are very important to investigate because the majority of vehicles used in Spain (including Barcelona) were produced by these companies. This is where collaboration with scholars outside of Spain can prove to be fruitful, and where this case study compliments the previous work of Estapé-Triay and Calvo. Additionally, few scholars have ventured into the analysis of how urban planning and design was affected by automobiles in emerging cities.[7]

Contextualizing Emerging Cities and the Automotive Industry in Barcelona

The impacts of mass automobile ownership were not felt in most European cities until after 1950, largely because it was only in the course of post-World War II rebuilding that car-friendly road systems were created

(Germany's autobahn being an exception). It was also in the emerging cities and towns that automobile design was successfully experimented with during the late nineteenth century. Early examples include Benz & Cie (1885, Mannheim, Germany), Laurin & Klement (1895, Mladá Boleslav, former Czechoslovakia), Oldsmobile (1897, Lansing, United States), and La Cuadra (1898, Barcelona).[8] However, the largest consumer markets for automobiles were among the upper economic classes in the metropolitan centers. Thus began the relationship of automobility between emerging cities, where automotive innovation was taking place, and metropolitan centers, where there was concentrated consumer interest. Automobile profits and order requests, in turn, were transferred back to the emerging cities, and the relationship between the two types of cities with regard to the automotive industry and consumer culture grew, expanding across international borders.

High concentrations of automotive manufacturers in emerging cities are most notably found in Barcelona and Turin for Southern Europe; Coventry, Gothenburg, Stuttgart and Boulogne-Billancourt for Northern and Western Europe's emerging centers; Mladá Boleslav, Pilsen and Kopřivnice for Eastern Europe; and Detroit, Cleveland and Toronto in North America. In Japan and South Korea (after 1950), the emerging cities of Osaka, Yokohama, and Ulsan served as cradles for the automotive industry in Asia.[9] Jordi Catalán defines these cities as "automobile-industry clusters," which corresponds with the emphasis of his scholarship on the early twentieth century emerging city.[10] Barcelona makes an intriguing case study because foreign manufacturers like Fiat, Ford and General Motors also located their subsidiaries in this emerging city, thus creating direct network links with Turin and Detroit. So, in Barcelona both native-industry and foreign-designed automobiles were manufactured side by side in the city. There were no special limitations from the government; in Barcelona there was a relevant group of artisans, technicians and engineers combined with an active bourgeoisie (with limited capital resources). This is in contrast to Italy, where the government prohibited many foreign – especially American – automotive manufacturers from establishing subsidiaries during the early twentieth century. The underlying key to success for emerging cities with clustered automotive industries was easy access to glass, steel, rubber and petroleum, as well as a core group of mechanically inclined and inventive entrepreneurs who were afforded sufficient access to investment capital to enable industrial development of automobile manufacturing.[11] Spain officially acknowledged the significance of the nascent automobile industry to its industrial and urban development as early as 1897, when King Alfonso XIII gave a Royal Order recognizing that:

> what will greatly influence the promotion of public wealth will be the transit of vehicles through public roads. These vehicles constitute a

> nascent and worthy industry of stimulus – of which it is legitimate to expect in the future a great [economic] expansion as a result of the speed and cheapness of the transports.[12]

Once the basic infrastructure for automobile manufacture and consumption was set, peasants from the countryside and immigrants from abroad flocked to the emerging cities to fill the labor shortages as well as improve their financial standing. This migration boosted the urban population and economy, and physically expanded the city in a way that encouraged the general public to own and use automobiles. Between 1900 and 1920, approximately 250,000 people migrated from the Spanish countryside to Barcelona, with many seeking factory employment. By the 1930s, tens of thousands of laborers were employed in the city, manufacturing automobiles or the associated components, with most working in allied supply industries (around 1920), such as textiles (47,872), metallurgy (27,131), and glass (5,112).[13] Some automobile companies also made engines and other components for airplanes and boats, so differentiating the people who worked on one type of vehicle manufacture versus another is complicated due to the complexities of economic innovation and product diversification by the corporations. According to historian James H. Rial, Spanish automobile production increased from 21,855 vehicles per year in 1925 to 36,928 in 1929. Further supplemented by foreign imports, the number of licensed automobiles in Spain climbed by 165 percent, from 89,910 to 238,547.[14]

Approximately 2,000 employees worked at Barcelona's Hispano-Suiza factory where they made automobiles and engines for airplanes.[15] By 1930, Ford had hired 600 workers at its Barcelona subsidiary.[16] As an example of how automobiles affected Barcelona's economy vertically, 12,000 workers were engaged in the production of General Motors' Marathon trucks, distributed across 145 different factories and workshops, most of which were small.[17] This economic complexity of industrial development, entailing automobiles, the supply of materials, and the manufacture of associated vehicles was a product of the networks created by the various actors. Automobiles were a central part of this network because they were the most widely produced and used vehicles under manufacture in the early twentieth century, serving as a great socio-economic symbol of modernity and success.

Companies that mass-produced automobiles intended them to be affordable so as to encourage their employees to buy their products, reinforcing the relationship between people, automobiles, and urban roads for commuting to and from work. Indeed, the agrarian and industrial-working population with its low purchasing power is precisely what caused the Ford Motor Company to establish a subsidiary in Spain in order to sell inexpensive Model Ts, tractors and trucks to ordinary people.[18] According to Per Lundin, most workers in Europe as a whole – not

Figure 11.1 Interior of the Hispano-Suiza factory, Barcelona c. 1910.

Source: Photograph by Frederic Ballell Maymí; with kind permission from the Arxiu Fotogràfic de Barcelona

just Spain – could not afford automobiles until the 1950s and 1960s, coinciding with the post-war economic boom. Prior to 1950, automobiles were the purview of the upper and professional middle classes. The labor movements frequently opposed the phenomenon of motoring, despite being the makers of automobiles.[19] But Spanish advertisements from the 1920s noticeably countered these sentiments, tying a nationalistic twist to automobile ownership, in an era consumed by nationalism following World War I.[20] Therefore, in emerging cities, the confluence of geographic locations in relation to specific resources, coupled with migrants seeking out factory employment, and capitalists with financial resources to invest in industry during the last decades of the nineteenth century was what formulated contemporary urbanized automobile culture – the first clusters or nodes of this specific actor network system.

As observed in 1915 by the internationally acclaimed city planner Werner Hegemann,

> [t]he recent advances in the automobile industry, combined with a sudden and continuous increase in the number of private machines, restores the individual vehicle [formerly horse-drawn] to an important

> role in modern city life and requires special provisions. This automobile traffic deserves special attention, not only because the fact of its connection with the wealthiest part of the city's inhabitants makes it of special interest to the retail merchant and the whole character of the retail trade in a business center.[21]

Hegemann would go on to visit and study Barcelona in 1933, and then fled to the United States to escape Nazi Germany due to his criticisms of Adolf Hitler.[22] The transfer of best practices for city planning during the early twentieth century, which emerging cities were very interested in applying, always centered around the idea that transportation efficiency was vital. The heart of modern urban mobility was the automobile.

Due to increasing globalization, Barcelona and other emerging cities with automotive start-up industries began to play a dynamic role in the international economy. Marián Šuman-Hreblay has researched makers of automobiles on a global scale. He begins in 1770 with Nicolas Joseph Cugnot's steam carriage in France and continues to 2000. According to Šuman-Hreblay, prior to 2000, there were approximately 10,693 makers of motor vehicles that traveled overland without the assistance of rails. This breakdown includes 5,394 makers of vehicles in the United States, as well as 4,834 makers for Europe, leaving 465 for the rest of the world. Within Europe, approximately 100 motor vehicle makers are attributed to Spain; these are primarily small firms such as Fenix, who, between 1901 and 1904, made a total of 25 automobiles at its shop in Barcelona.[23] Fenix is an example of the small, short-lived cottage industry automobile maker that once existed. Many early automobile makers began as manufacturers of other types of vehicles, such as bicycles, carriages and wagons. Thus, prior to 1930, the manufacturing of vehicles, whether they were powered by motor, pedal or draft animal, was sometimes a small business enterprise. Due to their limited production capacity, small makers of automobiles were unable to survive the competition from larger companies, especially during the Great Depression, since big companies were able to create their products more cheaply through economies of scale and globalized networks of suppliers and consumers. Therefore, it must be understood that most automotive companies failed – thousands of them – across Europe and North America before 1950.

Historians such as Estapé-Triay have tried to "answer the question of why no large Spanish motor company established itself during the first third of the [twentieth] century," and "why is it that all the companies founded during this period ultimately failed?"[24] It is not viable to simply compare the success of national-origin automotive manufacturers in the United States with the success of those in Spain, as Estapé-Triay does in his investigation. This is because the population, economy and territory of the United States are substantially larger than Spain's. Moreover, the transportation infrastructure in the two countries was also vastly different. While, in Spain, commerce transported by ocean-going vessel was greater than that by railroad in 1900,[25] in North America, maritime trade accounted for only a small percentage compared to that of railroad.[26] In the United States and Canada, there was already a precedent for overland transport by rail vehicles between cities, though overall road conditions on both continents were dismal at this time. Hence, comparing the continent of North America with the continent of Europe makes better sense, even though North America only comprises three countries. Considering the size and scale of Spain, comparing it to a US state or Canadian province is a better equivalent. Therefore, the failure of so many early Spanish automobile companies within a European continental context is not so unique when we consider that only the state of Michigan succeeded with Ford, Chrysler and General Motors in North America, and that all other states and provinces across the continent also failed. Calvo has identified that the leading causes for the failure of the Spanish automobile industry were the lack of infrastructure development planning, poor government administration, expensive fuel costs and poor road conditions outside of the urban areas.[27] These obstacles for a successful automobile industry were shared by many other parts of the world, too. In other words, if success is measured by a region's ability to produce a viable, major automotive manufacturer, early twentieth-century Spain is in good company among the many failures. The fact that the government tried again and succeeded with a new company, SEAT, in the mid-twentieth century is exceptional, even though SEAT was a joint venture between Fiat and the Franco regime. Fiat decided to set up operations in Barcelona (against the recommendation of the Spanish government) due to this city's history of vehicle manufacturing. Many countries with industries where automobiles are produced in large numbers are made by foreign-owned or licensed subsidiaries.

Spain's Early Automotive Industry

Spain had many national automotive manufacturers during the first half of the twentieth century, with some of the more renowned ones being Hispano-Suiza (1904–1938), Abadal (1912–1923) and Elizalde (1914–1928). These companies, as well as several others, were mostly located in Barcelona. The first recorded motor vehicle built in Spain was produced by Frances Bonet, who made motor-powered tricycles in 1889 with German-built Daimler engines. The vehicle was shown off to the public on an excursion along the Passeig de Gràcia, a thoroughfare in Barcelona that was improved early on to allow easier traffic flow.[28] The most successful early company was Hispano-Suiza, co-founded in 1904 by a Spanish artillery captain, Emilio de la Cuarda, and Marc Birkigt, a Swiss engineer, with entrepreneurial investment from Damià Mateu and Frances Seix. Prior to their collaboration, de la Cuarda had also begun building electric automobiles in Barcelona and Lleida several years earlier.[29] Spain's automotive industry was very important during these early decades because it symbolically represented a valuable and very modern diversification of the country's manufacturing economy. Other governments, such as that of the United States, were well aware of Spain's automotive market for the purposes of strategizing export opportunities. A report by the Department of Labor and Commerce from 1912, *Foreign Markets for Motor Vehicles*, explained:

> In Spain the *use* [author's emphasis] of the automobile has been developed principally in the Madrid district, this being the center of the country's official and social life, and containing a large number of people of wealth. . . . There is *but one automobile manufactory* [author's emphasis] in Spain, the Hispano-Suiza, which manufactures cars.[30]

Other Spanish emerging cities, such as Cadiz, Guadalajara and Málaga, also had some automotive industry after 1912, but Barcelona's reigned supreme, even over the capital.[31] Madrid was simply Spain's largest consumer market for automobiles, not a manufacturing center of them. In 1920, there were eight automobile factories within Barcelona, and at that time, the most significant Spanish facilities were those by Hispano-Suiza and Elizalde, respectively located at 275–279 Carretera de Ribes near the La Sagrera and Sant Andreu districts in the northern part of the city, and 149 Paseo de San Juan in the central part of the city. Later in the 1920s, Ricart established a factory on Carrer de Romans in the Gràcia district, in the western area of the city. Based on the known locations of automobile manufacturing in Barcelona, the industry does not appear to have been concentrated in any particular quarter of the city during this early period.[32]

Partnerships also developed between Spanish automotive manufacturers and those in other countries, such as in 1916 when Abadal established a relationship with Buick, an American company, to produce Abadals using Buick engines. At the same time, Abadal also made an agreement with Belgium-based Impéria to produce Impéria-Abadals in Northern Europe. In the 1920s, Škoda also had a license to make Hispano-Suiza automobiles for the Eastern European market at their factory in Pilsen, Czechoslovakia.[33] Contractual agreements were also made with Hispano-Argentina to produce Hispano-Suizas under license in Buenos Aires, but nothing more than a prototype and repairs to imported automobiles were accomplished.[34] Spanish delegations would also occasionally visit factories in other countries, such as Citroën in France, in order to learn current best practices of manufacture.[35]

Despite the iconic role Hispano-Suiza would maintain until the 1930s as Spain's car company, commercial automotive production gradually began in 1911 to shift to its French subsidiary located near Paris. The most acclaimed post-World War I automobiles by Hispano-Suiza were actually made in France. This was largely due to France's investment in Hispano-Suiza, whereby the company received a very valuable contract to develop aircraft engines for France's burgeoning air force and for a competition offered by the Spanish air force in 1914. The airplane engine, designed by Birkigt, performed as well as those made by the German company Benz, and was significantly lighter. The Hispano-Suiza airplane engines were also made under license by companies in the Allied countries of France, Italy, the United Kingdom, the United States, and Japan for a combined 40,000 engines. After World War I, the French government imposed the independence of the French Hispano-Suiza from the Spanish one. Birkigt remained the director of the French company and maintained ownership of the patents. Therefore, the great success of Birkigt's inventions benefited him extensively, and not just Hispano-Suiza. The license contracts further promoted Hispano-Suiza and Spain's international reputation as an exceptional builder of modern transport vehicles, providing additional evidence of the structure of the actor network.[36] The French Hispano-Suiza subsidiary was so successful that it even took over the French automobile manufacturer, Ballot, a company based in Paris. This was one of a number of instances when an automotive corporate entity in an emerging city planted itself a satellite in a primary metropolis, then subsequently took over a competitor based there.[37]

While Hispano-Suiza was the dominant Spanish automotive manufacturer in the eyes of the world, there were others in Spain, and they made significant contributions to the developing automotive heritage of the country. In its coverage of the Barcelona auto show of 1922, the American-based magazine *Automotive Industries* observed:

> Elizalde, although not as well-known abroad [as Hispano-Suiza], is just as important in the home country. [Elizalde] took advantage of the show to present an entirely new eight-cylinder in line automobile of exceedingly neat appearance. . . . España is another Spanish firm little known outside of its territory, producing a high grade car costly to build and having a certain general resemblance to the Hispano-Suiza.[38]

In addition to native Spanish companies, the American firm Ford in 1923 established its first subsidiary, where automobiles and tractors were built until the Spanish Civil War. General Motors did the same shortly thereafter, and used its Barcelona-based manufacturing operations to further distribute its products to other cities on the European continent for sale.[39] The Italian company Fiat partnered with the Spanish manufacturers Hispano-Suiza and Ricart to make cars in Barcelona. The Port of Barcelona also served as a major center of importation of motor vehicles.

Some manufacturers on the European continent, for example in France, transported automobiles to Spanish markets by railroad. Ford's Barcelona subsidiary also worked in a network with Ford subsidiaries in other European countries to make automobiles. In 1930, Ford moved its Italian subsidiary in Trieste to Genoa so that it could be closer to the Barcelona factory.[40] Using ship and rail transport, Ford and Citroën contributed the largest share of imported vehicles and parts in Spain. Until the 1920s, an average of 14,000 motor vehicles were imported into Spain per year, in contrast to the 2,000 or fewer that were manufactured by native Spanish companies, with the majority made by Hispano-Suiza.[41] Automobile production in Spain increased following the establishment of foreign-owned subsidiaries.

Network Exchanges of Urban Automobile Industrial Development

Many horse-drawn vehicle and bicycle makers converted their operations to automotive manufacturing in order to remain competitive, but eventually lost out due to their continued use of small industry methods. This is in contrast to the successful companies that adopted the *Fordism* assembly line approach of mass production. Indeed, the very term Fordism, referring to "the system of mass production that was pioneered in the early twentieth century by the Ford Motor Company," as well as the mode of "economic growth and its associated political and social order in advanced capitalism,"[42] was a side effect of the automobile actor network spreading out from emerging cities. Fordist production of automobiles from Detroit not only influenced manufacturing in the central metropolises of New York, London, Paris, Berlin and Vienna, but the process was also transplanted from Ford's Highland Park assembly plant near Detroit to the company's other factories abroad, including in Barcelona. Prior to the Civil War, Barcelona's collective industry – not just automobiles – had primarily comprised of small and medium-sized factories and workshops. By Spanish standards, Hispano-Suiza's factory of 2,000 workers in Barcelona during the 1930s was gigantic, but it was small within a Fordist production model. By comparison, the Highland Park factory near Detroit, where the Fordist manufacturing methodology was perfected, employed approximately 13,000 workers in 1914, producing more than 300,000 automobiles in that year alone.[43] It was not until the 1930s that the number of automobiles on Spanish roads would exceed this number. Fordist manufacturing processes went on to influence industries across Spain and other parts of Europe, further demonstrating how it can be through material objects, such as automobiles, that cultural and economic innovations can be transferred from one place to another within social networks. However, the adoption of Fordist

Figure 11.2 Interior of the Hispano-Suiza factory, Barcelona 1934.

Source: Unknown photographer, published in *El Día Gráfico*; with kind permission from the Arxiu Fotogràfic de Barcelona

manufacturing production did not become common in Spain until after 1950, when there was widespread economic restructuring and post-war factory rebuilding.

As Hupmobile, another Detroit-based automobile manufacturer which competed directly with Ford's inexpensive Model T, advertised in the September 1924 edition of the *Córdoba Automovilista*, "[Hupmobile makes] the most prestigious automobile of its category."[44] In other words, if you cannot afford the most luxurious of automobiles, purchase ours because it is the very best available within its price bracket. Here again, the automobile is playing the role of an actor within the social and geographic networks that connected people and also affected urban development. Virtually all other non-luxury automobile manufacturers (all of whom were of foreign origin) expressed these sentiments, as well. This marketing brought automobiles to the masses and contributed to a car-reliant culture and corresponding land-use development. An automobile-dependent society and the corresponding infrastructure within the landscape were defining features of twentieth-century urbanization.

The historian Valentina Fava has investigated the evolution of automobile manufacturing by Škoda in the former Czechoslovakia and Fiat in Italy between 1918 and 1948. Both companies had their own ties with Barcelona's automotive industry and were also seeking to learn from and improve their manufacturing methodologies from the success of the Fordist model. Fiat focused on improving efficiency and updating their factory machinery, but without reorganizing operations according to Fordist principals, whereas Škoda adopted the Fordist system of automobile production more thoroughly, especially after World War II when they had to rebuild their factories. The Soviets also adopted a purist strategy of Fordist mass production, which was a reinforcing influence across the Eastern Bloc.[45] When Spain resuscitated its industries in the 1950s, with SEAT as its primary automotive manufacturer, Fordism was adopted as the methodology of production, though with modifications to meet workers' needs because of Fiat who served as the corporate partner with the Spanish government.[46]

As in North America and Europe, many Spanish automotive manufacturers had already gone out of business due to the economic difficulties of the Great Depression, such as the government-backed company, Nacional Pescara. The Civil War was also incredibly disruptive to the country's automotive industry, both with regard to nationally owned companies and foreign-owned subsidiaries. Those companies that survived the challenging economic times of the Depression permanently closed their doors during the Civil War and did not return to Spain until the 1950s or later. The Civil War further exasperated the difficult economic situation, the uncertain times making it impossible to do business. Some factories in Barcelona literally became battlefields during the Civil War as various factions tried to control armament production, to which many facilities had been converted. The institutional culture of Spanish industrial manufacturing prior to the Civil War was not one that could synthesize well with a Fordist approach of production. Native automobile companies did not produce their products using the kind of assembly line that would make them economically available for the lower classes. It was not until the Franco regime and labor organizations had introduced total socio-economic restructuring throughout Spain that a Fordist model of manufacturing could be successfully applied – and one that came with the assistance of the Italian Fiat partnership.

Barcelona's Contributions to the Global Automobile Industry

Of all the early native Spanish manufacturers, Hispano-Suiza can be considered the most successful, both within Iberia and abroad. Not only did it flourish the longest, from 1904–1938, but the company also exported automobiles internationally for a period of time and established a foreign subsidiary, the Société Française Hispano-Suiza, near Paris. The French subsidiary was Hispano-Suiza's means of supplying automobiles to the French market. Again, the automobiles were the actors for Hispano-Suiza, attracting an upper-class following in France, the rest of Europe, and North America through the network of the fashion industry. When people saw that owners of Hispano-Suizas included celebrity fighter pilot André Dubonnet (1897–1980), 3rd Baron Rothschild (Nathaniel Mayer Victor Rothschild, 1910–1990), actress Dorothy Sturges (1889–1933) and King Alfonso XIII (1886–1941), the public desire to have an automobile increased, even if most people could not afford a luxurious Hispano-Suiza.[47] During the Civil War, Francisco Franco himself used a Type 68 Hispano-Suiza.[48]

What should be highlighted here is that Hispano-Suiza automobiles, in addition to those of other Spanish manufacturers like Abadal, were not intended for the masses. Their reputation was based on high-end luxury or racing automobiles that were made on an individual basis, similar to their horse-drawn carriage forbearers of the nineteenth century. An example of a Spanish-made cottage industry automobile is a Hispano-Suiza from 1926 held at the Boca Raton Museum of Art in Florida, which is documented as having been hand-built with silver plate detailing, with every piece individually numbered, and a custom-designed cabin interior by Paul Kellner of Paris.[49] The general public could not afford such a luxurious car, but nonetheless, automobiles such as this had a profound impact on people and urban culture that extended beyond an individual Hispano-Suiza, manifesting itself in an aura of consumer desire. Ford, Fiat, and other lower-end automobile manufacturers capitalized on this desire rooted in automobility, modern urbanity, technological advancement and consumption to sell their cars.

In foreign newspapers from the 1920s, such as the *Wall Street Journal* in the United States, automotive dealerships sold Hispano-Suizas alongside the other highly acclaimed brands of Rolls Royce, Pierce Arrow and Mercedes.[50] In comparison, Hispano-Suizas had a sleeker design than Rolls-Royces and Bentleys, which were boxier. The Hispano-Suiza design, by Bikgit, represented a faster and more powerful automobile than many of its competitors. This resulted in British-based Rolls-Royces adopting (under license) some Hispano-Suiza features for their cars. In the United States, Kissel Motor Car Company and General Motors also copied design aspects from Hispano-Suiza.[51] Indeed, Harley Earl (1893–1969), head of design for General Motors in Detroit, readily admitted when he spoke of designing the luxury La Salle Series 303:

> Well-to-do people would come from all over the country [the United States] and a lot of them drove foreign cars (non-American

> manufacturers). They began to bring them to me when they'd develop trouble and I'd patch them up but first I crawled all over them and took down every dimension. I was thinking of what I'd like to build for myself. Before long I began to get a good idea of what it took to make a good-looking car which was also comfortable. The Hispano Suiza was the apple of my eye – all the chic people who appreciated cars drove Hispanos. They were very light as against the heavier models American companies were making, and every line meant something. In fact, when I came back to Detroit to do the La Salle (he pronounced it La Sol), I stole a lot of stuff. You could tell I was looking at a Hispano.[52]

Thus, we have an instance of engineering and automotive design from an emerging city in peripheral Southern Europe influencing the product design of established industry in metropolitan Western Europe and North America. According to historian Steven Parissien, "[b]y 1930 the name Hispano-Suiza was, like Rolls Royce and Bentley, synonymous with quality and power."[53] Political power, of course, is often concentrated in urban centers, and luxury automobiles were becoming a symbolic representation of this modern milieu. The world over, including in Spain, the automobile played an important signifier role within fashion, symbolizing economic success and political influence, which was predominantly concentrated within cities. Due to the cultural importance of automobiles, which reinforced in many countries a sense of nationalistic pride, and because they were conceived of and produced in emerging cities instead of the already established metropolitan centers or capitals, the prominence and influence of places like Barcelona became elevated and their populations, economies and political influence grew.

The Image of the Urban Automobilist Projected From Barcelona

On 19 January 1928, a provocative advertisement was produced by Hispano-Suiza in the *La Vanguardia*, a Barcelonan-based newspaper targeted at a bourgeois readership. Considering Barcelona's industrial base, it is not surprising that *La Vanguardia* would market itself to Spanish and Catalan workers. Hispano-Suiza splits its full page add into three parts, with an airplane on the top, an automobile speeding across a bridge in the middle, and a speedboat racing past beneath the bridge. Most of the advertisement rhetoric is devoted to the recent speed and distance records achieved by airplanes and motorboats using Hispano-Suiza-built engines. But for all the featured vehicles, the keywords "*Fuerza, Velocidad, Lujo, [y] Elegancia*" ("strength, speed, luxury, [and] elegance") are used.[54]

The themes of these commercials epitomized Hispano-Suiza and the desired personification of Spanish automotive manufacturing was reflected in the media coverage of races, automobile shows and concours d'elegance of the period. Since the 1900s, automobile racing took place in Spain and was reported on in a plethora of newspapers. In June 1908, the Barcelona-based *La Ilustración Artística* dedicated an entire page to the coverage of the Catalunya International Cup. Though the French-made Peugeot was victorious, increasing the nationalistic rivalry between Spain and France, Spain soon won back its national pride when Hispano-Suiza won first place at Belgium's Ostend Cup, beating Peugeot, which came in second place; at the Boulogne Cup in France, Hispano-Suiza also placed first and third, with Peugeot coming in at second and fourth place.[55]

In addition to races, automobile shows played an important role in marketing the latest developments of the industry, with Hispano-Suiza receiving high acclaim at the 1906 and 1908 Paris car show, the Mondial de l'Automobile. This is an archetypal example of emerging city-made automobiles being put on display in the central metropolis, and is highly relevant to this case study of the ANT application. At the time, the Paris show, initiated in 1898, was the most exclusive and established event of its kind. Other prestigious shows were held in New York, London and Frankfurt-am-Main.[56] Emerging cities with robust automotive industries also developed their own shows, such as Barcelona and Detroit, but in the early years these events did not carry the same social or political influence as the shows of the metropolitan centers, as is shown by the media coverage of the 1913 auto show held at Barcelona's Turó-Park.[57] Hosted by the Royal Automobile Club of Catalonia, the 1913 auto show was the first in Barcelona. Hispano-Suiza, Elizalde, and Ford featured prominently. By 1924, Barcelona's auto shows were of great interest to the regime of Miguel Primo de Rivera (who ruled from 1923–1930). In 1927, the Automobile Industry Protection Act was established to provide protection for Spanish automobile companies and to encourage foreign subsidiaries in Spain to use more Spanish-made materials and parts.[58]

At the 1922 Barcelona auto show, 73 companies had exhibits, with the United States having the most vehicle manufacturers represented with 24, followed by 17 from France, and ten from Germany. There were seven from Spain, which included Hispano-Suiza, Elizalde, David, Elfe, Landa, Victoria and España. The Barcelona auto show of 1922 was exceptional in that it was the first in Europe after World War I to be hosted in a country that had been neutral in the war, so that automotive manufacturers from the former Allied Powers and Central Powers were, for the first time, gathered under the same roof, though the companies from Allied countries were much better represented. Through World War I, largely due to geographic proximity, French cars such as De Dion-Bouton dominated Spanish consumerism. Automobiles made by native Spanish companies never dominated the market before 1950. American cars became more popular after World War I due to a tariff war between France and Spain, which also strained the relationship within Hispano-Suiza between the parent company and its subsidiary near Paris. Indeed, it was during the Franco-Hispano rivalry of the 1920s, when there was conflict over trade and import duties, that the French subsidiary usurped the reputation of the Barcelona-based parent company.

By the mid-1920s, the auto show scene had become inverted, and the shows of the emerging cities with automotive industries took on a prestige of their own influence. As historian Beverly Rae Kimes found, people recognized that emerging cities like Barcelona and Detroit were now the tails wagging the dogs of Paris and New York in regard to automobility and the modern urban lifestyle associated with it. Automotive showing in Barcelona reached its climax in 1929–1930 when the city hosted the World's Fair – L'Exposició Internacional de Barcelona – where Hispano-Suiza had its own pavilion. While automobiles had been exhibited at previous World's Fairs, the 1929 exposition in Barcelona was the first to feature a pavilion dedicated exclusively to a single automotive company. This would inspire others, most significantly General Motors' Futurama at New York's 1939 World's Fair, where the advantages of automobile-dependent urban lifestyles were depicted.[59] There was one aspect, however, in which metropolitan centers maintained pre-eminence; in the words of Kimes, "the national events brought the industry together and gave company executives and dealers a chance to kibitz and have a holiday."[60] Through Primo de Rivera, the Spanish government became more serious about automobiles due to their becoming recognized symbols of urbanized modernity and industrial success, as portrayed at the L'Exposició and by the general media. During the 1920s, Spain's government thus began to provide greater financial support and legal protection for the automotive industry, as well as inter- and intra-urban infrastructural development. Iberia also began to enjoy greater economic prosperity than it had in previous decades, and automobiles were a sound economic investment for industry.

The newly established Ricart and Nacional Pescara companies were a result of Primo de Rivera's policies, and, in the case of Nacional Pescara, direct investment. Primo de Rivera was also the founder of the Unión Patriótica Española political party, which was conservative and sought support from political Catholics, technocrats and business-owning classes.[61] Automobiles fit well within the purview of the business-owning class, and the infrastructural development needed to support motor vehicles boded well for career technocrats. During the 1920s and 1930s, both Ricart and Nacional Pescara ran newspaper advertisements with the slogans "*Industria Nacional Metalúrgica S.A. Fábrica de Automóviles*"[62] and "*Fábrica Nacional de Automóviles*," because patriotism and automotive consumerism supported the political agenda of Primo de Rivera's regime and were endorsed by the monarchy. A photograph from the 21 September 1930 edition of *La Vanguardia* by Nacional Pescara bore the caption: "The King with the Marques of Pateras-Pescara in the new touring car [by Nacional Pescara]." However, as a striking contrast, the half-page advertisement below the photograph easily overpowers the King and Marqués of Pateras-Pescara with the announcement of "El Nuevo Buick,"[63] depicting an ordinary Spaniard driving a Buick. This can be seen as a better comment on the automotive reality: the future is going to be driven by the masses in mass-produced, affordable automobiles, and will not revolve around custom-made cars for the well-to-do.

Both Ricart and Nacional Pescara considered themselves "*el Fábrica Nacional de Automóviles*," and Barcelona was central to their production and distribution. On 30 October 1926, *La Esfera*, a Granada-based magazine with a focus on science, technology and culture, covered the grand debut of Ricart at that year's auto show in Paris, emphasizing their Barcelonan origins.[64] The wealthier, business-owning class would, of course, benefit from Primo de Rivera's affirmative stance on automobile consumerism because of the industrial expansion it would cause, especially in Barcelona. After World War II, this political message, sugar-coated through the joys of automobile consumerism, would also ultimately transform urban areas. While Franco's Falange party opposed free capital markets, automobile companies like SEAT continued to be beneficial to the government. Franco's technocrats also gained from the work it created to develop the automotive-oriented built environment after 1950. In a striking contrast, it should also be noted that Abadal-Buick does not appear to have touted itself as native Spanish national brand, like Hispano-Suiza or Ricart. Ford, which also had a subsidiary in Barcelona, technically making it made in Spain, marketed itself as "*El Automóvil Universal*,"[65] thus tying itself to no specific geographical location, but instead showing itself to be "based everywhere."

Evolving Urban Infrastructure in Spain for Automobility

Around 1920, out of a population of approximately 20 million, there were 7,000 registered automobile owners in the whole of Spain, which accounted for roughly 0.04 percent.[66] Many entrepreneurs in Spain and abroad saw this as a ripe economic opportunity to capitalize on. However, there were infrastructural obstacles that impeded the path of motor vehicle ownership. As observed by W.F. Bradley in 1922, a journalist for the American-based magazine, *Automotive Industries*:

> There is an indifference to the good roads movement in Spain, which stands out in sharp contrast to the progressive attitude of surrounding countries. On a road journey from Paris to Barcelona, conditions on Spanish territory were reminiscent of those prevailing in the midwest states of America fifteen or sixteen years ago. A few portions were good, but the majority of the road was bad, and some stretches were in such a condition that even with a big, well-sprung car it was impossible to travel more than six or seven miles an hour.[67]

The situation in Spain would not improve for many years. Indeed, considering that, as of 1900, the bulk of commerce was still conducted by boat, and not even railroad, there was little public motivation to change the means of moving goods from one place to another over land. Improvements to secondary roads also occurred faster than to national primary roads in Spain. The situation was very different elsewhere in Europe and North America, where railroads had flourished in the nineteenth century. The Spanish people were very set in their ways regarding transport, which, in addition to the country's rampant poverty, made the cost of recreational automotive use cost prohibitive for most people. This, in turn, fed into the stereotype among other Europeans and North Americans that Spain was backward.

In Spain, well into the 1920s, the "use of automobiles [was] confined to cities and to individual regions possessing good roads. There [was] no use of automobiles for long distance traveling, such as is common in France."[68] Main streets within major Spanish cities were relatively good and could handle automobiles. By 1906, a motor bus service was already operating in Barcelona, which was the third European city after London and Paris to have such a service.[69] The bus service was significant because, for a relatively low cost, the public could experience riding in a motor vehicle. For a time, Hispano-Suiza also made buses and set up provincial lines called "*Hispano Igualadina*" from Barcelona to Igualada.[70]

Street improvements had actually been part of an urban renewal process in Barcelona for many decades, beginning with the Passeig de Gràcia in 1853, originally intended for horse-drawn vehicles.[71] Bonet chose the smooth, paved road of the Passeig de Gràcia to parade Spain's first locally-made motor vehicle in 1889. Barcelona's Darder Plan of 1918 and Vilaseca Plan of 1932 each prescribed the widening of streets in order to encourage traffic flow.[72] The architects Antoni Darder and Joaquim Vilaseca simply revised the previous city plans of Illdefons Cerdà and Àngel Baixeras. After World War I, cities were so invested in the automotive future that planning for this mode of transportation was assumed even though not always explicitly stated. However, outside of cities, road conditions remained terrible. In 1910, Barcelona's Society for the Attraction of Foreigners, whose purpose was to boost tourism, embarrassingly advised sightseers against driving far out of the city due to poor roads and a lack of bridges.[73]

In 1928, the government proposed the construction of the country's first major improved highway, from Madrid to Irun, on the northwestern Spanish-French border, near the Bay of Biscay.[74] This proposal coincided with the successful starts of the government-backed Ricart and Nacional Pescara manufacturers, which had begun operations a few years earlier. Oddly, the proposed route completely bypassed Barcelona, the country's major automobile producer – the emphasis was on connecting the national capital to international Europe. The proposed highway was never realized due to the Great Depression and Civil War. By 1955 – one generation later – things had drastically changed. A travel guide warns that "when you drive in Madrid, Barcelona, or any of the big cites, because the control systems cannot even begin to cope properly with the recent massive influx of automobiles" expect there to be terrible traffic congestion.[75] It was Barcelona, and not Madrid, that would now provide the impetus for modernization in Spanish industry and the post-1950, automotive-dependent development of urban infrastructure in the country. Hispano-Suiza's nationalization was surprising given that the Spanish owners were loyal Franco supporters. Ford in Barcelona was converted to Motor Ibérica. The remaining Spanish pieces of Hispano-Suiza in Barcelona were obliged to be sold to the government, with some assets also going toward the new ENASA company, which produced Pegaso trucks in Barcelona. SEAT, a new car company also founded in Barcelona, would grow to become Spain's largest automobile manufacturer. In the 1980s, SEAT relocated to Barcelona's Zona Franca industrial district, in the southern part of the city. Today, Spain is the eighth largest manufacturer in the world, and SEAT by itself produces more than half a million automobiles per year.[76] As the vast road networks within and encircling the city can testify, as well as the smog that hangs overhead, automobiles are very much a part of modern urban Spain.

Conclusion

This case study investigates how in the first half of the twentieth century, a period that saw strong growth in production, automobiles served as actors within social networks in emerging cities like Barcelona. The purpose of automotive manufacturing companies was to make physical products, but they also played a pivotal role in the social structure, and thus the "coming of age" of twentieth century cities. The automotive industry was a matter of national pride in Spain and in other countries of the world as it symbolized modern urbanity.

Due to the mobility of motor vehicles, the significance of the specific geographic locations of manufacturing facilities became less relevant within emerging cities. Based on what can be ascertained regarding the places where production and exhibition occurred in Barcelona, there is no clear correlation other than what is likely to have been opportunistic at that time. The effects on the city's urban fabric were widespread, with road improvements emanating from arterial boulevards to smaller streets, though beginning as a city beautification and improvement project in the mid-nineteenth century for horse-drawn vehicles and improved sanitation and drainage. Urban streets brought private automobiles and public bus services to wherever could be reached within cities. In contrast, driving an automobile on rural roads was risky due to the likelihood that the vehicle would be damaged or the traveler injured or marooned. So, automobility from one city to another was more challenging during the early decades of the twentieth century. Rail and boat services remained a preference for intercity transportation, and beasts of burden for travel within rural areas. Rural motor vehicle transit between cities became efficient after 1950 with the development of sophisticated national and regional highway systems.

The historian Parissien observed that "[f]rom Benz to Birkigt, the inspired engineers and businessmen who developed the automobile into the principle mode of human transport during the first decades of the twentieth century succeeded in altering the global landscape beyond all recognition," most notably that of urban areas. "And it [urban areas] was an environment that, thanks to the car, was still changing with frightening speed" unto the end of the 20th century and beyond.[77] Automobile consumer marketing and government support for the industry and transportation infrastructure also played essential roles within the ANT system application. While the transformation of rural Spain to accommodate automotive use did not occur until the 1950s and later, five decades of important relationship building had already occurred, connecting people and cars on a number of levels. People, automobiles and the urban fabric are all actors within a *todos juntos* network of urban heritage.

Notes

1. See Bruno Latour, *Reassembling the Social: An Introduction to Actor-Network-Theory* (Oxford: Oxford University Press, 2005).
2. Dorothee Brantz, "Assembling the Multitude: Questions About Agency in the Urban Environment," *Urban History* 44, no. 1 (2017): 130–136.
3. Marián Šuman-Hreblay, *Automobile Manufacturers Worldwide Registry* (Jefferson, NC: McFarland, 2000).
4. *Revista de Historia Industrial* includes a bibliography with a number of relevant automotive history-related sources, see *Historia Industrial*, vol. 7 (Barcelona: Universitat de Barcelona Publicacions, 1995), 163. This is the bibliography of a paper by Elena San Román on the origin of SEAT.

5. Salvador Estapé-Triay, "The Spanish Motor Industry in the First Third of the 20th Century: A Lost Opportunity," June 2000. Universitat Pompeu Fabra Department of Economics Working Paper No. 470, available at SSRN, http://ssrn.com/abstract=235463 or http://dx.doi.org/10.2139/ssrn.235463.
6. Ángel Calvo Calvo, "Los Inicios de la Industria Automovilística," in *Història Urbana del pla de Barcelona: Vol. 1* (Barcelona: Ajuntament de Barcelona, 1985), 453–462.
7. Per Lundin, "Planning Experts and the Making of the 'Car-Friendly' City," in *Urban Machinery: Inside Modern European Cities* (Cambridge, MA: The MIT Press, 2008), 257–280.
8. See Šuman-Hreblay, *Automobile Manufacturers Worldwide Registry.*
9. "First Half of the History of Nissan," *Nissan Motor Corporation*, 2016, www.nissan-global.com/EN/COMPANY/PROFILE/HERITAGE/HISTORY/, accessed June 29, 2016.
10. Jordi Catalán, "The Life-Cycle of the Barcelona Automobile-Industry Cluster, 1889–2015," *Revista de Historia Industrial* 66, no. 26 (2017): 77–125.
11. Casares G. Tortella, *The Development of Modern Spain: An Economic History of the Nineteenth and Twentieth Centuries* (Cambridge, MA: Harvard University Press, 2000), 331–34; Alan Naldrett, *Lost Car Companies of Detroit* (Charleston, SC: History Press, 2016), 74–75.
12. Translated by author "*[s]e trata . . . del tránsito por vías de uso general utilizadas por vehículos que constituyen una industria naciente y digna de estímulo, de la que es lícito esperar en el porvenir un gran desarrollo como resultado de la rapidez y baratura de los transportes, que influirá en el fomento de la riqueza publica*" from "Real decreto aprobando el reglamento para servicio de coches automóviles por las carreteras del Estado," in *Colección legislativa de España: Parte 1. Legislación y Disposiciones de la Administración Central*, vol. 3 (Madrid: Imprenta de la Revista de Legislación, 1900), 387–388.
13. Angel Smith, "From Subordination to Contestation: The Rise of Labour in Barcelona, 1898–1918," in *Red Barcelona: Social Protest and Labour Mobilisation in the Twentieth Century*, ed. Angel Smith (London: Routledge, 2013), 17–43.
14. James H. Rial, *Revolution from Above: The Primo De Rivera Dictatorship in Spain, 1923–1930* (Fairfax, VA: George Mason University Press, 1986), 223.
15. Michael Seidman, *Republic of Egos: A Social History of the Spanish Civil War* (Madison: University of Wisconsin Press, 2002), 145.
16. "Ford Motor in Spain: Directors Decide to Close Factory New U.S. Tariff Blamed for Action," *Wall Street Journal*, August 2, 1930, 8.
17. Robert J. Alexander, *The Anarchists in the Spanish Civil War* (London: Janus, 1999), 540.
18. Pallares-Barbera, "Changing Production Systems: The Automobile Industry in Spain."
19. Lundin, "Planning Experts and the Making of the 'Car-Friendly' City," 257–280.
20. Advertisement, *La Vanguardia*, April 28, 1927, p. 4. Translation by the author.
21. Werner Hegemann, *Report on a City Plan for the Municipalities of Oakland and Berkeley* (Berkeley, CA: The Municipal Governments of Oakland and Berkeley, 1915), 80.
22. Christiane C. Collins, *Werner Hegemann and the Search for Universal Urbanism* (New York: W.W. Norton, 2005), 254.
23. Šuman-Hreblay, *Automobile Manufacturers Worldwide Registry*, 2–3, 112.

24. Estapé-Triay, "The Spanish Motor Industry in the First Third of the 20th Century."
25. Tortella, *The Development of Modern Spain*, 119.
26. Arthur Donovan, "Maritime Transport," in *The Oxford Companion to United States History*, ed. Paul S. Boyer and Melvyn Dubofsky (Oxford: Oxford University Press, 2001), 471–472.
27. Calvo, "Los Indicios de la Industria Automovilística," 453–462.
28. Catalán, "The Life-Cycle of the Barcelona Automobile-Industry Cluster, 1889–2015," 77–125.
29. Steven Parissien, *The Life of the Automobile: The Complete History of the Motor Car* (New York: St. Martin's Press, 2014), 67.
30. A.H. Baldwin, *Foreign Markets for Motor Vehicles* (Washington, DC: Department of Commerce and Labor, U.S. Government Printing Office, 1912), 102.
31. Estapé-Triay, "The Spanish Motor Industry in the First Third of the 20th Century."
32. L.C. Dawson, "Manufacture of Motor Vehicles in Spain," *Commerce Reports* 33 (February 9, 1920): 808; L.C. Dawson, "Hispano-Suiza: Kings of Engineering," *The Scarf & Goggles Social Club: Ripping Yarns from the Age of Adventure*, January 24, 2016, https://scarfandgoggles.wordpress.com/2016/01/24/hispano-suiza-kings-of-engineering/, accessed March 29, 2017; Pau Moliner, "Fabricación de automóviles (1909–1925)," *Fundación Elizalde*, 2017, http://fundacionelizalde.org/?page_id=12.
33. Nigel F. Piercy, *Tales from the Marketplace* (Hoboken, NJ: Taylor and Francis, 2012), 204.
34. See Howard H. Tewksbury, *The Automotive Market in Argentina* (Washington, DC: Government Printing Office, 1929).
35. *Revista minera, metalúrgica y de ingeniería*, vol. 74 (Madrid: Imprenta del Sucesor de E. Teodoro, 1923), 402.
36. Catalán, "The Life-Cycle of the Barcelona Automobile-Industry Cluster, 1889–2015," 77–125.
37. "The Cars of France," *Motor Sport Magazine*, July 1940, 5. See www.motorsportmagazine.com/archive/article/july-1940/5/cars-france, accessed March 22, 2017.
38. Bradley, "Spanish Show Forecasts Early Trade Revival," 1311–1314.
39. Montserrat Pallares-Barbera, "Changing Production Systems: The Automobile Industry in Spain," *Economic Geography* 74, no. 4 (October 1998): 344–359.
40. "Ford Plant to Move to Genoa," *Wall Street Journal*, August 15, 1930, 4.
41. "How to Save in Exports to Spain," *The Automobile* 30, no. 19 (May 7, 1914): 986; Catalán, "The Life-Cycle of the Barcelona Automobile-Industry Cluster, 1889–2015," 77–125.
42. Bob Jessop, "Fordism," *Encyclopædia Britannica*, May 17, 2016, www.britannica.com/topic/Fordism, accessed February 15, 2016.
43. "Ford's Assembly Line Turns 100: How It Changed Manufacturing and Society," *New York Daily News*, October 7, 2013, www.nydailynews.com/autos/ford-assembly-line-turns-100-changed-society-article-1.1478331, accessed December 27, 2017.
44. Translated by the author, "*el automóvil de más prestigio de los de su categoria*": "Hupmobile" advertisement, *Córdoba Automovilista: Órgano de los Automovilistas de la Provincia Revista Quincenal*, September 1, 1924, 2, 29.
45. Valentina Fava, "People's Cars and People's Technologies: Škoda and Fiat Experts Face the American Challenge (1918–48)," in *Expert Cultures in*

Central Eastern Europe: The Internationalization of Knowledge and the Transformation of Nation States Since World War I, ed. Martin Kohlrausch, Katrin Steffen, and Stefan Wiederkehr (Osnabrück: Fibre, 2010), 105–126.

46. Enzo Mingione, Marco Oberti, and Jose Pereirinha, "Cities as Local Systems," in *Social Assistance Dynamics in Europe: National and Local Poverty Regimes*, ed. Chiara Saraceno (Bristol: Policy, 2004), 35–79.
47. *The V-12 Hispano-Suiza*, No. 3, Profile Publications, 1966; "Miss Sturges's Auto Held at Customs," *New York Times*, July 6, 1930, 13; "Contents of Royal Garage of Spain's Motoring King," *Motor Age*, 15, 42, October 12, 1922, 33.
48. Beverly R. Kimes, *The Classic Era* (Des Plaines, IL: Classic Car Club of America, 2001), 565.
49. Steven M. Sears, "Automotive Gem Rolls into Boca Museum's Collection: Rare Hispano-Suiza Will Be Vintage Car Highlight," *The News* [Delray Beach], October 23, 1993, 1A.
50. Advertisement, *The Wall Street Journal*, October 3, 1928, 3 (upper left corner).
51. Kimes, *The Classic Era*, 92.
52. Barbara Holliday, "Harley Earl: The Original Car Stylist," *Detroit Free Press Sunday Magazine*, May 25, 1969, 13.
53. Parissien, *The Life of the Automobile*, 68.
54. Advertisement, *La Vanguardia*, January 19, 1928, 34. Translation by the author.
55. "Carrera Internacional De 'Voiturettes' Copa 'Catalunya'," *La Ilustración Artística*, 27, 1379, June 1, 1908, 374.
56. Mark Gessler, "Auto Shows: A Timeline," *Historic Vehicle Association*, January 17, 2013, www.historicvehicle.org/auto-shows-a-timeline/, accessed June 23, 2016.
57. "Barcelona – El Salón del Automóvil en el Turó Park," *La Ilustración Artística*, 32, 1633, April 4, 1913, 263.
58. Catalán, "The Life-Cycle of the Barcelona Automobile-Industry Cluster, 1889–2015," 77–125.
59. Pavelló Hispano-Suiza, "Exposició de 1929. Parc de Montjuïc. (1929–1930)," *Barcelofilia*, October 11, 2016, http://barcelofilia.blogspot.com.es/2016/10/pavello-hispano-suiza-exposicio-de-1929.html, accessed March 27, 2017.
60. Kimes, *The Classic Era*, 15.
61. Rial, *Revolution from Above*, 103.
62. Advertisement, *La Vanguardia*, October 11, 1929, 2.
63. Translated from "*El Rey con el marqués de Pateras-Pescara en el Nuevo coche de turismo*." Advertisement, *La Vanguardia*, September 21, 1930, 4.
64. "La Nueva Marca Española 'Ricart' Triunfa en el Salón de Paris," *La Esfera*, 13, 669, October 30, 1926, 47. Translated by the author.
65. Advertisement, *Córdoba Automovilista*, 17.
66. "Spain Fertile Field for Auto Salesmen," *Motor World for Jobbers, Dealers and Garagemen*, 61, October 1, 1919, 45.
67. Bradley, "Spanish Show Forecasts Early Trade Revival," 1314.
68. Ibid., 1312.
69. "Motor Buses in Barcelona," *The Chamber of Commerce Journal* 25, no. 152 (1906): 297.
70. Gabriel Pernau, *Barcelona Y El Coche: Cien Años De Amor Y Odio* (Barcelona: Lunwerg, 2001), 273.
71. Jesus Cruz, *The Rise of Middle-Class Culture in Nineteenth-Century Spain* (Baton Rouge: Louisiana State University Press, 2011), 141.

72. Olivia Muñoz-Rojas, *Ashes and Granite: Destruction and Reconstruction in the Spanish Civil War and Its Aftermath* (Eastbourne: Sussex Academic Press, 2011), 124–126.
73. "Highway for Tourists: Proposed Attraction for Foreigners," *Daily Consular and Trade Reports, New Series 1*, 23, July 10, 1910, 301.
74. "Foreign Trade News," *Good Roads: Devoted to Construction and Maintenance of Roads and Streets*, 71, January 1928, 78.
75. Temple Fielding, *Fielding's Travel Guide to Europe* (New York: Fielding Publications, 1955), 1187.
76. Tortella, *The Development of Modern Spain*, 318.
77. Parissien, *The Life of the Automobile*, 69.

12 Crossing the Iron Curtain

Milan's Museum of Technology and Transnational Exchanges Before and After World War II

Elena Canadelli

Science and Technology Museums as Local and Global Institutions

From the second half of the nineteenth century onwards, museums have been part of what scholars call *urban modernity*.[1] These institutions played a great role in the processes of modernization of the urban space and representation of the urban elites; for instance, in the designing of the South Kensington museum district in London and the Museum Island in Berlin. As historian Sophie Forgan argued, the study of museums' architecture and location represents a relevant research field within the history of science, especially in relation to urban history. The particularity of place, for instance, can help "to shape the museum's credibility and relation to knowledge," which in turn can help "to shape aspects of the urban landscape."[2] In this regard, industry, science and technology museums deserve special attention. Intended as beacons of progress, they strongly characterized the scenario of *modern* and industrial cities of the world. As it was in the case of international and national exhibitions[3] – with their galleries full of machines and technological devices – from the second half of the nineteenth century to the first half of the twentieth century, these museums offered, to the engineering and industrialist elites, an effective symbolic and public space of representation.

Created in the nineteenth century, science and technology museums expanded in the interwar years thanks to the financial support of both the state and private industry. Many industrial museums opened in those years, such as the Tekniska Museet of Stockholm (1924) and the Museum of Science and Industry of Chicago (1933), while many existing museums planned to transfer their collections and exhibitions into new and more spacious buildings, as in the case of two of the most iconic museums of this kind: the Science Museum in London, whose new galleries were completed and fully opened in 1928, and the Deutsches Museum in Munich, whose new building officially opened in 1925. During the same period, many others tried and failed to create technical museums. This happened in Barcelona with the Technology Museum of Catalonia and in Washington, DC, with the Smithsonian's National Museum of Engineering and Industry.[4] Due to the damages inflicted by World War II bombings, during the Cold War, many of these museums, especially in European cities, had to reconstruct their buildings and rethink their exhibitions. If we look to Eastern Europe, for example, the situation during the Cold War was particularly complex as a result of the Soviet annexation. During World War II and under communist regimes, museums such as the Narodni Technicke Museum founded in Prague in 1908; the Museum Tecniki in Warsaw, founded in 1955 as a continuation of the previous Museum of Technology, Industry, and Agriculture (1875); and the Kozlekedesi Muzeum, the Hungarian Museum of Transport opened in Budapest in 1899, experienced bomb attacks, lootings and profound changes of venues, aims, names and institutional memberships. Therefore, the presence and impact of these museums within the urban space was often not static but changed over time; as institutions, they were also very sensitive to societal and political changes and mainly devoted to the scientific and technical education of children and the general public. In many cases, their institutional affiliations also changed, from private organizations to the state or vice versa. Far beyond the nineteenth century, science and technology museums consistently contributed to shaping the debates about modernity and national identity in the urban space both in great European capitals and in the "emerging cities"[5] of Eastern or Southern Europe. Museums were important places of production, appropriation and dissemination of scientific and technical knowledge. They were the main actors in staging science within the dimension of the city and their location in the urban landscapes was a matter of primary importance.[6] In most cases, they were located in the city center, hosted in monumental buildings designed specifically for them.

From the very beginning, politics had a significant impact on the history of these museums and on the narratives they wanted to communicate. After World War I, as temples of progress, innovation and political and economic supremacy, many of these museums on both sides of the Atlantic flourished, directed by two opposing drives: on the one hand, a growing technological nationalism, and on the other hand, a strong ideal of internationalism among nations. As historian Tom Scheinfeldt argued, science and technology museums "have been simultaneously patriotic promoters of national achievements in science and industry and members of an international fraternity of similar institutions."[7] Even if "they were still essentially local institutions, best understood as products of 'local conditions, local requirements and the resources available,'" it is however true that they "have also enjoyed vigorous international engagement, both competitive and collaborative."[8] In a very unique way, these institutions are pervaded by the "dichotomies" described by historian Svante Lindqvist in 1993, being, at the same time, international and national, archaeocentric and contempocentric.[9] Each of these museums embraced an innate tension, which is the result of their historical development, between the rhetoric of national achievements and the rhetoric of internationalism, between the public display of a specific national scientific tradition and the universal values of science and technology, between the focus on the science of the past and the focus on present and future achievements. If science and technology museums always address local demands, mirroring the needs of specific communities and elites, it is also true that they deal with international models and standards, constantly looking to similar museums abroad. Thanks to these characteristics, they are simultaneously local and global, national and international, urban and interurban institutions. On the one hand, science museums play an important role in the urban planning of the cities that host them, shaping and influencing the development of entire districts. On the other hand, their stories are significant to understanding the dynamics of knowledge exchanges in the international context.

Science and technology museums all over the world historically shared a very high standardization of techniques of display and narratives. Those techniques were the result of an agenda pursued by the museums' organizers to imitate each other's architecture, exhibits and strategies of public engagement. In search of the best museological practices, delegations of curators and trustees of museums would travel across Europe and across both sides of the Atlantic, especially from the interwar years on. They visited exhibitions, interviewed colleagues and gathered all kinds of useful information. Until World War I, exchanges between science museums were, for the most part, unidirectional, with museums around the world following the examples of a very small number of leading institutions. Initially, these were mainly the Science Museum in London, the Deutsches Museum in Munich, the Conservatoire des arts et métiers in Paris and the Technisches Museum in Vienna. During the twentieth century, the panorama enlarged substantially, becoming more complex and fragmented. Exchanges between different museums became bi- or even multi-directional. Reciprocity, instead of unidirectional transfer, appears to be the right key to interpret these dynamics, especially during the second half of the last century.

On this basis, the case study of the Italian National Museum of Science and Technology Leonardo da Vinci of Milan (hereafter MUST) is particularly relevant for the case in point, since it allows us to focus both on the role of such an institution in the urban and national context and on the exchanges between museums in the international arena.[10] The museum was established in 1953 in Milan under the auspices of Guido Ucelli, an influential engineer working as general manager at Riva, a renowned factory assembling turbines and water pumps.[11] He was part of the city-based elites of Milan, one of the "emerging cities" in Europe's borderlands. Ucelli had been trying for a long time to create a museum of technical and industrial devices following the main examples in the field. The opening of the museum dedicated to the "genius" of Leonardo da Vinci was the result of a long and complex planning phase that lasted more than 20 years and had its roots in the 1930s. In his search for the best models and inspirations, before and after World War II, Ucelli and his collaborators contacted and visited a large number of technological museums around the world, including the Deutsches Museum, the Science Museum and the Tekniska Museet, but also, especially during the 1950s and the 1960s, several Eastern European museums, despite the Iron Curtain that divided Europe. Thus, the planning of the museum in the urban context of Milan involved consultation with other similar institutions abroad. At the time, the Milan institution itself became a model of inspiration to many of these museums, due to the peculiarity of the collections related to Leonardo da Vinci.

This chapter will analyze the still unexplored case study of the MUST, focusing on the Milanese, national, and international character of this institution. Following a chronological order, the first part will examine the foundation of the museum and its role in the urban environment of Milan as a symbol of modernity of the Milanese engineering and industrialist community, while the second and third parts will delve more into the interurban and international networks created by Ucelli and his collaborators, especially after World War II, focusing on several Eastern European museums.

The Urban Dimension: The MUST, Leonardo da Vinci, and the Shaping of Modern Milan

On 25 November 1937, the renowned Milanese architect Gio Ponti published in *Corriere della Sera*, one of the most influential Italian newspapers, an extensive article wherein he criticized the urban plans for Milan envisioned by the city authorities. In his argument against the official vision of the architectural development of the city, Ponti mentioned – among many other problems – the search for a suitable location for the Industrial Museum promoted by his friend Ucelli:

> Milan's citizens with their valuable initiatives, like the engineer Ucelli with his Industrial Museum and the engineer Semenza with his underground project, seem to suffer from fixation, since things easily realized all over the world take a long time here. Why is this? Because a neighborhood suitable to house the Industrial Museum (or, for that matter, the auditorium) has still not been designed. . . . There is only one problem and only one remedy: we must no longer think of Milan case by case, house-to-house, and year by year, and not just consider this street or the other, but ambitiously compare Milan with the largest and most beautiful cities of the world, taking action with daring and determined programs.[12]

In the eyes of Ponti, the debate on the foundation of MUST was part of a larger problem regarding the shaping of the "Milan of tomorrow,"[13] as the title of one of his articles published under the pseudonym of Archiatra reads.

As the architectural historian Lucy M. Maulsby wrote, Milan still "epitomizes the modern Italian city,"[14] the city of the future. Even if Milan is not the capital city, from the Italian unification in 1861 it was seen as a center of modern life and polytechnic culture marked by rapid population growth, industrialization, and a rich network of vocational and technical schools. Here the Polytechnic University had strong ties to the city's industrial and bourgeois establishment, as the case of Guido Ucelli clearly illustrates.[15] The state university was only inaugurated in 1924. Therefore, during the nineteenth century, the city had developed a significant network of collaborations between different technical-scientific institutions, like the Astronomical Observatory, the civic Natural History Museum, the School of Agriculture, the Veterinary School, the Polytechnic University, and many others. The bond between patronage, aid for the poor and vocational education of the working class was traditionally very strong.

In the late 1920s, the fascist municipal administration was determined to highlight the modernity of the city, reaffirming Milan's identity as a center for industry, engineering and commerce, as well as for arts and culture thanks to its theaters, museums, cultural associations, universities, libraries and archives. The museum, designed by Ucelli during the 1930s, was part of this strategy to create a place that brought together industry and culture. Therefore, in 1931, the *podestà* (mayor) of Milan, the duke Marcello Visconti di Modrone, an industrialist and a member of one of Milan's most noble families, appointed a new civic committee of around 50 experts, named Collegio dei consulenti di scienza ed arte. Its purpose was to prepare a coherent reform and development plan of the cultural, artistic and scientific institutions of Milan.[16] Beyond industry, Milan was the city of La Scala theater and the Pinacoteca Brera, of Leonardo da Vinci, Giuseppe Verdi and the Futurism avant-garde art movement. The Industrial Museum perfectly embodied the two souls of the *modern* Milan as a city of both technical and cultural advancements.

The Collegio was divided into nine subcommittees devoted to the improvement of municipal archives, libraries, theaters, and artistic and scientific museums, including the Museum of Arts and Industries, which still had to be established.[17] The commission for this museum was chaired by Ucelli and assisted by a group of engineers, who were part of the "urban elites"[18] of the city as industrialists, politicians, and men of institutions, and who attended the same associations and clubs, such as the Milan Rotary Club, where they discussed the strategies for the future development of the city. Among others, there was the entrepreneur and pioneer of aviation Gianni Caproni and the professor of electric technology at the

Polytechnic University and managing director of the leading Italian electricity company Edison Giacinto Motta.[19] According to the organizers, neither Rome nor Florence, with its Institute and Museum of the History of Science (1930), were suitable locations. In a time of political and economic autarky promoted by the regime, only Milan – as a lively center of industry and commerce – could host a national museum devoted to the technical and industrial education of the masses and young generations.[20]

The commission discussed the costs, the procuring of the collections, the coordination with other similar institutions in the city, the main purposes of the museum and the examples of other similar museums abroad, especially in Europe. The search for the museum's location was one of the most important issues in the dialogue with the municipal administration, engaged in those years in a broader urban reform plan, as also attested by Ponti's polemic articles. For engineers and entrepreneurs like Ucelli, the new museum had to be closely connected with other similar institutions of the city that could also provide the museum with collections, such as the Polytechnic University, the Milan Trade Fair and the international Triennale exposition of decorative and applied arts. To borrow the title of an article on Paris by the historian Miriam R. Levin, Milan at this time could itself be seen as a diffused museum of technology with many sites devoted to temporary or permanent exhibition of machines, scientific instruments and technological artifacts in general.[21] Examples of such sites were the International Exhibition of Foundry held in 1931 at the Milan Trade Fair, which also hosted two important Aeronautical Exhibitions in 1935 and 1937, and the successful exhibitions held at the Palazzo dell'Arte: The Exhibition of Italian Aeronautics (1934) and the Exhibition on Leonardo and the Italian Inventions (1939).

The initial debate on the foundation of the museum must be read within the context of the complex and often contradictory architectural and urban background that defined interwar Milan and its great need to improve and reshape infrastructures, municipal offices and cultural, health and educational institutions. With the advent of fascism, the debate on the transformation and renovation of the "Great Milan" increased consistently. The regime sponsored the development of public transportation systems and the construction of new buildings, avenues, squares and museums, from the new central railway station to the Palazzo dell'Arte, the new building close to the park of the Castello Sforzesco constructed to house the international Triennale exposition of decorative and applied arts.[22] In order to renovate and redesign the urban landscape of Milan, in 1926, the municipal government launched a competition for a new master plan. The first prize was awarded to Piero Portaluppi and Marco Semenza (both members of the Milan Rotary Club with Ucelli), while the second prize went to the group of architects named Club of Urbanists. Among them we find Gio Ponti and Ferdinando Reggiori, two architects very close to Ucelli.

During the 1930s, the urban reform initiated a long debate between municipal leaders, architects and engineers regarding the future of Milan, the way to transform the Old Town and the politics of enlarging the city.[23] The city's controversial master plan, prepared by the head of the city planning office, Cesare Albertini, would not be ratified until 1934 – but even after that, the criticism did not stop. Opponents such as Ponti and Reggiori publicly accused the municipality of Milan of having distorted the original plan by Portaluppi and Semenza, indiscriminately demolishing the historic center, with its monuments and gardens. At the time, many areas of the city needed a rearrangement, from the new site of the Milan Trade Fair to the slaughterhouse area, from the central San Babila Square to the new peripheral area of the young State University City founded in 1924. The national museum, envisioned by Ucelli for the industrial capital of Italy, was part of this complex urban debate, as its primary aim was to showcase the Italian and Milanese culture and technological advancements. Thus, it was no coincidence that Ucelli was in close contact with the architects' community of Milan, who helped him to promote the foundation of the new institution.

Ucelli was in search of a large building able to store future collections. During the 1930s, he and his supporters made many attempts and proposals. The most notable were the former building of the Milan Polytechnic in Cavour Square, close to the central green area which hosted also the Natural History Museum and the Planetarium, the former railway station area of Porta Sempione, known today as the elegant Pagano district, very close to the new site of the Trade Fair, and the Villa Reale in Monza, a small town close to Milan that hosted the international Biennale of decorative arts until 1930, before the transfer of the exhibition to the Palazzo dell'Arte.[24] In 1936, Ucelli, in association with the engineer Francesco Mauro and the architects Enrico A. Griffini, Portaluppi and Giovanni Sacchi, proposed the project of a "polytechnic institution" to be founded in close proximity to the Polytechnic University, recently moved to the new peripheral area of Città Studi. As they wrote, the museum was not designed as a center of "dead documentation, but instead, fostered by the relationship with the university, it was to be a place of living and 'speaking' instruments, capable of an effective propulsive action (machines in movement, films, phonographs)."[25] However, even this project, like the others, failed.

The outbreak of World War II, the Allied bombing that destroyed or damaged great portions of Milan, and the fall of Mussolini in July 1943 brought Ucelli's plans to a temporary halt. A completely new urban scenario began at the end of the war as the destruction of Milan was substantial, demanding a comprehensive action and a new master plan. In 1947, the authorities assigned to Ucelli the Villata barracks, which was the former Renaissance monastery of S. Vittore (Figure 12.1). It was a large, very damaged historical building in one of the most ancient

Figure 12.1 The former Renaissance S. Vittore monastery, Milan late 1940s.

Source: Archivio Fotografico Museo Nazionale della Scienza e della Tecnologia Leonardo da Vinci/AS_01652; courtesy of Archivio Museo Nazionale Scienza e Tecnologia Leonardo da Vinci, Milano

neighborhoods of the city that dates back to Roman times. The former monastery was close to the Basilica of Sant'Ambrogio and the Convent of Santa Maria delle Grazie, where the famous painting of the Last Supper by Leonardo da Vinci is housed in the refectory.[26] Moreover, the Castello Sforzesco with the Raccolta Vinciana, a research center dedicated to da Vinci, was not far from the museum of Ucelli. The project of converting the former barracks was designed by the architects Griffini, Portaluppi and Reggiori, with whom Ucelli had already worked with during the 1930s.

The renovation work of the building and the search for new political support took some time. The MUST finally opened its doors on 15 February 1953. Unlike the majority of science and technology museums, which were hosted in buildings specifically designed for their exhibitions, the MUST had to adapt to a pre-existing space. This constraint characterized Milan in a positive way, blending together art and science, history and modernity. At the same time, the site allowed for future architectural development and, in the 1960s, work began on a new monumental railway and aeronaval pavilions next to the main Renaissance buildings. Ucelli had more in mind than just a museum. Thanks to its many interior spaces, which included a state-of-the-art cinema and two cafés, it represented an ideal venue for congresses and film screenings. The MUST sought to present to the general public the manifold and ingenious crafts and abilities of mankind, from cutting-edge industry to handcrafts, and with a particular focus on Milanese industrial and scientific achievements. The exhibitions strongly recalled those of the Deutsches Museum. In the first two years of activity, 82 events took place in the museum building. According to Ucelli, the museum would play an ongoing role in the development of its neighborhood and of Milan in general after the devastation of World War II. As in the 1930s, one of the criticisms of the museum concerned its urban position in the new emerging Milan; many accused the institution of being too far from the city center, even though it was only a 20-minute walk to the museum from the Duomo cathedral.[27] The life of the MUST and the fate of a city in search of rebirth met again, illustrating the profound impact that this kind of museum had in defining the modernity of urban spaces in industrial societies, not only during the nineteenth century, but also in the twentieth.

The museum was inaugurated with an exhibition on the science and technology of the "genius" of Leonardo da Vinci, to whom the new institution was dedicated, in order to highlight the universal character of such a museum as well as its particular Italian and Milanese focus, which set it apart from other foreign institutions of its kind. In 1931, the engineer Camillo Cerruti pointed out in a meeting of the Milan Rotary Club, speaking of the future museum, that,

> a special feature that could make the museum of Milan extremely interesting in comparison with major foreign museums like those in London and Munich would be a collection of machines designed by da Vinci in his Codex Atlanticus. This kind of collection doesn't exist anywhere and might be of interest to many industries.[28]

Twenty years later, this vision was realized. Built in a neighborhood strongly associated with Leonardo, the MUST found the identity it was in search of under the name of one of the most iconic artists, engineers and scientists of all time. At the heart of the museum was (and still is) the Leonardo Gallery with its collection of machine models manufactured between 1952 and 1956, and based on interpretations of da Vinci's drawings.

Mobilizing Information: The Interurban Networks of Science Museums

From the very beginning, Ucelli was inspired by similar museums abroad. During the 1930s, while he was trying to establish his museum in Milan, he personally visited a number of major European museums, usually as part of business trips abroad, such as the Deutsches Museum, the Science Museum, the Conservatoire des arts et métiers and the Technisches Museum.[29] At this stage, Ucelli – as an individual traveling expert – used the foreign experiences as a lever in favor of the realization of his project rather than as a chance to build a transnational network for the purpose of exchanging expertise, as it was intended later on. To Ucelli, European technical museums served as terms of comparison in relation to the science exhibits and politics of science dissemination, proving the necessity of establishing an Italian national museum of science and technology. In his circle, Ucelli was not the only one interested in studying other museums. Many of his friends and peers, mostly engineers and industrialists, traveled in Europe and to the United States visiting science and natural history museums as a kind of grand tour. This was the case of the Milanese engineer Francesco Mauro, president of Cinemeccanica, the largest Italian manufacturer of film projectors, who visited many foreign scientific museums, especially the American ones, as a person interested in museum pedagogy and exhibitions.[30] As shown by the 1936 project of the "polytechnic institution," he was directly involved in Ucelli's plans. His case, among others, indicates a widespread museological culture and sensitivity to science and technology museums among the Milanese engineer and industrial community during the interwar years.[31]

In the 1920s and 1930s, the MUST was not the only example of a museum designed by a community of engineers and architects who, in looking to other museums of this kind in search of a model to be imported, organized grand transatlantic tours of curators, trustees and political delegations. As shown by the case of the New York Museum of Science and Industry, the first American industrial museums, which were created in the 1920s, looked to Europe in order to import what was seen at that time as a burgeoning urban cultural institution.[32] Pages and pages of reports, surveys, books, photos and films were produced as part of international exchanges between European and North American museums. The case of Charles Richards, an engineer involved in industrial education who was President of the American Association of Museums between 1923 and 1927, was exemplary. He traveled in Europe in 1924, visiting Paris, London, Vienna and Munich, publishing the survey *The Industrial Museum* one year later. Among many other tasks, Richards dealt with the architecture of the museums' buildings, techniques of display, educational activities and the internal organization of their staffs.[33]

Once the MUST opened, in February 1953, the search for connections became more stable and less sporadic, involving three young collaborators of Ucelli: the engineer Orazio Curti, the physicist Giulio Lenzi and the museum's secretary, Federico Morelli. After World War II, despite the Cold War, initiatives of internationalism and international cooperation among nations generally increased, especially with regard to science.[34] This trend had a profound impact on museums, leading in 1946 to the creation of the International Council of Museums (ICOM) under the auspices of the United Nations Educational, Scientific and Cultural Organization (UNESCO). From the very beginning, Ucelli was involved in this network, contributing two years later to the foundation of the Italian committee of ICOM.[35] With the birth of the Italian Republic in 1948, the new program of the museum stressed the idea of international cooperation through science and technology and consequently through the museums that preserved their history:

> Since they have to document origins and developments of research, discoveries, and applications, museums of science and technology are, by their very nature, international institutions. They transcend artificial borders and can thus effectively foster the understanding between peoples, documenting the interdependence between peaceful achievements of civilization and the necessity and fecundity of exchanges and mutual cooperation between nations.[36]

In the spirit of fostering international cooperation, events such as the International Campaign for Museums took place in October of 1956 with radio links between science museums in Milan, London, Paris and Moscow.

From 1953 on, international relationships between the MUST and other similar science and technology museums began to take different forms. On the one hand, international networks implied a movement of information such as books, official reports and leaflets produced by museums all over the world; on the other hand, they involved a real movement of personnel such as the directors, curators and trustees of the museums.

Regarding the circulation of information, in 1953, on the occasion of the third general conference of ICOM that took place in Milan, Bergamo and Genova, the museum hosted an international exhibition on similar foreign museums. An article in *Nature* describing the museum's opening reported that:

> A series of more than a hundred panels of photographs were contributed by more than twenty museums of science and technology throughout the world to illustrate their techniques and achievements. These are displayed around the principal lecture theatre in the Museum, and Dr. Ucelli hopes to retain them for some time to help him to show what other countries are doing and to obtain further interest in his own plans.[37]

A similar exhibition on the world's technical museums took place in April 1957 at the Narodni Technicke Museum in Prague, where a panel dedicated to the MUST was displayed (Figure 12.2). It was a traveling

Figure 12.2 Panel dedicated to the MUST at the Museum of Technology, Prague 1957.

Source: Fondo Musei, Musei europei, Cecoslovacchia n. 06. Praga, Museo Tecnico, Mostra "The foreign Technical Museums"; courtesy of Archivio Museo Nazionale Scienza e Tecnologia Leonardo da Vinci, Milano

exhibition that aimed at circulating ideas and information; after Prague, it was transferred into the Technical Museum of Košice in Slovakia and thereafter to the Branch Museum in Brno in Moravia.[38]

For Ucelli, the exhibition in Milan represented a seminal moment for gathering information on the functioning and organization of similar institutions, research that would steadily increase in the following years. Today, the archives of the museum preserve a large number of catalogs, leaflets, annual reports, photos, statistics and gray literature from scientific museums throughout the world concerning visitors, administrative organization, research departments and temporary exhibitions.[39] Part of this information was used by Ucelli in an official publication wherein he showcased the museum, with its unique focus on Leonardo da Vinci, alongside other similar museums.[40] In the text, he retraced the history and aims of institutions created in different periods, for different purposes, in different parts of the world and by different groups of people. Despite the "distinctive needs and attitudes in different countries,"[41] all these institutions aimed at educating people in science and technology.

Starting in the 1950s, contact was made with foreign science and technology museums on both sides of the Iron Curtain, which continued even after the death of Ucelli on 23 August 1964.[42] In the period from the Hungarian Revolution against the communist regime in 1956 to the Prague Spring in 1968, there was a regular and reciprocal cross-border transfer of materials and information. A similar exchange took place with the Polytechnic Museum of Moscow, illustrating how the action of placing Milan within an international network took a lot of time and effort, particularly in terms of translations: letters and reports written in Russian were translated into Italian and French, while answers were sent in French. In January 1965, the new director V.B. Yakovlev contacted the MUST in search of "friendly relations with other museums, . . . anxious to promote close mutual cooperation."[43] In the questionnaire, made up of 26 queries, Moscow asked for example: "Are you interested in the methods adopted in foreign museums? Do you try to use progressive methods?" The answer was of course yes, the MUST had "studied and compared various institutions. Some of the employees had visited major foreign museums of science and technology in order to gain a great number of ideas and lessons necessary for our achievements."[44] There were also questions such as: "How many visitors were children and how many of them adults?"; "How often do you renew the exposition?"; and "Are there aspects of the future of science and technology in your exhibitions?" Ucelli had already been contacted by Moscow in 1960 because the "Soviet Union expressed the necessity of establishing more and more close relationships between museums throughout the world as it was supported by UNESCO ideals,"[45] while the year before, Ucelli had asked Moscow for information about science museums in the People's Republic of China.

Moscow was not the only museum from a socialist country to ask Milan for information. In 1964, the Hungarian Transportation Museum in Budapest[46] wrote, asking for photos, catalogs and general information about the museum and its automobile and motorcycle collections, while connections with the technical museum of Prague date back to 1955. These documents prove how tight and mutual the relationships were between science museums at the time, despite the global and European political situation and considering, also, that Italy was governed at the time by the Christian Democracy party and that Ucelli, as a liberal moderate, was neither a supporter of Soviet politics nor of the Italian Communist Party. Recent historiography in the history of technology reconsiders the classical vision of East-West transfer of technology in terms of reciprocity in order to highlight relations between Eastern and Western Europe during the Cold War. Relations between science and technology museums appear to confirm the permeability of the Iron Curtain and the early interconnectedness between the two blocs.[47]

Based on a large study, summarized in a table dating back to 1953, Ucelli and his collaborators outlined the experiences of various museums according to different aspects of the life of these institutions: general objectives and names; exhibition area; number of visitors; special sections such as the planetarium in Munich or the Children's Gallery in London; sources of financing (private industries, state, university or civic funding); employees; library; different initiatives such as temporary exhibitions, catalogs of collections, radio broadcasting, film screenings, or the presence of an institute for the history of science; other activities such as photographic archives or publications; additional services such as cafés or restaurants; and last but not least, opening hours and tickets. Interestingly, once the MUST opened in the former monastery, Ucelli no longer considered the location of a museum to be information of primary importance.[48] As far as we know, only in a few cases have authors of these comparative surveys dealt with the location of museums, focusing more on issues such as scope, history, building, administration, collection and techniques of display.

After World War II, a greater number of international museums were taken into account than those chosen by Ucelli in the 1930s. They were: the Polytechnic Museum of Moscow, the Nederlandse Postmuseum of the Hague (National Post Museum), the Rijksmuseum voor de Geschiedenis der Natuurwetenschappen in Leiden (National Museum of the History of Science), the Conservatoire des arts et métiers and the Palais de la découverte in Paris, the Science Museum in London, the Technisches Museum in Vienna, the Tekniska Museet in Stockholm, the Franklin Institute of Philadelphia, the Smithsonian Institution in Washington, DC, the Museum of Science and Industry of Chicago, the Norsk Teknisk Museum in Oslo, the Narodni Technicke Museum in Prague and the Deutsches Museum in Munich.[49] Most of the museums are European, situated on both sides of the Iron Curtain, but some are US museums and most of them concern science and technology in general, except for the two Dutch museums. Comparing different experiences, Ucelli sought to shape his own Italian and Milanese museum devoted to Leonardo da Vinci.

In 1963, ten years after opening, the MUST promoted another survey in order to compare foreign science and technology museums, focusing on aspects such as the area covered by exhibitions, the annual number of visitors, museum staff and annual costs.[50] In addition to the museums previously taken into consideration, new additions included the Verkehrshaus der Schweiz (Swiss Transport Museum) in Lucerne, the National Maritime Museum of Stockholm, the National Science Museum of Tokyo, the City Museum and Art Gallery of Birmingham, the Museum Tecniki in Warsaw, the Museum of Applied Arts and Sciences in Sydney, the Museum of Applied Science of Victoria in Melbourne, the Glasgow Museum, the Norsk Teknisk Museum in Oslo, the Deutsches Bergbau-Museum (German Mining Museum) in Bochum, the Postal Museum in Bern and the Musée International d'Horologerie in La Chaux-de-Fonds. The range of considered museums continued to broaden and included more European than US museums, with a special focus on transport and handcraft. The number of Eastern European museums also increased.

Mobilizing Experts: From Milan to the World, and Back

The creation of international networks among museums also implied a real movement of people involved in the life of these institutions, such as directors, curators and architects. In the first years after the Milan museum opened, people moved in both directions: from Milan to the rest of the world, and back. Many foreign directors also came to visit the MUST. In June 1955, the director of the National Maritime Museum of Stockholm, Gerhard Albe,[51] spent time there, while in May 1958, a visit was paid by K.O.B. Jørgensen, director of the Danmarks Tekniske Museum in Copenhagen, who was making plans for a new building.[52] In search of inspiration, the Danish strategy was the same as Ucelli's:

> We are doing propaganda for our museum by means of articles in magazines and lectures, and in connection with this work we are most keen on showing the Danish industry how far behind other countries Denmark is and showing what beautiful museums you have abroad.[53]

Among the "beautiful museums" was the MUST, whose unique specialty was the focus on Leonardo da Vinci and the relationship between art and science. The museum that had been in search of a model had finally become a model itself.

Narrowing the focus on Eastern Europe, we did not find in the official letters exchanged between Milan and many museums in socialist countries any reference to political matters, but the difficulties encountered in obtaining a valid visa to cross the Iron Curtain was often the main reason behind the cancellation of visits. In April 1963, Josef Kuba, director of the museum in Prague, visited Milan in order "to discuss the problems within the scope of museum work and scientific collections, . . . and to promote active collaboration."[54] Only one month later, in May 1963, a Milanese delegation visited Prague in order to foster "rélations amicales."[55] Milan also looked to socialist countries closer to Italy like the former Yugoslavia. In October 1960, in a tour through Paris, London, Munich and Vienna, the director of the nascent Tehnicki Muzej Zagreb, Predrag Grdenić, visited Milan since he wanted to "take a closer look,"[56] discuss the criteria behind the MUST and exchange duplicates and models.[57]

Many times during the 1950s and the 1960s (also after Ucelli's death in 1964), the MUST staff visited foreign museums. One of the preferred destinations remained the leading institution of its kind during the interwar period, the Deutsches Museum.[58] "Emerging from the Second World War a battered institution,"[59] it had been restored by the mid-1960s against the background of a Cold War that divided East and West Germany. However, the Deutsches Museum was not the only destination; in the mid-twentieth century, the international panorama was far more complex than at the turn of the century. In July 1958, curators Curti and Morelli visited scientific and technical museums in Stockholm and Oslo, while in March 1959 they traveled to the United States, inspecting museums in Chicago, Washington, DC, and New York. After a few months, in August 1959, Morelli visited the Museu Nacional dos Coches (National Coach Museum) in Lisbon, while in July 1960, all the staff visited the Conservatoire des arts et métiers and the Palais de la découverte in Paris. One year later, in July 1961, they went to Switzerland, visiting the Swiss Transport Museum in Lucerne, the Bally Schuhmuseum (Bally Shoe Museum) in Schönenwerd and the Musée International d'Horologerie in La Chaux-de-Fonds. In July 1962, similar trips were made to Vienna and Zagreb.

With regard to Eastern European museums, in July 1963, the MUST staff visited the Narodni Technicke Museum in Prague and the Magyar Mezőgazdasági Múzeum (Hungarian Museum of Agriculture) and the Postamúzeum (Postal Museum) in Budapest.[60] Four years after Ucelli had died, in July 1968, in a time of intense political unrest on both sides of the Iron Curtain, a delegation traveled to Poland to inspect the Muzeum Techniki, part of the new Palace of Culture and Science in the very heart of Warsaw. Intended as a "Gift from Soviet Nations for the Polish Nation," the Palace had been constructed in 1955 (Figure 12.3).[61] Ten years before the visit, in 1958, Milan and Warsaw had already established contacts while the Muzeum Techniki was preparing the reorganization and modernization of its collections and was in search of "good practices."[62] In 1957, exchanges of collections were also discussed: Milan was to send models of Leonardo da Vinci's machines in order to start a new section dedicated to the Italian "genius" in exchange for a model of an electrical steel plant to be displayed in Milan in the nascent section of metallurgy and foundry.

Occasionally, first contact requests came from Eastern European museums, as in the case of the Hungarian Museum of Agriculture in 1964 or in the case of the small Museum of Komló in Hungary, which asked the MUST in February 1959 for a mineralogical collection for its new exhibition on minerals for students and workers. The Technické Museum Kosiciach in Košice, now in Slovakia, contacted Ucelli in 1957, while the Narodni Muzei in Ljubljana asked for advice on the museographic project. On other occasions, Milan took the initiative, as in the case of the Postal Museum in Budapest. In December 1957, Ucelli asked the director, Endre Vajda, to welcome his collaborators in order that they may "study the organization and the planning of the various technological sections."[63]

Figure 12.3 Museum of Technology, Warsaw, late 1950s.

Source: Archivo MUST, Corrispondenza II serie, b. 183, Musei esteri, Polonia; courtesy of Archivio Museo Nazionale Scienza e Tecnologia Leonardo da Vinci, Milano

Conclusions

While the choice made by the MUST of looking to the Deutsches Museum is not surprising – as it had long been an exemplary museum of its kind – the fact that, in the second half of the century, the Italian institution had intense and mutual exchanges with museums on the Eastern side of the Iron Curtain is particularly interesting. Considering that Eastern European museums had to face a great change under socialist regimes, these exchanges give us a unique insight into the dynamics of knowledge exchange in different political contexts. After World War II, the international panorama of science and technology museums throughout the world became more complex and the relationships between them became bi- or multi-directional, whereas, from the second half of the nineteenth century until the 1930s, only a small number of museums like the Deutsches Museum and the Science Museum had played a leading role.

Due to its history, the MUST covers both the pre-World War II period – when Ucelli tried to establish and find a home for the museum – and the post-World War II debate – when a museum now in operation had to act in a global context. On the one hand, this case study clearly illustrates the role that this kind of museum played in urban planning, from its foundation through to its enlargement and renovations over the years. On the other hand, it allows us to retrace the mechanisms of knowledge transfer and circulation. Compared to other aspects, the location of a science and technology museum in the urban landscape seemed to be determined more by local factors than by an interurban discourse, even if it is possible to retrace some constants in the monumentality of the buildings, their central position within the city and the profound impact they had on the environment of the districts that hosted them. With the emphasis on Leonardo da Vinci, Ucelli wanted to adapt the general narrative of this kind of museum to a local context, answering to the demands of the Milanese communities of engineers and industrialists. In doing so, he found his niche in the international arena.

Notes

1. Miriam R. Levin et al., *Urban Modernity: Cultural Innovation in the Second Industrial Revolution* (Cambridge, MA: The MIT Press, 2010); Miriam R. Levin, "The City as a Museum of Technology," *History and Technology: An International Journal* 10 (1993): 27–36, https://doi.org/10.1080/07341519308581833.
2. Sophie Forgan, "Building the Museum: Knowledge, Conflict, and the Power of Place," *Isis* 96, no. 4 (2005): 572–585, p. 574, https://doi.org/10.1086/498594. On this aspect see also pp. 579–581.
3. On technical museums and universal exhibitions, see among others: Elena Canadelli, Marco Beretta and Laura Ronzon, eds., *Behind the Exhibit: Displaying Science and Technology at World's Fairs and Museums in the Twentieth Century* (Washington, DC: Smithsonian Scholarly Press, 2019), https://opensi.si.edu/index.php/smithsonian/catalog/book/203, accessed June 25, 2019; Robert W. Rydell, "World Fairs and Museums," in *A Companion to*

Museum Studies, ed. Sharon Macdonald (Malden, MA: Blackwell Publishing, 2006), 135–151.

4. Arthur Molella, "The Museum That Might Have Been: The Smithsonian's National Museum of Engineering and Industry," *Technology and Culture* 32, no. 2 (1991): 237–263; Jaume Sastre-Juan and Jaume Valentines-Álvarez, "The Failed Technology Museum of Catalonia: Engineers and the Politics of the Musealization of Technology in Barcelona (1929–1939)," *Nuncius* 34, no. 1 (2019): 128–154, https://doi.org/10.1163/18253911-03401005.
5. Eszter Gantner and Heidi Hein-Kircher, "'Emerging Cities': Knowledge and Urbanization in Europe's Borderlands 1880–1945. Introduction," *Journal of Urban History* 43, no. 4 (2017): 1–12, https://doi.org/10.1177/0096144217705348.
6. On the relationship between science museums and the city, see Martin Willis, "Science in the City: Scientific Display and Urban Performance in Victorian Travel Guides to London," in *Staging Science: Scientific Performance on Street, Stage and Screen*, ed. Martin Willis (London: Palgrave Macmillan, 2016), 35–58; Carin Berkowitz and Bernard Lightman, "Introduction," in *Science Museums in Transition: Cultures of Display in Nineteenth-Century Britain and America*, ed. Carin Berkowitz and Bernard Lightman (Pittsburgh, PA: University of Pittsburgh Press, 2017), 1–10; Forgan, "Building the Museum," 572–585.
7. Tom Scheinfeldt, "The International Context and the Context of Internationalism," in *Science for the Nation: Perspectives on the History of the Science Museum*, ed. Peter J.T. Morris (New York: Palgrave Macmillan, 2010), 294–311, p. 294. More generally, see Andrea Meyer, Bénédicte Savoy, eds., *The Museum Is Open: Towards a Transnational History of Museums 1750–1940* (Berlin: De Gruyter, 2014).
8. Scheinfeldt, "The International Context", 307.
9. Svante Lindqvist, "An Olympic Stadium of Technology: Deutsches Museum and Sweden's Tekniska Museet," *History and Technology: An International Journal* 10 (1993): 37–54, p. 51, https://doi.org/10.1080/07341519308581834.
10. During its history, the museum has been called many names. From its inauguration in 1953 until 2000, the Italian name was Museo Nazionale della Scienza e della Tecnica "Leonardo da Vinci" di Milano. Afterwards, Tecnica changed to Tecnologia.
11. See the essays in *Guido Ucelli di Nemi. Industriale, umanista, innovatore* (Milano: Hoepli, 2011).
12. Gio Ponti, "Tempo di attesa," *Corriere della Sera*, November 25, 1937, 4 (all translations by author). In 1937, in the Milanese section of *Corriere della Sera*, Ponti published a series of articles under the title *Avvenire di Milano*, *The Future of Milan*. After World War II, on 25–26 June 1951, Ponti published another article pro-Museum: *Ci vuole a Milano un Museo della tecnica*. All the articles have been republished in *Gio Ponti e il Corriere della Sera*, ed. Luca Molinari and Cecilia Rostagni (Milano: Fondazione Corriere della Sera, 2011).
13. Archiatra, "La città di domani e l'esempio negativo di Milano," *L'Italia*, December 28, 1943. Ponti praised the urban development of cities like Barcelona, that "have developed according to independent plans outside the old town, preserving with love its genuine atmosphere." Conversely, according to Ponti, Milan had violated and dismantled the Old Town, replacing it with new buildings and districts in the name of a "politics of misinterpreted 'modernity.' "

14. Lucy M. Maulsby, *Fascism, Architecture, and the Claiming of Modern Milan, 1922–1943* (Toronto: University of Toronto Press, 2014), 3. See also the guide *Milano, Guida pratica* (Milano: Stabilimento grafico Ripalta, 1928).
15. On the technical-scientific community of Milan, see Elena Canadelli and Paola Zocchi, "Presentazione dell'opera," 9–12, and Elena Canadelli, "Introduzione. Alla ricerca del coordinamento: dal 'grande Politecnico' all' 'Università politecnica'," 17–45, in *La rete del grande Politecnico*, first volume of *Milano scientifica 1875–1924*, ed. Elena Canadelli and Paola Zocchi (Milano: Sironi, 2008). See also Pietro Redondi, "Introduzione," in *La città scientifica*, ed. Pietro Redondi (Milano: Guerini e Associati, 2012), 11–60. Abroad, the case study of Barcelona is particularly interesting under the aspect of the "urban science" and the similarities with Milan, see Oliver Hochadel and Agustí Nieto-Galan, eds., *Barcelona: An Urban History of Science and Modernity, 1888–1929* (London and New York: Routledge, 2016).
16. See "Conferenze del podestà alla 'Famiglia Meneghina'," *Milano*, no. 6 (June 1932): 267–275, p. 268. See also Katia Colombo, "Cultura e Fascismo a Milano," in *Milano fascista, Milano antifascista* (Milano: Guerini Associati, 2007), 13–142, pp. 101–104. For an overview on Milan and its institutions, Alessandro Visconti and Alessandro Molinari, eds., *Milano: storia, arte, scienza, economia, igiene, servizi pubblici, statistica, amministrazione* (Milano: Comune di Milano, 1928).
17. See *Regolamento del Collegio dei consulenti di scienza ed arte del Comune* (Milano: Industrie grafiche italiane Stucchi, 1931).
18. For the definition of "urban elites," I refer to Miriam R. Levin, "Dynamic Triad: City, Exposition, and Museum in Industrial Society," in Levin et al., *Urban Modernity*, 1–12. "Urban elites active in an international exchange of ideas constructed a modern, industrial-based culture by establishing new institutions, programs, and projects related to science and technology," p. 2.
19. See "Il Collegio di Scienza ed Arte. La Fondazione del Museo Industriale," *L'Ambrosiano*, January 9, 1931.
20. During the 1930s, Milan was not the only Italian city to claim to host such a museum. On the complex Italian panorama and the other attempts of establishing a science and technology museum in Italy, see Elena Canadelli, "Science versus Technology. The Exhibition of Universal Science in E42 Rome and the Museum of Science and Technology in Milan," in Canadelli, Beretta, Ronzon, eds., *Behind the Exhibit*, 132–156; in the same volume see the essay of Francesco Barreca, "From Instruments of Science to Instruments of History: Andrea Corsini and the Birth of the Museum Galileo," 51–68; Elena Canadelli, "Le macchine dell' 'ingegnere umanista': il progetto museale di Guido Ucelli tra Fascismo e Dopoguerra," *Physis* 51, no. 1–2 (2016): 93–104; Elena Canadelli, "I musei scientifici," in *Storia d'Italia*, Annali 26, *Scienze e cultura dell'Italia unita*, ed. Francesco Cassata and Claudio Pogliano (Torino: Einaudi, 2011), 867–893; Giovanna Baroncelli and Massimo Bucciantini, "Per una storia delle istituzioni storico-scientifiche in Italia: l'Istituto e Museo di storia della scienza di Firenze," *Nuncius* 5, no. 2 (1990): 5–52, https://doi.org/10.1163/182539190X00011.
21. Levin, "The City as a Museum of Technology," 27–36.
22. Maulsby, *Fascism, Architecture, and the Claiming of Modern Milan, 1922–1943*. See also Colombo, "Cultura e Fascismo a Milano"; Dario Franchi and Rosa Chiumeo, *Urbanistica a Milano in regime fascista* (Firenze: La Nuova Italia, 1972).

23. For an overview on Milan's urban development from the nineteenth century onwards, see Ferdinando Reggiori, *Milano 1800–1943: itinerario urbanistico edilizio* (Milano: Edizioni del Milione, 1947).
24. For a list of the proposed locations, see "Cronistoria 1928–1964," in A. Marazza, ed., *5 anni del Museo* (Milano: Alfieri & Lacroix, 1958), 1–29, pp. 1–3.
25. Francesco Mauro, Enrico A. Griffini, Piero Portaluppi, Giovanni Sacchi and Guidi Ucelli, *Schema di progetto per una istituzione politecnica in Milano* (Milano: s.n., 1936).
26. Ferdinando Reggiori, *Il monastero olivetano di San Vittore al Corpo in Milano e la sua rinascita quale sede del Museo Nazionale della Scienza e della Tecnica Leonardo da Vinci* (Milano: Silvana, 1954). On war damages and reconstruction after World War II, Agostino Giambelli, *Milano in cinque anni (sintesi della ricostruzione)* (Milano: Massimo Editore, 1951) and *Milano. Storia di una rinascita*, ed. Stefano Galli (Milano: Spirale d'idee, 2017).
27. For the debate, see *Il Museo della scienza e della tecnica come sede di congressi e convegni*, attachment to the *Bollettino*, no. 388 (November 16, 1954). Today this neighborhood is entirely considered part of the city center.
28. Attachment to the *Bollettino Settimanale del Rotary Club Milano*, no. 6 (February 17, 1931), *L'iniziativa del Museo industriale. Relazione del Comm. Ing. Guido Ucelli.* See Marco Beretta, Elena Canadelli and Claudio Giorgione, eds., *Leonardo 1939. La costruzione del mito* (Milano: Editrice Bibliografica, 2019).
29. The letters sent by Ucelli to his correspondents during the interwar period allow us to retrace his visits in many of these museums. See correspondence in the MUST Archive (hereafter ASMUST), series Museo industriale. To my knowledge, both the MUST and Ucelli's private archive (also conserved in the MUST) did not preserve any of Ucelli's detailed reports of his visits.
30. Mauro published detailed reports of his visits: See "L'organizzazione dei musei di storia naturale, l'educazione del popolo ed il progresso della scienza," *Natura* 21 (1930): 130–156; "Per un museo naturalistico dell'Africa orientale italiana," *Natura* 29 (1938): 21–31.
31. It is the case of Giuseppe Belluzzo, minister of National Economy and one of Ucelli's mentors at the Polytechnic University of Milan. In 1926, he recalled his 1905 tour of European scientific museums on the occasion of the International Exhibition organized in Milan in 1906. At the time, his proposal of installing a permanent pavilion of physics and chemistry and their industrial applications in Milan failed, and it was later developed by his pupil Ucelli.
32. Jaume Sastre-Juan, "'Science in Action': The Politics of Hands-On Display at the New York Museum of Science and Industry," *History of Science* (June 8, 2018): 1–24, first published on-line, https://doi.org/10.1177/0073275317725239. For another example regarding Sweden's Tekniska Museet and the Deutsches Museum, see Lindqvist, "An Olympic Stadium of Technology." In the late 1920s, the Science Museum of London also sent visitors to Munich, see Scheinfeldt, "The International Context," 299–301, 310. Another case is provided by health museums, with the diffusion of a popular exhibit like the German Transparent Man, which in the interwar years spread from the Deutsches Hygiene-Museum in Dresden throughout the rest of Europe and the United States. Elena Canadelli, "The Diffusion of a Museum Exhibit: The Case of the Transparent Man," in *Understanding Cultural Traits: A Multidisciplinary Perspective on Cultural Diversity*, ed. Fabrizio Panebianco and Emanuele Serrelli (London: Springer, 2016), 61–80.

33. Jaume Sastre-Juan, "Un laboratori de divulgació tecnològica: El New York Museum of Science and Industry i la política de la museïtzació de la tecnologia als Estats Units (1912–1951)" (Ph.D. Diss., Universitat Autònoma de Barcelona, 2013), 86–102; Jaume Sastre-Juan, "Pilgrimages to the Museums of the New Age: Appropriating European Industrial Museums in New York City (1927–1937)," *Science Museum Group Journal*, no. 6 (Autumn 2016), http://dx.doi.org/10.15180/160606, accessed October 9, 2018. See the survey of museums in Paris, London, Vienna, and Munich by Charles T. Gwynne, *Museums of the New Age: A Study of World Progress in Industrial Education* (New York: The Association for the Establishment and Maintenance in the City of New York of Museums of the Peaceful Arts, 1927).
34. Among others, Geert Somsen, "A History of Universalism: Conceptions of the Internationality of Science from the Enlightenment to the Cold War," *Minerva* 46 (2008): 361–379, https://doi.org/10.1007/s11024-008-9105-z; Harmke Kamminga and Geert Somsen, eds., *Pursuing the Unity of Science: Ideology and Scientific Practice from the Great War to the Cold War* (London and New York: Routledge, 2016). On ICOM, Sid Ahmed Baghli, Patrick Boylan, and Yani Herreman, *History of ICOM (1946–1996)* (Paris: ICOM, 1998).
35. Salvatore Sutera, ed., *ICOM Italia dalla nascita al 2016* (Siena: Cantagalli, 2016).
36. Guido Ucelli, *Programma e idealità del Museo nazionale della Scienza e della tecnica "Leonardo da Vinci": Onoranze a Leonardo da Vinci nel quinto centenario dalla nascita* (Milano: Off-Print, 1953), 7.
37. W.T. O'Dea, "The Italian National Science Museum at Milan," *Nature* 172 (August 29, 1953): 377–378, p. 377.
38. ASMUST, series Archivio MUST, Corrispondenza II serie, b. 176, letter of the Prague Museum to Ucelli, April 5, 1957.
39. See ASMUST, series Musei, www.museoscienza.org/collezioni/archivio-biblioteca/fondo-museo-albero.asp?fondo=musei, subdivided in European Museums 1884–1980; American Museums 1929–1976; African Museums 1950–1961; Asian Museums 1952–1959; Australian Museums 1940–1972. See also the correspondence exchanged by Ucelli and his collaborators with museums all over the world, preserved in the correspondence folders.
40. In the 1960s, brief articles on foreign museums were published in the journal *Museoscienza* edited by the MUST. See for instance, the case of Prague in November 1963, no. 21: 14–17 or Warsaw in December 1963, no. 22: 16–21.
41. Guido Ucelli, *Origine, realizzazioni e programmi del Museo Nazionale della Scienza e della Tecnica "Leonardo da Vinci"* (Milano: MUST, 1955), 20. As an important source of information, Ucelli also mentioned a publication of ICOM edited by the director of the Palais de la découverte, André Léveillé, *L'activité des Musées scientifiques et techniques et des planetaria* (Paris: ICOM, 1956).
42. See the 20 folders of correspondence exchanged by the MUST with other Italian and foreign museums from the 1940s to the 1970s, ASMUST, series Archivio MUST, Corrispondenza II serie, bb. 167–186.
43. ASMUST, series Archivio MUST, Corrispondenza II serie, b. 184, letter of Yakovlev to the MUST, January 28, 1965. The questionnaire is preserved in the same folder.
44. ASMUST, series Archivio MUST, Corrispondenza II serie, b. 184, answers of the MUST to the Moscow questionnaire.

45. ASMUST, series Archivio MUST, Corrispondenza II serie, b. 184, letter of Posdnjakov to Ucelli, December 22, 1960.
46. See Ralf Roth, "Introduction. Eastern European Railways in Transition," in *Eastern European Railways in Transition: Nineteenth to Twenty-First Centuries*, ed. Ralf Roth and Henry Jacolin (London and New York: Routledge, 2016), 1–23, pp. 19–20. On the history of the Budapest Museum, in relation to Germany, see in the same volume Zsuzsa Frisnyák, "Railway Heritage Protection Policy in Hungary," 343–354.
47. Valentina Fava and Luminita Gatejel, "East-West Cooperation in the Automotive Industry: Enterprises, Mobility, Production," *The Journal of Transport History* 38, no. 1 (2017): 11–19, https://doi.org/10.1177/0022526617698157.
48. However, in a questionnaire prepared in 1964 by the Nikola Tesla Société pour la propagation des connaissances scientifiques, the location of the buildings was a point in question, ASMUST, series Archivio MUST, Corrispondenza II serie, b. 183.
49. ASMUST, series Archivio MUST, Allestimento sezioni museali, Materiali preparatori, Principi scientifici generali, b. 1–2. In the same folder other documents are preserved probably dating back to the same period regarding the MUST sections: From communications technology to sources of energy, from raw materials to physiology. For each thematic subject, the cities taken into account were Munich, Paris, London, Chicago, Vienna, Budapest and Düsseldorf.
50. See ASMUST, series Archivio MUST, Corrispondenza II serie, b. 175.
51. Ibid., b. 184.
52. Ibid., b. 176, letter of Jørgensen to Ucelli, May 14, 1958.
53. ASMUST, series Archivio MUST, Corrispondenza II serie, b. 176, letter of Jørgensen to Ucelli, November 30, 1956.
54. ASMUST, series Archivio MUST, Corrispondenza II serie, b. 176, letter of Kuba to Ucelli, March 28, 1963 (trans. mine). Kuba visited Milan again in July 1969. Contacts between Milan and Prague dated back to 1955 and regularly continued thereafter. In 1951, the museum, founded in 1908 thanks to the initiative of professors of Czech technical universities, was nationalized and financed by the state. The construction of the new museum building on Letná commenced in 1938 and finished in 1941. See Dagmar Klepšová, "The Prague National Museum of Technology: A Survey," *Museum*, Special issue *Museums of Science and Technology* 38, no. 150 (1986): 108–114 and the official website, www.ntm.cz/en/en-muzeum/historie-muzea, accessed November 11, 2018.
55. ASMUST, series Archivio MUST, Corrispondenza II serie, b. 176, letter of Kuba to Morelli, May 22, 1963.
56. Ibid., b. 183, letter of Grdenić to Ucelli, September 29, 1960 (trans. mine).
57. ASMUST, series Archivio MUST, Corrispondenza II serie, b. 183, letter of Grdenić to Ucelli, November 14, 1960.
58. The Deutsches Museum was visited in May 1955, by the architects in charge of enlarging the MUST exhibition area; in June 1957, by some collaborators of Ucelli, Curti and Morelli, in charge of studying the exhibitions; in August 1959, by all MUST staff as a training opportunity; in October 1959, by the MUST's trustee and curator, Morelli and Curti, who inspected the naval collections; in May 1961, by trustee Vincenzo Grillo alone. See "Cronistoria 1928–1964."
59. Scheinfeldt, "The International Context," 298.
60. See "Cronistoria 1928–1964."

61. ASMUST, series Archivio MUST, Corrispondenza II serie, b. 183, report by Raffaele Massarotto, July 29, 1968. Here they also met with the director of the Science and Technology Museum of Moscow, G.P. Kozlov, who showed them a film on the Soviet Museum. After the visit, Massarotto said they were offered "cigarettes, coffee, and cognac."
62. ASMUST, series Archivio MUST, Corrispondenza II serie, b. 183, letter of the director of the Muzeum Techniki to Ucelli, June 22, 1958. The Museum in Milan tried to arrange a visit in Poland, but it probably never took place.
63. ASMUST, series Archivio MUST, Corrispondenza II serie, b. 184, letter of Ucelli to Vajda, December 27, 1957 (trans. mine). The visit never took place.

Afterword

Goodbye to Center and Periphery

Cor Wagenaar

In 1992, a remarkable book was published in Budapest. *An Architect-Planner on the Peripheries. Case Studies from the Less Developed World: The Retrospective Diary of Charles K. Polónyi* is the story of one of Hungary's leading planners.[1] In the 1970s, he was the head of Budapest's municipal department of urbanism, a position he occasionally gave up in order to work abroad, notably in African countries that had gained independence in the 1960s. Although these countries were no longer ruled from the capital cities in Europe, very few people would think of them as equal to their former colonizers – they represented the peripheries mentioned in the title of Polónyi's book. They were not only peripheral in a geographical sense, but lagged behind in almost every way, and these two qualities – being on the periphery and lagging behind – were two sides of the same coin. Planners from Europe and the United States were called upon to help these countries to catch up. Catching up implied that they learned from the experiences of allegedly more advanced countries (and for a time, Africa became one of the few places where experts from both sides of the Iron Curtain learned from each other's experiences).

Polónyi's accounts of his adventures in Africa alternate with stories about Budapest, suggesting that Budapest should also be seen as a peripheral city. In this way, Polónyi implicitly questioned the entire concept of the periphery. Hardly any European city can boast a more central position on the European continent. Moreover, it had been one of the twin capitals of one of Europe's major political powers, the Austro-Hungarian dual monarchy, and a leading city in the arts, literature, music – and above all, in urban planning. The master plan that gave Budapest its present shape represented a culmination of all the expertise accumulated in the nineteenth century – the two ring roads, the radial boulevards that lead outwards from the central ring road to the outskirts of the city, the embankment and the five bridges that mark the two ring roads, and the central axis that runs from the Danube to the main station. The plan also combined best practices from London (the embankment and the site of the houses of parliament), Paris (the boulevards cut through already built-up areas), New York (the island in the Danube that became the city's Central Park), and Berlin (the building code that resulted in the characteristic Budapest variant of the tenement block). A more "transnational" project is hard to find, and the project perfectly illustrates the inherently international nature of urbanism.

Whereas the twentieth century ultimately developed into the age of suburbia, the nineteenth century is the age of metropolitan cities, and in many ways, Budapest is the ultimate European metropolis. It instantly became a model that other ambitious capital cities began to emulate, and its urban structure would later be imitated, modified and expanded by planners elsewhere. When Stalin incorporated Hungary into the Soviet empire, Budapest was cut off from the cultural context that had helped to produce it and to which it belonged. Did that imply that the historical contributions of the city to European culture had become peripheral? Obviously not. Polónyi was well aware of the provocative undertones of incorporating Budapest in a book on underdeveloped, peripheral cities. It was a rhetorical trick – but it was also more than just a trick. It reflected historical perceptions about a city that, in reality, had never been peripheral. Forty years of socialism may not have done the city a lot of good, but Budapest was in no way comparable to, for instance, Accra. From the perspective of Moscow, Budapest may have been as peripheral as Accra seen from London, but in architectural and urban history, it was the result of one of Europe's innovative planning initiatives and was thus a modern metropolis that remained unparalleled in many ways. And yet, despite neither being on the periphery of Europe, nor in the periphery of historical realities, Budapest did become a "city on the periphery." It became peripheral in the minds of the people who, with or without valid reasons, believed they were at the center of things: the citizens of the countries in Western Europe and the United States, the regions that represented the cultural values that Hungary had shared before the Iron Curtain all but severed its ties with "the West."

Historical realities, and people's perception of the world and their place in it, are two very different things. What is decisive for people's (political) actions or for the way they value their own situation and that of their fellow citizens? What has a bigger impact on their opinions about world affairs and their place in it? Eszter Gantner, one of the initiators of this book, an outstanding scholar and, coming from Budapest, deeply aware of the abyss between realities and the way they are perceived, had her doubts when it came to the motivating power of historical realities. People behave on the basis of their beliefs, perceptions and interpretations, and a clear analysis of objective fact very often plays no role at all. For a historian (like myself), this is hard to stomach – but the rising tides of populism have proved Eszter Gantner right. In all likelihood, her observations are true for all times. If history is about reality, it does not count for much. Polónyi's Budapest – and Eszter Gantner's – are two cities in one: the real thing (a Central European metropolis and one of the pillars of "Western" culture), and a construct of the mind (a peripheral city in every sense of the word). Often, the notion of periphery appears to be a historical distortion.

This book is about the tension between historical realities and the way they are perceived. It brings together the work of scholars who share a common believe in the value of historical realities, but who are also very well aware of the dichotomies between these realities and public opinion. Distortions of historical realities come in many variants. Developments or historical situations that were of the utmost importance in their own time may be seen as irrelevant when the cities, regions or nations where they took place have lost their leading political, economic and cultural positions. Centers of power shift continuously; they move from one region to another, and in recent decades the scope of these shifts has become global. This process has been going on for centuries.

Of course, it does not affect the relevance of historical phenomena, but public opinion (and sometimes even historical professionals) tends to value these phenomena within the framework of contemporary power relations. Obviously, propaganda and the manipulation of public opinion also result in distorted views on historical phenomena. The mechanisms of deliberate distortion have become standard procedure in all populist movements, and sometimes even respectable parties resort to it – the Berlin venue of the Bonn-based Haus der Geschichte, for instance, skillfully evokes an image of former East Germany as a criminal state that produced inferior products and services, while continuously oppressing its citizens.

This view is, at best, one-sided; the suggestion that East Germany, the vanguard of the Soviet empire in Western Europe, was nothing more than a pathetic state in the backwaters of history is problematic, to say the least. Not far from the houses of parliament in Budapest, a statue of Ronald Reagan tries to convince passersby that the former US president has to be credited for the collapse of socialism in 1989 – nothing could be farther from the historical realities. The suggestion that the centers of power in the West decided the fate of the socialist empire in the East is similarly spurious. In both cases, the image of being peripheral was the result of political rhetoric in the aftermath of the Cold War. Historical distortions, whether a consequence of ignorance or propaganda, are not exceptional; they are the rule – and very often, politics and the processes of history are propelled by these distortions, not by historical realities.

The authors of the 12 chapters brought together in this volume are well aware of the continuous shifts of the geographical centers of political, economic and military power, which more often than not coincide with changes in the places that act as centers of cultural innovation. They emphasize the consequences of cultural geography and its dynamics, and question the tendency in public opinion – and sometimes also in historiography – to rank the importance of historical phenomena that took place in the past according to Europe's current political, economic and cultural landscape. In this respect, the case studies are examples of transnational studies that aim to correct distorted views on historical realities, as well as historiographical misrepresentations.

In the decades this book covers – from the late nineteenth century to the 1950s – the continent's cultural geography changed dramatically. The years around 1900, later dubbed the "Belle Époque," cannot be compared to the years between the wars or the reconstruction period of the 1950s, and from today's perspective, the geopolitical realities that underlie the stories collected here are very much history. The geography of power has, again, changed completely. That, of course, is the way of the world. As a consequence, however, the importance of past events tends to be obscured by various layers of later geopolitical realities. The authors accept this as a matter of fact and refrain from attempts to assess the degree or the causes of these inaccurate views; rather, these become apparent when they present their case studies.

Cities are at the center of all the stories collected here. Cities have been chosen as benchmarks that show the dynamics of cultural geography. The terms "periphery" and "peripheral" pop up time and again; they refer mainly to the cities' current geopolitical position and generate an awareness of the tension between their current place in world affairs and the historical phenomena that the authors set out to analyze, suggesting that the very notion of periphery is often the consequence of historical distortions. Most of the 12 case studies revolve around what the authors see as modernization processes, focusing on their cities' built substance – notably, their hygienic infrastructure.

They also targeted the urban structure, its performance in terms of providing a healthy living environment and its representative qualities. All of them demonstrate the mechanisms that guide the evolution of cities: the continuous process of emulating best practices, and avoiding the mistakes, of other cities. This, obviously, suggests a gap between local urban conditions and these best practices, and that may strengthen the notion of their "peripheral" qualities. This, however, would be beside the point: the processes of exchange operate in all cities at all times, irrespective of their geographical coordinates. Eszter Gantner and Heidi Hein-Kircher coined the term "emerging cities" for places that showed the ambition to catch up with their role models – in this respect, all cities that work on the improvement of their urban conditions should be seen as "emerging."[2] Paradoxically, the notion of being peripheral was often supported by the rhetoric of "backwardness," a term that the elites of emerging cities cherished and cultivated. They used it to underpin the need for reform, suggesting that their city lagged behind cities elsewhere; they used it to get their urban projects accepted (and position themselves as heralds of progress). Using this motif, however, was standard procedure everywhere and in no way limited to emerging cities. In the nineteenth century, the lack of proper sanitation in Amsterdam, for instance, led critics to compare the Dutch capital with cities elsewhere in Europe that were well known for their disastrous living conditions, such as Toledo.

The case study by Anna Mazanik on Moscow (Chapter 5), one of the leading capital cities in world history, and the capital of a huge empire that saw itself as a self-evident fact, illustrates how the elites there also constructed a notion of backwardness in order to promote their schemes for a sewage system. Remarkably, emerging cities looked to other emerging cities for inspiration, and for good reason: whereas cities like London and Berlin were among the first to introduce, for instance, state-of-the-art urban sanitation projects, best practices from later periods were more likely to be found in the emerging cities that emulated them. Thus, the Moscow sewage system adopted a model from Memphis, which had been identified as particularly efficient.

With the exception of Berdyansk and Milan, all the cities featured in this book are either national capitals or capitals of national minorities (or nations that had lost their independent status and had been incorporated in larger geopolitical units). Consequently, debates on the interventions they proposed to improve their technical and hygienic infrastructure was mixed up with the ambition to represent national values. Five of the 12 case studies deal with cities that once were part of the Austro-Hungarian dual monarchy, the multi-ethnic, multi-national and multi-religious political construct that between 1867 and 1918 was one of Europe's great powers, and from a cultural perspective, one of the most fascinating empires ever. In the literary world, it is also known as "Kakania," a term coined by the Austrian author Robert Musil who referred to the "imperial and royal" status of its civil servants "kaiserlich-königlich" in German, abbreviated as "k.u.k."). It is hardly surprising that the setting of such diverse cities as Prague, Lemberg (today Lviv) and Zagreb in the Habsburg Empire urged their national elites to promote their urban improvement projects for the representation of their status as national capitals (albeit for nations that were integrated in the supranational umbrella of the dual monarchy). One of the most peculiar cases presented in this volume (Chapter 6) is that of Lemberg, one of the major cities of Galicia on the northern fringe of the empire. After the Habsburgs granted most national minorities the right to use their own language for their internal affairs, the Polish citizens, who formed the majority in this multi-ethnic community, practically took over Lemberg (today Lviv) which now became known under its Polish name, Lwów.

Heidi Hein-Kircher describes how the municipality began to make plans for a thorough reconstruction of the city, which was to become the capital city of Poland, a country that was technically extinct: in the eighteenth century, it had been erased from the political map and divided between Prussia, the Austro-Hungarian empire and tsarist Russia. Warsaw was the provincial capital of the Russian partition, and after several revolutions, the authorities in Saint Petersburg introduced strict, oppressive policies supported by censorship and a strong military presence; although its size and history would have made Warsaw a more likely candidate to be the Polish capital, Russian rule prevented these ambitions. Lviv combined two strategies to realize its national ambitions. The first revolved around the construction of a hygienic infrastructure with a decent sewage system, the provision of clean drinking water and measures of slum control. The medical elite empowered the sanitation scheme; thoroughly scientific in its aspirations, they saw the introduction of a state-of-the-art hygienic infrastructure as a technical issue. Yet for some of them, these projects were linked to nationalism: the deplorable hygienic conditions were presented as an affront to feelings of national pride. Both the connection with technology and the emphasis on rational, scientific ways of doing things designated sanitation measures as part of a modernization campaign – the terms "modern" and "modernization" figure prominently in many of our case studies. However, since hygienic misery is always linked to urban poverty, and since the urban poor tend to concentrate in the city's least salubrious, ghetto-like neighborhoods, sanitation campaigns mainly affected the poor, who faced the consequences of large-scale demolition of the areas where they lived (sometimes for generations). Moreover, the rhetoric accompanying these urban reconstruction campaigns obviously pointed toward the most deprived areas and the people living there – in the case of Lviv, mainly poor Ruthenians and Jews. Thus, ethnic profiling and anti-Semitism tarnished debates about the city's technical infrastructure. The case studies on Prague and Warsaw demonstrate that here the exact same mechanisms were at work.

Intimately linked to the sanitation project, Lviv's second amelioration strategy targeted the representational qualities of its cityscape. Since the late eighteenth century, urban beauty was associated with community building – the aesthetic qualities of the city, it was believed, should foster a sense of civic pride. Lviv's urban planners took inspiration from the international state of the art, at the time epitomized by Vienna and Budapest. (Paradoxically, all national urban design idioms invariably evolved as regional interpretations of generic, international models.) Lviv adopted a monumental ring road that allegedly emulated the boulevards of Brussels and Paris, and crowned it with a grandiose theater. The city derived its architectural identity from the styles that had become popular all over the empire, but that did not prevent the authorities from promoting its urban make-over as a sign of Polishness.

In Prague, the demolition of the former Jewish ghetto acted as a wakeup call for the cultural elite, as Cathleen M. Giustino shows (Chapter 1). Medical professionals had promoted the radical slum clearance program and they had done so according to the generic, internationally accepted and scientific principles of their discipline, disregarding non-scientific motives in ways characteristic of most modernization campaigns. Prague's architectural scene was appalled: if the city's (Czech) identity was ingrained in its architectural and urban heritage, destroying it could hardly help to promote the city's role as the nation's capital (as was the case in Lviv, local people were allowed to run the municipality, and Czech had become the city council's official language). The former ghetto was surgically removed from the city's urban tissue according to the original plans. Giustino shows that while this clinical intervention was ongoing, Prague's architectural elite managed to increase its influence, which resulted in a more careful treatment of the city's cultural heritage and in attempts to create a national variant of mainstream "Habsburg architecture" – which, in the interwar period, triggered growing divisions about the importance of the nation in urban design (as the fate of Plečnik's proposal for the Prague castle demonstrates).

Highlighting key moments in the life of Géza Maróti, Eszter Gantner's Chapter 3 also revolves around the issue of nationalism in the arts, in this case the use of applied art used to embellish representative architectural projects in Budapest, one of the dual monarchy's two capital cities. Maróti's career peaked around 1900, when the new capital was in the final stages of realizing its brilliant urban master plan, and the city realized a range of buildings that are as impressive today as they were back then. Maróti was involved in several of these projects, notably the Gresham palace (a lavishly decorated office building that is nowadays one of the city's most expensive hotels), and the Franz Liszt music school that houses one of the world's most beautiful concert halls. Stained glass, mosaics, colorful tiles and many other features endow these buildings with a richness that has rarely been surpassed since. They represent the climax of an artistic trend that culminated in, as Eszter Gantner puts it, "regional-universal" art. In his personal life, Maróti saw it as a crowning his ambition to represent what it is to be Hungarian; originally Jewish, he finalized his own road to Hungarianism by converting to Catholicism in 1905. His early career demonstrates that nationalism in its liberal, inclusive form offers unique opportunities for social and, in this case, artistic integration, especially in a burgeoning hotspot like Budapest; it also shows that regionalism in arts and architecture does not contradict its international, universal qualities, and that these can be the source of international cooperation based on personal, but also professional networks. Although Maróti's art is closely linked to the cultural scene of Budapest in the "Belle Époque," the empire's demise did not end his career. His work on the national theater of Mexico City, and his collaboration with Eliel Saarinen and Albert Kahn in the United States underline the international qualities of art and architecture, which appeared to be perfectly compatible with local, regional and national aspirations. His personal fate in Budapest, the city he found difficult to leave behind, demonstrate that art's "regional-universal" nature made it acceptable in very different settings. This, however, was not true for the artist. Upon his return to Budapest, the Hungarian fascists who took control over the country in the 1930s deemed him to be incompatible with their exclusive, racist brand of nationalism. Even though Maróti saw himself as a nationalist, he suffered the consequences of Hungarian anti-Semitism.

These examples show that the Austro-Hungarian dual monarchy refrained from promoting its own imperial style in the multitude of nations it controlled. Rather, it allowed all regions to develop their own architectural and urban idioms – which, in practice, followed the models and innovations from its twin capitals, which as we have seen, absorbed the best practices of cities elsewhere in Europe. Maróti's art is characteristic of the way in which specific artistic languages could be based on generic models. Tamara Bjažić Klarin's case study on Zagreb (Chapter 4), another "Habsburg city," demonstrates that in architecture and urbanism similar mechanisms were at work. In the 1920s, after the dissolution of empire, the architectural elite of Zagreb embraced modern architecture as an idiom that marked a radical departure from the architectural styles of the Austro-Hungarian dual monarchy. Imbued with an ideology of fundamental innovation and the urge to break away from the past, modernism was perfectly suited for this purpose. Thus, modernism – the quintessentially international style – was associated with nationalism; this also happened in, for instance, Turkey and Israel. The most stunning feat of Croatian modernism was a general expansion plan with all the characteristics of international modernism. It was based on the designs by the winners of the competition, Erich Kotzer, Ewald Liedecke and Peter Koller, one of the 34 German teams of the 52 that participated. The brief asked for a regional traffic structure, a zoning plan, views on architecture and the positioning of public buildings and perspective drawings (complemented with photomontages). The slightly modified plan combined the winner's entry with selected elements from their competitors as well as with features inspired by Nikolay Milytin's linear city, the Sotsgorod. Bjažić Klarin recognizes the main features of the famous Chartre d'Athènes in this revolutionary scheme, one of the highlights of pre-war modernism that was debated on the Patris II, a luxury steam liner that hosted a Ciam-conference on urban planning while traveling from Marseille to Athens (the original plan to convene in Moscow had become impossible after Stalin's attacks on modernism). The proposal dissolved the traditional closed block with inner courtyards, proposed high-rise apartment buildings shaped as simple slabs and made up of minimum subsistence dwellings, and introduced sun, light and fresh air in a city that had become clogged and where slums for the working classes had emerged within walking distance of the center. Bjažić Klarin justifiably presents this project (which was never realized) as a definitive victory of modernism, and modernism as the definitive victory over traditional ways of doing things that were now associated with the period when the authorities in Vienna and Budapest had the final say in Zagreb's urban affairs. Judging from its qualities, the plan might have played a central role in international urbanism. The outbreak of World War II and the tragedies that followed, however, frustrated this perspective, though Bjažić Klarin and her colleagues managed to save the plan from oblivion. These events perfectly illustrate the dichotomies inherent in modernism: its protagonists stressed the need to connect spatial planning to the forces that were reshaping society, notably science and technology, and the way these transformed all aspects of life. These forces were universal, and modernism therefore continuously stressed its international nature. However, most of its manifestations, among them this remarkable plan, show the impact of regional circumstances and ambitions: the plan is an example of "regional-universal" art, to quote Eszter Gantner's characterization of Maróti's work.

The editors and authors of this volume address historical misconceptions of a specific type: all the case studies describe phenomena in cities that today are often seen as peripheral. Nevertheless, all of them deal with phenomena that have been central to European history in the last two centuries, and without exception the authors successfully debunk the notion of periphery. Celia Miralles Buil's essay on Barcelona's Central Dispensary (Chapter 7) does so very eloquently. This medical institution, an initiative of Lluís Sayé, a local doctor who became an expert in the fight against tuberculosis, gives the impression of a somewhat exotic experiment – the dispensary was a mix of an outpatient department and a medical support center specializing in the diagnostics and early treatment of tuberculosis patients. Ideally complemented with ambulatory dispensaries, the central facility was to become the spearhead of an extensive sanitation campaign that was to help "purify" the entire city. This campaign was inaugurated by the Generalitat de Catalunya, which, inspired by the health policies of the Soviet Union, ordered this project in 1934, two years before the outbreak of the Spanish Civil War. Designed by Joan Baptista Subirana, Josep Lluís Sert, and Josep Torres Clavé, it is a highlight of modern architecture. Sayé's approach, however, did not survive the end of the Civil War: Franco's fascists dismantled his system. Miralles Buil's chapter is saturated with notions that suggest the peripheral qualities of this unique project, being situated in Spain, in a city that suffered from the lack of an effective hygienic infrastructure such as could be found in cities in northern countries, and initiated by a local medical doctor. However, Miralles Buil goes on to convincingly deconstruct all these notions and proves that Subirana's dispensary was the outcome of the international networks of the well-traveled Lluís Sayé, the universal, Moscow-inspired aspirations of the local government (in which the health policies of the League of Nations also reverberated), and the adaptation of international modern architecture to the local needs of one of Europe's major metropolitan cities (which, as she explains, evolved as a local, Mediterranean brand of international modernism).

The Barcelona case also demonstrates the key role of elites – the medical elites (who, since time immemorial, had wanted to connect to the international body of knowledge and cultivated pragmatism), the political elites who, in this case, looked to Moscow for inspiration, and the architectural elites who embraced modernism and developed a regional variant within its generic, international mental framework. In other cases, directors of natural history museums and zoological gardens, the elite of managers and technicians, and the elites of diplomats and consuls, play similar roles: they were part of an international professional community for whom, as Oliver Hochadel suggests (Chapter 9), the notion of periphery is meaningless. In all these professions, learning from key examples was of the essence, while the conferences, journals and study trips designated the state of the art as thoroughly and quintessentially international. The world of ideas knows no borders (and, to quote Charles Polónyi once more: all history is world history). All disciplines linked to science and technology tend to cultivate the notion of objectivity – which, as Elena Canadelli's Chapter 12 on Milan's Museum of Technology demonstrates, usually implies that they are compatible with the entire palette of political ideologies, ranging from fascism to communism and the model of the social-democratic welfare state. Nationalism, on the other hand, also played a dominant role in many case studies. In its liberal, inclusive variant it could act as an emancipatory power (as was the case in the early career of Maróti). In its exclusive form, it often turned against national minorities and Jews. Paradoxically, nationalism could also be transnational, as Lucila Mallart's Chapter 10 on the intellectual exchange between Romania (Bucharest) and Catalonia (Barcelona) illustrates.

Peripheries, historical distortions, backwardness, emerging cities, modernization, nationalism, the role of elites – this book touches upon many aspects that have shaped Europe's recent history. Focusing on cities, its contents can be categorized under the heading urban studies; analyzing exchange mechanisms, its nature is transnational. Its subject matter is case studies: isolated and well-demarcated moments in the life of cities. Apart from their own historical evolution, they are subject to the consequences of dramatic geopolitical changes and their impact on the geographies of culture. All cases took place in settings that now belong to what appears to be a distant past.

How geopolitics affects cities can probably best be illustrated by the example of Lemberg. In 1918, after the Austrian-Hungarian dual monarchy imploded, Lviv was integrated in the newly established republic of Poland; Warsaw emerged as the capital city. The aftermath of World War II permanently erased Lviv's Polish heritage when the eastern part of Galicia was handed over to the Soviet Union and most of its inhabitants were forced to move to the former German territories added to Poland on its western borders; the Ukrainians who replaced them dubbed the city "L'viv." Warsaw tells a similar story: the events described by Clara Maddalena Frysztacka in Chapter 8 took place when the city was occupied by the Russians and the Polish nation had not re-emerged. In 1918, it resurfaced on Europe's political map, and in 1945, it moved about 150 km to the west.

The period covered by Giustino's comparative study on Prague ends shortly before the start of World War II. Still, it is worthwhile adding here that, once the interwar period ended, the concept of what it meant to be Czech became far more complicated with far more serious life consequences, and these changes also affected Prague's architecture, adding more layers to the city's history. First, Hitler managed to annex the Sudetenland, then he occupied the Czech part of the republic while the Slovaks voluntarily accepted becoming a satellite state of the Third Reich. The Nazis stressed the alleged German roots of Prague and wanted to eliminate everything with strong Czech nationalist associations; the Soviets who replaced them in 1945 stressed their own particular brand of internationalism which, I would argue, was to provide whatever Czech identity remained with a framework that was defined in Moscow. Only after the collapse of the Soviet Empire did Prague again become the capital of an independent republic (with the Slovaks splitting off within a very short time).

Prague provides just one example of the multi-layered histories of cities. These multi-layered histories remind us of the excavation work that is needed in order to overcome distortion and recover reality. Stated differently, before we can come to the essence of urban history, the consequences of historical distortions need to be eliminated. Understanding history requires a lot more than analyzing what is going on: it presupposes continuous processes of purification and constant efforts to deconstruct views and perceptions that, while often empowering public opinion, contradict historical realities. If this book contributes to the elimination of the notion of the periphery, one of the most persistent distortions, it has done what its authors have hoped for.

Notes

1. Károly Polónyi, *An Architect-Planner on the Peripheries. Case Studies from the Less Developed World: The Retrospective Diary of Charles K. Polónyi* (Budapest: P & C., 1992).
2. Eszter Gantner and Heidi Hein-Kircher, "'Emerging Cities': Knowledge and Urbanisation in Europe's Borderlands 1880–1945 – Introduction," *Journal of Urban History* 43, no. 4 (2017): 575–586.

Contributors

Tamara Bjažić Klarin is a senior research associate at the Institute of Art History in Zagreb. Her field of expertise covers twentieth century urban planning and architectural history, with a focus on the processes of modernization, mediation of concepts and public engagement by architects. She authored: *Ernest Weissman: Društveno odgovorna arhitektura, 1926. – 1939. (Socially Responsible Architecture, 1926–1939)*, 2015, and *"Za novi, ljepši Zagreb!" – arhitektonski i urbanistički natječaji međuratnog Zagreba, 1918. – 1941.* (*"For the New and Nicer City of Zagreb" – Architectural and Urban Planning Competition in Interwar Zagreb, 1918–1941*), 2020. She co-edited with Ljiljana Kolešnik: *French Artistic Culture and Central-East European Modern Art*, 2017.

Elena Canadelli is an assistant professor in history of science and natural history museology at the University of Padua and associate editor at *Nuncius: Journal of the Material and Visual History of Science*. Her research interests include visual and material aspects of science, with special attention to the history of science and natural history museums in the nineteenth and twentieth centuries. Recently, she co-edited *Behind the Exhibit: Displaying Science and Technology at World's Fairs and Museums in the Twentieth Century* (2019, with Marco Beretta and Laura Ronzon).

Clara Maddalena Frysztacka is a historian. She is currently a post-doc researcher at the Europa-Universität Viadrina in Frankfurt/Oder (Germany). Her research interests include history of historiography, history of Eastern Europe (with focus on Poland) in the nineteenth and twentieth centuries, as well as historical theories on modernity and time. Selected publications: *Zeit-Schriften der Moderne: Zeitkonstruktion und temporale Selbstverortung in der Polnischen Presse 1880–1914* (2020); "Kolumbus transnational: Verflochtene Geschichtskulturen und europäische Medienlandschaften im Kontext des 400. Jubiläums der Entdeckung Amerikas 1892," *Journal of Modern European History* (2017, with K. Herborn, M. Palli and T. Scheidt).

Eszter Gantner (1971–2019) was a post-doc researcher at the Herder Institute for Historical Research on East Central Europe (Marburg, Germany) with a background in urban history, intellectual and knowledge history, heritage studies and Eastern European Studies. Selected publications: Heike Oevermann, Eszter Gantner: *Securing Urban Heritage* (2020); Eszter Gantner, Heidi Hein-Kircher, Oliver Hochadel (ed.): *Backward and Peripheral? Emerging Cities in Eastern Europe*. Special Issue – *Journal of East Central European Studies*, 4 (2018); Eszter Gantner, Nicole Shea: *Contemporary Urban Research in the European City*, Special Issue of *Europe Now*, May 2018; Eszter Gantner, Heidi Hein-Kircher (ed.): Emerging Cities. *Journal of Urban History* 4 (2017).

Cathleen M. Giustino (Ph.D., University of Chicago) is the Mills Carter Professor of History at Auburn University and a Carnegie Fellow. Her research focuses on the politics of architecture, urban design and material culture in modern Central and Eastern Europe. Among her publications are her book *Tearing Down Prague's Jewish Town: Ghetto Clearance and the Legacy of Middle-Class Ethnic Politics around 1900* and her journal articles "Parlament, Letenská plán a panoráma Prahy za první republiky" (*Zprávy památkové péče*, 2018); "Rodin in Prague: Modern Art, Cultural Diplomacy and National Display" (*Slavic Review*, 2010); "Municipal Activism in Late-Nineteenth-Century Prague: The House Numbered 207-V and Ghetto Clearance," (*Austrian History Yearbook*, 2003).

Heidi Hein-Kircher is currently head of the department "academic forum" at the Herder Institute for Historical Research on East Central Europe. One important field of her research is the urban history of the nineteenth and twentieth centuries in East Central Europe. Selected publications: *Lembergs "polnischen Charakter" sichern. Kommunalpolitik in einer multiethnischen Stadt der Habsburgermonarchie zwischen 1861/62 und 1914* (2020); "Jewish Participation in the Lemberg Local Self-Government: The Provisions of the Lemberg Statute of 1870," *Simon-Dubnow-Institute Yearbook* 10 (2011); Emerging Cities. *Journal of Urban History* 4 (2017) (with Eszter Gantner).

Oliver Hochadel is a historian of science and a tenured researcher at the Institución Milá y Fontanals de Investigación en Humanidades (CSIC, Barcelona). His recent work deals with the urban history of science. He co-edited *Barcelona: An Urban History of Science and Modernity, 1888–1929* (2016), *Urban Histories of Science. Making Knowledge in the City, 1820–1940* (2018, both with Agustí Nieto-Galan), and *Saberes transatlánticos. Barcelona y Buenos Aires: conexiones, confluencias, comparaciones (1850–1940)* (2017, with Álvaro Girón and Gustavo Vallejo).

Victoria Konstantinova is the Director of the Research Institute of Urban History (http://ri-urbanhistory.org.ua/en/) of Berdyansk State Pedagogical University (Ukraine). The author of 21 books, focused on various aspects of urban history of the Southern Ukraine (the Northern Black sea and the sea of Azov region) between the eighteenth and the early twentieth centuries. With Igor Lyman she recently worked on the monographs *The Greek Community and Consuls of Greece in Berdyansk of the Nineteenth – early Twentieth Centuries* and *History of Prussian Consuls in the Southern Ukraine*.

Igor Lyman is professor, the head of the Department of History and Philosophy and the coordinator of international relations of Berdyansk State Pedagogical University. His recent publications include: *British Consul and Industrialist John Edward Greaves* (2017, with Victoria Konstantinova and Eugene Danchenko), *German Consuls in the Northern Azov Region* (2018), *The Ukrainian South as Viewed by Consuls of the British Empire (Nineteenth – Early Twentieth Centuries). Volume 1: British Consuls in the Port City of Berdyansk* (2018, both with Victoria Konstantinova), and *Descendants of the Zaporozhians: the Makhno Movement in the Northern Azov Region (1918–1921)* (2019, with Volodymyr Chop).

Lucila Mallart is a Juan de la Cierva Postdoctoral Research Fellow at Pompeu Fabra University in Barcelona. She received her Ph.D. in Modern European History from the University of Nottingham (United Kingdom) in 2016. She is author of *Josep Puig i Cadafalch. Visions, Identities, Cosmopolitism* (2018) and a number of articles and book chapters on visual culture, urban history, world fairs and intellectual history published in journals such as *Cultural History* and *Urban History*. She is currently researching knowledge transfers between Spain and other borderland countries such as Finland and Romania.

Anna Mazanik is a research fellow at the Rachel Carson Center for Environment and Society, Ludwig-Maximilian University, Munich. Between 2016 and 2018, she worked at the Central European University in Budapest where she curated the Russian-language archival collections at the Blinken Open Society Archives and was a lecturer at the History Department. Her research and publications focus on imperial Russian and Soviet environmental history, urban history and history of public health.

Celia Miralles Buil is an urban historian. She is currently an assistant professor at the University of Strasbourg (France). Between 2017 and 2020 she was a post-doc researcher at the University of Lisbon. Her research interests include history of health in Iberian cities in the twentieth century. One of her most recent publications is: “La tuberculose et la surpopulation urbaine en Espagne au début du XXe siècle" (*Histoire, Economie, Société*, 2017).

Barry L. Stiefel is an Associate Professor at the College of Charleston, where he is a member of Department of Art and Architectural History, Historic Preservation & Community Planning, and Urban Studies programs. He earned his Ph.D. in Historic Preservation from Tulane University, Master of Urban Planning from the University of Michigan, Graduate Certificate in Historic Preservation from Eastern Michigan University, and a B.S. in Environmental Policy (with a minor in Anthropology) from Michigan State University. His research interests concern how the sum of local preservation efforts affect regional, national and multi-national policies within the field of cultural resource management and heritage conservation.

Cor Wagenaar is full professor at the Department of History of Art, Architecture and Landscapes at the University of Groningen, head of the Expertise Center Architecture Urbanism and Health at the same university, associate professor at Delft University of Technology, and chairman of the Berlin-based advisory board of the European Network Architecture for Health (enah.eu); he wrote numerous articles and several books, among them *Town Planning in the Netherlands since 1800. Responses to Enlightenment Ideas and Geopolitical Realities* (2011, 2015); he led a team of authors who published *Hospitals. A Design Manual* (2018).

Name Index

Subject Index

Taylor & Francis Group
an **informa** business

Taylor & Francis eBooks

www.taylorfrancis.com

A single destination for eBooks from Taylor & Francis with increased functionality and an improved user experience to meet the needs of our customers.

90,000+ eBooks of award-winning academic content in Humanities, Social Science, Science, Technology, Engineering, and Medical written by a global network of editors and authors.

TAYLOR & FRANCIS EBOOKS OFFERS:

- A streamlined experience for our library customers
- A single point of discovery for all of our eBook content
- Improved search and discovery of content at both book and chapter level

REQUEST A FREE TRIAL

support@taylorfrancis.com

Routledge
Taylor & Francis Group

CRC Press
Taylor & Francis Group

Milton Keynes UK
Ingram Content Group UK Ltd.
UKHW020239020324
438793UK00013B/133

9 780367 609580